The Modern Nations in Historical Perspective Series

R. W. WINKS, *Consulting Editor*

The volumes in this series deal with individual nations or groups of closely related nations throughout the world, summarizing the chief historical trends and influences that have contributed to each nation's present-day character, problems, and behavior. Recent data are incorporated with established historical background to achieve a fresh synthesis and original interpretation.

THE
ARAB LANDS
OF
WESTERN ASIA

JOSEPH J. MALONE
University of Pittsburgh

48185

Prentice-Hall, Inc., *Englewood Cliffs, New Jersey*

Library of Congress Cataloging in Publication Data

Malone, Joseph J.
    The Arab lands of Western Asia.

    1. Arab countries—Politics. I. Title
DS62.8.M344   320.9′174′927   73-5948
ISBN 0-13-043968-1
ISBN 0-13-043950-9 (pbk.)

10 9 8 7 6 5 4 3 2 1

Printed in the United States of America

Prentice-Hall International, Inc., *London*
Prentice-Hall of Australia, Pty. Ltd., *Sydney*
Prentice-Hall of Canada, Ltd., *Toronto*
Prentice-Hall of India Private Limited, *New Delhi*
Prentice-Hall of Japan, Inc., *Tokyo*

To Lois, my wife

CONTENTS

PREFACE *ix*

1

LEBANON *1*

    Mount Lebanon, 2
    From the Crusades to the Fall
    of the Shihabi Emirate, 5
    The Shaping of Modern Lebanon, 9
    The Road to Independence, 13
    The Civil War of 1958, 19
    The Chehab Era, 25
    The Aftermath of the Six Day War, 28

2

SYRIA *36*

    The Umayyad Legacy, 37
    Syria Under the Ottomans, 39
    The French Mandate, 41
    The First Twelve Years of Independence, 47
    The Baathist Socialist Party and the UAR, 52
    Baathism and Neo-Baathism, 55
    Syria and Israel, 61
    The Place of Syria in the Arab World, 64

3

IRAQ   73

A Prize for Empires, 74
The Great Iraqi Revolution of 1920, 82
The Era of Nuri Pasha Said, 88
Abdul Karim Qasim, the "Sole Leader," 95
A Decade of Turbulence, 100
Iraqi Politics in the Seventies, 112

4

JORDAN   115

The Kingdom East of the River, 115
Damoclean Years for Hashemite Rule, 121
The Six Day War, 126
Hussein's Garrison State, 128

5

THE ARABIAN PENINSULA   135

SAUDI ARABIA, 142
SOUTH ARABIA, 169
1. The Yemeni Arab Republic, 169
2. The People's Democratic Republic
   of Yemen, 192
EASTERN ARABIA, 211
1. The Sultanate of Oman, 211
2. The Persian Gulf Shaikhdoms, 225

SUGGESTED READINGS   246

APPENDIX   255

AFTERWORD   257

INDEX   261

PREFACE

The editor's charge to authors of volumes in this series calls for a summary of the chief historical trends and influences that have contributed to each nation's present-day character, problems, and behavior. With respect to the Arab lands of Western Asia, the historian is confronted with the widely held interpretation, in the West, the Communist nations, the Arab countries, and the rest of the Third World, that there is an Arab nation transcending the artificial boundaries between, say, Iraq and Syria, or Jordan and Saudi Arabia. A common language, religion, and cultural heritage are advanced in support of this interpretation.

Yet in the past quarter of a century, the postcolonial era for most of the Arab lands of Western Asia, the "Arab Nation" has repeatedly revealed deep divisions. Some of the reasons for these divisions are rooted in the past, before the Ottoman era; others in a historical stratum nearer the surface, that of the European hegemony; while still others have come fully into force since World War II. Primary emphasis in this study is given to internal historical forces. But change has been shaped in Syria, Iraq, Lebanon, and Jordan—indeed, in the most remote statelet in the Persian Gulf—by the establishment and demonstrated viability of Israel, by the talented, restless, and stateless Palestinian population, and certainly by the charisma, ego, and ambition of the late Gamal Abdul Nasser. Vast petroleum reserves in the Arab lands of Western Asia and the global communications routes which traverse them assure that these countries will continue to be subjected to penetration and influence in many forms. Such factors form a backdrop against which historical development can be viewed with fuller understanding.

In preparing this volume I have drawn unreservedly upon the knowledge and good will of so many colleagues that full acknowledgement would constitute a "Who's Who in Middle Eastern Scholarship." Special thanks must go to friends with whom I collaborated for over a decade at the American University of Beirut—the late, beloved Nabih Amin Faris, my constant and patient mentors, Zeine N. Zeine and Yusuf K. Ibish, and a long list of A.U.B. specialists, high upon which must appear the names of Kamal Salibi, Mahmud Ghul, Khaldun Husry, Yusuf Sayigh, and E. Terry Prothro. So much was learned from my students in the Department of History and Middle East Area Program at A.U.B. that one has a feeling of role reversal. I am deeply grateful to D. J. D. Maitland, A. J. Wilton, Robert Walmsley, and D. C. Carden, who at various times directed that unique institution, the Middle East Centre for Arab Studies at Shemlan, Lebanon, to Albert Hourani of St. Antony's College, Oxford, Yusuf Shirawi of Manama, Bahrain and Muhammad Ahmet No'man of San'a, Yemeni Arab Republic. And how can one adequately express gratitude to resident editor, critic, typist, morale-booster, and wife, Lois Fleischhacker Malone? The answer is that one cannot.

Pittsburgh, Pennsylvania   JOSEPH J. MALONE

THE
ARAB LANDS
OF
WESTERN ASIA

1

LEBANON

Least Arab of all the Arab lands of Western Asia is Lebanon. It is a gateway to the Arab world, an interpreter of Western concepts and values for the Arabs, and of Arab aspirations and attitudes for the West. If it does not always succeed as a transmission belt, this is largely because of internal contradictions which affect Lebanese perceptions.

On the verdant slopes of Mount Lebanon are the villas in which shaikhs and wealthy businessmen of the Arabian Peninsula escape the blinding summer heat of their home countries. Christian villagers welcome the purchasing power they represent, and resent the mosques they have built in praise of God and his Prophet Mohammed. From much of Mount Lebanon, the capital city of Beirut is visible below, sprawling out in recent years toward the foothills and along the shore, but now lacking the well-scrubbed look once conferred by distance. Smog has taken care of that.

Beirut no longer is the unchallenged financial center of the Arab world but its narrow streets are thronged with people involved in every type of commerce, legal and illegal. Still greater distance has given Beirut the scarlet hue associated with smuggling, prostitution, and the narcotics trade. Yet the city's, and Lebanon's, strength derives from more legitimate pursuits. The business of Lebanon is indeed business. From executive suites in modern glass-and-steel skyscrapers as well as from cramped stalls in the Sursok market, the Lebanese businessman looks for buyers. The sophisticated, multilingual entrepreneur is daily involved in deals

1

spanning oceans and supplying markets in a dozen Arab countries. The stall merchant reduces his overhead by renting the exposed surface of his open door to an even smaller operator.

All of them are affected by the crises in the Arab world which close frontiers, establish curfews, and drive away customers. The large corps of Lebanese and foreign journalists may thrive on such events, but the hundreds of American, European, and Japanese businessmen resident in Beirut are as troubled by them as are their Lebanese and Arab counterparts. The pace of American and other foreign educational and philanthropic activity slows. Landlords, many of them absentee Kuwaiti, Qatari, Saudi, and other peninsular Arab millionaires, fear for the security of their buildings and mourn the declining return on their investments.

On the other hand, a *coup d'état*, a purge, or some other form of political change in the Arab world sends leaders into exile. More often than not they find asylum in Lebanon. There is a measure of security in this, for what Arab politician in power does not think about the time when he might have to emplane for Beirut?

For such reasons, the monument which characterizes most closely the ethos of Lebanon is to be found north along the Mediterranean from Beirut. It is the government operated *Casino du Liban*, where thousands of dollars change hands on a throw of the dice or a turn of the wheel.

Mount Lebanon

In 1920, French mandatory authorities drew the boundaries of what was initially known as the State of Greater Lebanon. This state was one of the four created when the French Ministry of Foreign Affairs deemed it expedient to carve up the historical and geographic unit which was Syria. The coastal plain and the Bekaa Valley, two invasion routes since antiquity, were thereby joined politically to the *massif* which gives the country its name. This arrangement was unsatisfactory to the predominantly Muslim population of the lowland areas, who regarded their future as bound up with the Sherifian leaders of the Arab Revolt and Damascus. But pan-Arabism was a new phenomenon. The long history of Mount Lebanon, stretching back to pre-Islamic times, best explains the artificiality of *Le Grand Liban*.

Mount Lebanon has always been a place of refuge for minorities and schismatics. Just as the highlands of northern Iraq have sheltered Kurds, Nestorians, and Yezidis, and the Yemeni mountains became the power base of the heretical Zeidi Imams, so the ridges and cliffs of Mount

Lebanon have acted as a shield against forcible incorporation into a succession of empires.

Thus many of the invasions which shaped the history of Syria (see Chapter 2) had but slight impact on the hardy cultivators of the mountain. Before the people of the coastal plain became Arabized and converted to Islam, they had undergone thousands of years of racial and cultural blending. They had witnessed the passage of many armies, at times northward bound but more often advancing upon the Nile Delta. The passage of Sumerians and Amorites, Egyptians, Canaanites, the mysterious Hyksos people, and the Hittites made the coastal settlements a frontier area between Egypt and the Land of the Two Rivers for twenty centuries before the rise of Phoenicia about 1400 B.C.

The term "Phoenician" is often glibly applied to the modern merchant republic of Lebanon. It suggests skill at the arts of commerce and finance, an advanced level of culture and sophistication, and a desire to seek opportunity beyond the horizon. In this context, twentieth-century Lebanon can be properly compared with its illustrious ancestor, famed for feats of navigation, for the founding of Carthage and other colonies, and for its seminal role in the evolution of written communication. Yet there is irony and paradox in the fact that in modern Lebanon a high proportion of the politically inarticulate and economically depressed section of the population lives on the coast—on the strategic and cultural crossroads where Phoenicia flourished for six centuries.

The reasons for this situation lie closer in time to the modern period. After Assyrians and Chaldeans moved through Syria, the Persians came, bringing, with Darius, something akin to an Augustan age. Decade followed decade of peace and prosperity. The Aramaic language made great progress, only to be forced to seek refuge, as it were, in the mountain areas with the advent of the Greeks in Lebanon. After the mighty Alexander swept by in 332 B.C., leaving the area to be disputed between his Seleucid and Ptolemaic successors, the more accessible districts underwent a degree of Hellenization. A decline in public order and prosperity must have made Pompey and his legions seem harbingers of peace and prosperity when they arrived in 67 B.C.

Parthians and Persians challenged Roman hegemony again and again, but the brunt was borne not by the people of the coast and the mountain, but by those who were closer to the "frontier"—in Damascus, Aleppo, and Antioch. Instead, the ancestors of the Lebanese prospered from ministering to the needs of their occupiers. Syria survived for seven centuries, during the last three of which the seat of imperial rule moved from Italy to Constantinople, and as a result the history of Syria is associated by Westerners with the name of Byzantium. In that part of it which would much later become the Republic of Lebanon, the Augustan peace long outlived the emperor who gave that prosperous era its name, and it was not until after Mohammed's birth in A.D. 570 that a new period of anarchy threatened.

From the victory of Islam's greatest general, Khalid ibn Walid, on the Yarmuk River (A.D. 636) and the establishment of the Umayyad Caliphate at Damascus (661), down through the many Fatimid-Abbasid-Byzantine rivalries which plagued all of Syria almost to the beginning of the First Crusade (1095), the future Lebanon was shaped by three important forces. One was the process of Arabization, as the result of which today's merchant republic has great importance as a repository and disseminator of Arabic culture. The other two, the development of the Maronite and Druse communities, stem from the mountain's significance as a place of refuge, rising above the coastal plain where Sunni and Shiite Muslims lived (and live today) in uneasy proximity.[1]

Probably in the late seventh century—the precise date is unknown—the priest Yuhanna Marun and some of his followers broke with the Byzantine religious hierarchy in Syria and found sanctuary on Mount Lebanon. By the ninth century considerable numbers of Maronites were present in the rugged hinterland of North Lebanon. With the coming of the Crusaders they found that Rome answered their religious requirements more successfully than had Constantinople, and therefore the Maronites became a uniate sect—in communion with the Holy See. Was it that the Maronites feared isolation in a Muslim sea and that their association with Roman Catholicism and the Crusaders were measures of desperation? Or did the remoteness of the Alban hills from the Lebanese highlands make the hierarchical relationship both valuable enough and tenuous enough to appeal to independent-minded Maronites who nonetheless were conscious of their vulnerability? Perhaps there is something in both lines of speculation, for the Maronites spent over three centuries establishing their own sense of "national identity" before Pope Urban II startled the Council of Clermont with his call for the recovery of Jerusalem. The Maronites assisted and advised the Franks as they had the Byzantines before them. But they maintained their independence in the sturdy, determined way of mountain people all over the world.

The Maronite community, one of modern Lebanon's major ethnic components, was followed into the country's highland region by another

---

[1]Another predominantly Shiite area in modern Lebanon is the Hermel region north of Baalbek in the Bekaa Valley. The Shiite sect, second only to orthodox Sunnism in numbers and geographical distribution, are followers of Ali, the son-in-law, whose martyrdom resulted in the first and most important division in the world of Islam. Shiites await the reappearance of a "hidden Imam" or religious leader embodying the legitimate succession from the Prophet. Their temporal leader is the Shah of Iran, a fact of considerable consequence in modern Middle Eastern politics.

sect, the Druses, who figure prominently in the country's historical development. The Druses had settled south of the Maronites on Mount Lebanon less than a century before the first Crusaders set off on their quest. Their origin is exotic rather than obscure, although in the course of its development the Druse faith has taken on some characteristics of a secret religion, fully comprehended only by an elect of its adherents. (The religious grouping to which the Druse faith has the closest relationship is the Shiite sect of Islam.) Its name is derived from that of Ismail al-Darazi, a follower of the "mad Caliph" of the Fatimid line, Hakim. Caliph Hakim was assassinated in Cairo in 1021 after claiming he was the Being whose earthly representative he had heretofore been. Ismail al-Darazi and a coterie of Hakim's disciples made their way to Mount Lebanon, where they formed the nucleus of another of modern Lebanon's ethnic components. Over the years, other religious groups would find freedom from oppression on the Lebanese *massif*. These included Greek Orthodox, Jacobites, Assyrians, and Shiites. As the Lebanese state took form, political and racial entities, including Palestinians and Kurds, came to seek a new start, or to thrive in a secure and tolerant atmosphere.

From the Crusades to the Fall of the Shihabi Emirate

In the era of the Crusades Lebanon became once again a march region. Bounded by the Latin Kingdom of Jerusalem and the County of Tripoli, the peoples of Lebanon came under European influence to an extent unknown since Pompey's time. Yet it would appear that the Crusaders were more shaped by than they were shapers of the land and people of that part of Syria which is modern Lebanon. In 1187, when Saladin was regaining Jerusalem, the third of Islam's Holy Places, the Crusaders occupying the territory between Acre and Tripoli were showing greater interest in the arts of commerce and in the "good life"—in the hedonistic rather than the missionary sense.

But Mount Lebanon could not remain a place of refuge when it was a "land between" such intractable enemies as the Franks, the Ayyubid heirs of Saladin, the Cairo-based Mamluks, and the dreaded Mongols, whose irruption out of the east seemed to herald another Dark Age. In the event, the mountain was spared the brief but horrendous visitation of Tamerlane; Damascus and Aleppo were not. In 1291 the vigorous Mamluk[2] rulers of Damascus expelled the Crusaders, devastated North Leba-

---

[2]The term Mamluk, "to be owned," refers to the slaves who served with the armies of Saladin and his successors, and who eventually rose to power on their own account For the most part they were converts to Islam.

non, and divided the area of modern Lebanon into two governates based upon Tripoli and Damascus. Political authority was fragmented on the northern section of the mountain. Turcomans were resettled in the Kisrawan district, for example, and for a time represented Mamluk interests. More remote areas were simply ignored by the governor of Tripoli, except for occasional tax-gathering expeditions. To the south, the hereditary authority of the Buhturid Druse family was recognized by the Mamluks.

Lebanon quickly recovered from the hammer blows of Mamluk armies and prospered from trade established during the Crusader period with the maritime and commercial republics of Pisa, Genoa, and Venice. Its role of transmitter of values and techniques between East and West was becoming more pronounced.

This role was not altered by the coming of Selim the Dread in 1517. The only major change was the establishment of the Ma'ni Emirate in place of the Buhturids, who had supported their Mamluk overlords until the battle of Marj Dabiq overthrew the old order. The Ottoman period has often been dismissed with the words "neglect and misrule," but it conferred many advantages upon Lebanon along with interludes of fear and tragedy. Although political authority continued to be confided to Druse emirs in what was, at least formally, a master-vassal relationship, the Maronite community did not suffer. So long as the Ottoman Turks did not give their direct attention to the affairs of the mountain, its several communities lived in relative harmony and understanding. The Maronites became organizers and administrators, the "makers and shakers" for the Ma'ni emirs. The two major groups came into closer proximity at this time, in what might be described as a process of Maronite "colonization" in the southern sector of the mountain.

The assumption that Lebanon, with the rest of Syria, suffered from the opening of a new trade route to the east in the wake of Vasco da Gama's epic voyage bears reexamination. Commerce declined, but not enough to invoke the tax-gatherer's wrath; perhaps Lebanon's prosperity diminished only sufficiently to minimize the interest and attention of the Sublime Porte (the gate of the Ottoman Sultan's palace, a term which came to denote the imperial government). The Maronite community continued to develop and build upon the link with the Holy See, which had been forged in the Crusader era and which was strengthened by the establishment of the Maronite College in Rome (1584) and the beginning of the Jesuit mission in Lebanon (1626). Was it the tolerance, the indifference, or the growing dependence of the Druses which permitted the evolution of a national experience among the Maronites? All of these factors played some role, but the relationship is not so easily explained.

Even though the Maronites understood that a local Druse ruler like the westward-looking Fakhr al-Din was far preferable to an Ottoman *wali*, their sense of exclusiveness and superiority remained unchanged. No feeling of community informed relations between the Druses and Maronites during the Ma'ni period.

The ethnic structure of modern Lebanon is based not only on the southward push of Maronite "colonizers" but also on Ma'ni success in exploiting Maronite economic and cultural superiority to expand their own role as territorial chieftains. By 1605 the ethnically heterogeneous Kisrawan, that part of the mountain rising above the coast immediately north of Beirut, was a Ma'ni domain, no longer answerable to the Pasha of Tripoli. Maronite appointees administered the territory. The al-Khazan family, Maronite aristocrats whose wealth came from a burgeoning silk industry (which flourished until World War I), did much to shape the structure of the clergy, and through them, the community. They made a vast contribution to the concept of a Maronite nation.

In time there occurred what might be considered a historic reversal. In an era when Rome's control over affairs of state was weakening elsewhere in the world, Maronite priests were becoming increasingly independent of Maronite patronage and Druse sufferance. After 1700, the mountain cultivators counted upon their clergy for economic as well as spiritual guidance.

The potency of reformed Maronitism is clearly exemplified by the conversion of the Shihabi emir to the Maronite faith about 1776. This family had established its ascendancy over the Druses in 1697 through the election of Bashir I by an assembly of the landed aristocracy after a half-century during which Ma'ni authority disintegrated. Its fiefdom was recognized as extending from the hinterland of Sidon to that of Tripoli. However, long before 1776 the Shihabi emirs were becoming Maronite clients. Even in the southern portion of the mountain, the secular hierarchy—the Junblatti and Yazbaki Druse factions—was reliant upon support from a Maronite peasantry and the entire country was undergoing a rapid shift toward Maronite social and political dominance. Leadership developed not only through pressures for clerical reform initiated by Rome and increased by the enthusiasm of younger members of the indigenous clergy, but also through the development of new economic and political opportunities.

Maronite opportunism, rather than sentiments deriving from the community's shadowy link with an earlier and more genuine Crusader, St. Louis (1250), explains the Patriarch's organization of support for Napoleon during the siege of Acre. This decision had no important results either for the French expeditionary force or for the Maronite community. Nonetheless, it signified Lebanon's debut on the stage of international politics and diplomacy. As the Eastern Question became more complex and the future of the Ottoman Empire more problematical, European capitals became interested in the "Lebanese factor."

International interest in Lebanon—indeed, in all of Syria—was not confined to diplomatic chanceries. The Jesuits had worked among the people of the mountain for two centuries before establishing their first school in 1833. Collaboration and improvement were regarded as imperative if the Maronite-controlled educational system was to withstand the challenge of other missionary and philanthropic endeavors which began shortly after the Napoleonic Wars.

The first American Protestant missionary enterprise took form in Lebanon in the early 1820s. But early zeal to proselytize among Muslims, Jews, Roman Catholics, Maronites, and Druses did not long survive the mission's arrival, for it was confronted at once by the monolithic, impenetrable nature of the Islamic community, the solidarity and protected status of the Jews (as an Ottoman *millet*), and the aggressiveness of the Roman Catholics, to which were added ridicule by the lower classes and the Byzantine scheming of native bishops. The attempt to define a policy for the American mission led to hypocrisy and delusion. The Americans claimed that Eastern Christianity must be reformed and cleansed to achieve a "pure" faith to be preached to the Muslims. This was a mere casting about for a *raison d'être*. The imperial and strategic aims with which the British and French missionary movements were linked, not only in the Levant but among the Christian communities of the Kurdish mountains, assured support at the highest levels in London and Paris, but such backing did not exist for the Americans. To give up and return to America was unthinkable, however, for these missionaries were of the same stock as the pioneers of the trans-Allegheny West. The mountains and coastal plain of Lebanon comprised their frontier. Ultimately, the educational activities and the publication of books which had supported the missionary movements became ends in themselves.

The British, in the meanwhile, had extended their patronage to the Druses of Mount Lebanon and to the native Jewish community of Palestine. As a result, a number of vital Western interests, political, cultural, and economic, were at stake when Mohammed Ali of Egypt moved to wrest Syria—and, if possible, all of the Sultan's Arab possessions—from the Ottoman Empire. The Egyptian viceroy's dispatch of an army into Syria under the command of his son Ibrahim Pasha was at once a thrust at the vitals of the Ottoman Empire, a dramatic phase of the historic Anglo-French struggle for hegemony in the East, and, because of French support for Mohammed Ali, a watershed in Lebanon's history.

If the Egyptian presence in Syria conferred certain advantages in the form of administrative reform and technical advancement, it spelled disaster for the Shihabi emirate in Lebanon. For in 1832 Emir Bashir II cast his lot with Mohammed Ali. This transformation—or usurpation—of a ruling institution which in previous decades had become a Maronite instrumentality led to rebellion. Sporadic resistance to the Egyptian *raj* developed into organized revolt, which reached a decisive phase in 1840 when it gained the sanction of the Maronite Patriarch.

The European powers followed these events closely. For Lord Palmerston, the architect of British foreign policy, the Maronite attack on the Shihabi emirate was a time of opportunity. In a series of brilliant diplomatic moves, supported by well-timed military measures, Palmerston secured the expulsion (with French acquiescence) of Ibrahim Pasha from Syria. The concurrent conflict between Maronites and Druses led to the collapse of the Shihabi emirate in 1841. Had Bashir II and his Druse followers not departed from the traditions of shared rule based upon personal associations and loyalties, and had they not abandoned the concept of Mount Lebanon's special position in relation to whomever ruled the coast and inland plains, the emirate would have survived. Instead, communal strife on the mountain, exacerbated by a revived Turkish presence in Syria, lasted for two decades. In 1842 the Great Powers had attempted to quell hostilities through an agreement with the Porte that the mountain should be split into a Maronite and a Druse district, each to be governed by a person chosen from the local inhabitants by the Pasha of Sidon. Thus the emirate ended, but the arrangement which replaced it was utterly unworkable.

The Shaping of Modern Lebanon

Proponents of reform can often count more victims than beneficiaries. This was true in mid-nineteenth-century Lebanon. The Great Powers encouraged Sultan Abdul Majid to achieve administrative centralization and a greater control over districts and provinces far removed from Constantinople. The result for Lebanon was an invasion of Turkish tax-gatherers whose official status was often maintained by encouraging or inciting local feuds. The next major reform which Great Power pressure forced upon the Sublime Porte was the decree of 1856 whereby Muslims, Christians, and other non-Muslim subjects were given equal status throughout the Ottoman Empire. Reactions to the *Hatt-i Humayun* were mixed and complex. To some Christians, it suggested a disturbing revitalization of the Ottoman ruling institution and thus a threat to their nascent nationalism and desire for independence. The church hierarchy saw in it a threat to its authority within its own religious community. There were instances of Christians and Jews making too much of their new position. Muslim reaction was especially intense in Syria and Palestine, where Christian and Muslim communities lived in close proximity to each other or were intermingled. On Mount Lebanon one outrage followed another. The new confessional arrangements were often the basis for the revival of hostilities rooted in the past. Muslims banded with Druses against the Maronites and chaos spread from north to south on the mountain. Although a truce was arranged by European representatives in Beirut, the virus of religious animosity had spread to Damascus, where Turkish troops joined the Muslim community in three days of seeking out and murdering the Christians of that city.

The Damascus massacres of 1860 had important consequences for Lebanon. With the reluctant acquiescence of Great Britain, French troops were landed at Beirut to assist the Sultan's special commissioner in restoring the communal balance. It was a highly complex situation. The Turks sought exculpation by singling out the Druses as initiators of the reign of terror. The British position was that the Maronites bore greater responsibility for the tragedy than the Druses, but that the root causes were Turkish scheming and incompetence. The French defended the Maronites vigorously, not only out of a sense of their historic role as protectors of Latin Christians, but out of the need to restore a relationship which had been damaged by their support for Mohammed Ali's Syrian venture. The Maronites saw in developments following French intervention an opportunity to gain complete control of the mountain and virtual independence from Ottoman Turkey. The church hierarchy aligned with its "freedom fighters," of whom the most redoubtable, Yusuf Karam of Zghorta (north Lebanon), has become a legendary figure to modern Lebanese nationalists.

It became French policy to seek the appointment of a Maronite governor of Lebanon with tenure for life, or at least for as long as the Great Powers could not agree on his removal. The British favored a Turkish governor, to be appointed by the Sultan after consultation with the Powers. But the Turkish hold on the rest of Syria, to say nothing of Lebanon, was precarious and a vigorous appointee might easily be tempted to emulate Ibrahim Pasha. After tortuous negotiations, it was agreed that Lebanon should be placed under a Christian governor who could not be a native of Lebanon, and who would be nominated by the Sultan and directly responsible to him. In practice, the organization of power being what it was, he would be equally answerable to the French consul in Beirut.

Thus the Maronite-Druse relationship, for so long based upon custom, accommodation, and personal ties, was formalized as a *mutassarifiya*, or governate, in 1861. The arrangement was guaranteed by France, Great Britain, Russia, Austria, Prussia, and that newcomer to the corridors of power, Piedmont-Sardinia. The first *mutassarif* was the remarkable Daud Pasha, an Armenian Catholic of wide administrative experience and prestige.

Daud Pasha was acceptable to the Powers and the Sultan, but not to the Maronites. The opposition of the Patriarch and of Yusuf Karam meant that his writ extended only a few miles into the hinterland of the coast north of Beirut. Further intervention of the Powers was therefore necessary, with the French finding themselves in the unenviable position of seeking to maintain their influence at the Porte and their special relationship with the increasingly intractable Maronite community.

The *Reglement* implemented in 1864 divided the mountain into seven districts, each represented in a largely advisory Central Administrative Assembly on the basis of confessional proportions. Yusuf Karam and his supporters were not pacified by the change and prepared for a full-scale uprising. As their plan went forward Daud Pasha attempted to recruit local Christians into a gendarmerie of about 1500 men. Before he succeeded, the challenge came and the governor was compelled to augment his small force of Christian dragoons (whose transfer from Constantinople he had earlier arranged) with Ottoman Muslim troops stationed in Beirut. The constraints under which Daud Pasha operated are indicated by the fact that he felt it necessary to obtain the approval of the French consul for this measure. It was given reluctantly, but the commitment of the Muslim troops to battle was so carefully orchestrated that there was no great support for the rebel movement. With Karam's departure into exile in Algeria in 1867, effective Maronite opposition to the *Reglement* was ended and Daud Pasha's authority consolidated.

The arrangements of 1864 also provided for a customs barrier between Mount Lebanon and the rest of Syria. With France committed to the concept of an autonomous Mount Lebanon, the sense of *apartheid* flourished until World War I. The Lebanese were not satisfied with their territorial limits, nor was Daud Pasha pleased with his status as chief executive of a governate. Thus in 1865, when Beirut ceased to be the capital of the *vilayet*, or province, of Sidon (that province being combined with Damascus to form the *vilayet* of Syria under Mohammed Rashid Pasha), interest was stirred in adding that port city to the governate of Lebanon. For the predominantly Muslim population of Beirut, the factor of religious animosity was second only to chagrin over the downgrading of the city as a result of administrative neglect and a measure of economic decline. Qualified enthusiasm for union with the mountain was reciprocated by some Maronite and Druse leaders, largely for economic reasons, although prestige was also a factor. Political union with Beirut would facilitate exports and increase profits from grain, raw cotton, silk, wool, dried fruit, and tobacco. Daud Pasha sought to bring Beirut under his control because he believed not only that this would ensure the economic viability of the mountain, but also that it would be the basis for raising the governate to the status of a province.

The French favored such an arrangement, but their defeat in the war with Prussia had reduced their influence in Constantinople. Moreover, a modicum of improvement in the economic condition of Beirut under the zealous regime of Mohammed Rashid Pasha prevented the formation of a political link between the city and the mountain. Daud Pasha's importunings resulted in his replacement by an Aleppine Greek Catholic in the Ottoman service, the first of a number of lesser men to hold the post of *mutassarif* of Mount Lebanon until the collapse of the Ottoman regime. Daud Pasha was more responsible for fixing the polity of Lebanon in its present mold than any other authority since the distant time when Maronites and Druses first fled to the mountain.

An event of the greatest importance to Lebanon and the entire Middle East occurred in Beirut as Daud Pasha and Mohammed Rashid Pasha vied for control of the city. In 1866 American missionaries opened the doors of the Syrian Protestant College, the name of which was to be changed in 1920 to the American University of Beirut. This was a beneficial and happy result of the failure to win converts to Protestantism during preceding decades. Instead of churches, schools were built, some of which survived to become preparatory institutions for the college when it was founded. Despite Bible reading, compulsory chapel, and the casting of Darwinism into the outer darkness, the Syrian Protestant College was never effectively a sectarian institution. The physicians, scientists, philosophers, engineers, historians, and, indeed, housewives who have obtained degrees from the S.P.C. and A.U.B. have played major roles in transforming and developing their countries.[3] The institution inspired emulation, first by the French Jesuits in the 1880s, and eventually by the Egyptians and the Lebanese themselves, making Beirut the home of four

---

[3]Increasing reliance upon the United States government for budgetary support and building funds in recent years has diluted the fine principles upon which the Syrian Protestant College was founded. The bureaucratization which inevitably accompanies the inflow of government money has isolated the university's administration from its students. Attempts to foster a neutral stance in Middle Eastern politics have been carried to extreme lengths, giving rise to charges that the university is a creature of a pro-Israeli American government, and that freedom of discussion is being stifled. The Faculty of Arts and Sciences, the heart of much of the university and repository of its century-old traditions, is the source of much of this criticism, and pride of place has been given by university administrators to an extravagantly funded Medical Center, the maintenance and operation of which are so costly as to threaten the existence of the institution. Meanwhile, no effective campaign to solicit support from other, and especially Arab, sources has been mounted.

universities and the leading center of higher education in the Middle East.

The Road to Independence

The Turks abolished the governate of Mount Lebanon in 1914, but it was revived once Ottoman forces were driven out of Syria. The sponsorship was French and the restoration of the *mutassarifiya* a temporary measure, pending the award of the mandate over Syria to France. Although the French initially may have overestimated their popularity in the rest of Syria, they had reason to be confident about their relations with the Maronites of Mount Lebanon. From the *Reglement* of 1864 until 1914, the French had pursued their *mission civilisatrice* on the mountain with such diligence that the Maronite community was by any standard—whether it be cultural development, economic advancement, or political astuteness—far ahead of the Druse and Muslim populations of Lebanon. The Maronites, in company with the Greek Orthodox and Greek Catholic minorities, had transformed predominantly Muslim Beirut into a business and professional center. Following the influx of Armenian survivors of the Turkish genocide after World War I, and with the eventual improvement of the Muslim educational level through the Maqassad (a local Muslim charitable foundation) and foreign philanthropy, something akin to equal opportunity began to develop in Lebanon. Such equality has yet to be achieved, but modern Lebanon is far different than *Le Grand Liban*, the State of Greater Lebanon, proclaimed on behalf of the French mandatory authorities by General Henri Gouraud in 1920.

The French colonial administration superimposed upon local forms of authority was vast and cumbersome. In the early years the great majority of officials were military officers. From the *Grand Serail* in Beirut, the High Commissioner supervised, organized, and chastised all four divisions of geographic Syria—Greater Lebanon, the Alawite State, Jebel Druse, and the State of Syria. This could only add to historic resentments, especially between Beirut and Damascus. But even more resented was the omnipresence of French officialdom. Nothing was beyond supervision. Intelligence and internal security service, the press and propaganda were concerns of the *Grand Serail*, as were finance, justice, communications, education, and every other aspect of public administration. So were the *Awqaf* (the Muslim charitable and philanthropic institutions) and archeology. There were a dozen inspectorates, and each office had its subordinate counterpart in the four states, all French-manned.

The political unit thus defined as *Le Grand Liban* included the coastal cities of Tripoli, Beirut, and Sidon, plus Tyre and its hinterland and the fertile Bekaa Valley which lies between Mount Lebanon and the range known as the anti-Lebanon. For the Maronites, the political entity thus established represented the achievement of a long-standing aspiration for full access to the Mediterranean and territorial expansion. For the French it was more than confirmation of their historic "special relationship." Events in Damascus had demonstrated the potency of Arab nationalism, unsuspected before Faisal ibn Hussein earned international prominence through the Arab Revolt. The State of Greater Lebanon, therefore, became France's Middle Eastern stronghold, and if the tenuous nature of its position in the Alawite Mountains along the Damascus-Aleppo axis and in the Jebel Druse was recognized, it was never admitted.

Of the peoples inhabiting *Le Grand Liban*, the Shiites of the Tyre region and the northern Bekaa Valley, a rural and to some extent tribal community, were, because of their poverty, backwardness, and dependence, acquiescent to incorporation in a state dominated by Maronites and to some extent by Druses. The Sunni Muslims, a largely urban community concentrated in Beirut, Tripoli, and Sidon, looked to their coreligionist, Faisal, for inspiration and dreamed of Arab unity, of a new Umayyad Caliphate. Under Ottoman rule before 1920, the Sunni and Shi'a communities had had scarcely any experience in politics; even those capable of speaking for their people did not, for the most part, participate in Lebanese politics because of sentiments of pan-Arabism, hostility to the mandate, and resentment of the Christians. Those Sunnis who accepted appointments were ostracized in their own community. Lebanon, in the Sunni Muslim view, was an artificial creation whose *raison d'être* was the protection of Christian interests. The rigid Catholicism of the first of the French proconsuls, General Gouraud, fortified this allegation. Today, it is easy to say that the Christians should have worked to improve the condition of the Muslims and to instill in them a consciousness of being Lebanese. Such statements can be made with facility from a distance in time of fifty years. In the early 1920s, however, the negative Muslim attitudes gave the Christians the opportunity to reinforce their dominant role, building on the experience gained in the era of the *mutassarifiya*.

There were other complicating factors. The paternalism of French colonial officials was resented. Far worse was their imposition upon Lebanon of an electoral system of which a Carmine de Sapio or Boss Crump would have been pleased to claim authorship. The list system, which has been described as a "new feudalism," ensured that moneyed or landed interests could secure an unshakable control of local politics.

Disbursements of cash, arrangements for sharing out patronage, political rewards, and the use or threat of violence won elections. They still do to a regrettable extent. In a district with a mixed representation, such as the Shouf, in which eight parliamentary seats are contested (three allocated to Maronites, two to Sunnites, two to Druses, and one to Greek Catholics), the possibilities open to a clan leader in constructing a politically potent list are manifold.

Another factor complicating Lebanon's development during the interwar period was the polarization of French politics. Acceptance of and collaboration with French authorities increased when the more liberal Catholic, General Maxime Weygand, succeeded Gouraud. But with the advent of the leftist, anticlerical Herriot regime in Paris in 1924, Weygand was replaced by the controversial, dictatorial General Sarrail. For years Sarrail's outspoken hostility to the Catholic establishment in France had made him the stormy petrel of the army and the darling of French radicals. Although there was an ecumenical quality to the aged soldier's hostility (see Chapter 2), he was hardly the man to break bread with the Maronite Patriarch.

In doing his part to bring about the Druse uprising in Syria, Sarrail gained for himself a more important place in Lebanese history than he otherwise would have deserved. His anticlericalism sorely tried Maronite Lebanon's loyalty to France, but the Druse rising and the spread of turmoil in Syria provided the admixture of fear which maintained the special relationship between the two countries. Indeed, fear consorted with Maronite particularism to bring into existence the Republic of Lebanon, proclaimed in 1926, through the promulgation of a constitution which remains in force today and which possesses an unmatched record for longevity in the Arab world. The 1926 constitution was a major defeat for Muslim proponents of Lebanon's incorporation into a larger Arab territorial unit, for it stated that the existing boundaries of the new republic were unalterable. It might possibly have been the occasion of civil disorders had not its provisions given the presidency to a Greek Orthodox lawyer and journalist, Charles Debbas, rather than to one of the leaders of the Maronite community. The constitution left open the possibility of political collaboration and interaction between the several religious communities, and it is this fact that best explains its viability.

Sarrail's successors to the High Commissionership, the journalist and politician Henri de Jouvenal, the persevering professional diplomat, Henri Ponsot, and Count Damien de Martel, another diplomat better remembered for his cynicism than anything else, were all failures, if less dramatically so than Sarrail. Supporters of union between Syria and Lebanon were angered by Jouvenal's emphasis upon the historic "special relationship." Ponsot, who brought great gifts to the task, was hampered by the unbending policy of the Quai d'Orsay, while Martel was more interested in the ceremonial aspect of his assignment. In the decade following the promulgation of the 1926 constitution, Lebanon's political life continued to be distorted by the prior claims given sectarian and personal interests over the welfare of the state. Corruption, official ineptitude, and the wasteful application of the country's meager resources were apparent, but there were no concerted efforts to effect reform. The repeated interventions of religious leaders in the domain of public affairs barred progress toward national solidarity and caused a temporary suspension of the constitution during Ponsot's term of office.

Yet the decade before 1936 was not completely devoid of political development. Sunnite participation in the parliamentary process began on a limited scale. The failure of treaty negotiations with France in 1936 (see Chapter 2) created unrest and dissatisfaction, but opposition was muted by an awareness that a French presence was preferable to the thrusting imperialism of Mussolini's Italy.

As economic conditions improved after 1936, Lebanon began to acquire the infrastructure of a modern state. The civil service was improved and advances were made in public administration. But factionalism persisted, nourished by the polarization of political life in Europe. The spread of fascist movements in France, Germany, and Eastern Europe invited emulation in Lebanon, thus giving rise to such political groupings as the Phalange (1936), a paramilitary organization enthusiastically supported by young Maronites who equated patriotism with opposition to any Lebanese compromise with pan-Arabism. Muslim reaction took the form of the Najjada ("Succour") Party (1937), also paramilitary and largely drawn from the Sunnite community in Beirut. Clashes between these groupings were not the only threats to the painful evolution of the parliamentary process in Lebanon. After 1930 extremism had been fostered by the *Partie Populaire Syrienne*, the creation of a Greek Orthodox intellectual, Antun Saadeh. The PPS was the only political grouping which was effectively multiconfessional, the leadership being largely Greek Orthodox and Protestant, with the ranks of its "storm troopers" swelled by Druses and Shiites. Until very recently, it opposed Lebanese particularism and called for a form of Fertile Crescent unity (Palestine, Lebanon, Syria, Iraq) with the inclusion, curiously enough, of Cyprus as "the star of the crescent." (The fact that Cyprus was deemed important for the defense of the rest of the envisioned state suggests that as a strategist Saadeh was no better than Disraeli.) All three organizations contributed to civil unrest until they were suppressed in 1939, and all three reemerged after the war. The Communist Party, originally dominated by the Armenians, became more "national" and better organized in the 1930s.

Despite the proliferation of various forms of political extremism and increasingly abrasive relations with Syria (which after 1939 demanded the cession of Tripoli as compensation for the loss of Alexandretta), conservative Maronite elements, allied with mercantile interests in Beirut and supported by the mandate authority, controlled the government of Lebanon through the outbreak of World War II. At the head of the government was France's man, Emile Edde. His principal rival, also a political veteran, was Bishara al-Khuri, who was to become the first president of independent Lebanon. Commanding formidable support among Christians and Druses, al-Khuri had something of a following in the Muslim community as well. But French support for Edde was the ultimate determinant.

The shape of things to come was to be seen in the guiding philosophies of the two major parties. Edde's National Bloc identified pan-Arabism as the principal threat to Lebanon's survival. The Constitutional Bloc, led by al-Khuri, took the position that Lebanon's integrity could be safeguarded only through Muslim-Christian cooperation. Before al-Khuri's formula could be put to the test, Hitler sent his armies into Poland and, with the conclusion of the Franco-German armistice on June 22, 1940, Lebanon became a Vichy colony.

World War II had two distinct phases for Lebanon. The first involved hardship for all levels of the population. General Dentz, the High Commissioner, made Lebanon into a police state and a base for further German penetration of the Middle East. Fortunately for the Allies, the Germans were incapable of taking full advantage of the facilities offered them in the Levant by the Vichy regime. The two years of the Dentz government ended with the invasion of Lebanon by Free French, British and Australian forces. This began the second phase, which entailed financial recovery achieved at the cost of stripping Lebanon of its forests and other natural resources in order to supply the needs of the Allies. The financial weakness of the victorious Allies and the strong demands on sterling and French franc reserves made by Middle Eastern countries as a result of the strong credit positions they had built up were to be significant factors in the immediate postwar era. A number of private fortunes made during World War II were to weigh heavily on the political scales of independent Lebanon.

This small country also had something to do with making the Cross of Lorraine so much of a burden for Winston Churchill. General de Gaulle, whose policy for Lebanon harked back to the days of his old commanders Gouraud and Weygand, sought to restore full French hegemony in the Levant. It was his understanding and assertion that the British had acquiesced in the paramountcy of French interests in Syria and Lebanon. But it was not to be. The tide of nationalism was at flood level as the war drew to an end, and in the eastern Mediterranean a new power, the United States, was attempting to define its interests and responsibilities.

Although de Gaulle condemned Great Britain for meddling in the affairs of post-Vichy Lebanon, it was in fact cooperation between the British and Americans which upset his plans and led to what the French community in Beirut described as "the second Fashoda." In the 1943 elections, General Sir Edward Spears, who headed the British mission, openly and energetically supported Camille Chamoun as a reform candidate for the presidency. This was a direct challenge to France's sturdy perennial, Emile Edde. Deadlock ensued and with it emerged the possibility of civil strife. Bishara al-Khuri was put forward as a compromise candidate, with Chamoun reluctantly agreeing to take the role of *dauphin.*

The compromise candidate turned out to be uncompromisingly anti-French. The new government introduced a number of constitutional amendments and proclaimed that all official ties with France were severed. French military authorities responded by rounding up the president, Prime Minister Riad as-Sulh, and the rest of the cabinet, including Minister of Interior Chamoun, and imprisoning them in Rashayya Fort. The constitution was suspended and Edde was designated as provisional head of state. But not for long. Faced with a general strike, spreading civic disorder, and relentless Anglo-American pressure, the French released the Rashayya inmates, stepped aside, and permitted the situation to revert to the *status quo ante.* French prestige in the Middle East was at its lowest ebb.[4]

Bishara al-Khuri and Riad as-Sulh were a potent political combination. The Maronite president had participated in Lebanon's political life throughout the mandate. The Sunnite premier had earned a reputation for astuteness and parliamentary skill before forming his first cabinet. Between them the concept of the National Covenant was evolved. Lebanese elders today recall having tiny paper Lebanese flags, the famed cedar tree against a red and white field, pinned to their lapels by Bishara al-Khuri in 1943, as he called for their support of the National Covenant. The Covenant was and remains an unwritten, oral agreement consisting simply of two principles. (1) Lebanon as an Arab state should never call upon a Western power for assistance if such action is detrimental to Arab interests; (2) Lebanese Muslims should manifest their

---

[4]But the last word would be deGaulle's, when his condemnation of Israel during the Six Day War of June 1967 raised the prestige of France to unprecedented heights in the Arab world.

commitment to the state by refusing to support efforts to incorporate Lebanon into some larger Arab political entity.

The balancing act had in fact begun during the mandate period. In the 1930s it had been established that the president should be a Maronite and the prime minister a Sunnite Muslim. Now, in 1943, the division of authority was carried much further. The Chamber of Deputies would be based upon a proportion of representation of six Christians to five Muslims (including Druses). A number of key posts, such as army commander and director of the *Sûreté Générale*, were reserved for the Maronites. In 1947, when the speakership of the Chamber of Deputies was set aside for the Shiite community, it was assumed that the post was largely ceremonial. In recent years, however, the Shiites have made considerable progress in organizing and articulating their political objectives, and as a result the speaker has come to play an important role in the cut and thrust of Lebanese politics.

Nor have other confessions been denied political influence. Although the Greek Orthodox and Greek Catholics do not have official positions reserved for them, their power finds expression in commerce and finance —and from time to time as veritable kingmakers. Political strategists will ignore the Armenian bloc in the Chamber at their peril. The Druses are a confessional group which has long had, and continues to have, political power disproportionate to its size. In part this derives from a martial reputation and an important place in Lebanon's history. More recently, the adroitness of Kamal Junblatt, who organized his faction into the Progressive Socialist Party in 1949, has conferred importance on the Druses. It also assured the ascendancy of the Junblatt faction over the rival Yazbaki Druse faction, led by the colorful Shaikh Majid Arslan, although the two have occasionally acted in concert.

The Civil War of 1958

Having achieved power in a newly independent Lebanon, President al-Khuri got on with enjoying what he considered to be the perquisites of his high office. His brother Salim took charge of political patronage while another brother, Fuad, divided his time between chairmanship of the cement trust and of the new international airport commission. Most foreign firms found it to be in their interest to retain a son of the president, Khalil, as legal representative. He also supervised the issuance of building permits and other similarly profitable official formalities. Politics in Lebanon before 1952 might be described as Tammany Hall East. Al-Khuri's actions prompted the veteran political leader of Sunnite Tripoli, Abdul Hamid Karami, to assert that the president thought of Lebanon as his personal plantation, to be plowed, harrowed, and reaped on behalf of the proprietor.

Lebanon resembled Tammany Hall also in the ruthlessness with which al-Khuri and Riad as-Sulh strengthened their political base by manipulating electoral lists. In the 1947 election the ward bosses did their work so thoroughly that government sponsored candidates won forty-seven out of fifty-five seats in the Chamber despite an economic depression. Complaints of electoral abuses, including the use of police power against opposition candidates, were disregarded.

Bishara al-Khuri lost his gifted accomplice to an assassin's bullet in 1951. Riad as-Sulh was gunned down in Amman, an act of retribution by the *Partie Populaire Syrienne* for the summary trial and execution of their leader, Antun Saadeh. Resentment over blatant corruption in the highest offices of the country spread, and a deepening economic crisis brought Lebanon to the brink of revolution.

Disclosure that the president had imported a large number of automobiles, duty free, to sell through middlemen brought about a temporary alliance between Camille Chamoun and Kamal Junblatt, who engineered a general strike. Al-Khuri, unable to find an acceptable Sunnite notable to form a cabinet, resigned in September 1952 and army commander Fuad Chehab served as interim prime minister until the Chamber elected Chamoun to the presidency.

Bishara al-Khuri's name will forever be associated with Lebanon's achievement of "independence." But in the years since 1945 that term has come to have a hollow ring for Lebanon. The al-Khuri regime exploited to the utmost the symbolic value of the departure of seventeen thousand French and British troops in 1946. But their departure also hastened the onset of an economic depression. Nor did the winding up of the mandate signify the end of the "special relationship." French educational, economic, military, and even political assistance increased rather than diminished after 1943 and was augmented by aid from other quarters. Lebanon would have become slightly more independent before 1952 had the governing clique sincerely concerned itself with economic development rather than merely using such development as a mask for personal aggrandizement. Likewise, Lebanon would have achieved greater independence after 1952 had the regime worked energetically to bring Lebanese Muslims more fully into the political life of the country and had it provided them with opportunities for education in political and social affairs. Instead, the political education of the opposition came from abroad, by way of the Voice of the Arabs, Radio Cairo, and the speeches of Gamal Abdul Nasser after King Farouk was deposed. Bishara al-Khuri seems not to have realized that the National Covenant was not just a political deal, but a contractual undertaking with many implicit obligations.

Lebanon was, to be sure, a founding member of the Arab League and a signatory to the Inter-Arab Joint Defense Alliance (1950), which was the source of some of the more reasoned and eloquent condemnations of Israeli policy. What is more, as a small state, she was more zealous than Egypt in enforcing the sanctions of the office which supervises the boycott of firms dealing with Israel. This could hardly have been otherwise, and it confers neither credit nor blame upon the successive governments. Such activities had their value in internal politics, placating Lebanon's Muslim population as well as giving the country a voice in regional affairs.

For the foregoing reasons, the name of Bishara al-Khuri evokes ambiguous reactions, making it difficult to answer the question of how effectively his political acumen served his country and how much it served himself. Such is not the case with Camille Chamoun, for his six years as president (1952–58) concluded with the country embroiled in civil war, its very future in jeopardy. There is great irony in this, for the Chamoun regime came to power pledged to implement political, economic, and social reforms, worked diligently to do so, and made considerable progress in some sectors.

Camille Chamoun continues to play a role in Lebanese political life in the 1970s. But in 1952 he was at the height of his powers, a born leader, handsome, an accomplished sportsman, fluent in English and French and, indeed, more fluent in Arabic than others who have held Lebanon's highest office since 1958. He entered office determined to dispense with a Chamber packed with al-Khuri supporters and to make electoral reform the wellspring of all other reforms in the country. While Radio Cairo and Radio Damascus criticized the feudal, clan-oriented nature of Lebanese politics, Chamoun sought the necessary remedies. The Chamber, aware of the possibility of disclosure of past dealings and sharings-out, provided for its own demise by authorizing revision of the electoral law and by voting, sixty-five to one (with ten abstentions), to confer authority upon the Chamoun government to rule by decree.

The seventy-seven-member Chamber of Deputies was thereupon replaced by one of forty-four seats, while the number of electoral districts was increased from nine to thirty-three.[5] Through this "gerrymander

---

[5]Eleven constituencies had two deputies each, and the other twenty-two each elected one deputy. The six-to-five confessional ratio was maintained with the following breakdown of seats: Christians (24)—13 Maronites, 5 Greek Orthodox, 3 Greek Catholics, 2 Armenian Orthodox, 1 representing other Christian minorities; Muslims (20)—9 Sunnites, 8 Shiites, 3 Druses.

in reverse" Chamoun and his advisors hoped to minimize the manipulation of electoral lists. With thirty-three less seats available and with smaller districts making for fewer divisions in the voting ranks, the records of traditional candidates would be subjected to closer scrutiny by voters whose support, it was felt, would no longer be based on the dispensation of cash, patronage, or threats. Candidates were required to deposit three thousand Lebanese pounds (nearly one thousand dollars) upon filing, which would be returned only if they secured 20 percent of the votes in their districts. For the first time women obtained the vote and provision was made to levy fines on males who failed to exercise their right to vote.

The Chamoun regime accomplished civil service reform and produced more orderly economic development planning and clearer annual budgets, but the scale of success was limited. This must be ascribed to the failure of the electoral reform law to accomplish its objectives. A nationwide agitation was directed against the reform program by the "electoral feudalists," and the elections of 1953 were held in an atmosphere of violence. Murders, abductions, and extensive street fighting led to the suspension of campaigning. Intimidated voters preferred to pay fines rather than risk going to the polls, since voting was a public process. Not more than 60 percent of the electorate actually voted and the result was hardly a reform-oriented Chamber of Deputies.

This election demonstrated that a truly modern and progressive political system was beyond reach so long as the confessional system was retained. No Lebanese leader has yet been strong enough to bring about the restructuring of the electoral process. Hence obstruction to proposals to carry out an official census continues, although obvious conclusions can be drawn from such factors as the high rate of emigration by Christians and the swelling Muslim birth rate. Nor are the Christians the only supporters of this conspiracy of statistical silence. Established Sunnite politicians fear that a census may reveal that the Shiite community is overtaking the Sunnites in numbers. With each year the potential of the population explosion as a primer for a catastrophic political explosion becomes greater.

As difficult as it was for Chamoun to carry out an effective domestic policy, it was in the arena of external relations that he was ultimately defeated. His long-standing ties and obligations to Great Britain, no less than his opposition to Nasser's policies, made it impossible for Lebanon to join other Arab countries in breaking relations with the United Kingdom and France during the Suez War of 1956. Chamoun's opponents did not take seriously the government claim that the country should not be cut off from the Lebanese diaspora in British- and French-controlled territories, especially in West Africa. A more flexible politician simply would have asked that the British and French envoys be temporarily withdrawn, a maneuver employed by the Helou regime with respect to the United States and Great Britain during the Six Day War of June 1967. Instead, Chamoun underscored his pro-Western policy by subscribing to the Eisenhower Doctrine in 1957. Syrian and Egyptian press and radio attacks on Lebanon's government reached a crescendo in April 1957 when the United States Sixth Fleet took up stations off the Lebanese coast in response to an impending civil war in Jordan (see Chapter 3).

As Lebanon's isolation in the Arab world developed, Sunnite leaders saw an opportunity to alter the country's political structure. President Nasser's extraordinary success in converting military defeat in the Suez War into political victory further stimulated pan-Arab sentiments. The proclamation of the United Arab Republic in February 1958 had an especially intoxicating effect on Muslim politicians such as Saeb Salam. After all, it was Salam's father, Salim Salam, who founded the Mu'tamar as-Sahil (Conference of the Coast) after World War I to oppose the concept of Lebanon as an artificial, Franco-Maronite instrumentality, and worked for union with Faisal's short-lived kingdom in Syria.

Saeb Salam skillfully organized opposition to Chamoun throughout 1957, playing upon every possible slight, insult, or hostile act experienced by Muslims, Druses, and Christians at the hands of Chamounites. Although he did not succeed in installing a nonpartisan government to supervise elections to the Chamber, a preliminary to the 1958 presidential election, Salam did succeed in organizing the first major opposition group under Muslim leadership to include a broad spectrum of confessional representation. Powerful Maronite presidential aspirants (such as Hamid Frangieh and Fuad Ammoun), Maronite supporters of Bishara al-Khuri, and even the traditional "first citizen of Lebanon," the Maronite Patriarch Peter Paul, Cardinal Meouchi, joined Salam's National Front.[6] So did the Druse leader Kamal Junblatt, who had broken with Chamoun as early as 1953. The Armenian community took sides and the pro-Soviet Hentchak Party lined up with Salam primarily because of Chamoun's support for the successful Tashnak Party candidate for Catholicos in 1956.

Having become disillusioned with electoral reform in 1953, Chamoun and his partisans demonstrated that they were as capable as anyone else

---

[6]Appointed by the Holy See in 1955, Meouchi was the first Patriarch to obtain the post in this manner, rather than by election by the College of Maronite Bishops. He later became a cardinal in the Roman Catholic hierarchy and remains in office today.

of organizing a traditional election. Chamoun supporters won a wide margin of seats in the new chamber, and the defeated candidates further swelled the ranks of Salam's National Front. The regime then organized support for a constitutional amendment which would give Chamoun another six years in the presidency. The reelection of Bishara al-Khuri had been made possible by a similar amendment in 1949 and no great difficulty was foreseen by Chamoun's National Liberal Party.

Shortly before the amendment was to be introduced in the Chamber, a journalist who supported Salam's coalition was murdered. The government was accused of complicity and a strike was called to prevent the parliament from meeting. Fighting broke out in Tripoli and in the Basta quarter of Beirut—both Sunnite centers—and quickly spread throughout the country. Rebellion became civil war. Syria, the "Northern Region" of the United Arab Republic, supplied arms, men, and financial support as well as radio and press attacks on Chamoun's "traitorous regime." Infiltration was an easy matter for the insurgents (as it would be again for the *Sai'qah* commando movement in late 1969), for the Lebanese government controlled only about seventeen miles of the Syro-Lebanese frontier. Chamoun's hope that his pro-Western friend, Iraqi Prime Minister Nuri Pasha Said, would bring pressure to bear on Syria and provide other forms of assistance ended with the Baghdad *coup* of July 14, 1958. The Baghdad situation, rather than the course of events in Lebanon, brought the United States Marines ashore south of Beirut on the following day, but the broader ramifications of American strategy were not to be apparent for some time.

More than the presence of American forces, the brooding personality of the commander of the army, General Fuad Chehab, was the key factor in the outcome of the Lebanese crisis. Chehab faced a situation ideal for a person who had already permitted his name to be listed among contenders for the presidency (all the while issuing denials and alleging that his ambitions lay elsewhere). Assuring Chamoun that the army would split into confessional factions if it were ordered to do more than attempt to prevent clashes between government and opposition supporters, Chehab refused to take offensive action to stop rioting. Heretofore, the army, an outgrowth of the *Troupes Spéciales du Levant* of mandate days, had a quasi-independent status. It was to be fully integrated with political authority once Chehab was established in the presidential palace, but in 1958 it was not available to President Chamoun as an executant of his policy. Hence the civil war was essentially a conflict between well-armed gangs.

Chamoun and his supporters will carry to their graves the conviction that he was betrayed by the United States. Chamoun supported the

Eisenhower Doctrine and considered it an example of how a small country could collaborate with a great power for mutual benefit. But in late 1958, Secretary of State John Foster Dulles was persuaded that King Saud ibn Abdul Aziz was hardly the Arab leader upon whom the United States could depend in efforts to construct a viable Middle Eastern policy. Only President Nasser might fulfill that role, perhaps to the extent of being able to overcome general Arab opposition to a negotiated peace with Israel. It would hardly do, then, to have American forces assist President Chamoun crush his opponents who at that time had Nasser's enthusiastic support. Thus President Chamoun's pro-American stance was sacrificed on the altar of improved Egyptian-American relations. The United States called for a political settlement of the Lebanese crisis and urged the election of a new president acceptable to both sides. The latter condition was not attainable, but as the least committed available Maronite, General Chehab was elected to the presidency by the parliament at the end of July 1958.

The Chehab Era

With the laying down—or burying—of arms in September 1958, the Chehab era really began. It was a period of quiet repression during which the president drew upon lessons from the previous regimes to ensure complete control of the country. An admirer of General de Gaulle, Chehab, too, claimed to be the personification of his country. Emulating de Gaulle's aloofness, he rarely appeared in public and worked through a few carefully chosen assistants and advisors, several of whom had been seconded from the French public service. A strengthened army with an improved and enlarged intelligence branch maintained close contact with developments throughout the country and worked with the *Deuxième Bureau* to stifle opposition and ensure tranquility. In reforming and modernizing the army and making it an instrumentality of political control, the president was only following the trend in other Arab countries where the army's principal function was the maintenance of internal security rather than the defense of frontiers.

Enlargement of the civil service provided additional patronage for the growing ranks of Chehab supporters, albeit at the expense of the quality of the service. Chehab assured that political activity would have more form than substance for at least three years by allying himself with Prime Minister Rashid Karami, the Tripoli Sunnite leader, and Kamal Junblatt, who took the portfolio of Minister of Interior. The reemergence of the Najjada and Phalange parties had little political significance beyond providing safety valves for the pent-up political emotions aroused by the 1958 civil conflict. To ensure full participation in the superficial political life of the country, a new electoral law was promulgated in April 1960. With ninety-nine members, the Chamber of Deputies was the largest in Lebanon's history.[7] The secret ballot was introduced and candidates were required to secure 25 percent of the vote or forfeit their deposits. The number of constituencies was reduced to twenty-six, which facilitated a recrudescence of local political activity dominated by clan leaders. The secret ballot did not put an end to complaints of rigged elections and no ballot since the introduction of the law has been free of substantiated charges of unlawful interference in the electoral process.

The political grouping least capable of coming to terms with the new dispensation was the *Partie Populaire Syrienne*, which had supported Chamoun in the 1958 fighting. The party had for the most part shelved its original program and now regarded Lebanon as the last bastion in the Arab world against socialism and a left-wing variety of pan-Arabism. Therefore, President Chehab's careful "balancing of confessions" appeared to PPS militants as a threat to Lebanon's heritage. A number of them believed that a PPS-dominated government in Lebanon might provide a base from which the leftist regime in Damascus could be overthrown. However, many others had the more limited objective of removing Lebanon from the ambit of Nasserite policy. On the last day of 1961, the PPS attempted a *coup d'état*, which was as remarkable for the ineptitude of the army and the security forces as it was for that of the perpetrators.

Following the attempted *coup*, over four thousand arrests were made and nearly two thousand persons were detained for further investigation through February 1962. Minister of Interior Junblatt rigorously enforced the detention of PPS members and their sympathizers, most of whom were Christian. It was considered in many quarters that Junblatt was taking revenge on the PPS for its role in the 1958 civil war. Pierre Gemayel, the leader of the Phalange Party, threatened that " . . . the Phalange will replace rifle for rifle and bullet for bullet from their private arsenal, arms taken from Christians by the government in excess of arms taken from non-Christians." The most stringent security measures were imposed for the following six months, and in September a military court condemned seventy-nine persons, only eleven of whom were in

---

[7]The six-to-five confessional ratio was maintained with the following breakdown of seats: Christians (54)—30 Maronites, 11 Greek Orthodox, 6 Greek Catholics, 4 Armenian Orthodox, 1 Armenian Catholic, 1 Protestant, 1 Minorities (they include Roman Catholic, Syriac Orthodox, and Syriac Catholics); Muslims (45)—20 Sunnites, 19 Shiites, 6 Druses.

custody at the time, to death for their part in the attempted *coup*. The executions were never carried out and the last of the prisoners was released in 1971.

During the Chehab years, Lebanon achieved a measure of economic independence by becoming a political satellite of Egypt. By following the Egyptian line, President Chehab ensured that the Muslim population of Lebanon would not disrupt the nation's economic development. The Beirut newspaper *an-Nahar* was suspended for ten days for publishing a cartoon depicting Lebanon as a province of the U A R. There was much truth in the cartoon's assertion, for the Egyptian Ambassador in Lebanon was frequently referred to as "the High Commissioner." After the breakup of the UAR, Lebanese identification with Egyptian causes created considerable difficulty with Syria. There were border clashes and frequent disruptions of the all-important transit trade from Lebanon through Syria to Jordan, Iraq, and the Persian Gulf states.

Chehab's term of office coincided with a period of relative quietude in international relations in the Middle East. As his term drew to a close, he frequently rejected petitions from various quarters to accept renomination. He knew that action to amend the constitution could cause another political crisis and preferred to sponsor a pliable candidate who would let him work behind the scenes. The selection of Charles Helou was regarded as a continuation of Chehabist policies and the best means of debarring Maronite stalwarts from Lebanese politics. Despite these efforts at pacification, political tranquility and economic progress did not continue for long, nor, for that matter, did Chehab's success in asserting influence over Helou once the latter had spent a short period in the presidential palace. The October 1965 failure of Intra Bank, the largest in Lebanon, with extensive international operations, was more fateful for the country than the subsequent Six Day War in June 1967. The collapse placed one of the country's most important economic activities in jeopardy. In the realm of banking, Lebanon was often referred to as the Switzerland of the Middle East. Within months, 90 percent of bank deposits in Lebanon were shifted to foreign-controlled banks.

The crisis tended to conceal for a time Helou's determination to be his own man, but this was dramatically asserted in 1966 by a ruthless administrative purge which earned widespread respect for the regime. Seventeen judges, fourteen high-ranking diplomats, and over fifty senior civil servants were dismissed at that time on charges of corruption and incompetence. The effect throughout the ranks of public servants was salutary.

The Arab-Israeli conflict of mid-1967 caused massive anti-Western demonstrations in Beirut. American institutions were especially threatened, but the security forces proved equal to the demanding tasks confronting them. The government requested and secured the withdrawal of the American and British ambassadors, an action which satisfied all but the most militant sections of the population. Nevertheless, there was considerable pressure upon the government to join the war against Israel, and many leading politicians, such as Prime Minister Rashid Karami, seemed ready to bow to it. But the army intervened to keep Lebanon out of the conflict, which doubtless would have established new Israeli frontiers on the south bank of the Litani River. From time to time since 1948, Israel had claimed that the Litani south bank was a "natural frontier." The more extremist Christians in Lebanon professed sympathy with Israel on this score, not because of any desire to lose some of Lebanon's finest agricultural land, but in order to restore the confessional balance by removing a predominantly Muslim area from the Lebanese political scene.

The Arab-Israeli war exacerbated confessional tensions in Lebanon and brought on a prolonged domestic crisis. European tourist trade nearly vanished and recovery was slow. (Arab tourism continued, however, at a fairly high level.) More important was the decline in Lebanon-based international commerce, which had the additional adverse effect of limiting the purchasing power of the resident foreign business community. To an economy attempting to shake off the effects of the Intra Bank collapse, the June war was a damaging second blow.

The Aftermath of the Six Day War

A grave new problem was introduced into the political life of Lebanon after June 1967 when Palestinian commando organizations began making extensive use of Beirut for their activities because it was the best communications center in the Arab world. Commandos frequently departed from Beirut International Airport on the first stage of operations, some of which involved the hijacking of commercial aircraft.[8] Throughout 1968 the commandos built up bases in southern Lebanon, and for the first time since 1948, the Libano-Israeli frontier was the scene of frequent clashes. The Israeli response to commando activities came in late December 1968 in the form of a massive attack on the Beirut International Airport during which a large number of Lebanese commercial aircraft were destroyed. The tactical brilliance of the operation was

---

[8]The hijackings were the work of the Popular Front for the Liberation of Palestine, a small but highly organized neo-Marxist group. The largest commando group is *Fatah*, the paramilitary wing of the Palestine Liberation Organization.

quickly overshadowed by its political ramifications. Not only was Israel widely censured for attacking a country which had long struggled to avoid involvement in the Arab-Israeli conflict, but now Lebanon was drawn inexorably into the nexus of that continuing tragedy. The Israeli action had the effect of stimulating further commando activity in southern Lebanon, which by late 1969 had grown to proportions alarming to both Lebanese and Israeli authorities.

Fighting between commando elements and Lebanese security forces in April 1969 punctuated an uneasy peace which had been maintained ever since the Syrian-sponsored *Sai'qah* commando group began infiltrating into southeastern Lebanon earlier in the year, led by regular Syrian army officers. The increasing tempo of its activities was a challenge to Yassir Arafat's *Fatah* organization, which asserts a *primus inter pares* position in the Palestinian liberation movement. Infiltration continued and as autumn wore on the prospect of spending a winter freezing for the cause on the slopes of Mount Hermon became increasingly unattractive to the commandos. A series of trials of strength resulted in Lebanese army attacks on commando units and brought on the crisis of October 1969.

In the October crisis, Arafat permitted himself and his organization to be drawn into the Syrian web, but the fact that Syria was something of a pariah in Arab affairs was of advantage to Lebanese authorities. The Sunni Muslim poor, whether Lebanese living in the Basta or Palestinians in the camps, tended to look to Cairo for inspiration. By 1969, President Nasser had had more than his share of setbacks at the hands of the Syrians and was disinclined to encourage their adventurism. Nor was he interested in appropriating an antigovernment insurrection in Lebanon for his own purposes, inasmuch as he was fully occupied on the Suez front and with challenges to his primacy at home. Moreover, the heightening of tension on the Lebanese frontier with Israel posed a threat to a general Middle Eastern settlement based upon United Nations resolution 242 of November 1967—a settlement which Nasser desired more than he dared to admit.[9] Therefore, Nasser was willing to act as a mediator between Lebanon and the commandos in an effort to reduce *Fatah*'s collaboration with the Syrians, which was in his interest as well as in the interest of Lebanon.

---

[9]The basic provision of Security Council resolution 242, which was adopted unanimously, is that Israel should evacuate all occupied territories and return to the pre-Six Day War frontiers. Adjustments were to be negotiable. The Arab countries, in return, would terminate any status of belligerency, recognize the right of Israel to live in peace within secure, established boundaries, and acknowledge Israel's sovereignty, territorial integrity, and political independence. The necessity for guaranteeing freedom of navigation through international waterways and for achieving a just settlement of the refugee problem was also affirmed in the resolution.

Peace was restored briefly on the basis of The Cairo Agreement of November 1969, which called for a "standstill"—i.e., the commandos would not be attacked by Lebanese forces if they would confine their activities to a specific area and would agree to no further augmentation of their strength. The Lebanese objective was to encourage the commandos to use their base in Lebanon for operations against occupied Syria (the Golan area) rather than for raids across the Libano-Israeli border. Although *Fatah* announced that a number of its members would be disarmed and that its offices in refugee camps would be closed, there was in fact a renewal of guerrilla activity.

Commando defiance of Lebanese authorities was stimulated by increasing evidence of divisions in the leadership of anticommando and antiarmy elements within the country. Among Maronite leaders, Camille Chamoun and Raymond Edde were opposed to the army, regarding it as a Chehabist instrumentality which had attempted to interfere with their campaigning in recent elections. Another Christian politician, Sleiman Frangieh from north Lebanon, was even more outspoken than either Chamoun or Edde in his opposition to the army in the weeks preceding the October crisis. Only Pierre Gemayel, leader of the Phalange, showed a more cooperative attitude and kept on reasonably good terms with Helou, Chehab, and the army.

Willingness to use the commando issue for partisan political ends was not limited to the Christian community. Farouk Muqaddem, the Tripoli lawyer whose family has been engaged in political rivalry *cum* blood feud with the family of Rashid Karami since Ottoman times, saw in the crisis an opportunity to broaden his local power base. He was also encouraged by the success of left-wing elements, underwritten by the Iraqi Baathist regime, in eroding Karami's position. More than any other section of Lebanon, Tripoli has continued to look to Damascus for guidance, a factor which became ominous when Muqaddem saw opportunities for himself in the "commando crisis."

Many Muslims, both established members of the middle class and new arrivals, were solidly behind the Lebanese authorities in the crisis. For them, the cost of confessional strife in 1958 was a painful memory, and even those who were too young to have benefited from that experience believed that their ambitions and expectations were more likely to be satisfied under a political and economic system which is the antithesis of Arab socialism. The Shiite community had additional reasons for supporting the status quo, drawn from the experiences of their coreligionists in Iraq. The leader of the Shiite council, Shaikh Musa Sadr, played a constructive, moderate role in the October crisis. Most important of all, the crisis demonstrated that the army was really a Lebanese army. Its adversaries in Damascus and in the commando camps must have expected it to be paralyzed by the confessional divisions which all but neutralized it in 1958, but this was by no means the case. Officers and men alike, whatever their backgrounds, responded admirably to the demands placed upon them. A call for volunteers met with over five thousand responses, a dramatic demonstration of the unifying effect of the emergency.

The commandos did not, however, remain quiescent. Their activities in 1970 caused a number of Israeli retaliatory raids into southern Lebanon. The resulting economic burden imposed upon Lebanon was severe, for nearly forty thousand Shiite agriculturalists fled the frontier area in early autumn, most of them settling in the outskirts of Beirut. Although many eventually returned, the situation in the south was a major issue in the electoral campaign for the presidency in 1970.

At the outset of the campaign, Fuad Chehab's return to the presidency was frequently predicted, leading Chamoun, Edde, and Gemayel to conclude a fragile alliance in opposition to him. It quickly dissolved, however, when the former president failed to rally the support of the politicians who had collaborated with him during his term of office, the most important of whom was Kamal Junblatt. Chehab's refusal to put forward the name of his principal advisor, Elias Sarkis, in time to organize support through traditional methods may be ascribed to his characteristic remoteness and disdain for open campaigning. When the Chamber of Deputies cast their ballots, the Chehabist candidate was defeated by one vote.

That vote was cast by the deputy from Zghorta, the Maronite stronghold of north Lebanon. The deputy was Sleiman Frangieh, who through his own ballot secured his election to the presidency. The perennial Maronite candidates, Chamoun, Edde, and Gemayel, had canceled each other out in pursuing their own ambitions once it was clear that Chehab was out of the running.

For years Sleiman Frangieh stood in the shadow of his more personable and better educated brother Hamid. His role was to organize support for Hamid, who was Zghorta's deputy and who held portfolios in several cabinets. When Hamid was paralyzed by coronary thrombosis, Sleiman stepped into the national political arena. He brought with him a reputation for toughness which has been manifested in office by his firm handling of commandos and other potentially disruptive elements. Less anticipated was his support for a young "technocrat" cabinet in preference to a coalition of old-line politicians. The only veteran selected was the durable Saeb Salam, who became prime minister. A moderate reformist program was implemented in the face of difficulties posed by traditionalism, economic depression, and the continuing Arab-Israeli crisis.

The principal problem inherited from the Helou regime was located in "Fatahland," a small strip of territory in southeastern Lebanon, to the east of the Hasbani River and in the foothills of Mount Hermon. From this sanctuary, Palestinian commandos launched rockets and mounted raids, continuously placing the stability of the Lebanese government in jeopardy. When the writ of the Lebanese authorities ceased to run in this area, it became the closest approximation of a Palestinian territory that that unfortunate people may ever achieve. Only the actuality and ever-present threat of Israeli reprisal prevented commando groups from expanding their activities beyond hit-and-run tactics. Because Israeli reprisals were not limited to this area, however, those who suffered most were the villagers and farmers in the entire border area south of the Litani River, which enters the Mediterranean near Tyre. Meetings were held between government and commando leaders in early 1971 as part of a continuing effort to keep the frontier from once more going up in flames. At the same time, various plans were announced and partially implemented to provide relief for the depressed agricultural population of southern Lebanon. Improved relations with Syria materially aided this effort, and critics of the politics of compromise, such as members of the Lebanese Communist Party, were arrested or otherwise intimidated.

But with the crushing of the Palestinian military capability in Jordan by mid-1971 (see Chapter 4), "Fatahland" once again became an urgent concern of the Beirut regime.[10] The Palestine Liberation Organization no longer functioned as a quasi-government in Jordan, and large numbers of commandos were flooding into Syria and across the Syro-Lebanese frontier. Frequent clashes occurred between commandos and security authorities in Lebanese cities. On many occasions Prime Minister Saeb Salam attempted to draw a fine distinction between support for the cause of Palestine and upholding law and order. Discontent over deteriorating security, however, was on the rise, especially after a spate of rocket attacks on Israeli positions in January 1972 and the beheading of an Israeli civilian near the frontiers by commandos. A new series of Israeli raids began, and once again the regime was faced with the choice of placing all of southern Lebanon—and perhaps the city of Beirut itself—

---

[10]The young and erratic dictator of Libya, Colonel Qaddafi, charged that Lebanon was collaborating with King Hussein in his campaign against the Palestinian commandos. But Lebanese authorities were relieved when Qaddafi, upon discovering that the Popular Front for the Liberation of Palestine held views antithetical to Islam, terminated his lavish financial support for those specialists in hijacking and terrorism. An alternative outlet for his fanaticism would soon be found—"Black September" (Chapter 4).

at the mercy of the ubiquitous Israeli armed forces or cracking down hard on the commandos. An Israeli ultimatum underscored the seriousness of the situation and was followed by strong anticommando measures by the Lebanese army and security forces. The Syrian regime cooperated by placing heavy restraints upon *Sai'qah*. After numerous conferences, Yassir Arafat agreed to a strict limitation on commando operations from "Fatahland."

Yet Arafat, quite obviously, was no longer the spokesman for the entire guerrilla movement, for in February more rockets were fired into Israeli positions. Israel retaliated with extensive land and air operations against the guerrilla bases. Refugee camps were strafed and bombed from the air, villages known to harbor guerrillas were demolished, and for four days beginning on February 25, what had been an autonomous Palestinian territory within Lebanon was under the full control of the Israeli armed forces. Great Power pressures expressed through the United Nations and regular diplomatic channels eventually convinced the Israelis that their objective had been accomplished and the action was broken off. But small bands of Palestinian guerrillas continue to be the determinants of Israel's policy toward Lebanon.

Internal turmoil was not solely of Palestinian authorship. Throughout 1971 Lebanon was plagued by strikes involving students, trade unions, bank workers, and communications specialists. In addition, the Lebanese Merchants Association struck when import duties on luxury goods were increased, thus threatening its flourishing trade with Lebanon's sybaritic wealthy classes. The tax decree was quickly canceled. Tensions were to an extent alleviated by minor wage increases and a rise in the level of the allowable minimum wage, but these measures did little for the student population, which remained a source of concern to the authorities. The several crackdowns on Palestinian guerrillas resulted in the student movement's becoming the channel through which various discontents were most clearly, and in some cases violently, expressed.

Yet Lebanon's economic position improved from about mid-1971. The tourist trade increased. Most spending in Lebanon, however, was attributable to the easing of restrictions on the private sectors of the Syrian and Iraqi economies, and to the purchasing power of Jordan, which remained high as a result of massive infusions of aid from various Western sources following the civil strife of 1970–71. Money derived from increased oil revenues poured into Lebanon's luxury shops, restaurants, hotels, and more importantly, into the bank accounts of Lebanese entrepreneurs and middlemen following the major victories scored by the Organization of Petroleum Exporting Countries in 1970 and 1971. However, the volume of this income was not as high as it would have been when Lebanon was unchallenged as a banking center. Although the salvaging of Intra Bank was successfully completed in 1972, much banking activity had shifted out of Beirut to Kuwait, Saudi Arabia, and other Persian Gulf states. And Lebanon, along with the rest of the Fertile Crescent, was beset by drought from 1971 into 1973. For all this, President Frangieh's unprecedented "technocrat" government dealt with continuing crises with sufficient success to gain a fairly strong vote of confidence in the national elections of 1972. Frangieh's supporters had no difficulty in retaining their seats. However, the election of several young leftists suggests that the cult of the personality, or at least the cult of older personalities, may be coming to an end in Lebanese politics.[11] Camille Chamoun went further into eclipse, succeeding only in electing two of his followers; his traditional rival, Kamal Junblatt, fared slightly better with five.

In the field of foreign relations, there was a slight alteration in course. For some years before the Frangieh regime came to power, there had been a drift away from dependence upon the French connection to more extensive ties with the United States and Great Britain. Personal preference and the opportunistic policy of the French government in the Arab world after the Six Day War were the bases of Frangieh's policy. There were frequent cordial exchanges of visits throughout 1971 and a high point was reached when, during a visit to Beirut, the French Secretary of State for Foreign Affairs assured Lebanon that France would come to Lebanon's defense should the country be exposed to an external threat. In January 1972 a military assistance agreement was signed between the two countries.

There was, however, another and much more unusual trend in Lebanese foreign policy. The need was perceived for an opening on the left, leading to a flurry of diplomatic exchanges and visits between Soviet and Lebanese officials in 1971. By November, the mutual courtship had developed to the extent that agreement for the purchase of Soviet military equipment could be announced. Nor was this all. On November 10, 1971, only a week after the agreement was announced, the Lebanese government made public the decision to establish diplomatic relations with the People's Republic of China. So completely did Lebanon adjust to its new and even-handed foreign policy that the government was encouraged to confer legal status on the Lebanese Communist Party. An international congress of Communist parties was held in Beirut in January 1972 under the auspices of the Lebanese Communist Party. Lebanon,

---

[11]Great interest was focused upon the election of Abdul Majid Rifai, a Tripoli Baathist with strong links to the Baghdad regime, and on Naja Wakim, a Beirut disciple of the late President Nasser, more remarkable for his age than for his political convictions. Wakim was twenty-six years old at the time of his election.

so long the center of communications and commercial interests in the Middle East, had now determined that her facilities should be shared by the Soviet bloc and, even more remarkably, the Communist Chinese. The punishment meted out in the 1972 Israeli raids, which reached a peak of intensity in September and October, was due to the sorties of Palestinian commandos across the frontier from positions in southern Lebanon as well as to an apparent shift in Lebanon's status (in the parlance of the Arab League) from that of a "support" to a "confrontation" country. This shift was signalled by the purchase of advanced weaponry from France, including Mirage jets, ground-to-air missiles, and a sophisticated radar system. It was a signal that Lebanon regretted, for it led to a governmental crisis accompanied by trials of highly-placed officials accused of corruption in weapons acquisition policy and procedures. Lebanon did not mourn the pushing of thousands of *fedayeen* into Syria, even though many commandos left conventional paramilitary formations to join urban terrorists groups of the "Black September" variety. (See also Chapter 4.) By harboring these groups, willingly or not, Lebanon remained vulnerable to the hammer blows of Israeli military power. By 1973, however, Lebanon's military contribution was clearly limited to the provision of early warnings to Syria when Israeli aircraft violated Lebanese air space enroute to attack Syrian positions.

The more pessimistic observers of modern Lebanon maintain that any government can achieve national consensus only if it limits its activities and suppresses creativity. Perhaps one of the more imperfect examples of parliamentary democracy in the world, Lebanon nevertheless stands in highly favorable contrast to the authoritarianism which surrounds it in the Arab world. Through its institutions much Western culture and technology have been transmitted to the larger world of the Middle East. Lebanon not only has been a place of refuge for political exiles from other Arab countries, but also has provided neutral ground upon which Arab adversaries could meet to try to resolve their differences. For such reasons Lebanon, a country about the size of Rhode Island (with less than two million inhabitants), has an importance unrelated to the statistics of area and population.

2

SYRIA

The Syrian Arab Republic is but a fraction of geographical and historical Syria. This fact determines the perspective of the Damascene who regards Jerusalem as a former provincial capital of an empire ruled from the city of his birth, or of the Aleppine who may himself be of an age to recall the day when Iskanderun, the entrepot port for northern Syria, was handed over to the Turks.

Geographical Syria is the area between the Mediterranean coast and the interior wastes of the Syrian Desert, and between the Taurus chain and the Sinai Peninsula. Historical Syria is less precisely defined. It can be considered to be greater in extent, as it was when the Umayyad Caliphate was at the pinnacle of its greatness, or lesser, as at the end of World War I, when Palestine and Transjordan became separate political areas. Irredentism and fear of further truncation both have left their imprint upon the politics of modern Syria.

Canaanites, Phoenicians, Hebrews, Arameans, Egyptians, Assyrians, Hittites, and Persians have figured prominently in Syria's rich history. The imprint of Alexander and of his Seleucid and Ptolemaic inheritors lies upon Syria as does, even more heavily, the long period of Roman and Byzantine rule.

Not two decades after the *hijrah* (or *hegira*, A.D. 622), Syria was incorporated by conquest into the Muslim Empire. The Sassanids, whose incursions into Syria had weakened Byzantine resistance, prepared the way for the Muslim Arabs. In another two decades, when Muawiya of the Umayya (a collateral branch of the Prophet's family) assumed the

36

title of Caliph in A.D. 661, Damascus became the capital of the Muslim empire.

The Umayyad Legacy

As the Hofburg and Palais Schonbrunn remind Austrians of Hapsburg greatness, when Vienna was the Imperial City and not the outsized capital of a small republic, so the Umayyad Mosque vouchsafes to Damascenes a glorious past. No ruler of Syria has been uninfluenced by the Umayyad legacy, handed down from a time when it was asserted that Damascus was the "center of the world," whose influence extended from Seville to the Oxus. In modern times, the Umayyad era has been employed to foster the myth of Arab unity. Close examination of tribal vendettas and blood feuds hardly lend substance to the myth, but history is determined by people reacting to what they believe to be true.

In recent years the symbolism of the Umayyad Mosque has been invoked by Damascus Radio, announcing that crowds of pious Syrians had emerged from Friday prayers in that historic shrine calling for war, revenge, or retribution in a form prescribed by their religious leaders— under pressure from the regime. Although, in the words of the distinguished Islamicist Carl Brockelmann, ". . . with the decline of the Umayyads not only the Syrians but the Arabs in general lost their absolute sovereignty in Islam . . . ,"[1] yet so strong is the pull of history that today a Damascene Sunni Muslim who visits the tomb of the Eighth Imam in faraway Meshed will be gently touched by Shi'a pilgrims who believe that in such contact there are *barakat*, or blessings. Small wonder, then, that the Umayyad legacy finds employment in modern Arab politics.

Umayyad supremacy engendered opposition and hatred to the east. The rise of the Abbasid Caliphate was the result of Perso-Iraqi collaboration, the denouement of which was a campaign of annihilation in Syria that ended in A.D. 752. Thus the way was prepared for the long sequence of invasions and occupations which have contributed as much to the formation of a Syrian consciousness as any recollection of Umayyad grandeur. The return of the Byzantine legions was a prolonged last phase of that empire's eastward venture. After an interlude in which the Egyptian-based Fatimids competed for influence with a number of local leaders, a new force, originating in central Asia, came to dominate Syria briefly. These were the Seljuq Turks, who arrived in the early eleventh

---

[1]Carl Brockelmann, *History of the Islamic Peoples* (London: Routledge and Kegan Paul, 1949), p. 106.

century and whose efforts to consolidate their hold were interrupted by the Crusader invasion.

The Crusader armies did not penetrate Syria deeply, but their presence set in train the events which brought the country under the sway of the brilliant Kurd, Saladin. His patron, Nur ad-Din, and his patron's father, Zengi, the skilled and dynamic Turkish ruler of Mosul, had taken the lead against the Crusaders. Saladin first demonstrated his mastery of the military arts in Egypt by ending the European occupation and with it the Fatimid era, making way for a Sunni renaissance. Saladin believed, as have rulers from Pharaonic times until today, that control of Syria would render secure his position in Egypt. This objective was achieved as the result of a twenty-year series of sieges and campaigns ending in 1192. Meanwhile, his brother Turanshah established an Egyptian hegemony on the southern Arabian shore of the Red Sea which lasted beyond Saladin's death in 1193. Understandably, many Arab rulers have sought to invoke the name of Saladin, despite the inconvenience of his Kurdish origin.

Saladin's death was followed by a long period of unrest, with frequent clashes between petty dynasts and confessional antagonists, until the first great Mongol invasion of 1260. This terrible visitation was cut short by the valor and ability of Baybars, a descendant of those slaves (hence the name Mamluk which attaches to his dynasty) who served with the armies of Saladin and his successors. With interruptions, such as the Ilkhan Mongol invasion and Tamerlane's awesome work of devastation, Syria remained under the Mamluks until the Ottoman conquest in 1517. The luminosity of Mamluk rule was confined to Egypt itself; as one of Egypt's provinces, Syria did not prosper. Rather, it experienced a long period of economic decline and recurrent rebellions, making it an easy prey for Selim the Dread.

The nearly eight centuries which separate the fall of the Umayyad Caliphate and the beginning of Ottoman rule should not be dismissed, however, as a dark age of bloodshed and cruelty. The character of modern Syria was shaped by the religious sects which developed during this period, the most important of which were the Alawi and the Druse.[2]

---

[2]The Alawis are a semi-Islamic sect at two removes from the Shiite persuasion. To the acceptance of Ali's cause they added a concept of a body of religious knowledge denied to all but a few of the "chosen." This belief was borrowed from the Ismailis, the sect presided over by the Aga Khan, who split with Shiism following a controversy over the succession to the Imamate. The Alawi liturgy is largely derivative from Christian sources, and pantheistic accretions are also identifiable. The Druse community migrated from south Lebanon during the strife-torn eighteenth century, giving their name to the hill country east of the plain of Haurani. (See Chapter 1 for details on Shiism and the Druse religion.)

The Crusader presence reshaped the local Christian communities in various ways. Syria was a rich prize, and throughout history its conquerors have patronized its artists and artisans (with the exception of Tamerlane, who abducted them). Poets and philosophers also found encouragement, and the life of Usamah ibn Munqidh, the warrior-poet of Shayzar, scourge of the Franks and companion of Saladin, must have special meaning for modern Syrians. In his declining years Usamah wrote: "How many sword cuts and lance thrusts I have received! How many wounds with darts and arbalest stones have been inflicted upon me!"

Nevertheless, he could conclude, "The sword of Indian steel becomes rusty when kept long in its sheath."[3]

Syria Under the Ottomans

The four centuries of Ottoman rule in Syria (beginning in 1517) provided no great contrast to the period which preceded the Turkish conquest. Except at the very outset, the Turks failed to exploit the country's situation as a strategic base in Arab Asia, and eventually others used the base against them. The wealth and potential of Syria were recognized, as were the talents of the Syrian people, but the Turks, content to collect taxes, did nothing to develop these resources. Of course, due acknowledgement was made of the special status of the Pashalic of Damascus, where the devout from all over the world of Islam began the supreme act of faith, the pilgrimage. As governors of Syria and commanders of the pilgrimage, the al-Azms of Damascus were grandees of the Ottoman Empire.

The heyday of the al-Azms was the eighteenth century, but long before that the sinews of empire had slackened. Syria had been divided into several pashalics, which did not render Ottoman administration effective but did enhance feelings of apartness between, for example, the cosmopolitan and mercantile community of Aleppo and the more truly Syrian Arab Muslim city of Damascus. Indeed, the elite troops of the Janissary garrisons, rather than the patronage of the Pasha's *diwan* (court), were the means by which power was gained and augmented by ambitious Syrians. Such alliances as developed were productive of conspiracies, assassinations, rebellions, and sieges, all incidental to personal gain, until the firm control of the al-Azms brought temporary respite. But

---

[3]Philip K. Hitti, *Memoirs of an Arab-Syrian Gentleman or an Arab Knight in the Crusades* (Beirut: Khayat's Oriental Reprints Number Seven, 1964), p. 9.

it was no more than that. Factional strife revived and continued until most of the country came under Jazzar Pasha, a sadistic Bosnian whose harsh rule ended only with his death in 1804.

The Syrian situation, bad as it was, was less of a spur to the reforming energies of Sultan Selim III than were the corruption and the incompetence he found nearer home. However, Syria benefited from his efforts until he was removed from office in 1807. The further extension of imperial neglect and indifference permitted Mohammed Ali to consolidate his power in Cairo, so that Egypt once again became the arbiter of Syria's fortunes. Beginning in 1830, Egyptian occupation by Ibrahim, Mohammed Ali's son, was the watershed in the modern history of geographical Syria. This was due less to firm rule, vigorous tax collection, and rough justice, evenly dispensed, than to European intervention which the Egyptian presence and Egyptian ambitions north of the Taurus invited. Landlords and peasants alike hailed Ibrahim's departure, for at the end his officials had been as harsh as they were ubiquitous.

The Syria from which Ibrahim Pasha retired in 1840 was now subjected to Western influences to an extent unknown since medieval times. Tradesmen, missionaries, promoters, and adventurers all played their roles, but it was European pressure for reform which was of the most vital importance. Regardless of whether European policy was based upon concern for the security of minority groups, born of a desire to keep the empire intact, or upon a desire to secure additional advantages in Ottoman lands, the result was nonetheless a half-hearted and awkward effort, under Mahmud II and Abdul Majid, to modernize and centralize administration. Many abuses were committed in the name of reform. There is some merit to the assertion that the Turks fared reasonably well in their Arab provinces until they set out to emulate Western administrative methods.

Nevertheless Syria achieved some progress in the last years of Ottoman rule. Commerce, agriculture, and the arts advanced, although development was not as remarkable as in Lebanon. Such improvements were jeopardized by the accession of Sultan Abdul Hamid II in 1876. Although he patronized Syrian notables and made a show of concern for Syrian welfare, his policy was little less brutal there than elsewhere in the empire. It was during his rule that an Arab independence movement crystallized. Its members cheered the Young Turk Revolution of 1908, only to learn that they had cheered too soon; the ruling Turkish Committee of Union and Progress was hostile to Arab aspirations. Abdul Hamid, stripped of his powers, was emperor in name only after 1908, although as Caliph he retained a claim upon the loyalty of Arab Muslims. Arab opposition to the Committee's policy was predictably vigorous and extensive, and Syrian participation in the many overt and covert societies founded in the last decade of Ottoman rule befitted the Syria which in future would so energetically seek identification as the heartland of the Arab nationalist movement.

The French Mandate

Hussein-McMahon, Sykes-Picot, Sazonov-Paléologue, Balfour, St. Jean de Maurienne—this litany sums up the folly and covetousness of the eastern policy of the Great Powers during the 1914–18 war.[4] All but the last of these agreements and declarations affected Syria. While diplomats negotiated arrangements for a post-Ottoman future, Syria suffered the cruel administration of Jamal Pasha. Corruption, incompetence, crop failures, and locust plagues brought famine and disease which killed nameless thousands, while the gallows of Jamal Pasha provided Arab nationalism with a roll of honor.

The liberation of Damascus by Allied and Sherifian forces on October 1, 1918, led to the establishment of a provisional government under Emir Faisal, co-architect, with T. E. Lawrence, of the Arab Revolt. There followed eighteen months of bitter wrangling over the future of Syria. The Arabs relied on British commitments to Sherif Hussein, Faisal's father. The French refused to be bound by negotiations in faraway Hejaz to which they were not a party, and cited not only the Sykes-Picot Agreement, but made an elaborate claim to special interests in Syria reaching back to Bohemond, Baldwin, and Reginald of Chatillon.

The American King-Crane Commission found no enthusiasm for French rule, but these findings had no influence on Syria's future. This was no time to consider the enthusiasms of the Syrians, for British forces found themselves overextended and were compelled to pull back from Syria, leaving a vacuum that drew the powers deliberating in Europe toward the award to France of a mandate for Syria. Postwar exhaustion and demands for retrenchment in England made this decision irrevocable, and Emir Faisal came to understand that wartime comradeship counted for little at the councils of the Great Powers.

---

[4] The correspondence between Sherif Hussein of Mecca and Sir Henry McMahon, High Commissioner of Egypt, contained the commitments and provisions leading to the Arab Revolt. Subsequent negotiations between Sir Mark Sykes and Georges Picot made Syria a twice-promised land and the Balfour Declaration did the same for Palestine. Russian claims were incorporated into Sykes-Picot by negotiations between S. D. Sazonov, the Russian Foreign Minister, and Maurice Paléologue, French ambassador to St. Petersburg. St. Jean de Maurienne was the site of negotiations which authorized Italy to annex territory in southwestern Anatolia, but the Italians proved that Bismarck had been correct in stating that they "have large appetites but poor teeth."

History presses heavily upon Syria, and no portion of it more so than the brief life of Faisal's kingdom in Damascus, from March through July 1920. The reservation with which the Sherifians had been received in 1918 was quickly broken down by the dignity and presence of Faisal, who had spoken for Arab interests in Europe with a courage which complemented his valor under fire. The kingship was accepted without illusions, for both the offer and its acceptance were acts of defiance. For a few months in 1920 Syria experienced a unity under Arab rule unknown since Muawiya proclaimed his Caliphate at Damascus thirteen centuries earlier. Then came the "Day of Maisalun," the title given by Sati al-Husri to his account of General Gouraud's military triumph over Faisal's forces at Maisalun, a village on the high road between Beirut and Damascus. Although Faisal was destined for a major place in the history of modern Iraq, his years of desert war and his rule in Damascus are much more a part of the story of the Arab's struggle to be master of his own destiny.

The French separation of the mandate territory into four units—Greater Lebanon, Syria, Latakia (the Alawite state), and Jebel Druse—was regarded as a classic example of *divide et impera.* Except for changing the character of Lebanon by adding the Bekaa Valley and other predominantly Muslim areas to it, the French made administrative arrangements for areas whose "apartness" was rooted in history. There was, however, considerable satisfaction when the Jebel Druse and Latakia were annexed to the Syrian state in 1936. Indeed, in 1920 the fractious population of the Jebel Druse had provided sufficient rationale for a policy of compartmentalization, and the same was true, to a lesser extent, of the Alawites. Later, in the process of reinterpreting their past, the Syrians would conclude that France had acted to restrain Syrian nationalism.

There was no grand design. The weakness of the mandatory power excluded such a possibility. It was this very weakness that prepared the way for the loss of the Sanjak of Alexandretta (*vilayet* of Hatay) as early as 1921, although the actual transfer did not take place until shortly before World War II. The Sanjak, whose Turkish population was considerably less than one-half of the total, was placed under a special French administration as a part of the Franklin-Bouillon (Ankara) Agreement of 1921. This also provided for the withdrawal of French forces from Turkish Cilicia and redrew the Turco-Syrian frontier as (delimited in the ill-fated Treaty of Sèvres) in such a way as to deprive Syria of about nine thousand square miles of territory and to remove from Franco-Syrian control the railroad line to Baghdad.

This was not the sort of arrangement to which the guardians of

France's reputation for imperial grandeur could readily acquiesce. The forces of Mustafa .Kemal Pasha (Ataturk), their armaments replenished after the *sauve qui peut*, which was the principal feature of the Italian venture into mainland Turkey, had inflicted defeat upon France. No assistance could be expected from the British, with whom the split was now complete. It was remarkable that the French held on to the Sanjak of Alexandretta for as long as they did. But this did not assuage the bitterness of the Syrians, who as recently as December 1968 thronged the streets of Damascus calling for the restoration of Iskanderun. Nor is the argument that Kurds, Circassians, and Turks populated the territory lost in the 1921 treaty acceptable to Syrians. (Despite the support of Kurdish levies for the French authorities in the rebellion of 1925–27, the Syrians were pleased during the Ankara negotiations of 1929 by the expansion of the Jazirah province to the Tigris, an area containing a sizable Kurdish population. The area gained has proved to be of considerable economic value.)

Many Frenchmen regarded the mandate as a preliminary, or an obstacle, to outright annexation. They tended to emphasize the concept of their country's special *mission civilisatrice* in Syria after 1861. Syrian intellectuals considered this a false premise. They believed that the French exerted cultural influence after 1861 in Lebanon, but not in Syria. Rather, the Syrians—Muslim and Druse alike—told and retold their version of the French armed intervention of 1860 in order to cast the mandatory authority in the role of usurpers and occupiers.

Undue emphasis has been placed on the fact that most French officials in Syria had earned their spurs in the Algerian hinterland, or Senegal, or Indochina, and dealt in the most governessy, colonial-office manner with an articulate, politically minded, economically advanced population. Actually, the principal problem the mandatory authorities faced was the need to maintain a facade of representative government in order to gain the endorsement of the League of Nations Permanent Mandates Commission. There seems to have been a relationship between the spread of inefficiency and the need to satisfy the League on the propagation of democracy. Direct rule, even if disliked, would not have been tainted by hypocrisy and would have been more beneficial.

Ever since Syrian independence, the Druse rebellion of 1925–27 has been represented as a rising against French tyranny. (From time to time after 1945, depending on Druse relations with the Damascus regime of the moment, Sultan Pasha al-Atrash would be brought from Suwaida to preside over observances honoring this phase of the national struggle.) In fact, the rising was largely attributable to the zeal for social reform of a French governor, Captain Carbillet. His rigorous efforts to protect the peasantry from the exactions and injustices of Druse notables bred hostility, and the rebellion was sparked off by the discourteous and treacherous treatment of a Druse delegation to the High Commissioner, General Sarrail. The affair was given the color of a national rising because the Druses left their own territory and attacked Damascus.

Although the Druses were convinced of their capacity to sustain a "forward" policy, their invasion of Damascus did not bring about a general rising. Syrian nationalists were not emboldened by this challenge to the French forces, and into 1927 the only substantial forces, other than the Druses, were bands of brigands. No efforts were made to organize resistance until various nationalist elements realized the advantages to be gained by prolonging the rebellion until the 1928 meeting of the Permanent Mandates Commission, where an unfavorable report could mean the end of French rule. This nationalist move came too late, however, for a determined French counterattack, including several heavy bombardments of Damascus, deprived the rebellion of momentum.

The pendular nature of French policy and a series of economic misfortunes, rather than a vigorous nationalist movement, weakened the French position in Syria before the Vichy era. Syria was at the mercy of bitter party politics in France at a time when moderation was the victim of a deteriorating political situation throughout Europe. Each new high commissioner brought a new policy identified with the rightist or leftist views of his patrons. Those who lived under bombardment in Damascus would have found some irony in Premier Herriot's statement to the Chamber of Deputies that the appointment of General Sarrail provided "an opportunity for the government to recognize this distinguished republican general." Apparently the fact that his predecessor, General Weygand, was a respected and reasonably effective high commissioner was not sufficient grounds for his retention. Later, when those who would be known as the "Gravediggers of France" dominated French politics, the Agreement of 1936, which might have provided an orderly transition to independence, was destroyed. (See below.)

Syria's economic problems, stemming from wartime deprivation and exhaustion, increased when the stable Turkish gold pound was replaced by the rapidly fluctuating French franc. What is more, the currencies of the British mandates were relatively strong. As a result, trade across frontiers became difficult—a situation especially disastrous for a community which thrives on commercial pursuits. Syria's economic distress quickly spread to her agriculturalists.

Many French politicians and statesmen wanted to give up the mandate, and perhaps would have done so had it not been for the unanswerable question. "How could we do so without a fatal loss of prestige in our Muslim possessions?" Another consideration forcing France to hold on was the very eagerness of Mussolini's Italy to replace her as the mandatory power. Thus when American destroyers were sent to Beirut during the Druse rebellion, the High Commission asked that they be withdrawn because their presence provided Italy with a pretext for a naval demonstration. In retrospect, they seem to have acted wisely, for an established Italian colonial regime in Syria would have complicated the Mediterranean and Middle Eastern strategies of the Allies in World War II.

Syrian political life under the French Mandate, although circumscribed by French policy objectives and interventions, was nonetheless vigorous and contentious. The principal political objectives of the main groupings, the People's Party and the National Bloc, were (1) reorganization of the territories of the French Mandate into a unitary state; (2) complete and immediate internal autonomy; and (3) an early achievement of independence and the removal of French armed forces. The political leadership was notable for its qualities of sagacity, courage, and executive ability in the persons of Hashim al-Atassi, Abdur Rahman Shahbandar, Jamil Mardam Bey, Faris al-Khuri, Haqqi al-Azm, Shukri al-Quwatli, and others. Three factors limited their effectiveness: (1) the extent to which their attention was captured by problems which could be solved only if Syria were an independent, unified state; (2) internal disputes concerning the extent to which cooperation with the High Commission was permissible; and (3) the divisive effect of local interest groups, which meant that the main parties were in fact uneasy alliances rather than unified political organizations.

The external problems were, of course, the increasing strength of political Zionism and attendant developments influencing the future of Palestine as well as the pursuit of the will-o'-the-wisp, Arab unity.[5] Despite domestic and foreign distractions, and indeed because of such external developments as Iraq's qualified independence, its entry into the League of Nations, and the Anglo-Egyptian Treaty of 1936, progress was made toward Syrian independence. Strikes and militancy first met with repression, then earned concessions from the High Commission. A Popular Front government emerged in Paris, ready to concede the legitimacy of Syrian demands. In 1936 a draft treaty was negotiated providing independence for a Syrian state which earlier in the year had been enlarged by linking the Jebel Druse and the Alawite state to the Damascus government.

But Syrian hopes were built upon sand, for the treaty was not rati-

---

[5]In the interwar period the most compelling expositions of these themes were to be found in the writings of Shakib Arslan, a Druse emir living in exile in Switzerland.

fied. Its fate was bound up with the eclipse of democracy in Europe. The weakening of Léon Blum's left-liberal government in Paris gave the clergy and the military—opponents of Syrian independence—a powerful voice in colonial affairs. The search for allies against Hitler and Mussolini gave all the high cards to Turkey in the bidding for the Sanjak of Alexandretta. Particularism in the Jebel Druse, the Alawite region, and even the Jazirah indicated that the writ of Syrian leaders in Damascus was severely limited. For some at least, the coming of Vichy authoritarianism was initially more of a relief than a trial.

Such feelings were soon replaced by fear that the war would bring back to Syria the famine and disease which had swept it during the 1914–18 war. For Syria there was also the humiliation of being held in thrall by a defeated nation. Thus, when Vichy confirmed its status as a Nazi satrapy by resigning from the League of Nations in April 1941, Syrian nationalists concluded that the legal basis for French rule had disappeared. General Dentz was a determined High Commissioner, but he was not Jamal Pasha, and the equally determined opposition of Shukri al-Quwatli and other resistance leaders forced further concessions. Before these concessions could take effect, however, developments in Iraq threatened to transform Syria into an advance base for the *Luftwaffe* and the German army. The Allied response was a British, Commonwealth, and Free French invasion in June 1941, which was preceded by a statement by General de Gaulle's deputy, General Catroux, recognizing the independence of Syria and Lebanon.

Yet the Free French could not and would not relinquish the special position of their country in the Levant states. Their situation was replete with irony as well as difficulty: it was as if some of the 1919 pages of Syrian history had been torn out and reinserted at 1941. The invasion was primarily a British and Commonwealth affair. British forces shored up the new Free French administration and Syria quickly became a part of the sterling area. Pronouncements of Allied solidarity notwithstanding, it was assumed that a clash between the British and Free French was inevitable. When it came, two new factors had to bear on the situation which tended to push the British further than they wished in sponsoring reforms and self-determination. These were the rudimentary beginnings of an American policy for the Middle East and the emergence of the Arab League as a rallying point for the support of Arab causes.

The first major confrontation occurred in Lebanon in 1943 (see Chapter 1). As the war dragged on, a desperate French policy, based on the premise that Syria and Lebanon were years away from real independence, attempted to ensure that the entire Arab world east of Tunis should not become a British preserve. Such measures were embodied in two draft treaties between France and Syria and France and Lebanon containing the substance, if not the form, of the mandate and the *mission civilisatrice*. French troops were landed to provide the ultimate argument in the treaty negotiations, touching off strikes, riots, and other forms of resistance that were answered by a French bombardment of Damascus in May 1945. But it was British military force that decided the outcome (even though the crisis found its way onto the agenda of the fledgling United Nations Organization), and it was from the British Commander in Chief, Middle East, that the civilian governments of Damascus and Beirut took over full responsibilities in 1946.

The First Twelve Years of Independence

It was to the veteran nationalist, Shukri al-Quwatli, that the National Bloc gave the task of governing Syria after independence. Until the "time of the colonels" (1949–54), governing responsibilities would be confined to a few upper-class families, all with good nationalist credentials from the mandate period. But habits of opposition and rebellion were not easily transmuted into qualities of political leadership, and very quickly al-Quwatli and his colleagues became objects of the obloquy earlier directed against their country's occupiers. The task of building a polity among an individualistic and articulate people who were accustomed to suspect and mistrust their rulers would have been difficult in the most favorable of circumstances, and no favorable circumstances were present.

Postwar Syria experienced a meteoric rise in the cost of living. Those who had made or increased fortunes in wartime could pay the prices, but poverty was widespread and the gap between classes, already great, increased. The need to develop industry, to modernize agriculture to match the sophisticated level of the commercial class, and to strengthen administration from the municipal level upward was recognized, but there were many other claims on the attention of the politicians. Some were real problems, such as the need to secure the loyalty and confidence not only of the Druse and Alawite communities, but also of the small, politically advanced Christian minority, in order to withstand the centrifugal forces which threatened to divide the state. Others were simply diversionary, such as the fear of Turkish designs on Aleppo, or manifestations of irredentism involving Tripoli, Sidon, and the Bekaa.

Attention was also being given to various "Greater Syria" and "Fertile Crescent" proposals, providing outsiders their first real appreciation of the durability of European-designed frontiers, but arousing among army officers and civil servants fears that their rank, status, and future prospects were in jeopardy. Most distressing was the feeling of helplessness in a new and confusing world of international politics, particularly as proponents of Israel went from strength to strength. Such distractions, combined with all the frustrations involved in dealing with problems for which in former times the French could be blamed, quickly sapped the energies of the first independent regime.

Disillusionment with the National Bloc government spread as evidence of corruption was added to its obvious failure to grapple with social and economic problems. The crisis was intensified by defeat in the Palestine War, the most traumatic experience in the history of modern Syria. The unpreparedness, the failure of leadership, the shabby equipment, and the supply breakdowns demonstrated that corruption was not a civilian monopoly. In the contest to assign responsibility for the state of affairs, the government struck first but the army struck hardest. Several army officers were arrested on charges of corruption. The riposte by the chief of staff, Colonel Husni Zaim, took the form of a swift and bloodless *coup d'état* in 1949. Whether Zaim acted because Premier Khalid al-Azm was about to sign a warrant for his arrest, or because the villainy of the politicians had to be established before an armistice with Israel could be signed is immaterial. Popular reaction to the *coup* was favorable because of widespread discontent. A parliamentary transfer of power might have been achieved earlier had not the al-Azm government been sustained by good harvests and the anticipation of revenues from projected oil pipelines across Syria to the Mediterranean from Iraq and Saudi Arabia.

It was Husni Zaim's aspiration to be Syria's Ataturk, but he brought no great ability to the task. His principal claim to a place in modern Arab history is that he showed the way to power to other colonels, most notably to Gamal Abdul Nasser. Neither his external policy, based on friendship for Egypt and France and an ungovernable hatred for Iraq's Nuri Pasha Said, nor his internal policy, which cost him the support of the Druses, served to consolidate his position. Still more transitory was the rule of his executioner-successor, Colonel Sami Hinnawi, whose tenure might have been less fleeting had he been content to exploit continuing bitterness over the Palestine War. When it was revealed that Hinnawi was collaborating with elements of the Aleppo-based People's Party in negotiations seeking union with Hashemite Iraq, his residence was surrounded by military units who reportedly chanted, "We are republican—we do not want a king!" The order for Hinnawi's arrest was signed by Colonel Adib Shishakly, whose rise to power had been briefly interrupted when Husni Zaim recognized his abilities and imprisoned him.

Zaim, Hinnawi, and, for the first two years of his rule, Shishakly operated behind a facade of veteran politicians. Until November 1951 discussion continued, reasonably openly, on such issues as Syria's international alignments. Subsequent condemnations of military ties with non-Arab countries have tended to obscure the fact that in 1951 there was a considerable body of Syrian opinion favoring links with the West through a Middle East Defense Organization. Undoubtedly some Syrians were less interested in Western ties than in the modern weapons which could be obtained through such an arrangement. Others hoped that the process of politicization which the Syrian army was undergoing could be halted. But this was not to be, and the "time of the colonels" was one in which new political elements—the Arab Socialist Party led by Akram Hurani and the Arab Baath (Resurrection) Party, the creation of Michel Aflaq and Salah ad-Din al-Bitar—won over scores of young officers. The Baathists were especially influential in the Homs Military Academy, Syria's West Point or St. Cyr.

The most effective opposition to pacts with non-Arab countries came from politicians and intellectuals who argued that Syria must remain neutral in the expanding bipolar struggle. For the same reason, participation in the American Point Four program was rejected, although in this case opposition also was based upon American assistance to Israel, suspicion that the program would provide a cover for other activities, and the desire of landowners to keep the reforming zeal of American Point Four officials at a distance. Dr. Ma'ruf Dawalibi was one of the early supporters of Syrian neutralism and thus earned the unwarranted title of "the Red Shaikh" from the American news media.

It was Dawalibi who, with courage and forthrightness, asserted the primacy of civilian authority in Syria in November 1951. His efforts landed him in the Mezze prison, just outside Damascus, along with many other politicians who had not gone into exile. From that time, Shishakly's regime was an outright military dictatorship, although his rule was described as temporary, "pending the restoration of normal parliamentary life." The ritual statement, "I do not want to become a dictator, I am a simple colonel," was repeated with the customary earnestness. Initially, Shishakly made good use of his opportunity to rule Syria without the interference of the politicians. His record as a nationalist and as a soldier who had seen action in Palestine gave him a measure of popularity, which he increased by exploiting the enduring bitterness over Turkish possession of the former Sanjak of Alexandretta. Although he sought close ties with revolutionary Egypt, he kept Syria isolated from involvement in international affairs and even from the cut and thrust of inter-Arab politics. His "Movement of Arab Liberation" was called into being for domestic purposes and it served admirably for a time.

Economic prosperity was on the increase when Shishakly assumed full control of the government apparatus, and the dictator bent his energies to the continuation of this trend. Syria's postwar political life had been rich and varied, its participants excelling at diagnosis and pre-scription, but failing to make the patient take the medicine. Shishakly changed that situation by implementing legislation already on the·books and by initiating a comprehensive program of social and economic re-form. The army was used to carry out the Shishakly program, in the process becoming a political machine accorded privileged treatment. The system worked well until the military leadership began to feel its special status threatened by Shishakly's increasing isolation from the army. In addition, the Druse element in the army was alienated by Shishakly's repressive policies in their home area. Combining with these internal sources of dissatisfaction was the Iraqi money spent to purchase intrigue against the dictator. (This marked the beginning of a period of heightened effort to bring Syria somehow under Hashemite control.) These developments coincided with an agricultural depression, the effects of which spread quickly to other sectors of the economy. It was in this atmosphere that the military rebellion of February 1954 occurred, send-ing Shishakly across the frontier.

There could be no return to the politics of the pre-Shishakly era. The army was too completely involved in politics and its inner tensions were based on shifting political loyalties as new groups developed to challenge traditional alignments. The fusion of the Arab Socialist and Baathist parties in 1954 introduced a powerful new element into Syrian politics and aroused religious leaders throughout the country to demon-strate against its "atheistic tendencies." Yet the elections of 1954, the freest and most honest in Syria's history, promised a mature government, attuned to popular needs and aspirations.

The promise went unfulfilled. The country was plunged into a series of crises arising from the irruption of revolutionary Egypt into Arab politics, Western attempts to include Syria in a defense system, and Iraqi ambitions. Abdul Illah, whose career as Regent of Iraq ended in 1953 when Faisal, grandson of Syria's ruler of 1919–20, attained his majority, still aspired to be proconsul of Syria. Among old-line politicians there was a significant amount of support for a policy aimed at realizing what amounted to a form of Hashemite Fertile Crescent. Western plan-ners were encouraged by the reportedly sympathetic reception given Mohammed Ali's advocacy of the advantages of adhering to a pact with Turkey and Pakistan when the Pakistani statesman visited Damascus. But opposition crystallized with the conclusion of the American-spon-sored Turco-Iraqi treaty of January 1955.

Baghdad viewed the treaty as a step toward union with Syria on Baghdad's terms. Elsewhere in the Arab world it was regarded as a violation of the canons of Arab unity and solidarity. Seen in this light, it did as much to align the policies of the Cairo and Damascus regimes as did the major Israeli raids directed against both countries in 1955 at Gaza and Tiberias. A Syro-Egyptian military alliance was signed in March 1955 and resulted in an immediate Turkish troop buildup on Syria's northern border. The crisis atmosphere continued into 1956 and through the Suez War.

The position of Syrian political moderates, who after Shishakly's fall had been attempting to reduce the effects of some of the more socialistic reforms sponsored by the dictator, was undercut by the Suez affair. It gave leftist elements in the army an anti-imperialist pretext for punishing the Iraqis by blowing up the Iraq Petroleum Company pipeline. More importantly, Suez greatly enhanced the position of the Arab Socialist Baath (Resurrection) Party, the Soviet embassy, and the Syrian Communist Party, the latter under the gifted leadership of Khalid Baqdash, known despite his Kurdish origins as "the Arab Togliatti."

Like Jordan, Syria failed to come to the aid of Egypt during the Suez crisis of 1956, citing the tense northern frontier as the reason. Because of the Turco-Syrian crisis, the United States—regarded in Damascus as the author of every Turkish maneuver—failed to gain among the Syrians that brief moment of approbation which the Americans won elsewhere in the Arab world by intervening to frustrate the designs of Britain and France. The Eisenhower Doctrine of 1957 was considered another attempt to force Syria to take sides in the Cold War. Syria's policy position was made manifest by the arrival of Egyptian troops at Latakia in October 1957 to bolster defenses against "the Turkish agent of Western imperialism." Nikita Khrushchev assured the world that in any aggression against Syria, Turkey would not last one day. At the same time, reports of American and Iraqi sponsorship of plots against the regime, not all of them baseless, were published in Syria. It was a moment of opportunity for the Baath Socialists and Communists. Although the hysterical tone of the Western press created the impression in Western Europe and America that Syria had become a Russian fiefdom, no overt moves were made by socialist and communist factions. Rather, it was the traditional political leadership, disillusioned and shocked by ill-conceived, heavy-handed Western policies, which spoke out in favor of an "opening on the left."

The now familiar series of pilgrimages to Moscow began, and promises of extensive economic and military assistance quickly followed. In the confused local political situation, the Syrian Communist Party was the principal beneficiary. American policy in the Middle East seemed near to achieving what presumably it had been designed to prevent. But Baqdash and his followers overreached themselves. A fairly conciliatory approach to "front" politics—which meant cooperation with the Baath Socialists—was replaced by an aggressiveness widely regarded as preliminary to a *coup d'état*. No less fearsome than the prospect of a *coup* was that of a strong Western reaction, possibly in the form of armed intervention.

As the crisis developed in late 1957 and early 1958, the army was in no position to intervene. The chief of staff, General Afif al-Bizri, favored collaboration with the Soviets. The position of Colonel Abdul Hamid Sarraj, the intelligence chief, was less clear but he was assumed to be a man of the left. The establishment of Baath Socialist and Communist cadres in the armed forces, in addition to the customary divisions between Sunni Muslims, Alawites, and Druses, made the military a microcosm of the fragmented polity of the nation. The traditional political leadership and a number of army officers who retained some measure of influence, therefore, turned with greater or lesser reluctance to Cairo for a solution. The Baath Socialist Party supported this move.

The Baath Socialist Party and the UAR

The Baath Party was built upon the friendship and convictions of two Syrian intellectuals, a Christian and a Muslim, who met as students at the Sorbonne in the late 1920s. Michel Aflaq, the Christian, become the philosopher of the party, Salah ad-Din al-Bitar its political manager. Their detractors would point out that the Baathist constitution, drawn up long before the party achieved power, has all the merits of the 1936 constitution of the Soviet Union, which came as near perfection as any ever formulated, and has been as little implemented. Its fundamental, "unalterable" principles are (1) the Arab land constitutes an indivisible unity ("present dissimilarities and dissensions are contingent and not essential, superficial and not substantial, and will disappear with the progress of a national consciousness"); (2) the Arab nation is characterized by its capacity to revive and recreate itself, and its revival is proportionate to the freedom of the individual; hence freedom of speech, association, and belief are sacred and inalienable; and (3) Arabs should fraternize with the rest of the nations of the world for the sake of the common welfare and world peace.

The Baathist ideology attracted international attention and support, largely among intellectuals and members of the professions, long before the party established a base in Syria. The Arab Socialist Party, with which the Baathists became associated in 1954 in their search for power, was led by Akram Hurani, who had for a time collaborated with Shishakly, and whose greatest strength was in Homs and Hama. The Baathist centers of influence were Damascus and Deir az-Zur; thus the new Baath Socialists gained a much needed broader base. After 1954 the Baathists became an important factor in Syrian politics, participating in coalition, penetrating the government apparatus, and widening their appeal to bring industrial workers into the ranks along with intellectuals and professionals. Baathist success among the peasants of northern Syria was facilitated, ironically enough, by the high degree of organization of the region's agriculture under the management of mercantile interests of Aleppo. By 1958 the Baath Socialist Party had thirty thousand members and many more supporters, but much more important was its success in gaining a following in the armed forces.

The political conquest of Egypt had long been a Baathist objective. In 1958 Aflaq and al-Bitar were not apprehensive about the possibility of a Sovietization of Syria, and for them union with Egypt was not so much a rescue operation as an ideological goal. The Egyptian concept of Arab socialism was not to be formulated until 1961, so that in the late fifties only the Baath Socialists possessed a program for the achievement of socialist unity in the Arab world. The party had small but articulate and growing groups of supporters in Lebanon, Jordan, and Iraq, but in early 1958 it regarded Egypt as the key to eventual success in recasting the Arab world in the image evoked by the writings of Michel Aflaq. The Egyptian power structure could supply the motive force in spreading Baathist ideology.

By August 1958, six months after the Baath Socialists helped to precipitate the United Arab Republic, Syria's political left was expressing regret that the revolt against Nuri Pasha Said and Hashemite rule had not occurred in time for Syria to make the more natural and profitable link with Iraq. Such sentiments were aroused more by Egyptian policy than by any understanding of the aims of Iraq's Abdul Karim Qasim. Much later, Gamal Abdul Nasser would state that the union should have been limited to the areas of foreign policy and defense. But initially there was enthusiasm for the UAR in both the "Southern Region" and the "Northern Region."

Syrian instability facilitated the merger. It was to be expected that the remedies would be prescribed in Cairo. There was some benefit to be gained from an enforced internal political truce, as in the Shishakly period, and needed economic reforms were included in Nasser's decree legislation. Yet the Syrian partner in the UAR had an impressive record of economic progress before 1958, and feeling was widespread that Egypt had little to offer in this field. Between the end of World War II and 1958 the Syrian gross national product had doubled, and it was increasing at the rate of 8 percent annually when the UAR was formed. With a population not greatly ·exceeding four million, the potential Syrian contribution to the union's economy was limited. But it was soon clear that Nasser intended to make the most of the situation, extending to free-enterprise Syria the mechanisms of extensive government control. The two cabinets were merged, the dissolution of Syrian political parties ordered, a drastic agrarian reform law introduced, and widespread nationalization of industry implemented. An early indication of the true nature of Egyptian policy was seen in the exchange of army officers, the Egyptians occupying key positions in the "Northern Region" while Syrians cooled their heels in unimportant posts in support services. Syrian officers were bypassed in the chain of command in Syria itself and many were placed on the inactive list. The unfailing Egyptian penchant for giving themselves the characteristics of an occupying force was once again demonstrated.

Nasser's policy was almost immediately jeopardized by drought and crop failures. Previously an exporter of grain, Syria was now forced to rely on grants of American wheat. As discontent spread, the Egyptians sought to assign responsibility for the country's difficulties to the Baath Socialist Party. It was a logical move in the game of power politics, for Nasser feared the party's appeal in the Arab world and especially in Cairo and Alexandria. For a time his persecution of Baath Socialists also purchased a measure of cooperation from right-wing elements in Syria. With the efficient help of Colonel Abdul Hamid Sarraj, purges of Baathists and other left-wing elements in the government were carried out. In January 1960 the five Baath Socialists in the central government, headed by Vice President Akram Hurani, resigned.

Reports of clashes between Syrian and Egyptian troops and information concerning an incipient rebellion by Syrian army units decided Nasser on the appointment of his brother-in-law, Marshal Abdul Hakim Amer, to be his proconsul in Damascus. Further measures of control over civil servants and army officers were planned, but the opportunity for implementation never came. In the final analysis, Nasser's program of centralization and socialization briefly linked the Syrian right, center, and left in the much more elemental or traditional stance of anti-foreignism. In 1961 it was "Syria for the Syrians," and for once the army had the support of the populace. Proponents of the union went to ground and the impression of monolithic opposition to Cairo's rule put a checkrein on Egyptian retaliation. Lebanese authorities, who in the civil war of 1958 had direct experience of Egypt's willingness to employ Syria as an infiltration base, now had the satisfaction of facilitating the return, via Beirut, of Egyptian paratroops landed near Latakia in the early hours of the anti-UAR rising.

To President Nasser, the Syrian defection of September 28, 1961, was a major reverse. The union had been to Egyptians an assertion of their Arabism, so often doubted or denied in the Arab East. It was considered a step forward in the "three circles" policy in which Egypt was the leader at once of the world of Islam, of Africa, and of the Arabs. It had been founded amidst risings against pro-Western regimes in Lebanon and Jordan, at a time of increased pressure on France in Algeria, and was followed shortly by the bloody overthrow of Nuri Said and his Hashemite patrons. But now the Arab revolution appeared to have lost its momentum, and perhaps even its rationale. In Syrian mythology, on the other hand, the union became clear proof of Syria's vanguard role in Arab politics, a demonstration of Syrian capacity to seize the initiative. If it failed, it was because Egypt was unworthy. There is a direct connection between Syria's promotion and rejection of the UAR and Syria's most remarkable accomplishment of modern times—the Six Day War of June 1967.

Soviet pleasure over the failure of the United Arab Republic may be measured by the alacrity with which the restored Syrian government gained full recognition.

Baathism and Neo-Baathism

Upon secession from the UAR, the Baath Socialists, not yet recovered from Egyptian persecution, were unable to form a government even on a coalition basis. The army's transient popularity was based on its opposition to "Egyptianization," which was in fact opposition to the Egyptians themselves, although as an organization heavily influenced by Baath Socialist ideology, it was in essential agreement with the UAR program of economic and agrarian reform. As a result, a great deal of UAR decree legislation remained in force. To this already unsettled situation were added the complications of the December 1961 election, which was a clear victory for moderate and moderate-conservative elements. In these circumstances the army sponsored, or permitted, the formation of several governments led by veteran politicians.

Western officials and political commentators, who had in general come to consider Baath Socialism as the Arab equivalent to the European social democratic movement, regarded these politicians as "restored

Bourbons." This assessment was manifestly unjust to such leaders as Nazim al-Qudsi and Ma'ruf Dawalibi, whose ministries sought to adapt the UAR program to Syrian realities. The agrarian reform act was amended to make it workable and although some companies were denationalized, sections of the UAR social legislation were extended. The army's attacks on these ministries, which included charges of corruption and intrigue and stressed the need for "constructive socialism," masked fears of another "Fertile Crescent" project. Although it was natural that Qasim should cheer the collapse of the UAR and send his foreign minister, Hashim Jawad, to seek some basis for understanding in Damascus, the Syrian army remembered well the pro-Iraqi orientation of the People's Party leadership which was once again at the helm of the government.

The crisis developed in Damascus as President Nasser, who in 1961 had joined his Arab nationalist movement to socialist doctrine by comprehensive nationalization and sequestration decrees, introduced the concept of "Arab socialism" to regain the prestige he had enjoyed throughout the Arab world before the collapse of the UAR. Inclusion of the element of class struggle strengthened the hand of the revived unionist element in Syria. A number of politicians concluded that some new form of association with Egypt was the only alternative to an arrangement between the Syrian "old guard" and Qasim's Iraq. To Western observers, Syrian apprehensions were almost incomprehensible, for they tended to consider Qasim as virtually a captive of the Iraqi Communist Party. But in the Middle East the possibility was taken seriously, and a military mission was dispatched to Cairo to discuss the threat of a Syro-Iraqi merger.

Most Syrian politicians who had experienced the workings of the UAR at first hand were not eager for another association with the "new" Egypt. They were led by former UAR Vice President Akram Hurani, who employed his considerable prestige and political skill in opposition to any renewed link. His tactics split the Baath Socialists, many of whose leaders, including Aflaq and al-Bitar, continued to favor some form of union. Hurani then revived his Homs- and Hama-based Arab Socialist Party, from the platform of which he accused Egypt of "betraying the cause of Palestine in exchange for American aid."

For several months the Syrians and Egyptians jousted in the press and on the radio, each side extolling the merits of union while submitting lists of conditions which had to be met before union in fact could be achieved. Following several bomb explosions in Aleppo and Damascus, vigorous suppression of pro-Nasser demonstrations, and the announcement of the capture of Egyptian plans for a campaign of terrorism and sabotage, relations were restored to their normal level of vilification. Once again Syria was isolated in the Arab world. To make matters worse, increasing army interference with the regular functions of government frustrated plans for the economic rehabilitation of the country. Baathist-influenced officers interpreted the incorporation of UAR economic decrees into Syrian law and practice as an indication of pro-Nasser sentiment—a sentiment that may have existed among the masses but was not present in the several post-UAR governments of Syria between 1961 and 1963.

The Baathists were swept into power in 1963 on a groundswell of enthusiasm following the bloody downfall of Qasim and the emergence of a Baathist regime in Iraq. As a reflex reaction to the death of a despot whose contempt for Baathism and Nasser had been fully and frequently expressed, another United Arab Republic came briefly into existence, and for several weeks a third star in the UAR flag represented Iraq.[6] Although this tripartite experiment served little purpose other than to emphasize the immutable divisions existing between Cairo, Damascus, and Baghdad, the two Baathist regimes were able to cooperate, for a time at least, on the military level. A military union was agreed upon, with the Iraqi defense minister, General Saleh Mahdi Ammash, designated as supreme commander of the united army. The Syrian "Yarmuk" brigade entered northern Iraq and participated in operations against the Kurds.

But Baathism did not fare well in Baghdad, and by the end of the year a presidential *coup d'état*, supported by the army, ousted the Baathist ministry, after which the party was declared illegal. The Iraqis assailed the Syrian Baathists in newspapers, television, and radio. At the coffee-house level the story was repeated throughout the Arab world that President Abdul Salim Aref's favorite description of Michel Aflaq was "that Christian disciple of a Jewish atheist." The two adjectives were as important as the terminal noun.

The new dispensation in Syria encountered strong resistance from the commercial classes and religious leaders. In April 1964, when strikes and demonstrations against the Baathist regime occurred in Damascus and Hama, the president and chairman of the National Revolutionary Council, Lieutenant-General Amin Hafiz, promised that opposition would be quelled by "the most ruthless methods." The promise was kept. The regime also introduced an extensive program of nationalization. Exchange controls were imposed and by early 1966 the banks, foreign trade, and most industries were in the government sector. In the process the Baathists did serious injury to the economy of one nation in the *tiers*

---

[6]After September 1961 the Egyptian regime continued to employ the term "United Arab Republic" as the country's official name, and the flag remained unchanged.

monde—perhaps the only one—with sufficient resources to develop itself without outside assistance. But, having been spared natural catastrophe or enemy occupation, the economy remained viable, if not vibrant. Domestic policies therefore caused no dissension within the regime, and middle-class opposition was dealt with firmly. Rather, it was conflicting concepts of foreign policy, as well as the thirst for power—which is, after all, the most basic force in politics everywhere—that generated the unrest which developed within the ruling establishment.

From the Baathist rise to power in 1963 until the *coup* of February 1966, the maneuvering for influence and privilege within the party and government was a continuation of earlier controversies. The lines were drawn, primarily between the army and the civilian apparatus of the Baath party. On the surface it appeared as if the armed forces were firmly in control. But they were divided into factions headed by prominent officers seeking alliances and promoting vendettas. The concessions made by Hafiz to veteran civilian Baathists such as Aflaq and al-Bitar were part of a complicated balancing act rather than the measures of a firmly entrenched ruler.

The power struggle changed in early 1966. The contest within the regime became one of youth *versus* seniority, and in the ensuing and quite bloody *coup d'état* it was youth that took over. This was the ninth *coup* in seventeen years. What was now considered as the Baathist "old guard" went into prison or joined politicians of the center and right in expensive exile in Beirut. Their places were taken by the "neo-Baathists," restless and impatient younger officers and civilians. The term "neo-Baathism" suggests that in the hands of the new men who seized power in February 1966, the movement ceased to have an ideological basis, if by ideology is meant something more than a formula for obtaining and consolidating power. In fact the "new men" of 1966 broadened their political base not by socialist nostrums but by the vigor with which they espoused the cause of Palestine.

No Arab politician can ignore the Palestine issue. His success or failure in some measure depends on whether he employs it or permits it to be employed against him. The three leading civilians in the new Syrian regime, Nur al-Din al-Atassi, Yusuf Zu'ayyan, and Ibrahim Makhus, were all seventeen years of age at the time of the Palestine War. Having been brought up on the stories of secret deals and sellouts—the amalgam of fact and fiction which has poisoned inter-Arab relations since 1949—they were determined to take the initiative on Palestine, and thereby assert the primacy of Damascus over Cairo. Much of their inspiration was drawn from the Algerian revolution, and particularly from the element of class struggle which they read into it.

Unlike the Palestine War, the Algerian conflict appeared to have had no vested interests bound up in it. The people had nothing to lose but their lives, which was assumed to increase their revolutionary ardor. In contrast, President Nasser, as the neo-Baathists saw it, had vested interests which dictated the avoidance of war. It was recalled that when Israel's plans for irrigating the Negev with water drawn from the Jordan became known in 1963, Syria called for immediate war while Egypt was forced to admit unreadiness. Nasser's summit diplomacy was considered in Syria to be an excuse for inaction. It was also asserted that Nasser took the initiative in developing the Palestine Liberation Organization in order to keep the refugee element from becoming an embarrassment to Egyptian diplomacy. Under Ahmed Shukairy, hand-picked by Nasser, the PLO seemed to be a pale reflection of the Algerian FLN. Although PLO militancy was to catch the Egyptians and Jordanians off guard in May and June 1967, the emphasis in 1966 was on words rather than action. Palestinian militants who favored commando operations against Israeli installations were completely disillusioned until they found a sympathetic response among the neo-Baathist leadership of Syria.

The *fedayeen* ("those who sacrifice themselves") have a long tradition in Islam, although in their modern manifestation the religious sanction for their deeds is combined with, or even replaced by, such temporal aspirations as recovering a homeland or removing the stain of humiliation. Their devotion to their cause has made them into a force with which not only Israel but also Arab regimes and even the Great Powers have had to reckon. Syrian sponsorship gave them their opportunity. "Popular war," as exemplified by the Viet Cong, was extolled to give further emphasis to Syria's revolutionary zeal, and while the *fedayeen* trained with new Soviet weaponry and made tentative forays across the truce line, the neo-Baathists implemented other aspects of an ambitious program.

Even before the pipeline blockade, Jordan had been singled out for special attention. In early December 1966 the Syrian head of state, Nur al-Din al-Atassi, broadcast a plea to the Jordanians urging them to overthrow King Hussein, whose government al-Atassi described as "the stumbling block in the way of the liberation of Palestine." As *fedayeen* activity increased, so did tension with Jordan, which had frequently paid the price for Syria's Israel policy. Syria's virtually unlimited capacity for disturbing the peace is to some extent attributable to the fact that its common border with Israel before June 1967 was little more than twenty-four miles—even less than the Israeli-Lebanese border—much of it backed by highland territory, conferring enormous tactical advantages upon the Syrians. Often Israeli raids across the long, exposed Jordanian frontier were responses to Syrian bombardments or forays from well-fortified positions on the now famous Golan Heights.

In mid-1966 Syrian-based commandos began infiltrating Jordan, from whence they mounted attacks into Israel, adding a new dimension to the tense situation. Syria thereby emphasized its militancy and increased its pressures on the hated Jordanian Hashemite regime. Neo-Baathists spoke of the "joining of revolutions," a special Armageddon in which Algeria, Egypt, and Syria would overturn the governments of such "nonliberated" states as Saudi Arabia, Kuwait, Libya, Tunisia, and Jordan, at which time the last act of the Palestine drama would take place. How seriously such objectives were regarded by those in power must remain a subject of conjecture. Rhetoric outdistanced reason, and not only in Syria.

The Jordanian regime, worried by a large, restless refugee population and irritated by the belligerency of PLO leader Ahmed Shukairy, willingly provided haven and support for Syrian elements opposed to the neo-Baathists. An almost total deterioration of relations occurred after the bloody Israeli "reprisal" raid on Samu, Jordan, in November 1966. Again, Jordan paid heavily for the presence of *fedayeen* along her borders and responded with mass arrests of activists and pro-Syrian elements. These acts gave further credence to assertions of the "reactionary" and "collaborationist" character of King Hussein's government. Relations were broken in May 1967 after a bomb outrage at Deraa, the Jordanian frontier post which is part of the legend of T. E. Lawrence. Syria had succeeded in increasing pressure on the Jordanians to such an extent that the only alternative to war with Israel in June 1967 would have been a Hashemite capitulation to the Palestinian activists.

In December 1966 the Iraq Petroleum Company's pipeline was blockaded by the Syrian army. As in 1956, when the pipeline was blown up, this act provided an opportunity to reap praise from various quarters for a selfless act of anti-imperialism while at the same time inflicting economic reverses and otherwise weakening an Iraqi regime which Syrian leaders held to be reactionary. Iraq's revolutionary character was acceptable to Egypt but was not pure enough for Syria.[7] The pipeline strategy was, after protracted and tense negotiations, a financial as well as a propaganda success for the neo-Baathists, although it did not topple the Iraqi regime.

---

[7]Syria considered Republican Yemen as an ally fighting the lackeys of imperialism on another front. Lebanon was pictured in the Damascus press and radio as a haven for playboys and greedy shopkeepers, and the Muslim community was encouraged to oppose the regime. With the emergence of Saudi Arabia's King Faisal as a vigorous and determined traditional leader in 1964, there had been a further polarization between what was described in the Cairo, Damascus, and Algiers press as "liberated" regimes (the UAR, Syria, Algeria) and those which were placed in the "nonliberated" category.

Syria and Israel

Before 1966, the Israeli tactic of massive responses to Arab infiltrations had purchased periods of peace. But after the Israeli artillery and aircraft attack on the Baniyas water diversion project in Syrian territory in July 1966, the tempo of *fedayeen* activity increased. The subsequent Israeli raid on Samu, Jordan, only spurred the commandos to greater efforts. Concurrently, Damascus Radio energetically developed the theme of "Crush Israel"—a fact which becomes more than a footnote to recent history when it is recalled that educated Arabs often have remarked that Syrian broadcasts reflect what is in the minds and hearts of Arabs more faithfully than any other media.

In Israel, a struggle for political power made the government more responsive to public opinion than it had been for years. And public opinion wanted action against Syria. In the early months of 1967 Syria's provocative policy and the Israeli strategy of reprisal achieved new heights of extremism. For twenty years Syrian politicians had employed the issue of Palestine to divert public attention from the poverty and corruption of their policies. They exploited the passions of the enthusiastic youths who served as their proxies in martyrdom, and in the process Israel came to be regarded in many parts of the world as a beleaguered and vulnerable state. In 1966 tension had increased to the point that *The Economist* (London) captioned a report from Israel, "Will the Public Stand It?" As David Ben-Gurion's Rafi Party turned the screw on Levi Eshkol's shaky government, thereby eliciting public threats against Syria, the neo-Baathists assumed that the warnings were "good politics" intended for internal consumption and refused to allow Egyptian aircraft and army units on Syrian territory.

The seriousness with which Tel Aviv regarded the situation was indicated by the revival, after a long hiatus, of Israeli participation in the Israeli-Syrian Mixed Armistice Commission (ISMAC). From 1951 Israeli cooperation with ISMAC and its parent organization, the United Nations Truce Supervisory Organization, had been minimal, although Israel held a slight edge in the number of complaints of border violations filed, out of a total exceeding 65,000. In three months, beginning with the last week of January 1967, ISMAC received just under eight hundred Israeli complaints—a testimony to *fedayeen* success in keeping pressure on army units and settlements across the frontier.

Syrian news media did not give undivided attention to the call of "Crush Israel," for some of their time and space was devoted to allegations that Egypt was hiding behind the United Nations Emergency

Force. Villification increased as Arab capitals were swept by rumors of Israeli troop concentrations on the Syrian frontier, rumors recklessly fostered by the Soviet Union.

The next major clash was touched off in April by intermittent Syrian shelling of Israeli cultivators in the demilitarized zone. Israeli reaction was the most intense since the Samu raid seven months earlier. Ground action, however, took second place to an air battle in which six Syrian MIGs were shot down. The Syrian response was a series of incursions into Israeli territory on a larger scale and with greater frequency than previously. At the same time the neo-Baathists were giving much attention to questions of internal security. Possible centers of disaffection were closely watched and the business community and religious leaders were provided with examples of the cost of disloyalty.

A new factor was introduced into this tense atmosphere when Israel threatened in mid-May to march on Damascus and overturn the government. The motivation for this has been ascribed to outright calculation, a display of nerves on the part of the Eshkol ministry, a response to the prodding of "hawks" in Israel, pressures generated by internal political and economic crises, and a misreading of the domestic situation in Syria. It could have been a combination of such factors. But one question was not asked in Israel—could President Nasser once more afford to back away from conflict?

This crisis produced another in the series of treaties of mutual assistance between Cairo and Damascus. Veteran observers saw the treaty as an Egyptian device to keep the neo-Baathists in check, but as in Bismarck's treaty of 1879 with Austria, the junior partner became the determining factor. Ignoring Egypt's military involvement in Yemen (see Chapter 5), the Syrian media reflected with eloquence and sarcasm on the passiveness of the Cairo regime. These verbal attacks combined with Syria's continued pressure on Israel amounted to grave challenges to Nasser's leadership of the Arab world. Hence the fateful Gulf of Aqaba strategy—the announced blockade of the entrance to the Gulf and the Egyptian demand that the "shield" of the United Nations Emergency Force be forthwith removed. From this point in time Syria had little to do with the shaping of events, but was swept along in a historical continuum that its rulers had set in motion.

Nasser's Aqaba strategy was described authoritatively in the West as "a sophisticated further step in Cairo's attempt to show public support for the Syrian government while privately urging caution." It would appear, until closely examined, to have been a departure from his accustomed emphasis on words for Cairo and deeds for his supporters abroad.

The strategy was based on four considerations (1) that Israel did not make idle threats; therefore (2) Syria was to be, as Damascus claimed, the target of an attack which could be averted by taking a hard line on the Gulf of Aqaba, the closure of which (3) had an arguable basis under international law but (4) would not be countenanced by the United States and Great Britain. Nasser was to state, on July 13, 1967, that his country could not fight the United States but that its intervention would have served his propaganda purposes while removing pressure from the Syrian border. It seemed an inexpensive means of demonstrating revolutionary purity and willingness to make sacrifices for the Arab cause.

Eshkol's miscalculation of Nasser was serious, but Nasser's miscalculation of the United Nations, and especially of its Secretary-General, was fatal. In the future, however, the removal of the United Nations Emergency Force may be regarded not as the product of an Egyptian blunder but as the result of the inability of the United States and Great Britain to bring their joint influence to bear in keeping the UNEF in place. Instead, Lyndon Johnson and Harold Wilson contented themselves with speeches on the sanctity of international waterways and the Soviet Union made last-minute efforts to extinguish the fire it had helped to ignite.

An account of Syrian participation in the June war is necessarily short. Apart from hit-and-run activity by small units and the bombardment of the upper Jordan Valley, plus baseless claims that Syrian aircraft had destroyed the Haifa oil refinery and left Tel Aviv in flames, Syria's participation was limited to rejections of the United Nations call for a cease-fire. The Syrian expectation was that, as in 1948–49, the Golan Heights would not be attacked. The Israeli view was that Syria must be made to pay, and the Golan Heights must be in friendly hands.

Israeli air attacks, which began on June 8th, produced a Syrian request for a cease-fire. The Israeli attack on the escarpment meanwhile met determined resistance by reserve officers and their men. What had been described as "front-line" units were deployed in and around Damascus, Homs, and Aleppo to protect the regime. By announcing the fall of Kuneitra, some distance behind the combat lines, the neo-Baathists broke the will of their own armed forces to continue resistance, so that it now became important to increase pressure for the cease-fire which three days earlier had been contemptuously rejected and in which the Israelis now showed no interest. The outpouring of sympathy and generosity with which the Syrian population greeted units returning from the Golan Heights was more than a manifestation of the traditional qualities for which Damascus has long been famous; it was their way of demonstrating opposition to an entrenched regime which imprisoned and executed other military men who had ventured from their places of asylum and returned to fight for Syria.

The Place of Syria in the Arab World

Diplomatic relations with Jordan were resumed after the June war, and Syrian standing in the Arab world improved because of the loss of men and territory under fire. Feelings of solidarity in defeat were all the more compelling because of widespread Arab acceptance of charges of Anglo-American collusion with Israel. Nonetheless, Syria remained isolated. Its militancy contrasted sharply to the hesitancy and introspection of the Egyptian and Jordanian regimes in the first months after the war. Only faraway Algeria took a stronger line. The Syrian government operated as if under siege conditions, with Nur al-Din al-Atassi assuming the premiership while remaining head of state and secretary-general of the party. In view of the Israeli preoccupation with consolidating its hold on the Golan Heights, and in view of general popular indifference to all but questions of economic survival, it is difficult to understand why such emergency steps were deemed necessary.

Colonel Salah Jedid, the secretive Alawite who emerged as the strong man in support of the Atassi-Zu'ayyan-Makhus triumvirate after February 1966, was responsible for this situation. Earlier connections with extreme right-wing political elements raised questions about his objectives, but he was assuredly an admirer of Soviet security practices. Before the June war his purges of the armed forces placed hundreds of officers, from Russian-trained pilots to hardened infantry commanders, on the retired list for "political unreliability." These actions helped to determine the deployment of troops during the fateful six days. Afterward, Jedid labored to align Syria with Soviet Middle Eastern policy, which had swung back to a highly aggressive phase. The "state of siege" strategy and other manifestations of militancy won for Syria expressions of full Soviet support. President Podgorny's visit in July 1967 and journeys to Moscow by Syrian delegations, including Jedid himself, produced a new infusion of Russian weapons and instructors.

The Syrian government further emphasized its hardline apartness by boycotting the Khartoum "summit," where a formula was worked out according to which the oil-producing Arab states would be reunited with their Western or Western-organized markets, and would give financial support to countries that had direct experience of the Israeli *Blitzkrieg*. There was little enthusiasm at the meeting for including the absent

Syrians in the formula finally settled upon, but the persuasiveness of the Algerian delegation on this score won reluctant acceptance. However reluctantly offered, this was a gesture of solidarity. But it did little to shake the Syrian government from its intransigent aloofness, for Syria was less reliant than Jordan and Egypt on Kuwaiti, Saudi Arabian, and Libyan largesse thanks to increased returns from oil pipelines, some improvement in cotton production, and export and agricultural surpluses that gave her a heady feeling of independence despite the fact that her overall trade deficit continued.

The neo-Baathist regime directed its greatest outpourings of scorn and hostility at efforts to achieve a negotiated Arab-Israeli settlement. The round of talks in which Dr. Gunnar Jarring, U Thant's special representative, participated with King Hussein and Egypt's Mahmud Riad was condemned as a policy of surrender.

But Syrian policy did not go unopposed. The Arab Nationalist Movement, which generally supported Nasser's objectives in the Arab east, ordered its Syrian branch to join with the Arab Socialist Party of Akram Hurani in blaming the Syrian regime for the outbreak of the June war and for a policy which could lead only to further reverses. The Palestine Liberation Organization, in seeking more tangible support than was provided by the largely verbal nature of Syrian aggressiveness, also got onto bad terms with the neo-Baathists. More significant was the Baghdad *coup d'état* of June 1968 which returned to power Baathist elements which had been closely identified with those who had ruled Syria before February 1966. This stimulated considerable activity among exiled Syrian politicians of every persuasion, and there were rumors of negotiations for a "popular front" in opposition to the Damascus regime. These rumors probably originated in Damascus, for the issues which divided the political exiles of the pre-Baathist era from those who held power between 1963 and 1966 were insurmountable. Inevitably, the Syrian government discovered and announced the crushing of a plot in which Salah ad-Din al-Bitar, Ma'ruf Dawalibi, and Akram Hurani were listed as collaborators. A by-product of these alarums and excursions was a press and radio campaign against Lebanon for harboring hostile elements, which not only did violence to an honored tradition but assured an unenthusiastic Lebanese reception of Syrian political exiles after the bloodless *coup* of the following October.

Colonel Salah Jedid's close identification with the Soviet Union placed him in an uncomfortable position when the Russians began moderating and qualifying their support of Arab objectives. Serious differences arose in the highest councils of government, and in October 1968 a new strong man came forward. General Hafiz Assad, Minister of Defense and air force commander, demanded a more "Arab" policy, which in his view involved cooperation with Iraq and Jordan in military arrangements on what has become known as "the Eastern Front." His policy prevailed, and Zu'ayyan and Makhus went into eclipse. Atassi, despite early expressions of reluctance, remained in office as the front man for Assad. Shortly afterward, regular units of the Syrian army moved into positions in northern Jordan.

The new arrangement was also marked by increasing cordiality with the People's Republic of China. It may have been designed to dramatize the lessening of Syrian dependence on the Soviet Union, but it seems to have caused concern in Moscow out of proportion to the Soviet stake in the Syrian regime. The value of this initiative in terms of weaponry, credits, and other forms of assistance was inconsiderable, but it enabled Syria to assert once more its reputation for militancy.

The Assad-Atassi regime at first seemed no more prepared than its predecessor to challenge Israel militarily. A safer objective was Lebanon, whose social and economic system, Western orientation, and special position in the Arab world caused particular resentment in Syria and among the Palestinian refugee communities of the two countries. At no time since independence have relations been cordial, but bad feeling usually had been expressed by propaganda attacks, minor border affrays, or levies and restrictions on the trade transiting Syria from Lebanon to Iraq, Jordan, Kuwait, and Saudi Arabia, which had become both more lucrative and more vulnerable after the closure of the Suez Canal. Lebanon had given employment to great numbers of Syrians and Syrian-domiciled refugees who entered the country to work on construction sites, on the docks, and in agriculture, while keeping their families in Syria where the Lebanese pound had more purchasing power. But such considerations were ignored in early 1969.

The Syrian regime after June 1967 kept a close rein on units of the Palestine Liberation Army (the conventional force of the Palestine Liberation Organization) based in Syria, and upon the several *fedayeen* organizations. Among these was *Sai'qah* ("Thunder"), directly controlled by the neo-Baathist regime. It was apparent that with little effort it would be possible to exacerbate confessional and political tensions in Lebanon by introducing a *Sai'qah* force into the country. The force encamped in the Marjayoun-Mount Hermon area, intimidating local security forces with superior weaponry and announcing their intention to train for attacks on Israel from positions in Lebanon. As observed earlier, only a firm stand by the Lebanese army high command during the Six Day War had vetoed the potentially disastrous policy of "opening a front." Frustrations increased after the Israeli raid of December 28, 1968, on the Beirut International Airport. Now the *Sai'qah* presence was an invitation to extremism. Clashes occurred between supporters of unrestricted commando activity and security forces, and between *Sai'qah* elements and units of the Lebanese army. There were a number of deaths and many wounded. The government fell and Lebanon was on the verge of civil war. From the standpoint of the Syrian junta, the strategy could be counted a success until the newly elected Lebanese president, Sleiman Frangieh, imposed measures limiting commando activity late in 1970.

The first major intrusion into Israeli-occupied Syrian territory occurred in June 1969 when members of the Popular Front for the Liberation of Palestine blew up the Trans-Arabian Pipeline (Tapline) in the Golan Heights. The objective may have been to pollute the Sea of Galilee but the operation did greater damage to Arab interests. Whether it was undertaken with governmental sanction has not been established. Two months later, however, Syrian regular army units and jet aircraft engaged in operations on a significant scale against Israel for the first time since the 1967 war. Thus another step was taken toward the brink of catastrophe.

Meanwhile major dissensions divided the neo-Baathist regime. At the root of the difficulties was a simple struggle for power in which al-Atassi, as head of state, hoped to sustain himself by playing upon the rivalry of the two military strongmen, Jedid and Assad. Both Assad and Atassi felt that Jedid's blatantly pro-Soviet stance weakened whatever ideological appeal the Baathist variety of pan-Arabism still could generate. Internal maneuverings continued into 1970, until a crisis was precipitated by civil war in Jordan, which began with severe clashes between Palestinian commando units and the Jordanian army in late August.

The principal combat zones were Amman itself and northern Jordan. On September 1, Salah Jedid ordered Syrian armored units across the frontier and into battle against the Jordanian army. It was an ill-starred venture and within forty-eight hours the Syrian units were withdrawn. The retreat was due more to Russian and Egyptian pressure on Damascus, combined with General Assad's refusal to provide air cover for the Syrian tanks, than to Jordanian army resistance. The Russian disavowal of Jedid after American moves to buttress King Hussein's regime provided Assad with a great opportunity. He seized it with such thoroughness as to remind the entire Arab world of the Alawite reputation for secretiveness and skill in intrigue. Moreover, the death of President Nasser in October suggested that Egypt might no longer be available to save Syria from the penalties of adventurist policies.

For a time Assad attempted to collaborate with al-Atassi, but clashes on foreign policy objectives soon forced a showdown. Al-Atassi demonstrated considerable skill in rallying support in the Baathist high command, but more significant was Assad's success not only in broadening the base of his support in the armed forces but also in winning popular opinion to his side. Assad strengthened his power base by means of what purported to be a reform of the Baathist party and of the armed forces. In the latter case, "reform" consisted of a blending of retirements and promotions which made the army more thoroughly an instrument of Assad's personal authority. At the same time, his cautious advocacy of the concept of a multireligious community won support among Syrian Christians (whose intellectual resources are disproportionate to their small numbers) and the Druses, whose militancy and cohesion constantly challenged earlier regimes.

In organizing support, Assad often promised to broaden participation in the governing process. Yet there were economic constraints which made him reluctant to perform on his promise. The economy was depressed and consumer goods were in short supply. After extensive consultation and preparation of public opinion, Assad opened negotiations with Tapline in an effort to remedy this situation. In January 1971 repair of the pipeline was authorized and operations recommenced on terms very favorable to Syria. Almost simultaneously, al-Atassi was placed under house arrest—a move that accomplished more than simply the elimination of a powerful rival, for the removal of al-Atassi made improved relations with Lebanon possible.

New revenue and unprecedented cordiality between the Damascus and Beirut regimes enabled Syrian merchants to stock their shelves with consumer goods purchased through middlemen in Beirut. A further orchestration of the economy led to increased family allowances for workers and a rollback in price ceilings on essential foods.

Such was the background of the plebiscite held in March 1971 to elect Assad to the presidency of Syria. He ran unopposed but the size of the vote and the festive atmosphere in which the results were announced in Damascus, Aleppo, and other Syrian cities were more than manifestations of the power of the man who controlled both the armed forces and the mechanism of the ruling party. They were in some measure indications of popular approval. Once this hurdle was passed, the new president addressed himself to dealing with internal forces and external pressures responsible for making Syria reliant upon the Soviet Union for military and economic assistance to the extent that the country had become a client state. To this end, the Baath Party structure was thoroughly purged throughout the spring and summer of 1971. In August, five potential rivals, including Michel Aflaq and Amin Hafiz, were sentenced to death *in absentia.* (These sentences were subsequently commuted to life imprisonment.)

Assad and his supporters were aware that continued hostilities between Palestinians in Jordan and the Royal Jordanian Army posed problems for Syria. A large Palestinian refugee population was concentrated in and around Damascus and sympathy for the Palestinian cause was widespread and deeply rooted in the Syrian population. In April 1971, therefore, Assad dispatched the chief of staff of the Syrian army on a conciliation mission to Amman, hoping to restore peace between the two groups. This effort continued through July, with mediation attempts by several military delegations while Assad met frequently with commando leaders, including Yassir Arafat. These attempts did not bear fruit, and eventually the extreme measures embarked upon by the Royal Jordanian Army, accompanied by border clashes brought about the severance of diplomatic relations on August 4, 1971. (See Chapter 4.) Only in the last days of 1971 was the border reopened and Jordanian freight impounded in Syrian ports or held up at the Lebanese frontier released.

Despite the fact that friendly relations with the Beirut regime brought high-ranking Lebanese delegations to Syria and led to a flurry of commercial activity, Assad was initially less successful in improving ties with Iraq. Communication between the two countries was, however, greatly improved with the completion of the Damascus-Baghdad highway in September 1971. Progress on such central problems as the sharing of the Euphrates waters and transit trade was facilitated by the removal from the Syrian Baathist Party structure of a number of the more resolute opponents of the Iraqi neo-Baathist regime.

By early 1972, Syria's improved economy as well as her improved status in the Arab world permitted President Assad to initiate a series of sweeping changes in the structure of government. A National Progressive Front was formed, through which Assad reduced the potential of various left-wing groups for challenging his authority by soliciting and gaining their participation in the governing process. In the new government only ten of eighteen ministers were Baathists. Four other organizations—the Syrian Communist Party, the Social Unionists, the Arab National Movement, and the Arab Socialist Union—were each given two ministers. A further balancing of forces was provided in the municipal elections of 1972 in which conservative elements made gains throughout Syria. The local administrative councils in Homs came under the control of the *Ikhwan* (Muslim Brotherhood) while a slate endorsed by religious leaders took control of the Damascus inner city. The success of Assad's policy was manifest in the subsequent split in the Syrian Communist Party over the decision to participate in the National Progressive Front. To further improve his popular standing, Assad authorized a further easing of restrictions on the private sector of the Syrian economy.

Nor was Assad idle in inter-Arab politics and the broader international sphere. He spoke often and with enthusiasm of the projected federation of Egypt, Libya, and the Sudan (proposed in 1971), and expounded upon the importance of Syrian participation in the project. Finally, on April 17, 1972, Assad announced the creation of the Federation of Arab Republics, to include Egypt, Libya, and Syria, with Sudan joining when circumstances permitted.

During this same period, Assad courted the Palestinians by emphatically condemning any settlement of the Arab-Israeli dispute based upon the United Nations resolution of November 1967. He balanced his endorsement of cooperation with the Soviet Union and other countries of the socialist bloc with an endorsement of free and more extensive relations with France. Less publicized but of equal significance was the further development of political and economic relations with Italy. In Syria as elsewhere in the Arab world the United States had so completely assumed the mantle of Western imperialism as to make it impossible for any leader to make overtures in that direction. With regard to the People's Republic of China, a policy was not so easily defined. China's advocacy of violence in solving the Palestine problem gained many sympathizers, yet Syria's dependence upon the Soviet bloc made it important that the country not become involved in the Moscow-Peking rivalry. Hence relations with China were proper but restrained.

President Assad's plans for a Syria-Egypt-Libya axis were disrupted in mid-1972 when Egypt downgraded the Cairo-Moscow relationship, the most dramatic aspect of which was President Sadat's request for the withdrawal of the immense Soviet military mission from Egypt. The Syrian government was immediately subjected to new external and internal pressures, and Damascus replaced Cairo as the focal point of Russian activity in the Arab world. Moscow emphasized its special relationship with Iraq, its improved relationship with the Palestine Liberation Organization, and Syria's continuing need for military, economic, and technical aid—the latter especially in connection with the Euphrates High Dam project. The Russians, still smarting from the Egyptian debacle, indicated that such aid would be generous but conditional upon Syrian rejection of Egyptian overtures.

Assad's position was complicated further by the influx of three thousand Palestinian commandos from Lebanon after the massive Israeli raids of September and October. To maintain control of the governing coalition, Assad was forced to pledge renewed support for the Palestinian movement, and the Syrian Communist Party made sure that the Marxist Popular Front for the Liberation of Palestine was included in Assad's embrace. The response of Libya's Islamic fundamentalist Colonel Qaddafi was predictable and immediate—to the great satisfaction of the Communist Party, the Syrian Arab Socialist Union, and the Arab Socialist Party, all of which condemned Qaddafi, Egypt's President Anwar Sadat, and the Egyptian-Libyan federation project.

Hence Assad was compelled to return to the lonely and dangerous policy of his predecessors. The *fedayeen* were given free rein, and by early 1973 their attacks on new Israeli agricultural settlements on the occupied Golan Heights had drawn the armed forces of Syria and Israel into the bloodiest fighting since the Six Day War. The USSR quickly replaced Syrian aircraft lost in the fighting—the fiftieth MIG to be shot down since 1967 was recorded—and airlifted anti-tank weapons and ground-to-air missiles to Damascus.

If the USSR's planners hoped to improve their Middle Eastern stance by advocating a vanguard position for the Damascus regime in a pro-Moscow combination of Syria, Iraq, and the Palestinians, they had to be aware of historical forces militating against such a development. More important than the fractiousness of the Palestinians is the ancient hostility between Damascus and Baghdad, now manifested by the claim of each regime to possess the "true faith" insofar as Baathist ideological purity is concerned. Nor were relations helped when Assad employed the leverage provided by the fights over Golan in order to extract higher oil pipeline transit payments from Iraq.

For all this, Assad has shown remarkable staying power in a country that has known a long succession of *coups d'état* since the Palestine War of 1948. His long-term objectives are unknown, but if modern Syria's history continues to run true to form, it will be the policies of some as yet obscure conspirator, civilian or military, and not those of President Assad, that will determine the future course of the Syrian Arab Republic.

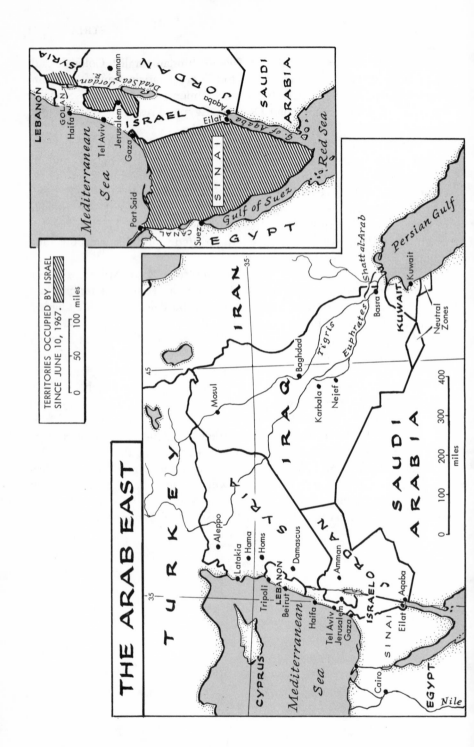

THE ARAB EAST

TERRITORIES OCCUPIED BY ISRAEL
SINCE JUNE 10, 1967.

0   50   100 miles

Inset map labels: LEBANON, SYRIA, JORDAN, SAUDI ARABIA, ISRAEL, SINAI, EGYPT, Mediterranean Sea, Red Sea, Gulf of Aqaba, Gulf of Suez, Dead Sea, Jordan R., Golan, Amman, Haifa, Tel Aviv, Jerusalem, Gaza, Eilat, Aqaba, Port Said, Suez, CANAL

Main map labels: TURKEY, IRAN, IRAQ, SYRIA, LEBANON, ISRAEL, JORDAN, SAUDI ARABIA, KUWAIT, EGYPT, CYPRUS, SINAI, Mediterranean Sea, Persian Gulf, Red Sea, Neutral Zones, Tigris, Euphrates, Shatt al-Arab, Nile, Aleppo, Latakia, Hama, Homs, Tripoli, Beirut, Damascus, Haifa, Tel Aviv, Jerusalem, Gaza, Amman, Aqaba, Eilat, Cairo, Mosul, Baghdad, Karbala, Nejef, Basra, Kuwait

miles 0 100 200 300 400

3

IRAQ

Iraq is less governable than Syria, for reasons rooted in the country's history and geography. Its great rivers have not served a unifying purpose. The flood plains and swamplands of southern Iraq and the mountains of the north have for thousands of years been areas of refuge, where habits of defiance against central authority developed. They remain today.

Eons ago, the head of the Persian Gulf retreated, as a result of the deposit of alluvial soil, from above the site of Baghdad to a point south of modern Basra. The process provided a lasting demarcation, most readily identifiable in the contrast between flood plain and rich, rolling pastureland, but apparent as well in human attitudes, characteristics, and concerns. How far this demarcation goes back is an open question, for archeologists only recently have begun to speculate on the lives of the earlier peoples who dwelled in the challenging environment of southern Mesopotamia. Stages of pre-Sumerian development were not categorized until after World War I, but since then the time-frontier of our knowledge has been pushed back to the sixth millenium b.c. There has emerged, at least in outline, a story of advances in building, decorative arts, and communication by peoples who migrated from the Turkish and Persian highlands to begin a new life in the Land of the Two Rivers.

Much more is known of Sumer and Akkad from Layard's discovery of the tablets at Nineveh and from one of the world's earliest adventure stories, *The Epic of Gilgamesh*. Sir Leonard Wooley's claim that Sumerian civilization lit up "a world still plunged in primitive barbarism" is well founded. Yet the observer of the contemporary Iraqi scene must be forgiven if he finds more understandable the story of Sargon the Akkadian, which is one of power gained by *coup d'état*, power consolidated by subduing the tribes of the north, and power lost at the hands of an assassin. Nor can he avoid pondering the thought that of the greatest names of pre-Achaemenid Iraq—Hammurabi of Babylon, the Assyrian Sennacherib, and the neo-Babylonian Nebuchadnezzar—only the first is known less for a *Drang nach Westen* to the shores of the Levant than for his talents as an administrator and codifier of the law.

With the arrival of the armies of Cyrus in the sixth century B.C., their way having been prepared by Median assaults on Assyria and Babylonia, Iraq became successively a Persian, Achaemenid, Parthian, and Sassanid colony, lasting for over one thousand years. The Alexandrine and Seleucid interval (331–129 B.C.) left no important imprint. Of even less significance were the forays of Julian, Belisaurius, and Heraclius. Nor did the rapid rise and expansion of Islam in the seventh century A.D. transform Iraq into an Arab colony after Khalid ibn Walid's momentous victory over the Sassanids at Qadisiyah.

A Prize for Empires

It hardly could be expected that these primitive and deprived Arab warriors could withstand the Persian civilization in whose midst they found themselves. They were overwhelmed by Persian culture. The fact that the Arabic language prevailed was due almost exclusively to the quality of sacredness bestowed upon it by the Koran. This made it an element in the process of cultural synthesis and also tended to foster the myth of an early Arab unity.

As important in the shaping of modern Iraqi society were the historical forces which made Iraq the base of operations and ultimately the site of the violent deaths of Ali and Hussein, son-in-law and grandson of the Prophet. Their burial places, the shrine cities of Nejef and Karbala on the Euphrates, became the most venerated Shiite places of pilgrimage. In time, the Shiite persuasion would prevail in southern Iraq and the rulers of Iran would be regarded as the defenders of this sect, most often against Sunnite governments in Baghdad.

In Damascus, persecutions and corruption kindled opposition to the Ummayads, giving the Abbasids, descendants of the Prophet's uncle, their opportunity. With Persian help, the time of Iraq's greatest glory began. To be sure, there was a Persian patina to this Arab glory, but

Mansur, the builder of Baghdad, and his grandson Harun al-Rashid must be considered in some measure responsible for the modern Iraqi aspiration to have a decisive voice in Arab affairs. The prosperity of Abbasid Iraq, with Baghdad as its marketplace and gilded *caravanserai* for all the East, is another portion of the historical legacy likely to induce melancholia in recent times. The Abbasid Caliphate survived for five centuries, from 750 to 1258, but the period of Abbasid greatness did not stretch to two. Then came a century of servitude to the Buwayhids—once again a period of Persian ascendancy—after which the dust of Mesopotamia was stirred by Seljuk and Mongol armies. The Seljuks are remembered for the peace they imposed and for their patronage of Omar Khayyam. The Mongols are remembered for their devastation in some cases and their neglect in others, as in the case of the irrigation system which was the basis for the flourishing agriculture of Iraq. The Mongol era and its Turcoman aftermath were truly Iraq's burden, for the damage they wrought has yet to be fully repaired.

In spite of this destruction, Iraq was a prize to its next conqueror, the Persian Safavid, Shah Ismail, who aspired to extend his rule over the Shiite shrine cities. His armies occupied the country in 1509 and a stratum of Persian officials was established as the ruling class. Persian rule over Iraq coincided with a period of explosive Ottoman Turkish expansionism. The first clash between Persians and Ottomans took place in Asia Minor, at Chaldiran in 1514, where Sultan Selim's legions massacred thousands of Ismail's Shiite followers. It was a portent of future bloodlettings, brought on by conflicting imperial ambitions. Scarcely eight years after Shah Ismail had imposed his heavy-handed rule upon Baghdad, Selim the Dread occupied Damascus; sixteen years later an Ottoman army was on Iraqi soil, and only one more year had passed when Selim's son Sulaiman raised his standard in Baghdad in 1534.

Iraq would never again be so Turkish as during this first phase of Ottoman rule, which lasted just over eighty years. The luster of Harun al-Rashid's caliphate and the opportunity to strike a blow for Sunni orthodoxy encouraged great efforts to secure Baghdad and the surrounding country to the Turkish interest. But the energy with which reconstruction and reform were carried out did not long survive Sulaiman's return to Constantinople. The loyalty, much less the cooperation, of the local population could not be obtained by these foreign rulers.

A major obstacle was the deep division of the urban population. Baghdad was heavily Persian, with Shiite followers of Ali and Hussein living in uneasy proximity to the Sunnite ruling class. It was also the home of many thousands of Jews who engaged in banking and a variety of commercial occupations. Kurds and Turks had settled there in numbers long before the Ottoman conquest. Jews, Christians, and an Indian community lived in Basra. The Christians included Armenians, Indians, and a few Arabs, while the Indian community was further divided into a Hindu element and a number of Islamic sects. Perhaps half of Mosul's population was Christian. The ethnic and religious groupings had little to do with one another except for routine business transactions. And when to these divisions and subdivisions within the communities are added those of trade and craft, it is readily understandable that the rulers could do little more than hope that they would not clash and would deliver up tax money in satisfactory amounts.

A still greater gulf divided town and tribe. From the marshland and riverine villages of southern Iraq, Shiite tribespeople brought their dates and rice to market in Basra. Somewhat less sedentary were the buffalo breeders of the marshes who were joined by date and rice cultivators in levying tolls on Euphrates and Tigris river traffic whenever the opportunity arose. There were a few settled tribes working market gardens around Baghdad. Christian Arab villagers in the hills north of Mosul supplied foodstuffs to that city, as did settlements of Sunnite Turcomans nearby. But far greater in number were nomadic (beduin) Arabs who roamed vast areas in search of pasturage. In addition to tending camels, sheep, and goats, the beduin exacted passage money from caravans and looted villages, towns, and each other. Drought induced acts of desperation, but there were also blood feuds, often many generations old. The failure or success of raids, marriage arrangements, disputes over pasturage, and the sharing-out of loot were responsible for a constant shifting of alliances among the beduin. Many years would pass before great tribal confederations would emerge—among them, the Anezah and Shammar on Iraq's western and southwestern marches, the Muntafiq between Baghdad and Basra. At times they posed a threat to Ottoman rule, but there were periods in which they paid tribute and even participated in military operations against more recalcitrant tribal groups. Their sixteenth-century forebears, however, had scant contact of a peaceful nature with townspeople apart from the occasional exchange of livestock for food and cloth.

The Kurds were divided between nomads and settled cultivators. In Sulaiman's time they were ruled fairly effectively from Ardalan (Persian Kurdistan). Ottoman inroads into the Kurdish mountains would come much later. To the south, Arab and Persian tribes crossed and recrossed the undemarcated border of the Safavid and Ottoman empires, fighting thousands of unrecorded battles, mostly over pasturage and water rights. In time, their concerns would be translated into international incidents involving European powers.

Hence there was more form than substance in Ottoman administration of Iraq, a situation found also in other provinces of the empire. More often than not the authority of Baghdad's rulers was secure in the city itself and derisive in the surrounding countryside. In 1621 the empire's feeble administration finally collapsed into anarchy, opening Baghdad's gates to Shah Abbas.

The new Persian regime put heavy demands on its chroniclers for terms adequate to describe either the hatred which inspired it or the barbarity which the hatred produced. The Sunni population was cut down by torture, murder, and commitment to slavery. No Hafiz or Sa'di could alter the reputation for savagery gained for the Persians by the actions of Shah Abbas in Iraq. Yet no one did more to carry out the Persianization of the regained province. The few years of the second occupation (1621–38) passed under almost continuous Turkish pressure. Baghdad had become a symbol for Turks and Persians alike, for its possession bespoke the primacy of empire, its loss the deepest humiliation. In Persian hands it was the key to sacred Shiite shrine cities as well as to commercial opportunity. The Turks had no very precise idea of the advantages of possessing Iraq beyond the additional scope it gave to an expanding, contentious, and voracious aristocracy.

In Sultan Murad IV the Turks found leadership equal to their ardent desire to again raise the Ottoman standard over Baghdad. The organizational and operational skills which marked the march and siege of 1638 reached a level never again attained in Ottoman history, even in the famous Kuprulu campaigns in Europe. Murad may have intended that the final act of his campaign would be one of clemency to a defeated foe, but he was unprepared for the fanatical resistance he met and could not have anticipated the explosion of the city's arsenal at the height of battle. Both spurred excesses which, in the name of Murad, drenched Baghdad in blood no less completely than had the deliberate policy of Shah Abbas seventeen years earlier. In the long term, the greatest sufferers were the Arabs and Kurds of Iraq.

Ottoman determination to regain Baghdad stands in striking contrast to Constantinople's neglect of the province once it was secured. In peace Baghdad became a backwater; in war, it remained a glittering prize. The century which divided Sultan Murad's campaign from Nadir Shah's first invasion was hardly one to inspire chroniclers. There were no inducements to settled pursuits for the restless tribes. Forays by garrison troops produced neither submission to authority nor revenue to sustain the imperial garrison. They were productive primarily of severed heads, grisly mementoes of useless victories, of a legacy of hatred among Kurds and Arabs, and of a mutinous spirit among the troops. Only occasionally did concerted tribal action threaten Turkish rule, even though the tribal population grew with the great migrations out of Nejd. Iraq was divided in many ways; one was between those who collaborated and those who did not.

On a smaller scale than at Constantinople—the stakes were not nearly as high—Baghdad was the scene of recurring plots, intrigues, and Janissary revolts. As plague, famine, and floods added to the misery produced by man, the habit of opposition spread. The mountains of Kurdistan remained beyond any measure of Ottoman control, and the rise of the Kurdish Baban dynasty in the late seventeenth century assured organized resistance to later attempts at Ottomanization. The Pashalic of Baghdad expanded and contracted in relation to the energy and good fortune of successive governors. But at the best of times the relationship between the Baghdad government and those of the cities at the extremities of Iraq—Basra, Mosul, Kirkuk, and their dependencies—was remote to the point of meaninglessness.

Basra in particular looked in an opposite direction—to the Persian Gulf. Its fortunes were bound up with the Portuguese, Dutch, and English struggle for maritime supremacy, with the slave and coffee trades, and with southwest Persia, which was both a market area and the base for successive invasions of southern Iraq. Indian and Persian merchants were numerous, and the Jews and Christians of Sindbad's city, like their coreligionists in Baghdad, took the avenue of commercial and financial enterprise to achieve prominence and influence disproportionate to their numbers. Among the Christians, the Armenian community was especially successful. In the north, despite the fact that numbers of Nestorians and other Christians turned to mercantile pursuits, their strength remained in the communities of sturdy village cultivators and herdsmen of the hill country, living in close and uneasy proximity to Kurdish settlements.

The dullness and mediocrity of Turkish rule were forgotten in the third decade of the eighteenth century with the Afghan challenge to the Safavid dynasty in Persia and to the Ottoman hold on Iraq. The Afghans swept aside a feeble Persian administration, thereby encouraging the Turks to take up arms and secure a share of the prostrate Shiite state. But neither Turk nor Afghan reckoned with the Persian capacity for resistance and renewal. On this occasion it was manifested in the person of a Khurasani buccaneer who would become known to history as Nadir Shah. For two decades after ridding Persia of its Afghan occupiers and pushing the Turks across their old frontiers, he deployed his talents and resources in a campaign to make Iraq Persia's westernmost province. Yet his brilliance, ruthlessness, and qualities of leadership were not enough, for the Turks possessed that steadfastness in adversity which has survived into the republican era. The Persian challenges to Baghdad, Mosul, and Basra, ending only in 1743, once again made Iraq the brightest jewel in the Sultan's crown. In Othman Pasha and Ahmed Pasha the Ottomans found military leadership akin to that of Marlborough or Sobieski.

In organizing Baghdad's defenses, Ahmed also provided the ground-work for the extension of authority over remote corners of Iraq. The frontier settlements retained little independence from Baghdad, but Baghdad achieved a considerable degree of independence from Con-stantinople. This situation survived the death of Ahmed Pasha with the rise to power of the Georgian Mamluks. These converts to Islam, many of them gifted and energetic and all of them ambitious, made the most of the rights and responsibilities bestowed upon them by the Ottoman Turks. Some attained high rank in imperial service. In Iraq, at least, they gave little in return. The trend toward independence of the Porte was accentuated, and if loyalty was measured in soldiers, supplies, and re-venue provided for imperial purposes, then loyalty scarcely existed. Soon virtually every position of consequence in the Pashalic had a Georgian incumbent. The Sultan's efforts to end the "slave regime" came to noth-ing. Remedies for periods of incompetent or corrupt rule came not from Constantinople but from the Georgians themselves. Three of them, Sulaiman Pasha (1749–61), Buyuk Sulaiman Pasha (1780–1802), and Daud Pasha (1817–31), showed remarkable qualities of leadership, on occa-sion accompanied by a ruthless determination and tenacity which would become more widely recognized in another Georgian's rule in twentieth-century Moscow.

The splendor of the Georgian court at Baghdad, the pageantry, the scale of daily life, and the extravagant gifts sent to Constantinople upon receipt of the imperial *firman* (the decree renewing the Pasha's mandate) left little surplus to remit to the Porte. The Sultan would have preferred to dispatch a punitive expedition in place of a *firman*, but European pressures and concerns denied him this alternative.

The Baghdad authorities spent little money on improvements and much upon tax-gathering and pacification operations, especially when Wahhabi incursions from Nejd and Hasa in the first decade of the nine-teenth century added another dimension to the problem of unruly Arab and Kurdish tribesmen. Yet there were stories of immense accumulations of wealth, borne out by the ferocity with which the succession at Bagh-dad was contested and by the fact that the year 1831, which marked the end of Georgian rule, did not mark the beginning of the rule of Con-stantinople. Ali Ridha Pasha wrested Baghdad from Daud in the name of the Sultan but kept it for himself. Two more decades were to pass before Iraq was governed by Turks animated less by the commandment *"enri-*

chissez-vous" than by the Porte's interest in and concern, however faint, for reform.

A series of disasters hastened the depopulation and general economic decline of Iraq before the Georgians were displaced in a *Gotterdammerung* scene of violence and treachery in the midst of floods and plague. A cycle of severe winters and early summer heats in the mountain regions caused ruinous floods almost annually. Such natural calamities were factors in causing the Persians to abandon their hold on Basra in 1776 and later, in the era of Daud Pasha, raised a Persian siege of Baghdad. But they also reduced the capacity of the Pashalic to support its population. Thereafter, the violence with which grazing lands were fought over, tribute collected, chieftanships contested, and taxes exacted, made for a dark period in an already tragic history.

Yet none of these developments, which took Iraq to the lowest ebb of its fortunes by the end of the Georgian era, made possession of Baghdad less attractive to the Egyptian viceroy, Mohammed Ali. The Arabian and pan-Islamic strategy of the Egyptians had the occupation of Iraq as an objective. In the early 1830s Mohammed Ali's warrior son, Ibrahim, ruled Syria, and the British political agent at Baghdad claimed that the city's miserable inhabitants would have happily thrown open the gates to an Egyptian invader. The spectre of an Islamic confederation, including Persia and Afghanistan and energized by an imperial Egypt, seemed to threaten British India. Lord Palmerston responded by marshaling a European coalition to frustrate Mohammed Ali's grand design. The Egyptian threat to Baghdad evaporated.

Other concerns accounted for the presence of a British political agent at Baghdad. The East India Company had been active at Basra since early in the seventeenth century. For one hundred fifty years trade had never been good enough to give .confidence nor bad enough to bring about complete withdrawal. But chaos in Persia made Basra seem preferable to Bundar Abbas or Bushir, and jealous rivalry with the English merchants of the Levant Company suggested that it might be worth hanging on in Iraq. Ultimately, the decision was the result of Napoleon's Eastern design, and in particular his brief occupation of Egypt, which .conferred upon Iraq an importance it had not known since the days when it was the heartland of an Islamic empire. Once the French threat, if such it was, had receded, another challenge to British paramountcy was discerned in the southward drive of Russia. Iraq was considered as a strategic counterbalance to the Russian occupation of Georgia. The high standard of British representatives, of whom Sir Henry Rawlinson was the best known if not the most attractive, was an indication of the importance placed upon the Iraq assignment. A permanent residency was established at Baghdad at the end of the eighteenth century, and from that time the British political agent ranked second only to the Pasha in official precedence and very frequently exceeded him in the capacity to shape events.

Iraq, as suggested earlier, felt little of the reforming spirit which was manifested in Constantinople at various times throughout the nineteenth century. Midhat Pasha, during the three years he governed Iraq, was more interested in regaining the patrimony of Sulaiman the Magnificent than in projects of detribalization or administrative improvement. Before the advent of his government in 1869, there had been unsuccessful efforts to make Basra a base from which Ottoman rule might be extended down the Arab shore of the Persian Gulf and on to Muscat. Midhat's "Nejd expedition" won a hold on only a few strongpoints, which were retained until World War I through a vast expenditure of blood and treasure.

For more than a century before Turkish rule gave way to British occupation, the influence of the British political agency at Baghdad steadily increased. Ottoman attempts to reduce the Kurds to subject status, to impose unwelcome government nominees as shaikhs of such tribes or tribal confederations as the Anezah, Shammar, Al Bu Mohammed, Beni Lam, and Muntafiq of southern Iraq, to protect caravans, or to prevent river blockades by Arab "blackmailers," repeatedly led to hostilities which were ended only by the political agent's mediation. When coming to Baghdad to make his submission, a tribal chief preferred the British agent's guarantee of his safety to a pasha's oath on the Holy Koran.

At times of acute Turco-Persian tension—prompted by Wahhabi raids on the Shiite shrines, the extension of Persian authority over Mohammerah (Khorramshahr) and the Ka'b districts,[1] restrictions on Persian *mujtahids* (religious leaders) within the Pashalic, or any of the countless disputes over frontiers, grazing rights, the status of border-crossing tribes, or reparations for raids into each other's territory—the political agent's role was central. And well it might be, for a clash between the two ramshackle empires was considered to be a threat not only to the extensive buffer zone beyond India's northwestern frontiers, but also to India itself, for a Turco-Persian war could provide opportunities to other

---

[1]Long before the nineteenth century the Ka'b Arabs had settled in the region stretching eastward from the shoreline of the Shatt al-Arab. When the Turks found it necessary to recognize Persian hegemony over this area, the negotiations effectively made the Shatt al-Arab a Turkish waterway. The Turco-Persian boundary was not in midstream, but on the Persian shoreline. This unusual arrangement has frequently, most recently in mid-1969, caused tension between Iraq and Iran, as have occasional Iraqi claims to Khorramshahr and an extensive Iranian hinterland referred to as "Arabistan."

powers with imperial ambitions. Thus the reports, recommendations, and requests from the political agent in Baghdad were studied carefully in the embassies at Constantinople and Teheran, and by high officials at Bombay, Calcutta, and London. Further involvement came through interest, especially during Stratford de Redcliffe's embassy at Constantinople, in the welfare of Christian minorities of the northern Pashalic. No less important were the vigorous British commercial firms, one of which, Lynch Brothers, followed up the pioneering work of the Chesney expedition in the early 1830s with the establishment of the Tigris and Euphrates Steam Navigation Company. The introduction of the electric telegraph, improvements in postal services, and other westernizing projects were given official patronage, but it was the British who made them work, and in the process they gained greater influence than that which would be conferred by the mandate of the League of Nations.

The Great Iraqi Revolution of 1920

Not until war clouds had gathered in Europe and the storm was about to break did a class of educated Iraqis emerge prepared to challenge Ottoman rule. The peoples native to Iraq were for the most part onlookers to the Mesopotamian war. A series of grim campaigns, their costs increased tremendously by resolute Turkish resistance and incompetent British generalship, culminated in the surrender of Baghdad after nearly four centuries as capital of an Ottoman province. No empire left fewer traces after such a long reign than did the Turks upon their departure from Iraq.

The war delayed the development of an Iraqi nationalist movement, but by 1920 the nationalists were ready to strike at their new occupiers. It made little difference that the British variety of foregn rule provided public works and civil improvements on a scale which the Turks had not attempted. Nor did it matter to the nationalists that they lacked the human resources necessary for organizing a state on modern lines. The Iraqi goal was self-determination. Bolshevik propaganda may have played some part in influencing their thinking but more important was the influence of nationalists from abroad, and particularly that of Iraqis who had served with Faisal in Syria. The educated class saw salvation in the principles of Thomas Woodrow Wilson, but instead they were subjected to the paternalism of Arnold Talbot Wilson, the young British official in overall charge of the conquered province until October 1920. The result was *al-Thawra al-'Iraqqia al-Kubra*, the Great Iraqi Revolution in the language of the nationalists, or the Iraqi Revolt of 1920 in the more jaded terminology of historians of empire.

The storm broke with the announcement that a mandate for Iraq had been offered to Great Britain at the San Remo Conference. From Mosul the insurrection spread down the Euphrates and over the entire country. Baghdad alone remained quiescent, but the tribesmen, as always, could not or would not join forces in a concerted effort. They, and not the city-dwelling nationalists, suffered the heavy blows of punitive expeditions. The revolt, short-lived but more widespread than the Druse Rebellion in Syria, was a further drain on Britain's already depleted financial resources. Account books rather than position papers argued the wisdom of replacing the mandate with an acceptable treaty.

Meanwhile, the Kurds demonstrated their fractious instability to British well-wishers who sought to bestow autonomy upon them: "Kurdistan for the Kurds" was also promoted by *emigré* groups, the most notable of which were to be found in Istanbul, but British involvement took the project beyond the stage of rhetoric. The emigrés' candidate for the central role, in spite of extensive evidence of his unsuitability, was Shaikh Mahmud of Sulaimaniyah, and it was his personal ambition that was decisive in bringing about the collapse of the British proposal. His claim to rule an independent Kurdistan was no more acceptable to Kurdish tribal leaders and townspeople than it was to Turks and Iraqis. Reluctantly, the British decided that the Kurds must be integrated into the Iraqi state. Implementing such a decision was another matter.

The inflexibility of British bureaucracy played a part in the Iraqi Revolt. The need to scale down commitments, if Britain was indeed to be made into a country fit for heroes to live in, would seem to have commended any plan for an early bestowal of self-government on Iraq. However, the decision-making process was slowed by conflicting viewpoints of the Indian government, the London government, and all their supporting agencies and officials in Baghdad. There were too many interests and too many committees. The general opinion was that things might have gone better had not the experienced British Civil Commissioner, Percy Zachariah Cox, been compelled to undertake a special assignment and leave the affairs of Iraq to young Wilson as Acting Commissioner. More recent research suggests that any person in that position would have become a scapegoat for the mandarins in the great government ministries. Wilson ran Iraq as if it were a district in India, but the system turned out not to be transferable. Idealism—and there were British officials devoted to building an independent Iraq—counted for less than the assiduity with which taxes were collected. The use of Indians in subordinate positions, to the exclusion of Iraqis who had been officials before and during the war, caused great resentment. Iraqi weakness in English and English weakness in Arabic may have been the operative reasons for these exclusions, but the accepted explanation was discrimination.

British troop reductions, the arrival of civilians to impart Wilson's recommended five years of tutelage, border-raiding from Faisal's Syria (both offenders and defenders being supported by British subventions), the agitation of Turkish agents, "caliphate nostalgia" among the Sunnis, and heightened antiforeignism in the Shiite community made the attainment of stable government seem remote.

To be sure, a provisional government was formed at Baghdad late in 1920 and met with a fair degree of success, attributable in part to the influx of Iraqi administrators which occurred after the French turned Faisal out of Damascus. It was hardly a representative government, for like so many of its successors it was predominantly Sunnite. But the restless, ruthless dynamism of Sayid Talib Pasha Naqib, a powerful southern Iraqi landlord and politician, and the organizational talents of such Sherifians as Ja'far Pasha Askeri and his brother Nuri Pasha Said helped Iraq through a difficult period. The way was paved for more permanent arrangements by the settlement of border disputes with the French and improved internal security arrangements.

A fascinating and complicated period of maneuver and intrigue followed in the autumn of 1921, with Winston Churchill at stage center, Wilson, Cox, Gertrude Bell, T. E. Lawrence, St. John Philby, and other *dramatis personae* in the wings. Iraq had to be provided with a king since a republic was unthinkable to those burdened with the country's destiny. Apart from Faisal, only Sayid Talib took his own candidacy so seriously as to necessitate his being decanted from the genteel atmosphere of one of Lady Cox's tea parties into exile in Ceylon. The others—among them Abdul Aziz ibn Saud of Nejd, the Agha Khan, and Faisal's older and less capable brother Abdullah—did not press their qualifications or were not given serious consideration. Once Faisal agreed to serve, a one-question plebiscite was arranged, and arranged so very well that 96 percent of the electorate supported Churchill's solution for Iraq. The show of unanimity may have impressed outsiders, occurring as it did before such plebiscites were organized in more advanced countries.

More important is the fact that Faisal's qualities of leadership quickly earned him support at all levels of Iraqi society. Pressure on the northern borders eased when the League supported the Iraqi claim to Mosul, a judgment made viable by sound military arrangements and effective British diplomacy. The sanguinary Saudi resolution of a rival dynasty's challenge—that of the house of Rashid—made for trouble on an extended, ill-defined Saudi-Iraqi frontier area (see Chapter 5). A settlement was reached in 1930, after Abdul Aziz ibn Saud had obtained a high Iraqi decoration and Iraq had received a Saudi compensation of £30,000, which was in fact an indirect British subsidy. Throughout the greater part of Iraq, and especially near centers of population, security was improved, an administrative structure was begun, and some progress was achieved in the field of education. Faisal deflected or contained forces which, if unchecked, might have destroyed the basis for his regime. Characteristically, he did not attempt to avoid difficult decisions. Convinced that indignant international public opinion was preferable to a hazardous internal security situation, he accepted the necessity of a "final solution" of the Assyrian problem. His biographers have since attempted to shift responsibility elsewhere for the massacre of the Assyrian Christian levies raised under British auspices. This would not have pleased him.

Faisal and a few determined politicians, greatly assisted by a more subtle British tutelage than Arnold Wilson had advocated, made possible a workable Anglo-Iraqi treaty that was ratified in 1930 and led to independence and membership in the League of Nations two years later. The question of Iraq's readiness for independence did not arise. If the criteria for independence include an economic and administrative infrastructure, a national consciousness, a stable polity, adequate social services, and an absence of major internal divisions, Iraq was utterly unprepared in 1932. But none of these factors were prerequisites for nationalism, and the magnanimity of Great Britain is best understood against a backdrop of world economic crisis and a feeble home government.

In recent years it has become clear that Faisal was fully cognizant of the shaky foundation of Iraq's independence. His brief kingship of Syria was much more than a distant memory; indeed, it was a permanent obsession. His perspective was much more Umayyad than Abbasid. Later, the terms "Fertile Crescent" and "Greater Syria" would be employed by the *Epigoni* who followed him. Faisal was convinced of the advantages to be gained by mobilizing the Sunni majority to end the precarious nature of Baghdad-based minoritarian governments; he recognized that a greater Arab majority would reduce the Kurdish problem to manageable proportions, and he knew the value of Syrian entrepreneurial skills, intellectual attainments, and diversified resources. He knew, too, that he could combine all these resources in an association latterly made attractive by the prospect of Iraqi oil revenues. But he did not have long to speculate about such possibilities, for he died in 1933, at the age of forty-eight.

Independence, especially in an era before Egypt began to assert its Arabism, gave Iraq an importance in Arab affairs which it did not regain after World War II. Baghdad became a haven and a platform for leaders of the Arab Revolt in Palestine and a wide variety of other Arab causes. Independence also meant diplomatic relations and all the activities—constructive, ceremonial, or nefarious—which such establishments made possible. From 1936 Dr. Fritz Grobba energetically represented Germany's new order in Baghdad.

The presence of such elements in the midst of a faction-ridden political scene inevitably stimulated attacks on Britain's special position in Iraq. Political maneuvering left little time or inclination to cope with the genuine ills of Iraqi society. Corruption was most obvious in the sharings-out of agricultural lands, which increased already serious tribal unrest, but it was present in many other forms as well. Lawlessness in the Kurdish districts multiplied until it was too great for government forces to handle. Elsewhere, attempts to enforce military conscription only increased resistance to Baghdad's authority. Another problem was the relationship of the Palace to the government. Young King Ghazi had none of his father's political intuition. His charm and high spirits earned him a popular following, but his interventions in political affairs increased the divisions in the country's leadership. Some progress was made in public works financed by the new oil royalties, but in general the picture was gloomy. Such circumstances seldom fail to produce a man on horseback. In the Iraq of 1936 he was a Kurd, General Bakr Sidqi. His principal fellow conspirator, Hikmat Sulaiman, was a vigorous and able proponent of Ataturkian methods. Thus the politics of the *coup d'état* began for Iraq, and for the first time an Iraqi air force bombed Baghdad.

Less than a year later Sidqi was gunned down by an Iraqi soldier. Much blood was on Sidqi's hands, including that of the distinguished patriot Ja'far Pasha Askeri, but Sidqi's assassination was not an act of revenge. Factionalism within the armed forces, rivalries spurred by preferential treatment, and a general conviction among the officer corps that the army should have a greater share in the direction of the country were responsible for the shots which killed Sidqi at the Mosul airport. The same factors were to be present in the *coups* of 1938, 1940, and 1941, as well as in some of the postwar upheavals.

The influence of pan-Arabism in the officer corps must not be overlooked, for when Sati al-Husri made his way from the ruins of Maisalun (see Chapter 2) to the Ministry of Education in Baghdad in 1921, it was with the goal of creating a generation of fervent Arab nationalists. Many young graduates in the officer corps believed that the army must be the vanguard of the Arab nationalist cause. These youthful officers were but one element in a struggle which continued from 1936 to 1941, and frequently, as in the introduction of the Palestine issue into Iraqi politics, their idealism was exploited by those who sought power for personal gain, vengeance, or particularist objectives.

The rivalries of this period, which lasted through the outbreak of World War II and until the Rashid Ali Ghaylani episode of 1941, destroyed the possibility of achieving some sort of forum in which Iraq's basic problems could be identified and analyzed. Tribal revolts, Sunni-Shiite animosities, and chaotic conditions in Kurdistan belied Iraq's claim to nationhood. The views of young Arab socialists and communists were irrelevant and unimportant, so handicapped were they by a perfervid internationalism. External relations (such as the Shatt al-Arab dispute with Persia), difficulties with Kuwait over an alleged *carte blanche* to smugglers (together with a few hints of an Iraqi claim to the emirate), and attempts to obtain modern military equipment were given undeserved prominence. King Ghazi's contribution to statecraft was a clandestine radio station which attacked Iraq's neighbors and supported the Arab Revolt in Palestine. His death in 1939, after losing control of a speeding automobile, brought his cousin Prince Abdul Illah to the center of Iraqi affairs as regent. The habitués of Baghdad's coffee-houses took note that the new regent was a person who could work with Nuri Pasha Said, for Nuri was convinced that Ghazi had conspired in support of Bakr Sidqi and in the murder of Ja'fer Pasha. Collaboration between Abdul Illah and Nuri did not begin until after 1941; before that time there were no serious attempts to establish a basis upon which the political life of the country could be organized or upon which Iraq could shake off the burdens of tribalism and religious prejudice and become a modern state.

The "Golden Square" uprising of 1941, to employ the name given to the group of four highly placed, disaffected officers whose cooperation made Rashid Ali Ghaylani's *coup d'état* possible, marked the beginning of a new era in Iraqi history. It was not the era the conspirators envisioned, for their project ended with what became known as the second British occupation. It has been widely accepted that Nazi money, rivalries, and jealousies within the services as well as thrusting ambition, especially that of Rashid Ali, brought about the *coup*. In fact, all of these factors were present except the first, but once the *coup* occurred, the Germans moved quickly to take advantage of it. The Germans, however, were only slightly less mistrusted than their Italian allies, whose colonial aspirations were blatantly obvious.[2] For this reason the usual explanations

---

[2]In 1940 Iraq attempted to counter British influence by establishing diplomatic relations with, and seeking military assistance from, the Soviet Union.

of the *coup* are inadequate and another factor must be considered if the Rashid Ali episode is to be understood—the factor of Iraqi concern for its position and prestige in the Arab world.

The changed circumstances of wartime Middle East, particularly with Britain and France in retreat, provided opportunities for Iraq to strike a blow for the Arab cause. To do so, Iraq needed to preserve its neutral status. It could not become, in the words used long ago by John Quincy Adams, "a cockboat in the wake of the British man-o-war." Or so Rashid Ali and his colleagues hoped. They failed, but among Arab nationalists their failure counted for less than their attempt to rid Iraq of British influence.

The Era of Nuri Pasha Said

After a brief hiatus provided by the ineffectual ministry of Jamil Madfai, Nuri Pasha Said took office in October 1941. He had first served as prime minister before independence, and his reputation as an Iraqi patriot was made in pre-1914 Baghdad, before he went to the Hejaz to join Faisal and T. E. Lawrence on their great quest. Nuri served as prime minister from October 1941 until June 1944 and formed many cabinets after that. Indeed, the entire period from the autumn of 1941 until a day of bloodshed in July 1958 may properly be regarded in Iraqi history as the era of Nuri Pasha Said.

Like so many other Arab leaders from King Faisal I to Gamal Abdul Nasser, Nuri looked beyond the borders of his country for his place in history. Before the Palestine disaster it was possible to support a program for union of the states of the Fertile Crescent, grounded upon close cooperation with Great Britain, and with the avowed intention of defeating the Zionist aim of establishing an independent Jewish state in Palestine. Even after 1949, Nuri continued to believe that the welfare of the Arabs could best be secured in partnership with the West.[3] His unwillingness to take seriously enough the Egyptian claim to a voice in Arab affairs was an important miscalculation. Still more decisive, and in more ways than one, was his attitude of "the public be damned."

During the last years of World War II, an illusion of tranquility developed in Iraq because of the imposition of martial law and the removal

---

[3] By "West" he really meant Britain, inasmuch as he considered America to be the motive force behind the Zionist organization and his attitude toward France had been formed in Syria in 1920. He often emphasized the value of the British connection by pointing to their anti-French stand in Syria and Lebanon at the end of World War II and asserted that if the British had not moved against the French in Damascus, he would have sent the Iraqi army into action.

through internment of elements whose activities and enthusiasms were considered dangerous. Nuri surrounded himself with members of the old guard with whom he had collaborated since 1920, and seemed unmoved by evidence of corruption. The flourishing state of agriculture and the high level of employment resulting from wartime markets and the presence of a large, free-spending military force crippled effective opposition. Oil revenue had fallen off markedly, but progress was being achieved on irrigation facilities, Allied logistical requirements conferred major infrastructure improvements, and in 1942 Iraq, which had declared war on the Axis after the defeat of the "Golden Square," became the recipient of American Lend-Lease support. It was a period of good relations between Nuri and the Regent, although later, when Abdul Illah became more involved in politics, the friendship would for a time be strained.

The withdrawal of Allied forces from the Middle Eastern theater caused the collapse of markets and the rise of unemployment at a time when amnesties and expired sentences were returning the regime's opponents to their meeting rooms and editorial offices. Nuri encouraged his supporters to take a hard line against the communists, who were a more pragmatic and effective group than their predecessors a decade earlier, but neither he nor those with whom he shared power attached importance to the rising tide of anti-Western sentiment as Palestine's hour of decision approached.

Nuri Pasha Said's patronage permitted the installation of a government under Iraq's first Shiite prime minister, Salih Jabr, but the effect of this important step was lost in the campaign of violence which greeted the signing of the Portsmouth Treaty in January 1948 and continued with scant interruption until after the Palestine War. No attempt had been made to prepare public opinion for this Anglo-Iraqi treaty, which gave the Royal Air Force landing rights at Iraqi bases and authorized the dispatch of British troops to Iraq if general war threatened. In return, Britain undertook to equip and train the Iraqi armed forces. Although the terms of the Portsmouth Treaty—at least in comparison to those of earlier treaties—granted concessions to Iraq, in the changed conditions of 1948 any treaty with a Western country was considered "concealed colonialism." The tenth ministry of Nuri restored order with firm police measures, but the country was in desperate straits. The more violent the Baghdad mobs became over Palestine, the more pessimistic became the Kurds in the north and the Shiites in the south over their prospects in an Iraqi state.[4] The economy had been crippled by bad harvests and by the loss

---

[4]The fate of the Iraqi Jewish community must not be overlooked, but space does not permit the detailed treatment which the subject would require, for a thorough discussion of this subject would have to include current problems faced by the remnant of a formerly influential minority which had prospered and contributed

of oil revenues from the Haifa refinery, now in Israeli control. Food shortages spread discontent, especially when it was learned that landowners and speculators were exporting wheat in highly advantageous circumstances. The scope for demonstrations was almost limitless and a cycle of martyrs and mourners was introduced as the death of a demonstrator was the occasion for funeral processions in which further violence among the mourners created new martyrs to be mourned. There would be difficult years ahead until burgeoning oil income made major development projects possible and also provided Nuri Said with the means of purchasing stability.

The "Old Nationalists," of whom Nuri was *primus inter pares,* based their hopes for Iraq on a fruitful Arab-Western relationship which was placed in jeopardy after the establishment of the Israeli state. The spectacle of Great Britain "folding its tents, leaving behind a vacuum" after the Palestine debacle left Nuri feeling unarmed and unshielded until the alternative which became known as the Baghdad Pact was offered to him. The man who had ridden with T. E. Lawrence was again prepared to employ an external factor to achieve Arab objectives.

This is, however, to anticipate. Nuri was unprepared for the sharp decline in British postwar power in the Middle East and even less prepared for dealing with the "new" Britain whose cooperation he sought. The factors which encouraged a British electorate to turn out Winston Churchill in favor of a Labor government were incomprehensible to Iraqis of the old school. Less obvious, but perhaps more significant, was the influence of the postwar generation of British personnel who accepted employment in Iraq. Baghdad in the late 1940s and the first years of the 1950s still had an atmosphere and appearance which, while giving evidence of considerable Persian influence, also bespoke the *raj* and British India. It was an anachronism, for its decaying, yellow brick structures no longer housed the paternalistic, quondam district commissioners whose concerns were keeping the roads open and secure, collecting the revenue, and improving public utilities. Representatives of the new Britain were often more interested in socialist theory than in parliamentary democracy, the exportability of either being left unquestioned. Together with British-educated Iraqis, they made the university and the schools into forcing houses of doctrines half understood but enthu-

---

to the advancement of the country. Iraqi Jewish payments to the Palestine Defense Fund were not solely motivated by fear, but by a feeling that the vigor of European Jewry, under American sponsorship, would bring into being a state in which they would be more alien and less likely to succeed. Eventually most of Iraq's Jews went to Israel, under circumstances which make their anti-Arab animus more understandable than that of their compatriots whose origins are European.

siastically espoused by a generation brought up in a mood of defensive suspicion, aware of corruption and of the gulf between the few rich and the many poor, and yearning for the millenium which was to arrive with the victory of Arab nationalism. Journalism became less a means of mass instruction than a catalyst for disorder. There was an inevitability about the process.

One of the more obvious paradoxes was that even as the young nationalists talked and agitated and demonstrated for the cause of Arab unity, other forces were at work creating vested interests for the maintenance of the "San Remo" frontiers. New tariffs were being devised, civil services were undergoing expansion, national airlines developing. It could hardly be expected that men of humble education, providing for their families by stamping passports, checking visas, and glancing at inoculation certificates, would view with equanimity the abolition of frontiers between Arab states.[5] A much more persuasive factor was oil revenue. The prospect of sharing it has consistently dampened unionist enthusiasms. By 1950 an Iraqi Development Board was established. Vistas opened for restored irrigation systems and flood control programs that would make Iraq once more, as in the Abbasid era and before, into a granary capable of supporting a population many times larger than that which currently subsisted in rural and urban poverty. Such a development inevitably would shift the balance of power in the Middle East and make Iraq a nation in every sense—especially in the sense that she would be capable of challenging the political supremacy of Egypt. Yet the possibility of resettling Palestinian refugees in underpopulated areas to work in agricultural development schemes gained no serious support, nor were the reservations all on the Iraqi side.

The Arabian American Oil Company set a new pattern by agreeing in 1950 to a fifty-fifty profit-sharing program with Saudi Arabia. Negotiations quickly began between the Iraq Petroleum Company and the government. An understanding was reached on a similar formula in 1952 shortly before the new thirty-inch pipeline from Kirkuk to the Mediterranean at Banyas, Syria, was placed in operation. Thus the Old Nationalists, in the year of the Egyptian revolution, obtained a major increase in income, facilitating the construction of a despotism which hid behind a facade of elections and parliamentary forms and was re-

---

[5]Such reservations were not restricted to holders of menial positions. For many years before the Iraqi-Jordanian federation came into being, suggestions along this line were occasionally considered. Although it was made to appear that the plan was of Jordanian inspiration, there was great Iraqi reluctance even as, on the Jordanian side, fear for the continuation of the Jordanian branch of the Hashemite royal line was a restraining factor.

garded as benevolent by those who did not attempt to question or oppose it. Yet Nuri Pasha Said, who gave his attention only reluctantly to domestic political concerns, never lost interest in a closer association with the other states of the Fertile Crescent and saw Iraq's improving economic situation as an inducement for Syrian cooperation. His overtures to two of Syria's rulers, Husni Zaim and Adib Shishakly, were totally unsuccessful, heightening the impression that Iraq was exposed and without friends.

After the British departure from Palestine, Western observers heavily emphasized the opportunities for Communist expansion provided by the semi-feudal social systems and the increasingly precarious interstate relationships in the Middle East. In 1952 Winston Churchill, who doubted the capacity of the Arab states to effect reforms and increase security as much as he doubted the ability of the British to wield any great influence on these states, took what was, according to his lights, the logical course and called for an association, or coordination, of American and British policy in the Middle East.[6] This was a policy that commended itself to Nuri and his followers, although they could hardly say so in public. By 1954, Nuri was attempting to reap maximum political advantage from demands that the Anglo-Iraqi Treaty of 1930 be terminated, especially because provisions for British assistance in maintaining internal security had ceased to be relevant. Nuri's program was carefully orchestrated and the treaty was not abrogated until 1955, a year after the United States had approved an Iraqi request for military assistance and the preliminary maneuvering had begun to bring Iraq into treaty relations with the "northern tier." In his 1954 election manifesto, however, Nuri made a definite miscalculation by including in his policy the termination of the British treaty and its replacement with a "regional arrangement." Had Nuri confined his program to opposition to communism and the endorsement of economic and social reforms, he would have placated conservatives and progressives without antagonizing the nationalists.

Widespread contemporary criticism of "entangling alliances" contrasts sharply to the enthusiasm with which the West greeted the Turco-Iraqi Pact of 1955. Ratification of the treaty in February was followed in rapid succession by visits to Baghdad by Foreign Minister Anthony Eden, President Celal Bayar of Turkey, and, in quite another spirit, Khalid al-Azm of Syria. The new arrangement permitted the scrapping of the Anglo-Iraqi Treaty of 1930 and the adherence of Great Britain to the

---

[6]Before a joint session of the U.S. Congress in 1952. The corollary, of course, was his opposition to the 1956 Suez adventure unless the United States was willing to go along.

Turco-Iraqi Pact, all of which gave a hollow ring to Iraq's protests of devotion to the Arab League and Arab collective security arrangements. This was the high point of Turco-American relations and the "realists" of the period seemed to assume that the new treaty would soon have the Iraqis behaving like Turks. There were comments on the "likemindedness" of the two countries, and Turkey's renewed political and economic interest in areas "abandoned" after 1918 was considered an encouraging portent, at least in Washington and London. Turkey was described by a Western authority as the Middle Eastern country least exposed to the "unpredictable and destructive xenophobia which makes stable government so difficult . . . so little obsessed with the existence of Israel," and able to see so clearly "the real and immediate danger on the doorstep." Nuri Pasha Said was transformed into an Iraqi Everyman and optimism abounded. Some Iraqis were no longer plagued by a feeling of isolation, and the prospect of a regional Islamic grouping was pleasing to many segments of the population.

On the domestic side, scarcely a year separated the new treaty arrangements and the completion of two of the Iraq Development Board's major flood control projects on the Tigris and Euphrates. Reclamation projects were planned involving upward of six million acres of land. Funds were allocated for ambitious community development projects. The vast revenues now available to the regime enabled it to strengthen internal security. The army was purged and purged again. The rewards for simply avoiding the wrath of Iraq's rulers were considerable. Yet no army can be purged of its last dissident element. Economic interests may have bound tribal and religious leaders and entrepreneurs to the state apparatus, but only a few intellectuals had such commitments. Police power grew in some sort of proportion to the oil revenues. The mob, better rewarded on construction sites than by organizers of demonstrations, briefly lost its reputation for ferocity. An illusion of permanence was fostered. Even the particularism of the Kurds caused no great concern.

Nevertheless, the storm warnings were up for those who could but see. The mildest reaction to the Turco-Iraqi Pact in the Arab world came from sources which insisted that the minimum price for acceptance of the treaty should be a return of the Sanjak of Alexandretta to Syria and Turkish suspension of diplomatic relations with Israel. And there was no support for the pact from Saudi Arabia, where a long tradition of enmity for Iraq was strengthened by anti-Hashemite sentiments. Jordanian attempts to affect a *rapprochement* between Cairo and Baghdad were soured by Iraq's acceptance of American economic aid which Egypt had refused. The "Voice of the Arabs" asserted that Gamal Abdul Nasser "would not forsake the Iraqi people, whatever their government," and Egyptian, Syrian, and Russian propaganda media called for the overthrow and assassination of Nuri. Diplomatic relations with the Soviet Union were severed in 1955.

To make matters worse, a crisis was reached in Iraq's program of development, which had passed beyond the stage of flood control and expanded irrigation, a stage where a relative handful of directors and engineers, many of whom were expatriates, could organize the efforts of a largely unskilled and uneducated labor force. Nor could the overcentralized bureaucracy effectively handle the large sums of money allocated to the next phase of the development, which required abilities which the Iraqi population did not possess. Bribery and corruption in the letting and performance of contracts were favorite topics of conversation among the regime's detractors. Moreover, it was becoming obvious that the Iraqi Development Board's projects were steadily increasing the value of untaxed land, much of which was owned by wealthy landlords. Iraq's chances of evolving from the status of a preindustrial society seemed slight in such circumstances.

Then came Suez. The thoroughness of Nuri's security network helped the regime survive a situation which saw Iraq's partner in the Baghdad Pact, Britain, fighting alongside Israel. It also survived the dynamiting of the IPC pipeline by the Syrian army, a gesture of Arab solidarity which cost Iraq £1 million weekly and could not have failed to encourage thoughts, especially by Nuri and Abdul Illah, about the desirability of placing Syria under new management. The regime believed that the masses had been given a stake in society, as indicated by the relatively mild demonstrations over Suez in a capital city which was in the midst of a building boom. The formula was simple: revenues from oil meant employment and employment was the best guarantee against mob action. But in the event, the mob became a factor only after the army struck.

In the interim, the regime continued unreceptive to new ideas. The formation of the short-lived federation with Jordan was simply Iraq's unenthusiastic application of a long-proferred nostrum as her way of responding to the establishment of the United Arab Republic. Those in power were more interested in dealing with the restless educated class by familiar methods of police roundups, night visits, censorship, jamming of broadcasts, and the closing of schools. But there are always oversights and opportunities, and in July 1958 they combined to favor Brigadier Abdul Karim Qasim.

The names of victorious revolutionaries are usually better remembered than those of their victims. Sam Adams of Boston stands the test of time better than General Gage. Yet even the last miserable act in Baghdad belonged to Nuri Pasha Said. Until he was killed, the revolution was in peril. It was Nuri's death that relegated to the background the equally violent ends of Faisal II, Abdul Illah, and the nearly four decades of Hashemite rule in Iraq. His passing marked a major stage in the declension of the Western position in the Arab world. Although the death blow was struck by one of the Baghdad mob, it may nonetheless be argued that Nuri was the victim of Israel. Over the years from 1948 he had argued that his position and that of his Western friends depended not on the sharing out of economic aid and weaponry to Israelis and Arabs nor in deliberations and condemnations in the United Nations, but in the application of Western political power to the settlement or stabilization of the Israeli question. He was convinced that negotiations on the basis of the United Nations resolutions of 1947, which he was willing to undertake, could be forced on the other parties. But no sign came from the West, and as Israel went from strength to strength, the position of the Old Nationalist steadily eroded. It all seems so very long ago.

Abdul Karim Qasim, the "Sole Leader"

Although Brigadier Qasim in time became accessible to the point of giving marathon press conferences, his early reticence gave the center of the stage to Colonel Abdul Salim Aref, whose passionate espousal of union with Egypt soon resulted in his being stripped of vice-presidential powers. In 1958 this pro-Egyptian enthusiasm was shared by the Iraqi Baathist Party, which was soon to follow Aref into political limbo. Qasim had only the vaguest ideas of a political program, but they definitely did not include a sharing out to Egypt and Syria of Iraqi oil revenues in the name of Arab solidarity. He was much more interested in domestic affairs than his predecessor. Qasim sought a broadly based program of development to secure his own popularity, which he feared would otherwise be transient. Nor was President Nasser encouraged by developments in the "Northern Region" of the United Arab Republic to embark upon another unionist experiment.

Within Iraq, widespread satisfaction over the destruction of Nuri's police state was taken in the early period to mean a full endorsement of Brigadier Qasim. This impression was supported by the selection of a government which was broadly representative of elements suppressed by the previous regime. From the first, the energy and high level of organization of the Iraqi Communist Party was a revelation to those who had accepted the myth of the capacity of Nuri's counterintelligence forces to penetrate and neutralize all centers of opposition. The ubiquitousness of the Communist Party and especially the extent to which it came to control communications media and educational policy alarmed Arab nationalists and caused a brief revival of interest in a merger with the United Arab Republic.

The landowning class, however circumscribed its capacity to assert its views, remained a power group opposed to both the nationalist and the communist groupings. The urban poor, known as "the street" to connoisseurs of rebellion and the *coup d'état*, were courted by Qasim to such effect that for years after 1963 many of them remained unconvinced of his death and awaited his return as a *Mahdi*.[7] He was less successful with religious leaders and the Kurds, although it was at his personal invitation that the most effective leader of the Kurdish oppositionists, Mullah Mustafa Barazani, returned from long exile in the Soviet Union. Qasim had no real understanding of the strength of the forces which divided Iraq, just as he had no concept of governmental organization. His acceptance of the title of "Sole Leader" was as much a mark of his inability to delegate, cooperate, or negotiate as it was an indication of an unstable personality. In view of these weaknesses, it is possible to believe that Qasim considered that the televised trial proceedings of the notorious Special Supreme Military Court, presided over by his cousin Colonel Fadil Abbas Mahdawi, would have the effect of unifying the country behind him.[8]

Apart from reestablishing diplomatic relations with the USSR, broadening relations with the Communist bloc countries, denouncing the Baghdad Pact, and proclaiming solidarity with the Algerian revolutionary movement, Qasim's energies in the field of foreign policy were consumed in a campaign against Gamal Abdul Nasser.[9] The origins of the Nasser-Qasim feud are obscured in a cloud of acrimonious rhetoric. If Nasser was unenthusiastic about incorporating Iraq into the United Arab Republic, he also was concerned lest Iraq, under new and revolutionary

---

[7]Qasim's principal contribution to the urban migrants was the "new towns"—thousands of cement block structures pressing in on Baghdad and devoid of the most basic amenities. Nuri's policy had been to send them back to the rural areas from whence they had come.

[8]The technique, at least, caught on. After the Baathist regime came to power in 1968, Iraqis awaited with fear and fascination the televised tribunal which came to be known as "the spy of the evening program."

[9]Funds also were dispensed to less-known Arab revolutionary movements such as the Saudi Arabia-based Free Omani group. Some evidence suggests that Iraqi money also was available to an underground organization with the aim of overthrowing the Saudi regime.

management, become a rival center of Arab nationalism. Trouble with Syria doubtless magnified his fears and made him more receptive to Colonel Aref's expressions of fealty when the latter arrived in Cairo instead of going meekly off to comfortable exile as Iraq's ambassador to Bonn. This was before Nasser undertook his purge of Syrian Baathists, who were then in a position to call for measures against Qasim because of his rough handling of the Iraqi branch of the party. But the whole affair is further clouded by the fact that several influential Syrians, most notably the intelligence specialist Abdul Hamid Sarraj, apparently took initiatives which exceeded Nasser's intentions. In any case, Qasim believed that Aref's "unauthorized return to Iraq" and his attempt to raise the standard of revolt in October 1958 were sponsored by Cairo.

It was clearly a time of opportunity for the Iraqi Communist Party. Emphasis on "guided democracy" in the cabinet suggested that Ibrahim Kubbeh, who held portfolios of National Economy, Agricultural Reform, and Petroleum Affairs, was an agent of penetration. The security structure was dominated by men of the left and the functions of censorship, publishing, and broadcasting were conducted along lines satisfactory to the Iraqi Communists. Foreign publications available in Iraq and the type of news releases emanating from Baghdad indicated a Communist bloc monopoly. Communist domination of action committees, trade unions, peasants' unions, and professional and educational associations, as well as their development of paramilitary forces revealed a degree of organization, a sense of priorities, and an instinct for the political jugular never before witnessed in Iraq. Nasser was no longer concerned about Iraq as a rival center for Arab nationalist leadership, but as a base for the communization of the Arab East. References to the threat of a "Red Fertile Crescent" appeared in Cairo broadcasts. The Egyptian leader was dismayed by speeches delivered in Eastern Europe by the Syrian Communist leader Khalid Baqdash attacking Nasser and describing Iraq as the "unconquered bastion of the Arab nationalist movement."

But Nasser's challenge to Qasim was too little and much too late. The Mosul rising of March 1959, led by Colonel Abdul Wahhab Shawwaf and involving army units and large numbers of the Shammar tribe which had long been accustomed to the largesse of Nuri, was a bloody fiasco. The Kurds showed their preference for the status quo over any unified state, plus their appreciation of an opportunity for looting, by swarming into Mosul to assist in repressing the revolt. The "street" participated in massive anti-Nasser demonstrations. But the big gainers were the Communists, or so it appeared. For a time the Iraqi Communist Party exerted an even greater influence over the affairs of the country than had formerly been the case. To the chagrin of Arab nationalists throughout the Middle East, Great Britain acknowledged the extent of their success by concluding an arms agreement with Iraq, hoping to check the country's drift toward satellite status. It was an admission of the bankruptcy of Western policy.

The Communists, however, overreached themselves. Their activities deepened the basic divisions in Iraqi society. Baghdad's control over outlying districts weakened and the army was more than ever rent by factionalism. Commerce was fettered by unrealistic regulations and labor unrest brought about a marked decline in production. In July 1959 a mutiny among army units in Kirkuk touched off fierce fighting among rival elements in the city. The divisions were racial as well as political, involving Arabs, Kurds, and Turcomans, but before order was restored it was obvious that a Communist bid for greater power in Iraq's major oil-producing region lay at the root of the disorders.

Thus began the struggle for power between Qasim and the Communist Party leadership. Widening divisions within the Iraqi Communist Party and purges in its governing apparatus permitted Qasim to increase his authority through 1960. Soon Soviet newspapers were accusing the regime of "arbitrary acts against the Iraqi working class." But Qasim carried his campaign beyond the Communists in an attempt to eliminate all forms of political expression. The effects of repression were magnified by the near failure of the grain crops in 1959 and 1960 and by ill-advised economic measures, such as a drastic increase in petroleum export duties which quickly cut down the volume of sales. The only class which prospered was the officer corps, sedulously courted with pay raises, improved housing, and a variety of perquisites. Internationally, Iraq became increasingly isolated. Executions of pro-Nasser officers involved in the Mosul rebellion—it was assumed that to be anti-Qasim was to be pro-Nasser—earned Qasim widespread condemnation by Arab news media. In many quarters outright regret was expressed at the failure of an attempt on the dictator's life in October 1959. Only the Algerians avoided criticism of Qasim in order to encourage Iraq's substantial donations to the provisional Algerian government.

Before the end of 1960 Mullah Mustafa Barazani, who had revisited the Soviet Union during that year, realized that his hopes of obtaining autonomy for Kurdistan from the Qasim government were groundless. After consolidating his position in the northern highlands, he began leading anti-government activities. In 1961 hostilities commenced, and by the time of Qasim's death the war was costing the regime $60 million annually. The Iraqi armed forces had air power, rockets and napalm, tanks, and heavy equipment. They could blast houses and burn crops, but they could not master the terrain or defeat commando tactics. Kurdistan was Qasim's Dienbienphu.

Even as the first shots of the Kurdish war were fired, the regime was preparing for a remarkable adventure in external relations. This was the Iraqi claim to Kuwait, based upon vague nineteenth-century relationships between the ruling Sabah family and various Ottoman authorities. A case might be made that at one time or another the paramount shaikh of Kuwait had accepted the almost meaningless title of *Qaimaqam* (which, depending on the circumstances, could mean anything from viceroy to deputy governor) from the Turks, safe in the knowledge that the Ottoman writ scarcely ran beyond the walls of Basra. Qasim, as ruler of the successor state, asserted this claim only days after the abrogation of the 1899 Anglo-Kuwaiti treaty in which responsibility for defense and foreign affairs had been entrusted to the British. Although there was no buildup of Iraqi forces, the announcement was enough to bring British troops back into the emirate. Saudi contingents also arrived following a request by the shaikh of Kuwait. Eventually an Arab League force arrived, permitting the departure of the British and the safeguarding of Arabs by Arabs. It is not clear whether Qasim thought that Kuwait could be blackmailed, or that something was to be gained by causing Britain to move a military force back into Kuwait ("this tyrannical imperialistic aggression," as the Iraqi radio described it), or that a restless army and a discontented civilian population could be placated by the prospect of more oil income. But whatever he thought, his suspension of diplomatic relations with countries recognizing the independence of Kuwait was one more aspect of a ridiculous policy. Doubts were cast on Qasim's stability and intelligence but not on the absolute nature of his authority, for no responsible person within Iraq dared to question his Kuwait policy. Once the crisis had subsided, it was seen that the ill wind from Baghdad had blown some good along with it. As much as anything else, the Iraqi threat impelled the foundation, later in 1961, of that excellent example of how to win friends and influence people known as the Kuwait Fund for Arab Economic Development. (See Chapter 5.)

There was a sameness about the last eighteen months of Qasim's rule which makes it impossible to single out a date or event after which it could be said that time was running out for the dictator. The security and counterintelligence organizations had succeeded in shutting down overt political activity. The extent of their success prompted amnesties which released from Iraq's prisons some of the most determined opponents of the regime. No agency was developed, however, to infiltrate and expose clandestine groups, despite the example set by the Iraqi Communist Party. Censorship remained strict and news was "managed"— not very adroitly—in what the regime considered to be its interest. The extent of the Kurdish debacle was kept from the general population and the country's economic position improved slightly. If Qasim no longer commanded any sort of a following among the educated classes, he nonetheless seemed to be unchallenged as "Sole Leader." A student strike at the end of 1962, sparked by a minor incident, briefly recreated the tense atmosphere of 1959 and early 1960 but did not appear to present a threat to the regime. The strike ended in mid-January 1963 and the next major political event occurred three weeks later. This was the revolution known as "the fourteenth of Ramadan."

A Decade of Turbulence

February 8, 1963, near the middle of the Muslim month of Ramadan, was earlier than the date initially selected by the group of Baathists and army and air force officers for their rising against Qasim. But there had been arrests and the undertaking seemed in jeopardy. The revolutionaries, however, made good use of armor and air power, won over units of the armed forces, captured key installations, and eliminated hard-core Qasimites with dispatch and with effective support from the Baathist "national guard." The revolutionaries seized communications media and presented on television the grisly scene of Qasim's execution.

If the former regime's internal security network had derived no lessons from the Iraqi Communist Party, the Baathists certainly had, as was demonstrated after events in Syria made it no longer necessary or possible to collaborate with the pro-Nasser Arab Nationalist Movement. High priority was given to the elimination of centers of Communist power. The list of victims of all ranks was long. But the rivalry of political parties should not obscure the fact that the operative element was the armed forces, as it was in 1958 and as it would be again. Among the conspirators were officers who had worked closely and in concert with Qasim, just as Qasim had worked with Nuri Pasha Said in an atmosphere of amiability. The army and air force had been purged frequently and some of the conspirators had been in enforced retirement. There were legitimate grievances, but the army had long since become what it remains today, an insatiable brute, kept in check by the lavish expenditure of oil revenues. It must be added, however, that in the Arab world outside Iraq, the rapt attention given to the Nasser-Qasim feud meant that for many there could be only one explanation of Qasim's murder—the blame (or credit) for tyrannicide ultimately must reside with Egypt's president.

The "new men" of 1963 stated that their objective was to "return to the principles" of the 1958 revolution. Delegations were sent to the "liberated" Arab states—Egypt, Algeria, and Yemen—to carry news of the great happenings in Baghdad. As noted earlier, a three-starred—cynics would say ill-starred—United Arab Republic consisting of Egypt, Syria, and Iraq was a short-lived result of the intoxicating period just after the fourteenth of Ramadan. Negotiations for union were far different from those which led to the establishment of the UAR in 1958. Separate armies, arrangements for independent national economies, the rejection of the concept of a single unitary state, which had facilitated Egyptian domination of Syria, were all indications, however, that practical concern about "legitimate national interests" weighed at least as heavily in the deliberations at Cairo as the quasi-religious concept of Arab unity.

It is significant that Abdul Salim Aref, the new president of Iraq, had far more to do with the planning of the revolution of 1958 than that of 1963. The prime minister, Brigadier Ahmed Hassan Bakr, was a Baathist, but more important than the formal governmental structure was the National Council of the Revolutionary Command, with its slogan of "unity, independence, freedom." Now was the time for the Baathists to go about consolidating their hold on power, using their paramilitary "national guard" for tasks similar to those undertaken by the Communist Party's Popular Resistance Force after 1958. But Iraq was not ready to return to the purges and oppression which it had known under Qasim and resistance to Baathist policy was soon evident. Nor did all resistance come from outside the party, for the party itself was split between moderate and extremist factions. Of greater importance, however, in determining the shape of things to come was the deterioration of relations between Gamal Abdul Nasser and the Syrian Baathists, consequent upon the Syrian regime's rigorous suppression of the elements responsible for a pro-Nasser insurrection in Damascus in July 1963. This was an invitation to President Aref to choose Iraq's future alignment in the Arab world. His choice took the form of an anti-Baathist presidential *coup d'état* on November 18, 1963. Supported by the army, Aref declared the Baathist Party illegal. The invective of the government broadcasting stations of Baghdad and Damascus plumbed new depths.

The fourteenth of Ramadan *coup* brought a brief cessation of the war in Kurdistan while the intentions of the new regime were being assessed. But fighting quickly resumed, further embittered by open Soviet assistance to Barazani. This was Russia's repayment for what was described by *Pravda* as "the wave of terror and persecution of Iraqi democrats" by the new regime. Soon Baghdad authorities were accused of adopting "Nazi methods of mass extermination" in the north. The new Soviet policy gave prominence to the leader of a left-wing faction in Barazani's Kurdish Democratic Party, Jalal Talabani, who was sent to

Europe to present the Kurdish case before various groups. There he used his considerable talents to suggest a much closer identity of views between the Kurds and the USSR than in fact existed. But in 1964, after Aref broke the Baathist power structure, he concluded a truce with Barazani which resulted in Talabani's being forced into exile in Iran.

Aref and Nasser had long been on good terms, in part no doubt because of the touch of sycophancy in Aref's attitude toward the Egyptian president. Personal esteem was one thing, however, and political union quite another. Having had the trying experience of attempting to govern Syria, Nasser must have had greater reservations about Iraq. Yet he could not be completely negative on what passed for an article of Arab faith, and as a result, union was cautiously encouraged. Both parties agreed that a period of transition, to last until 1966, was necessary in order that Iraq might develop institutions and policies on an Egyptian model. During this period of "Egyptianization without Egyptians," no role was taken by the considerable number of Egyptian civilian and military personnel stationed in Baghdad to assist in "protecting the revolution."[10] In order to give the regime a broader base, an Iraqi version of the Arab Socialist Union of worker, peasant, professional, and student organizations was formed in association with its Egyptian counterpart. In Iraq, nationalization of banks, insurance companies, and industries, as well as the imposition of new taxes and profit-sharing arrangements followed the socialist program initiated by President Nasser in 1961.

But once again the venerable maxim that "a Jacobin in power is no longer a Jacobin" was borne out. With each month, Aref's enthusiasm for union diminished. Perhaps Acton's famous dictum applied as well. The pace of preparation for union slowed, and in mid-1965 a cabinet reshuffle resulted in the dismissal of a number of conspicuously pro-Nasser ministers. But there was no shortage of enthusiasts for union, and September witnessed an attempted *coup* by air force Brigadier Aref Abdul Razzak. With this, President Aref called on Dr. Abdur Rahman Bazzaz to form a government. He was the first civilian premier since the destruction of Hashemite rule. His was a course of moderation, although he shared the aspirations of Arab nationalists.[11]

Bazzaz's answer to Iraq's problems was "prudent socialism." He

---

[10]Soon this assignment would be used as a kind of psychological decompression chamber for Egyptian troops returning from Yemen, in order that they should not arrive home with fresh accounts of that costly campaign.

[11]Dr. Bazzaz was imprisoned for activities opposing the regime in 1969. His standing in the Arab world was such that appeals to the regime on his behalf were made by both President Nasser and King Faisal. He was tortured while in prison and, near death, was released in mid-1971 and allowed to go to London for hospitalization.

rejected what he described as "slavish imitation" of Egypt in favor of a program based upon Iraq's potential and her requirements. Private and foreign investment was encouraged and a strong effort made to transform the country's five-year plan into a viable instrument. Bazzaz favored decentralized authority as a means of injecting enthusiasm and imagination into the direction of the economy. His most courageous policy was an all-out attack on a self-serving, overpaid, underproductive, and cumbersome bureaucracy—a guaranteed method for acquiring enemies. Yet this was an obvious prerequisite to overhauling the Iraqi economy, and it was Bazzaz's capacity for diagnosing Iraq's more complicated ailments which made his early departure from the premiership so regrettable.

Despite the profligacy with which it was expended, oil income, helped by some improvements in manufacturing and service activities, had kept the overall national income on the upgrade. A chaotic land reform program, a run of bad weather, the cost of the Kurdish war, and a political atmosphere in which the business community could hardly be expected to be optimistic had slowed the pace of development after 1958. But the economy was not stagnant, and Dr. Bazzaz envisioned an early achievement of an annual 8 percent growth rate of the gross national product. This goal was frustrated by changes in internal policies, Syria's blackmailing blockade of the Iraq Petroleum Company's pipeline late in 1966, and the Arab-Israeli war of the following year. But Bazzaz succeeded in restoring Soviet participation in developmental projects to a significant level after relations had cooled because of President Aref's anti-Baathist measures in late 1963. He hoped to foster a dualism in which development of heavy industry would be a government responsibility while private investment, under adequate guarantees, would build up the consumer goods sector.

Dr. Bazzaz knew that "socialist planning" in Iraq, as in Syria, had been little more than a catchphrase. He also knew the implications of labor-intensive and capital-intensive programs in creating what has been described as an "explosive model." Landlord-dominated agriculture, the drift of the rural poor to the cities, and government emphasis on capital-intensive industrial development were all features of the economic situation Dr. Bazzaz had inherited. As the population expanded and social legislation increased labor costs, the proportion of wage earners in the total population declined while the size of the service sector, bordering on starvation in menial and occasional employment, continued to rise. Concurrently, the government, especially during the Qasim years, supported grandiose projects, often based primarily on considerations of prestige. Private enterprise also emphasized capital-intensive investment in conditions of surplus population. Many of the projects called for "technological transplants" which the patient, Iraq, rejected. Planners should have been intimidated by thoughts of constructing machinery consisting of hundreds of parts, made from a wide variety of materials, and involving thousands of manufacturing steps, to say nothing of budgetary and quality controls. But in the new climate of international relations that existed after 1945 it was not to be expected that developed countries with interests in Iraq would advise its leaders that the economic environment was not conducive to the assimilation of an advanced technology. The admission had to come from the Iraqis themselves, and since Dr. Bazzaz was the sole economic realist to occupy a position of major authority in two decades, it could only have come from him had his tenure of office been longer.

There were other problems to be solved before Iraq's development rate could increase. First priority was given to the Kurdish situation. The winter campaign of 1965 resulted in heavy losses on both sides and created renewed interest in negotiations. By June 1966 the government announced its readiness to introduce a development program (preceded by emergency relief), an amnesty, a status equal to Arabic for the Kurdish language, early elections to national and provincial assemblies with proportional representation for the Kurds, equality of government employment opportunities, and other significant concessions. It was widely assumed that Bazzaz had brought the Kurdish war to an end.

In the international field, Dr. Bazzaz proceeded on the sound principle that if a country's relations with its neighbors could not be cordial they should at least be proper. Inasmuch as two of the neighboring regimes, those of Iran and Saudi Arabia, were of a conservative cast, this policy was as unpopular with intellectual and political groupings as was his conciliatory Kurdish policy with the army. A new approach to Saudi Arabia resulted in a Saudi initiative that improved Iraqi-Iranian relations. The significance of this development for the Kurdish problem was immediately apparent, for the prospect of losing an area of asylum and recovery combined with the threat to supply lines implicit in any understanding with Iran inevitably reduced Kurdish intractability. The venerable Shatt al-Arab dispute was also shelved for a time. Improved relations with the Soviet Union, marked by a successful official visit to Moscow, lessened Iraqi feelings of isolation as well as conferring certain economic benefits.

Dr. Bazzaz managed to steer the country through the succession crisis in which General Abdur Rahman Aref became president following his brother's death in a helicopter crash in April 1966.[12] Three months later, Brigadier Aref Abdul Razzak returned to the charge with a second

---

[12]Help was provided by President Nasser, who dispatched Marshal Hakim Amer to Baghdad as his representative and arbitrator.

attempt at a *coup d'état*. Although again unsuccessful, it was a nearer thing and made it clear that militant voices were gaining authority. The army was exacting a price for its support of President Aref during the Razzak rising, and in little more than a month Dr. Bazzaz handed in his resignation.

Major General Naji Taleb became the new premier. He had taken a key part in the 1958 revolution and was an admirer of President Nasser. His cabinet had strong military representation. Although it did not want any deterioration of relations with the Soviet Union, which had become outspoken in support of the Kurds during the winter campaigns of 1965, the new government was unenthusiastic about the Bazzaz peace plan. Any dilution of Iraq's "Arab" character through recognition of the Kurds as equals was considered a threat to projects of Arab unity. The government's flirtations with the Talabani faction, which stood to the left of Barazani in the Kurdish Democratic Party, were intended to be provocative. But President Aref showed unexpected determination to keep the peace in the north, personally inspecting rehabilitation projects in Kurdish areas and receiving delegations from Barazani in Baghdad. It appeared to observers that the president, having kept his bargain with leftist forces by securing the resignation of Dr. Bazzaz, was attempting to retain his policies.

The most important challenge to the regime came from Syria. What initially appeared as tough negotiations between the Iraq Petroleum Company and the Damascus authorities on the Syrian demand for increased transit fees developed into a Syrian political offensive based upon closure of the pipeline. The Syrian Baathist regime welcomed an opportunity to divert attention from its domestic problems, and the IPC crisis was incorporated into a feverish propaganda campaign featuring monopolies, imperialism, and Zionism. No less important was the Syrian interest in reviving the fortunes of the Iraqi Baathist Party. When dwindling oil revenues brought Premier Taleb to Damascus in 1967 for uncomfortable negotiations (during which he was accused of being an agent of the Western oil cartel), he was told that a few Baathist appointments in the Baghdad cabinet might improve the atmosphere. The Syrians, who were engaged at that time in a highly provocative phase of their policy against Israel, caused considerable annoyance in Cairo with their posturing as revolutionary Arab socialists. But because of Nasser's concern that his military agreements with Syria should not be placed in jeopardy, he took a cautious line when Aref arrived in Cairo seeking his support. There was some comfort for the Egyptians in the fact that the pipeline closure caused an improvement in his Suez Canal revenues from tanker traffic.

President Aref won the support of moderate and conservative elements in Iraq by refusing to give in to pressure for "strong measures," which could only have had disastrous effects. When the Syrians relented after months of obstructionism and oil began to flow through the pipelines once more—at greater cost to the IPC—the loss of revenue served only to increase tension between Aref and a ministry which stood considerably to the left of his position. The implementation of projects and reform programs, especially in the agricultural sector, was delayed. The critical shortage of funds had an obvious effect on a free-spending government, but continued quiet in Kurdistan kept the financial problem within bounds until oil revenue began to build up once more.

The frustrations were too much for Naji Taleb, however, and he resigned in May 1967. President Aref, in attempting to broaden the base of his support by bringing representatives of various groups into the cabinet, briefly took on the premiership, and there was significant Kurdish participation in the new government. Relations with Iran continued to improve and overtures·were made to Turkey to end a long period of coolness between the two countries. These developments, constructive in themselves, created no optimism, for once again the attention of the Arab world had become fixed upon Israel. Iraqi troops were moved across the frontier to positions in Jordan and the government identified its policies on the crisis with those of Egypt. The long truce in Kurdistan made it possible for the Iraqis to plan full-scale cooperation with other Arab armies.

Israel took the Aref government's resolve seriously enough to include Iraqi airfields in their preemptive strikes of June 5, 1967. Iraqi infantry and armor were active on the Jordanian frontier and a small unit was present in Sinai. The debacle has been fully described in a spate of publications appearing since June 1967.

Anti-Western demonstrations in Iraqi cities, touched off by charges of American and British "collusion" with Israel, led to a rupture of diplomatic relations with those two countries. Resumption of relations with Great Britain occurred in May 1968; the United States remains without representation in Baghdad. Meanwhile, the French ambassador, because General de Gaulle was willing to defy public opinion and condemn Israeli policy, began studying English in order to better appreciate Iraqi sentiments of appreciation and goodwill.

The most significant Iraqi action of the June war was to call a meeting of Arab oil-producing states, at which the decision was taken to place an embargo on oil shipments to American and British markets. Shortly after the war President Aref, who was giving his attention to the numerous inter-Arab meetings where attempts to frame a common postwar policy were being made, resigned the premiership in favor of Lieutenant

General Taher Yahya, who had served Aref's brother in that position. Emphasis was placed on preparing the country for another round of warfare against Israel and the structure of the cabinet was altered to exclude more moderate opinion. Implicit in the new arrangements was the abandonment of serious efforts to conciliate the Kurds.

The Iraqi contribution to shaping a postwar Arab policy was important. The eagerness of the conservative oil-producing regimes to end the embargo of Western markets generated tensions and made a mockery of "Arab solidarity." President Aref took a particularly militant pro-embargo stand, but soon shifted his position, making it possible for Iraqi delegates to play a key role at the Khartoum conference. There a formula was worked out for oil-producing countries to support those states that had felt the full force of the Israeli attack. The essentially conservative character of the Jordanian regime assured that Saudi Arabia, Kuwait, and Libya would not object to placing King Hussein on the dole. The provocative policy of Syria, which was correctly regarded as responsible for the disaster, and the dismal showing of the Egyptian armed forces, plus antipathies of longer standing, engendered no similar enthusiasm for budgetary support for those two states. It was, nonetheless, provided. In all other respects, the Iraqis remained squarely on the side of the "progressive" regimes, and President Nasser had no more effective supporter than President Aref. Thus Aref's part in working out a formula for inter-Arab relations at Khartoum caused increasing political tensions in Baghdad.

A long period of internal crisis ensued. Demands for elections were heard, as were calls for an end to socialization measures and, ominously, criticism in the army of a policy of "appeasing" the Kurds. The fact was that little was being done to honor the 1966 agreement with Barazani, who by the end of 1967 was openly threatening to renew the insurrection. In an attempt to rally support for their government, Aref and Yahya removed some of the restraints under which the university and school systems had been operating. This only increased tensions, as manifested in demonstrations supporting a more militant anti-Israel line and favoring contributions to *fedayeen* operations within Israel and the occupied territories. The regime was becoming more of a holding operation than a government. Purges of army and air force officers betrayed the uneasiness of Iraq's rulers. Charges of corruption were circulated relating to arrangements with a French firm on concession areas relinquished by the Iraq Petroleum Company. The return of Communist groups to overt political activity, in uneasy cooperation with Baathist elements, was another sign of impending changes.

The first *coup d'état* of July 1968 was led by a curious combination of Baathist and conservative army officers, politicians, and functionaries. It was an almost bloodless affair. Aref was allowed to leave the country but Yahya was imprisoned. The new president, Major General Ahmed Hassan Bakr, had been a prime mover of the rising against Qasim in 1963, but his Baathist orientation cost him all influence when Abdul Salim Aref purged his government later that year. The new government emphasized reform, preparation for elections, and improved relations with the Kurds. There were predictions that the "Bazzaz approach" would once again become operative. Then the second *coup* took place. Only two weeks separated the two actions. The conservative supporters of the first *coup*, proponents of elections and moderation in economic policy, were pushed aside by elements better versed in conspiratorial techniques.

President Bakr extended his authority to include the premiership, command of the armed forces, and chairmanship of the Revolutionary Command Council, which, as in the immediate post-Qasim period, became the real locus of power in Iraq.[13] Political authoritarianism and radical economic policies calling for further state intervention were in prospect. The new regime had a narrower base of support in the country than any of its predecessors going back to the Hashemite era. Relations with the Kurds deteriorated.

Two months after taking power, the Bakr government foiled a *coup* attempt by conservative and pro-Nasser elements, including supporters of former President Aref. Many arrests were made, including a large number of army officers. This marked the beginning of the long series of spy trials and allegations of Zionist, CIA, and British intelligence plots, punctuated by executions, some public and others private. Pressure on the regime took the forms of renewed fighting in the Kurdish areas and "street" demands for more active support of commando groups on Israel's frontiers.

The prospects for the Bakr regime were unpromising, and observers predicted an early changing of the guard in Baghdad. The division of the Revolutionary Command Council into factions seemed to sustain this view. The differences had to be resolved either by bargaining, by a purge, or by another *coup*, but as 1969 wore on there was no evidence of a

---

[13]The inner core of the Revolutionary Command Council reportedly was directed by a young revolutionary, Saddam Hussein al-Tekriti, who earned his spurs in an attempt to assassinate Qasim in 1959. He is less an *eminence grise* than a proponent of violent solutions. His collaborators were Bakr, Defense Minister General Hardan al-Tekriti (who was assassinated in early 1971), Interior Minister General Saleh Mahdi Ammash, General Hamad Shihab al-Tekriti, chief of the general staff, and Colonel Sa'dun Ghaidan, commander of the "republican guard" and the Baghdad garrison.

resolution of conflict in the higher levels of government. There was agreement only that the reign of terror should continue, as it did throughout that year. It seemed to have become the government's *raison d'être*.[14]

The drain on Iraq's resources caused by the Kurdish war and the support of twenty thousand Iraqi troops on the "Eastern Front" in Jordan combined with internal unrest to force the neo-Baathist regime to reexamine its policies. A comprehensive and completely unpredicted agreement was reached in March 1970 with Barazani. It was largely a restatement of the unimplemented Bazzaz program of 1966, but in 1970 it succeeded in stopping the shooting in Kurdistan. The March agreement provided for five Kurdish cabinet appointments and a formulation of revenue apportionment for development and social welfare projects. Autonomous status, based upon a census of Kirkuk Province, was written into the agreement. Instruction in Kurdish was to be provided in the school system and the language was to have an equal standing with Arabic in areas of mixed population.

The agreement sharpened divisions within the Revolutionary Command Council. Conciliation of the Kurds was opposed by General Ammash, who also demanded nationalization of the Iraq Petroleum Company. The final sorting out began in March 1971 with the assassination of Hardan al-Tekriti in Kuwait by unknown assailants. Six months later Vice President Ammash and his most effective supporter, Foreign Minister Abdul Karim Shaikhly, were purged. (Ammash subsequently was appointed ambassador to Moscow.) These developments were represented as victories for President Bakr, but his health had deteriorated and he was unable to take full advantage of them. Saddam Hussein al-Tekriti, heretofore without a government portfolio, now came forward as a clearly identifiable strongman. With his elevation from the secretary-generalship of the Baath Party to the vice presidency, the Revolutionary Command Council fell completely under his control. In September 1971 the neo-Baathists had been in power in Iraq longer than any other regime since the fall of Qasim in 1963.

The Iraqi army and an efficient, relentless secret police were the filters through which the regime obtained its perceptions of popular opinion. Their grip upon the reins of government was strengthened by systematic purges of possible or suspected centers of resistance in the army and civil service. The new vice president, however, looked for more conventional sources of viability for his regime. After dropping the surname "Tekriti" because of its unfortunate and parochial associations

---

[14]The execution of fifteen Iraqis, including several Jews, in August 1969, just after the fire at al-Aqsa Mosque in Jerusalem, effectively deprived the Arabs of any opportunity to make international political capital out of this tragic event.

(deriving from the bloody history of the town of Tekrit, north of Baghdad on the Tigris), Saddam Hussein sought the means of implementing a sophisticated five-year plan. His efforts were jeopardized by the increasing restiveness of the Kurds, who, after desisting from the use of force for over one full year, now demanded specific concessions if they were to continue honoring the spirit of the March 1970 agreement. Barazani now called for a minimum government investment of 10 percent of the national budget in Kurdish regions. Equally important was his insistence that the Kurds be given representation on the Revolutionary Command Council, clearly the locus of power. He now saw that cabinet representation was meaningless and feared that continued payment of some fourteen thousand of his troops by the Baghdad regime would only erode their loyalty to him at a time when no real progress toward autonomous status was being achieved.

Throughout 1971, there were government appeals for increased participation of the private sector in Iraqi industrial development. Efforts also were made to encourage trade. More consumer goods were made available through increased oil revenues, for Iraq had followed the precedent set by Iran in November 1970 of increasing taxes on the price of crude oil. But the Kurdish problem, the rising cost of internal security, and an expensive foreign policy contributed to a severe inflation. Rather than curbs on spending and administrative reform, the regime looked for additional revenue from oil production. President Bakr warned repeatedly that his government's economic planning depended upon a greater share of income from oil. However, the Baghdad regime did not immediately follow Libya's lead, as manifested by the nationalization of British Petroleum in retaliation for Britain's failure to prevent Iranian seizure of Abu Musa and the Tumbs, three small islands dominating the Straits of Hormuz, the entry to the Persian Gulf (see below).

Iraq's deepening crisis provided opportunities for the Soviet Union. Already in mid-1971 the USSR had agreed to undertake a number of technical and developmental projects. Most important by far was the undertaking, on behalf of the Iraqi national petroleum authority, to bring into production the North Rumeilah field, a portion of the southern Iraqi structure taken over from the Basra Petroleum Company, a subsidiary of the Iraq Petroleum Company. The Bakr regime was apprehensive about this agreement because of poor Soviet performance on previous development projects, which seemed to provide the USSR with the means for exchanging obsolete machinery and shoddy workmanship for diplomatic advantages. But in 1971 Iraq's dependence on the Soviet Union had greatly increased and there seemed to be no other choice.

The North Rumeilah field would not soon rival the Iraq Petroleum

Company as a source of income. Negotiations with IPC, therefore, began in January 1972 and Baghdad called for drastic changes to make Iraq the major shareholder in the company, with an Iraqi majority on the board of directors. They could not have begun at a less propitious time. Europe was experiencing a mild winter and the demand for petroleum products had been severely reduced. Even as Prime Minister Kosygin arrived in Iraq for ceremonies marking the opening of the North Rumeilah field, Iraq Petroleum was cutting the flow of oil by pipeline from Kirkuk to the Mediterranean by 50 percent. Projections indicated that unless production was resumed at full capacity, Iraq's revenue for 1972 would be reduced by one-third, with a catastrophic impact on the economic plan. Iraq Petroleum continued to export oil at full capacity from its installations in southern Iraq. It was possible to ship Iraqi crude oil around the Cape of Good Hope in supertankers for delivery to Mediterranean and Western European ports at prices lower than those which had to be charged for Iraqi oil entering the market via the expensive trans-Syrian pipeline.

The economic realities of the situation were lost on a desperate Iraqi regime. On May 1, 1972, Baghdad issued an ultimatum to IPC to either resume full production or relinquish its concession. The deadline passed without action by the company. This led to an Iraqi announcement of nationalization in early June. Some observers saw in the situation a great opportunity for the Soviet Union, which faced formidable production and marketing difficulties with its own vast oil reserves. Until resolved, there would be great advantages to be had in purchasing Middle Eastern petroleum production to offset Soviet production. The latter could then be sold in Western Europe for much needed hard currency. The possibility of incorporating Iraq into a vast barter agreement involving the exchange of petroleum products for Russian and Eastern European consumer goods loomed large. The traffic of official visits by high-level Soviet, Eastern European, and Iraqi officials to each other's capitals became heavy in the wake of these developments. However, the Iraqis did not lose sight of the fact that France depended upon Iraqi petroleum for nearly a third of her requirements. These were obtained through participation of the *Compagnie française des petroles* (CFP) as one of the four major shareholders in Iraq Petroleum.[15] French policy on Israel was anything but a mirror of popular opinion but it conferred advantages in Franco-Arab negotiations. In June 1972 Saddam Hussein flew to Paris for talks with President Pompidou on CFP's future relationship with the

---

[15]French, British, American, and Dutch companies all are involved, each with 23.75 percent, the remaining 5 percent belonging to Gulbenkian interests.

Iraqi regime. It was subsequently agreed that France would purchase Iraqi (IPC) production in proportion to the CFP shareholding.

The Iraqi action fell short of full nationalization, but it provided a convenient means of achieving the desired participation in the company without forsaking managerial and production skills and access to a wealthy industrial market. The precedent of a consortium along the lines of the one worked out for the Anglo-Iranian Oil Company after the "Mossadeqh crisis" of 1952 may be followed. By early 1973 a financial crisis, compounded by Syrian exaction of increased oil pipeline transit payments, created a new atmosphere of realism in Iraqi petroleum policy. Despite any advantages gained from the USSR in the North Rumeilah deal, Iraq was now prepared to reconsider its hard-lining policy against the other "majors" represented in the IPC. The vast and expanding Western market and the related attractions of Western investment capital replaced IPC iniquity and the future of Iraqi-Soviet relations as primary concerns. The shift in attitude was strengthened by complaints from other Arab quarters over the fierceness of Soviet competition, especially in seeking markets for natural gas, in Europe, the United States, and Japan. In the economic sphere, at least, many Iraqi bets were being hedged by 1973.

Iraqi Politics in the Seventies

The Iraqi regime also was concerned with the continued strengthening of the Iranian position in the Persian Gulf. Before 1971, Baghdad's search for a larger role in Arab affairs had caused the regime to enter into a number of economic arrangements with the People's Democratic Republic of South Yemen. It continued to take extreme positions in the Palestine problem and a more aggressive policy in the Gulf began with the visit of units of the Soviet fleet to Umm-Qasr on the Shatt al-Arab in early 1971. Iraqis rejoiced in the concern this visit occasioned in Teheran, remembering the humiliation of 1969 when Iraq and Iran were on the verge of war over the status of the waters of the Shatt. In mid-1971, the neo-Baathist regime attempted to reassert Iraq's influence in the Arab world, dispatching ministerial delegations to Arab capitals with plans and exhortations on the subject of a united front against Israel and on the "Arab" character of the Persian Gulf. The tempo of this campaign increased as the date for the termination of Britain's various protectorate treaties neared. The effectiveness of the Iraqi diplomatic offensive was diminished by widespread Arab condemnation of the neo-Baathist regime for refusing to order Iraqi troops stationed in Jordan to go to the rescue of Palestinian guerrillas beleaguered in Jerash and Irbid by regular Jordanian army units. By November of 1971, diplomatic activity reached an unparalleled level of frenzy, but to no avail. With the Iranian take-over of Abu Musa (a dependency of Sharjah) and the seizure of the Tumbs from Ras al-Khaimah at the end of the month, Iraq severed diplomatic relations with Britain and Iran.

Iraq's geographical position gave it additional importance to plan-ners of Soviet international policy. Its ports figured largely in Russian naval strategy. Indeed, as the struggle for dominance in the Persian Gulf intensifies, greater attention will be focused on the client relation-ships of Iraq and Iran to the Soviet Union and the United States respec-tively. Prime Minister Kosygin's visit to Iraq in April 1972 was followed by President Nixon's state visit to Teheran in May. During both visits there were clashes almost daily on the frontiers between Iran and Iraq, largely the result of Iraqi provocations although the Iranians contributed their share of provocation by announcing their readiness to provide military assistance to the Iraqi Kurds unless peace were restored along the long frontier.

The Iranian regime sought a long period of quietude in which rela-tions with the newly formed Union of Arab Emirates could be consoli-dated. The seizure of Abu Musa and the Tumbs disrupted what had been a relatively cordial relationship between Iran and the most powerful of the rulers of the southern Gulf, Shaikh Zayid of Abu Dhabi, and even earned the condemnation of the Kuwaiti government. Hence the desire for a hiatus during which fence-mending activities could be carried out was genuine. But, with the Iraqi foreign minister touring the Gulf states to excite further opposition to Iranian policy, any lessening of tensions seemed unlikely. Moreover, in the era following the Strategic Arms Limita-tion Agreements of May 1972 between the United States and the Soviet Union, it may very well be that Iraq and Iran will provide channels to express old, deep seated rivalries and animosities for the two super-powers.

The intensification of Iraqi-Soviet relations made it possible for the Revolutionary Command Council to take long-contemplated steps to broaden the base of its support in the country. In November 1971 Presi-dent Bakr announced a "Charter for National Action," inviting various political groupings to form a coalition with the ruling Baath Party and providing for the formation of "People's Councils" at provincial, mu-nicipal, and village governing levels. Little progress was made in the achievement of a national front until the signing, in April 1972, of a fifteen-year Soviet-Iraqi friendship treaty. The implications were clear to left-wing forces in opposition to the neo-Baathists, and by May two members of the Iraqi Communist Party and two members of pro-Communist organizations had taken seats in the cabinet. This was a victory for the Baath Party, which made no concessions in securing the collaboration of the two groups, each with a considerable following in the country. It seemed unlikely that the national front arrangements would be quickly enshrined in a permanent constitution. The rapid deterioration of relations with the Kurds in late 1972, accompanied by the breakdown of negotiations between the Baathists and the Kurdish Democratic Party and an Iraqi army buildup in Kurdish areas in 1973, also support that conclusion.

The most salient fact of Iraqi political life remains that only members of the Baath Party can hold positions of high command in the Iraqi armed forces. Broad-based support of any Iraqi regime continues to be a transient phenomenon, and not every group which organizes the seizure of power in Baghdad enjoys even a brief moment of mass approbation.

4

JORDAN

The Kingdom East of the River

It is with the land beyond the River Jordan, the weak and riven desert kingdom where, against all odds, King Hussein still keeps his throne, that this chapter is concerned. To be sure, the Hashemite kingdom must be considered at the moment of its greatest size geographically (between 1948 and 1967), but only in the context of one inescapable fact: historically, the Jordanian claim to the West Bank territory is little better than that of the Israelis. The West Bank is Palestinian. The most accurate title Hussein could assert is the one long held by his grandfather —Emir of Transjordan.

The Biblical names associated with the area of Transjordan—Gilead, Ammon, Moab, Edom—are set apart in many ways from those of Samaria and Judea farther westward. The region supported a greater population in antiquity than it does today, even considering the large number of Palestinians who have taken refuge there or have sought to make a new start east of the Jordan after 1948, and especially since 1967. Amman was an Amonite capital and stronghold. The tides of Assyrian, Chaldean, Persian, and Seleucid conquests left few traces. Of greater consequence was the Ptolemaic thrust from Egypt about 2500 B.C. It was in this era that Amman prospered under Philadelphus and took his name. Some of the people whose lives Philadelphus tried to organize were beduin who had slowly made their way into this transitional zone from the Arabian heartland. The first important clash between an Arab and a Mediterranean culture came later, when Pompey made Jerash a Roman city in 64 B.C.

The Arab Nabateans based in Petra struggled for power and influence in Jordan. The importance of Petra derived from its defensibility and water supply. The Nabateans made it a commercial center and, as visitors since its "rediscovery" by Burckhardt in the nineteenth century have come to know, a place of surpassing beauty. But for all their vigor, the Nabateans could not withstand Roman pressure. In A.D. 106, during the reign of Trajan, Petra fell and Nabatean power was eclipsed.

After Constantine's conversion to Christianity, Jordan became the site of yet another contest. The very considerable appeal of this new monotheistic faith to pagan Arabs, and possibly to Jewish Arabs, increased among those simple people through its identification with secular, material strength, so that, until Arab Islam arose to challenge Byzantium, the impact of Christianity upon Jordan was considerable. Khalid ibn Walid's great victory on the Yarmuk in 636, of enormous significance in Muslim history, was likewise a major turning point in the history of Transjordan. As the new faith penetrated ever deeper, under the first Caliphs and then under Umayyad rule, the region's predominantly Arab character became Muslim as well.

Yet Transjordan remained almost entirely outside the mainstream of events, in contrast to Palestine, where Jerusalem became one of Islam's holiest cities. Even during the Crusades Transjordan was little more than a source of recruits for the long series of struggles. Nor did four centuries of Ottoman hegemony, beginning in 1517, significantly alter its character. Its importance as an area to be traversed on the holy pilgrimage to Mecca was established before Selim the Dread's conquest and survived the Ottoman Caliphate. It gained some strategic importance at the end of the Ottoman era through Abdul Hamid's Hejaz Railway project.

When Emir Faisal's forces occupied Aqaba in 1917, Transjordan was briefly the subject of worldwide interest. This lasted as long as it took Faisal, T. E. Lawrence, and their followers to move north of Jerash. The region was hardly mentioned at the Paris Peace Conference and figured almost in a negative sense in the negotiations on the mandates. There was little discussion of internal arrangements for Transjordan; its importance derived only from its geographical position in defining the frontiers of the Syrian and Palestinian mandates.

Faisal's expulsion from Damascus in 1920 conferred a measure of importance on Transjordan. Future policy for the Emirate of Transjordan was worked out in a series of meetings between Colonial Secretary Winston Churchill and Faisal's brother Abdullah, and the details were confirmed at the 1921 Cairo Conference. As Emir of Transjordan, Abdullah headed an autonomous Arab government under a British mandate. Such were the beginnings of another Hashemite dynasty. A firm British checkrein on Transjordan's ruler prevented further deterioration of Anglo-French relations.

This arrangement gave little satisfaction to the British. Abdullah took second place to Faisal in every respect save in pleasure-seeking. That he was not deposed was due more to the unsuitability of alternative candidates than to any display on his part of an ability to govern. Yet it was necessary that Transjordan remain peaceful and secure, for it was a base from which the British could move to protect their interests in the Persian Gulf, Palestine, Suez, and the northern Red Sea area. It was also a strategic link between Baghdad and Jerusalem. Once a certain amount of pacification had been imposed upon local tribes, the newly constituted Arab Legion was used for similar missions in the frontier area between Iraq and the Kingdom of Hejaz and Nejd and its Dependencies, the forerunner of modern Saudi Arabia. In the first years, the Legion also dealt with major incursions by Wahhabi tribesmen who supported the Saudi claim to territory as far north as Ma'an.

The Treaty of Jeddah (1927), which eased pressures upon Transjordan's southern frontier, was facilitated by the British-officered Arab Legion and the Royal Air Force. When the long quiet era of economic stagnation and political apathy ended in the late 1930s, it was Transjordan's military strength which determined the country's role in World War II. The Arab Legion's service to the Arab cause in action against the Vichy regime in Syria is a dim memory. Its support of British forces during Rashid Ali Ghaylani's 1941 uprising in Iraq is better remembered in Baghdad, Damascus, and Cairo—a fact that is considered to be early evidence of the "nonliberated" nature of the Jordanian state.

After World War II, a treaty with Great Britain signified the end of an era of tutelage but the special relationship remained strong. It also promoted Abdullah to kingly status. Negotiations went smoothly in an atmosphere of friendship and good will. It could hardly have been otherwise, for there was no nascent nationalism in the tribal community of Transjordan and economic survival took precedence over political progressivism at every level of Jordanian society. The treaty assured that Jordan would continue to be available to Britain as a *place d'armes* and would be subsidized by the British. Without this treaty, the people of the new kingdom would have been less well off than before and would have been restricted to the activities of their Nabatean ancestors, dealing in animals from Saudi Arabia and engaging in a small amount of entrepot trade. There were discussions concerning the possibility of a Hashemite federation with Iraq and calls for closer relations with Palestine, but little enthusiasm was generated for either.

In 1948 Jordan's Arab Legion provided the only significant opposition to the military forces of the newly proclaimed State of Israel. This can be ascribed to training and leadership rather than zeal for the Palestinian cause. The Jordanian occupation of a large block of territory west of the Jordan River was a military success but a political liability. What had been a unified economic region was now divided by a border which slashed indiscriminately through rich agricultural areas, especially north of Jerusalem, often cutting farmers off from their fields and wells. The long exposed boundary would be crossed thousands of times between 1948 and 1967 by raiders and vengeance seekers. Just as significant was the fact that the armistice arrangements doubled Jordan's population. A traditional and largely beduin society was immediately challenged by an advanced, articulate, embittered, and politically sophisticated community, including a large refugee element from the territory upon which the State of Israel had been founded.

Palestinian participation in the Jordanian government began before the armistice of April 1949. When formal annexation of the West Bank territory took place a year later, the Palestinians were assured of half of the seats in the Council of Representatives.

The act of annexation could be regarded as King Abdullah's death warrant. In 1950 the same Cairo meeting of the Arab League Council which described Israel as a "figment of imagination" referred to Abdullah as a "potential traitor." Charges of his collusion with Israel during the Palestine War gained credence when the king called for negotiations with the Israelis on outstanding issues ranging from mutual access to the Holy Places to trade and tourism. At the same time, Jordan was being weakened by the spread of bureaucratic incompetence and corruption and by the polarization of political life arising from the regime's tendency to equate radicalism and progressivism with communism.

The shots which killed King Abdullah at al-Aqsa Mosque in July 1951 obstensibly united the Arabs, for a "summit" meeting was called. The assassination had been carried out by the "Sacred Struggle Organization," led by Hajj Amin Husseini, ex-Mufti of Jerusalem. Extreme nationalist elements, whose numbers were growing rapidly, approved the assassination. Before long, these same elements would deride Hajj Amin's ineffectual leadership.

Abdullah was a man out of time. His politics were influenced by the traditions of the desert Arab and by his contacts with Europeans. His training in statecraft was limited to learning the tasks of a tribal shaikh— the mediation of disputes, the reconciliation of differences, and the apportionment of censure and responsibility. His sketchy knowledge of European history convinced him that a country's interests counted for more than its alliances and enmities. Abdullah was killed, however, because his country's borders expanded as the result of a war which was a disaster for the vast majority of Arabs. The humiliation of defeat in the Palestine War created an atmosphere in which proponents of negotiation and conciliation could not function.

The brief passage of the irresolute, perhaps mentally incompetent, King Talal (1951–53) would have been a de facto interregnum but for the strong-willed members of his family, not the least of whom was his wife, Queen Zayn. Rumors of union with Iraq as the only way to ensure Jordan's survival recurred frequently, but no initiatives were taken in Amman or Baghdad although the subject was debated in the Jordanian Chamber of Deputies. Anti-British feeling mounted because of resentment over the extent of British control of the Arab Legion, the existence of British bases on Jordanian territory, and the general opinion that British influence was an insidious form of neocolonialism. Critics pointed out that budgetary expenditure on the armed services was excessive and that little was being done to develop the national economy.

The departure of the patriarchal figure of King Abdullah and the pressures generated by politically conscious Palestinians prompted initiative toward a more truly representative government. In November 1951 a new constitution was approved by the Chamber of Deputies. An appointive and largely ceremonial Senate was provided, but the most important change made the Council of Ministers responsible to the Chamber of Deputies. A two-thirds vote by the Chamber could secure the resignation of the Council. The Chamber consisted of forty members, twenty from each side of the River Jordan.

Adjustment to parliamentary government was difficult. There were frequent boycotts of Chamber proceedings, usually by West Bank representatives. These were accompanied by anti-government demonstrations in cities and towns. The suppression of opposition newspapers occurred regularly. Yet the Chamber of Deputies succeeded in focusing attention on Jordan's serious economic crisis. It became clear to Western observers that a British subsidy (£1,250,000 in 1953) could hardly sustain government operations. Western strategic planners realized that if Jordan was to continue to warrant the description "Faithful Ally," a program of economic development would be required.

A month before Hussein's eighteenth birthday (May 2, 1953) and his elevation to the kingship to succeed his ailing father, a technical assistance agreement was signed with the United States government providing for $1,915,000 in development funds. The United Nations Relief and Works Agency at this point was spending about $14 million annually through the Jordanian Development Bank. At the end of the year, the British government made up the Jordanian budget deficit with a

£750,000 grant and provided an interest-free development loan of £1.6 million. This was followed in mid-1954 by an $8 million U.S. Foreign Operations Administration grant for road construction, reforestation, and related projects. Amman took on the aspect of a boom town, with communications and water requirements continually outdistancing the planners. Poverty was unrelieved elsewhere in Jordan, for only about 10 percent of the land was potentially cultivable. Prospects for the future were grim.

Yet there were those who were undaunted by statistics and projections. In 1953 the Arab Development Society, an inspired creation of Musa Alami, opened its training center. It was a fine example of the concept of self-help and an indication that the Israelis had no monopoly on determination to make the desert bloom. Quite obviously, full and effective utilization of the country's water resources was central to any development plan for Jordan. Consequently, the progress of United Nations and United States surveys of potential utilization of the Jordan Valley waters was watched with great interest. Already in 1952 the Jordanian government had held discussions with Syrian representatives concerning a cooperative plan for utilizing the Yarmuk River. These talks led to a proposal for a "Yarmuk High Dam" which not only would have been an extremely costly undertaking but also would have created a situation wherein a vast amount of water would have been lost through evaporation.

It was in response to this proposal that President Eisenhower appointed Eric Johnston as a mediator seeking agreement on the utilization of the Jordan Valley waters, including the Yarmuk system. There was great concern in Jordan, Syria, and Lebanon over Israeli hydroelectric and irrigation planning, for it was widely believed that the Israelis sought to monopolize the water supply and would go so far as to seek control of the Litani River system to irrigate lands formerly watered by the Jordan, using Jordan water for hydroelectric purposes and then piping it to the Negev.

The question of utilization of the Jordan Valley waters had been studied by the United Nations and a survey had been completed in 1949. The Johnston study was completed in 1953. Both drew heavily on American experience with the Tennessee Valley Authority. There was optimism over Johnston's efforts. In drawing up their own proposal in 1954, the Arabs recognized the principal of sharing the waters with Israel. (Egypt played a constructive role before 1956, perhaps because of awareness of its own "downriver" status.) But the Unified Development Plan which emerged from the consultations, based upon agreement by technical representatives of all riparian states, failed to receive the endorsement of the Arab League Political Committee in October 1955. The tone of that meeting had been set, unfortunately, by a massive Israeli raid into the Gaza strip.

Everyone lost with the failure of the Johnston plan, but Jordan was the biggest loser—not only because of what an agreement could have accomplished for the Jordanian economy, but also because the United States had a second objective in the negotiations: refugee settlement. It is precisely the unsettled and therefore exploitable nature of the refugee community which kept up border warfare between Israel and Jordan over the years and which expanded the ranks of the *fedayeen*. Since 1955, no feasible alternative to the Johnston plan for international agreement on the Jordan waters issue has been suggested.

Damoclean Years for Hashemite Rule

Even if programs of economic development had achieved broad success, it seems unlikely that Jordan could have continued to be regarded in London as the "Faithful Ally." This was dramatically asserted in 1955 by the riots that resulted from General Sir Gerald Templer's abortive mission aimed at incorporating Jordan into the developing structure of the Baghdad Pact. Widespread unrest indicated a decline in effective, reliable police and security authorities and pointed to the growing strength of pro-Nasser sentiments in the army. Time was running out on Glubb Pasha, long-time commander of the Arab Legion, and he could hardly have appreciated an article in a contemporary British publication which referred to him as the "uncrowned king of Jordan." Glubb's decision not to attempt to turn back the clock by resisting King Hussein's dismissal order early in 1956 may have spared Jordan the trials of civil war for more than a decade. At one stroke young Hussein became a "hero of Arab nationalism."

Much was made of this defeat for Great Britain. There were bitter assertions that much of Transjordan would have been overrun by Jewish forces in 1948 had not the Arab Legion been led by British officers. Yet it is clear that Glubb's dismissal enabled the Hashemite regime to weaken internal resistance and at the same time maintain the British connection. Jordan not only refused to join the Baghdad Pact but also avoided commitments implicit in the offer of a subsidy by the "Damascus Pact" states (Egypt, Syria, and Saudi Arabia). The king had been carefully coached, but in time he developed his own adroitness in dealing with internal and external challenges.

The delicate situation provoked by the Templer fiasco, the Glubb dismissal, and an attempted *coup* by a Nasser-inspired "Young Officers' Movement" (subsidized in part, ironically, by Saudi Arabian money) convinced British and American planners that many assumptions upon which Middle Eastern policy had been based were no longer applicable. This conclusion was strengthened first by intense attacks by Cairo and Damascus Radio in which Jordan was described as a British colony and then by the elections of October 1956, which for the first time returned a West Bank majority to parliament.

King Hussein's fondness for British things and ways did not extend to an appreciation of British tutelage. Nobody was more aware of this than Major Aly Abu Nuwar, who was promoted from a junior post in Paris to be aide-de-camp to the king, where he used his special position to urge the "Arabization" of the Arab Legion. Glubb's dismissal led quickly to his promotion to the command of what was now known as the Royal Jordanian Army. At this point the kingdom easily could have shifted into the "progressive" camp, in which hereditary dynasties were long out of fashion. Popular enthusiasm for such a shift, following the drastic reduction of British influence in the armed forces, was coupled with widespread resentment over Sir Anthony Eden's Guildhall speech urging the Arabs to accept a permanent settlement with Israel following frontier and other concessions by the latter. These developments placed the young monarch in a belligerent mood, and only the counsel of experienced politicians such as Samir Rifai and Bahjat Talhouni prevented him from courting disaster.

The quickening pace of events in the Middle East gave Jordan new importance in the view of Western policy-makers. If the Glubb dismissal was a slap in the face, it seemed wise to turn the other cheek. Fear of another Russian-engineered "Czech arms deal" prompted the dispatch of additional Western armaments to the Royal Jordanian Army. In late 1956 there were indications that Aly Abu Nuwar was organizing a revolutionary command council in the army, not unlike the instrumentality of Nasser's rule in Egypt. By early 1957 Jordan was moving toward a closer relationship with the Cairo-Damascus axis, with Abu Nuwar closely coordinating his activities with Colonel Abdul Hamid Sarraj, the *eminence grise* of the Syrian military establishment. But Abu Nuwar and his supporters in the army moved too rapidly for many civilian politicians, who were themselves not enthusiastic for Hashemite rule. Disagreement over tactics and goals led inevitably to security breaches, so that when Abu Nuwar's challenge to Hussein came, the king and his supporters were prepared and carried the fight to the rebels. After a brief struggle, Hussein regained control and Abu Nuwar fled to asylum in Damascus, thence on to Cairo.[1] The dispatch of units of the American

---

[1] Abu Nuwar eventually was permitted to return to Jordan. He now prospers as a businessman with extensive interests in the Arabian Peninsula and is very much Establishment Jordanian.

Sixth Fleet to the eastern Mediterranean at the time of the crisis may have strengthened Hussein's hand, or at least discouraged external intervention in the showdown. But of more immediate consequence was the advice and guidance of pro-Western strategists such as Samir Rifai and Sulaiman Tuqan. Many arrests and imprisonments followed the *coup* attempt and political parties were banned.

It was the dismissal of Prime Minister Sulaiman Nabulsi which had isolated Abu Nuwar and caused him to bid for power prematurely, relying only on his supporters in the army. Nabulsi, a Palestinian, had attained the premiership as the result of the 1956 elections which returned a majority of anti-Hashemite West Bank candidates. Shortly thereafter, he abrogated the Anglo-Jordanian treaty and obtained pledges from Saudi Arabia, Syria, and Egypt for financial support which previously had come from London. Only Saudi Arabia lived up to this undertaking with the payment of $1,400,000. Egypt provided useless credits in blocked Egyptian currency while Syria sent a bill for the expenses of Syrian troops which had been moved into Jordan at the time of the Suez crisis. At the height of his power after the termination of the treaty with the United Kingdom, Nabulsi pressed for "Egyptianization" of the educational system and then further increased his popularity by making threatening remarks on the future of the Trans-Arabian Pipeline Company (Tapline) and other American interests. Had he been content to move cautiously in purging beduin and other loyalist elements in the civil service, he might have ended Hussein's primacy. But his attempt to change the composition of the royal household made him vulnerable and, in a society where traditional values count heavily, his decision to extend diplomatic recognition to the Soviet Union enabled Hussein to rally support for Nabulsi's dismissal. The Abu Nuwar fiasco that followed in the wake of Nabulsi's downfall as well as some civil disturbances inspired by Baathist elements brought martial law and "beduin" government.

The Hashemite position was further improved by Saudi Arabia's increasing disenchantment with the regime of Gamal Abdul Nasser. King Saud's visits to Baghdad and Amman and the subsequent talks between the Saudi monarch and Iraq's Abdul Illah in Washington were ascribed to the influence of Crown Prince Faisal. The burgeoning Nasserite threat to traditional regimes acted to place Saudi-Hashemite animosity in cold storage.

Efforts to market the Eisenhower Doctrine of 1957 at this time of crisis were as maladroit in Jordan as in other Middle Eastern countries. Even as Hussein fought for survival, his friends in Washington attempted to provide him with a contract that would give him tenure as an instrument of Western policy. He undoubtedly was just this, but he was much less likely to be an effective one by advertising his commitment through signing on the line. (Only Lebanon was taken in by this example of Dullesian baroque diplomacy, and she paid dearly for this mistake.)

The next challenge to Hussein came in 1958 and was timed to coincide with the *coup d'état* in Iraq which ended Hashemite rule and installed Abdul Karim Qasim in power. Prime Minister Samir Rifai, known as "little Nuri," was more alive to the developing threat than was the old master in Baghdad. The Hashemite regime in Amman survived with British assistance in the form of a virtual occupation of Jordan by British troops for three months.

Once Iraq was lost to the British interest—in political and strategic terms, if not in the economic sense because of such factors as the Iraq Petroleum Company—Jordan's value to the United Kingdom became largely sentimental. Fortunately for Hussein, the British Foreign Office did not recognize this hard fact. So long as Nuri and the Hashemites ruled Iraq, it made a certain amount of sense to maintain the viability of a country such as Jordan for use as a communications zone. But in 1958, revolutionary elements within Jordan were emboldened by developments in Lebanon and Iraq. Henceforth the Hashemite regime's survival would depend more upon the suffrance of Israel and Egypt (and to a lesser extent Syria and Iraq) than it would on Great Britain.

This was not immediately apparent. In mid-1958, as British paratroopers patrolled the streets of Amman and an American airlift assured the flow of vital supplies, Jordan sundered diplomatic ties with the United Arab Republic. The Syrian *Deuxième Bureau* and Lebanese revolutionaries were accused of subsidizing terrorists in Jordanian cities. With Jordan's economy sustained by large American grants-in-aid, the country's place in the polarizing conflict between tradition and revolution then underway in the Middle East seemed obvious.

Yet Jordan fared remarkably well in the Middle Eastern political jungle of the late 1950s and early 1960s. The United Arab Republic experiment was in some ways reassuring to the Hashemite regime, for in Syria there was none of the docility with which President Nasser's policies were accepted in the Nile Valley. King Hussein and his ministers repeatedly expressed concern and dissatisfaction over the "enslavement" of Syria. Moreover, the deterioration of Iraqi-Egyptian relations provided opportunities for Jordanian officials to accuse President Nasser of plotting against Abdul Karim Qasim. Not waiting upon events, King Hussein sought to turn regional political developments to his advantage.

Opposition to Hussein was not far below the surface in Jordan. The regime increasingly became identified throughout the Arab world as traditional and even feudal. Jordan's early and outspoken support for the Imam of Yemen against the revolutionary elements which brought "republican" rule to San'a was further proof of the regime's ultra-conservatism. Governments headed by such conservatives as Wasfi Tal and Samir Rifai were barely able to keep the lid on the steaming cauldron of Jordanian politics. A 1961 census established that the total population of Jordan was 1,690,000, of which the West Bank component was 805,880. More specifically, 460,000 were "indigenous" Jordanians, 460,000 were West Bank Palestinians, 596,000 were classified as Palestinian refugees, and another 105,000 as Palestinian exiles. The situation hardly could have been more explosive, and by 1963 seasoned observers were talking in terms of "King Hussein's last stand." A typical editorial in an Arab nationalist newspaper held that "Jordanian isolation can no longer be upheld" now that Syria, Iraq, and Yemen were firmly in the revolutionary camp. The 1963 crisis was the most serious since the Palestine War. Widespread rioting east and west of the Jordan impelled King Hussein to dissolve parliament and call upon his uncle, Sherif Nasser—"the most hated man in Jordan"—to form a caretaker government and to provide full internal security. Jordan's isolation seemed complete. No meaningful assistance could be expected from Saudi Arabia nor, in the Kennedy era, could sorties by the Sixth Fleet into the eastern Mediterranean in support of a beleaguered Jordanian monarch be imagined. But Hussein held on, encouraged as much by his comprehension of the essentially verbal nature of Arab solidarity as by his uncle's repressive measures.

Arab solidarity was put to the test in 1964 with the disclosure of Israeli plans to divert water from the Jordan in upper Galilee for piping to the northern Negev. Although the resignation of Sherif Nasser and his replacement by Bahjat Talhouni made inter-Arab cooperation more possible, Arab reaction to the Israeli plan was limited to threats in the press and radio and the deployment of modern Syrian artillery units in the Golan Heights—hardly an overpowering response, even though it did cause one Israeli official to remark that "we are living in a fish bowl."

If such demonstrations of impotence partially explain the survival of Hashemite rule, they also encouraged the rise of paramilitary organizations comprised of Palestinians, and an admixture of supporters from various Arab countries, who had lost faith in repeated pledges by Arab governments to regain for them their homeland. Today the Palestine Liberation Organization and the various commando groups which function to a greater or lesser extent under its auspices—*Fatah*, the Popular Front for the Liberation of Palestine (PFLP) and others—receive daily mention in the international press. But already in 1965 *Fatah*, as a result of its raids into Israel from Jordanian territory, had become a major source of concern to the government. The Palestine Liberation Organization (PLO) demanded a semi-autonomous status which would permit the collection of taxes as well as open recruitment. In refusing, the Jordanian cabinet correctly concluded that such measures would create a state within a state, although its assumption that such a situation also would divide the allegiance of the refugee population was incorrect inasmuch as the majority of the refugees felt no loyalty to the Amman government.

The Six Day War

Several American oil companies spent considerable time and money in an unsuccessful search for oil in Jordan. By the middle of the 1960s it seemed clear that there would be no easy path to economic self-sufficiency. However, the large increase in tourism was encouraging. Six hundred thousand tourists visited Jordan in 1966, a fivefold increase over 1960. Much progress was made in agricultural production, especially after the opening of the American-financed East Ghor Canal. Income from phosphates also increased. During a 1966 visit to the United Kingdom—for which he was roundly criticized by the Palestine Liberation Organization and the Soviet Union—King Hussein gave details of the economic plan through which Jordan expected to achieve financial viability in 1970. This was a seven-year plan, superseding the 1962–67 plan, and was altogether better coordinated, with provision for expanded irrigation in the Yarmuk and Jordan Valleys, the further development of mining (phosphates, copper, and potash), railroad development, and hydroelectric projects on the Yarmuk. But economic plans make no provision for natural or manmade disasters.

On November 13, 1966, Israeli units struck at Samu in reprisal for commando raids, some of which, it was alleged, were made possible by the collaboration of inhabitants of that border village. It was a heavy raid, supported by air strikes, and resulted in extensive damage and many casualties. The United States, Great Britain, France, and Russia achieved a brief unanimity in condemning the raid. There was speculation that Israel's basic motivation was to bring about the overthrow of the Hashemites as a preliminary to a once-and-for-all showdown with a Palestinian-dominated successor state. The commando organizations and their supporters called for a general mobilization, leading to four weeks of sporadic rioting. This was accompanied by a barrage of anti-Hussein invective from the Syrian, Egyptian, and PLO press and radio. Along with its grave political implications, the new crisis underscored the fragility of the Jordanian economy. The optimism of a few months earlier evaporated.

The Jordanian military effort during the Arab-Israeli War of June

1967 may have been comparatively better than the efforts of its nominal allies, but it was nonetheless apparent that the Royal Jordanian Army was little more than a pale shadow of its illustrious ancestor, the Arab Legion. Jordan was drawn into a war it did not want, perhaps in some measure encouraged by an Egyptian guarantee of air cover which, after the first few hours of conflict, was no more available to the Egyptians than to the Jordanians. What is more, the quality of Jordan's statesmanship during the war was no higher than her standard of performance militarily. King Hussein's prestige in the West was badly damaged by his unquestioning—and public—acceptance of the myth of Anglo-American collaboration with Israel in air operations against Egypt.

The Israeli government provided world press and television with full coverage of the rout of the Egyptian army and the destruction of Nasser's air force. Within weeks, there were tourist excursions to the Mitla Pass and Sharm as-Shaikh. These and the dramatic Israeli seizure of Syria's Golan Heights overshadowed the fighting on the West Bank and disguised the fact that Jordan had been dealt the hardest blows. Half of its entire agricultural production was destroyed along with approximately one-third of its earnings from agricultural exports. The West Bank's potential for earning foreign exchange from tourism passed into Israeli hands.

It was as if history had been rolled back thirty years, for the Hashemite Kingdom of Jordan was once again nothing more than a desert emirate. Nearly 250,000 West Bank refugees crowded into Amman, although some 30,000 eventually returned to their homes. There was no more talk of economic self-sufficiency by 1970 or any other future date, nor could there be without the West Bank. Almost before the shooting stopped, proposals were advanced from various quarters for the establishment of an autonomous state or Palestinian entity in the occupied territory of the West Bank. Israeli proponents of such formulae found little support. Arab and Israeli intransigence in the face of efforts to bring them to negotiations, either direct or indirect, indicated that the West Bank's Palestinians faced an extended period of colonial administration with only the most tenuous links with their compatriots beyond the Jordan. In the intervening period, the various missions of Dr. Gunnar Jarring, the special United Nations negotiator, Big Four diplomacy at New York, and the probings and soundings at other levels have produced further proposals for the occupied West Bank, all of which suggest that there is little possibility of reincorporating the West Bank into the Hashemite Kingdom, should the Hashemites in fact be on hand to reassert their authority.

In the months following the Six Day War, King Hussein, with texts and various cosmetic effects provided by Western public relations firms, became a most eloquent spokesman for the Arab cause before the United Nations, in Washington, and in European capitals. While the peripatetic young monarch was on yet another mission to Washington, his peace overtures were negated in the most violent fashion by a *Fatah*-organized rocket attack on Eilath, the Israeli port and a vital link with Asia and Africa (and especially Iranian oil) on the Gulf of Aqaba. Coming from Jordanian territory, the attack was a forceful reminder that the Palestinian policy remained one of "no compromise"—with either Israel or the last Hashemite dynasty. Although the perpetrators were arrested, it was necessary to release them almost immediately to avoid a clash between the shaky regime and the increasingly confident *fedayeen*.

Nineteen-sixty-eight visited more misery upon Jordan, with the escalation of fighting along and across the Jordan River. In March there was a massive Israeli raid on the permanent refugee camp at Karameh in retaliation for extensive *fedayeen* activity—a battle in which Israeli forces were badly bruised and the prestige of the *fedayeen* enhanced. This in turn forced the Jordanian government to make further concessions to the commandos and meant that still more of the meager funds available for development would be diverted to rearmament. Inevitably, the Israeli setback at Karameh led to further reprisals, including the destruction of the East Ghor Canal, an irrigation facility upon which much of the country's agricultural production depended. Meanwhile, fruitless efforts to maintain a military balance continued, with Jordan receiving tanks, fighter aircraft, and other military equipment from the United States and Great Britain. Much of it was destined to be deployed against Palestinian commando groups, rather than to contribute to the Arab-Israeli standoff. Nonetheless, it achieved its primary purpose of keeping King Hussein's government in the status of a Western satellite.

Hussein's Garrison State

During the three years following the Six Day War, energies and resources which might have been deployed in the search for economic viability in the truncated Jordanian state were consumed in political maneuver and occasional violence. It appeared to observers, however, that the leader of the Palestine Liberation Organization, Yassir Arafat, and King Hussein had reached some form of accommodation by which an all-out showdown could be averted. Instead, a remarkable affirmation of the platitude that the road to hell is paved with good intentions precipitated hostilities in September 1970. American efforts to secure a cease-fire on the Suez front between Egypt and Israel had succeeded beyond all expectations with President Nasser's acceptance of proposals by Secretary of State Rogers. When Hussein associated himself with the Egyptian leader's momentous decision, the Palestinians charged that their cause had been betrayed by a cowardly act of political expediency. The call for action quickly found an answer from the hard-line, Marxist-oriented PFLP. It took the form of the "day of the hijackings" (September 6, 1970), which ended with American and Swiss airliners in guerrilla control at Dawson's Field (now "Liberation Airport") in northern Jordan and an American "jumbo jet" blown up by its hijackers shortly after landing in Cairo. Three days later a British VC–10 was hijacked to Dawson's Field while inbound to Beirut from Bahrain. The aircraft in PFLP hands were subsequently blown up and much political capital was made from the hostages—not only among the Arabs and the inhabitants of the refugee camps where they were shown off, but even among the hostages themselves.

After their early successes, the commandos proved incapable of sustaining their momentum. A severe blow was the withdrawal of Syrian armored units which had entered Jordan to support the Palestinian offensive. Only intervention by President Nasser saved hundreds, and perhaps thousands, of commandos from annihilation during the Royal Jordanian Army's "Black September" offensive. Although the commandos' tactics posed a threat to the general Middle Eastern settlement under United Nations auspices that Nasser favored, his emotional ties to the Palestinian cause would not permit him to abandon them. His intervention was his last act on behalf of the Palestinians and occurred a month before his death.

The truce of September 27th only delayed the "final solution" sought by King Hussein and his beduin supporters, who were augmented by mercenary tribesmen from Iraq and Saudi Arabia. Hussein employed the truce period to prepare to sweep Jordan with the iron broom of his army. Fighting resumed before the year was out. Mile by mile, commando-controlled territory was regained. Commando camps in the Jordan Valley were closed down and their militia disarmed. The hard core of armed guerrillas was progressively isolated from the towns and refugee camps which had been sources of support. The last paragraphs in a tragic chapter of the history of the Palestinian liberation movement were written in July 1971 in the hills above Jerash and Ajlun. A major Jordanian offensive took over one thousand prisoners. Hundreds of guerrillas escaped into Syria and eventually made their way to camps in Lebanese territory on the slopes of Mount Hermon. Still others chose surrender to Israeli border guards in preference to a doubtful future in the hands of Hussein's soldiers.

Throughout the renewed fighting, King Hussein and his capable

Prime Minister, Wasfi Tal, and a corps of dedicated military and civilian advisors insisted that the commando issue was a domestic affair. The Arab League's mediators were received with courtesy and frustrated in every attempt to carry out their orders. By April the chief civilian mediator, a Tunisian ex-premier, had given up in disgust and departed. He was preceded by the Egyptian general who headed the military observation team. A mutual effort to mediate was made by Saudi Arabia's King Faisal and Egyptian President Anwar Sadat. It, too, was fruitless except in achieving a measure of improvement in Saudi-Egyptian relations. There was no Nasser to come once more to the rescue of the commandos. On June 30, 1971, a confident King Hussein rejected a Saudi-Egyptian plan for cooperation between the Palestinian movement and the Jordanian government.[2]

The price paid by King Hussein's government for its commando policy was not high. Diplomatic relations were severed by Iraq and Syria and their frontiers were closed to all trade and commerce. This action affected 75 percent of Jordan's exports. Yet Iraq had resumed trade relations by October, and Syria followed suit soon after. The suspension of diplomatic relations by Algeria was meaningless and Colonel Qaddafi's claim that Libya was ready to send its armed forces to the aid of the Palestinians if another regime were willing to do likewise was hardly damaging to the Amman government.

The Jordanian economy was weakened as much by the flight of private capital to safe havens in European banks and the resultant interruption of commerce as by protracted fighting. These were temporary

---

[2]The plan assumed a spirit of cooperation among Palestinian leaders which had never existed. Long before July 1971, greater fissures appeared in the movement, caused by the question of negotiations with the Jordanian government. Earlier disputes were over tactics. The leader of *Fatah* and the leaky umbrella which was the Palestine Liberation Organization, Yassir Arafat, favored negotiation and opposed terrorism and hijackings. George Habbash of the Popular Front for the Liberation of Palestine, which professed a "Marxist-Guevarist" orientation, opposed negotiation and supported terrorism, hijackings, or any other spectacular act which, in Habbash's flawed logic, emphasized Palestinian determination to regain their homeland. The Marxist but less activist Popular Democratic Front for the Liberation of Palestine headed by Naif Hawatmeh opposed negotiation. Habbash's hand had been strengthened by the support of Libya's strongman, Colonel Qaddafi, who in February 1971 provided the PFLP with nearly $1 million for its hijacking program. Some of the money went into a publication fund, with the result that, as indicated in Chapter 1, the Marxist content of PFLP writings alienated the Libyan leader and dried up this source of support. Habbash was further weakened by the defection of younger PFLP members in March 1972. The split followed the hijacking to Aden of a Lufthansa aircraft enroute from India to Europe. The splinter group denounced air piracy as diversionary and called for a campaign to achieve a united Palestinian movement. Their failure suggests that the various groups have become institutionalized, but their defection was a boost for Yassir Arafat when he needed it most.

inconveniences, quickly rectified by generous emergency aid. Grants and loans from Great Britain, the Federal Republic of Germany, the United States, and the World Bank had been secured by November 1970. President Nixon requested congressional approval of a $30 million military aid package to the Hussein regime at the same time, shortly to be followed by a $10 million International Monetary Fund loan to underwrite highway and school construction. Nor did all of the largesse come from the West. Saudi Arabia, Abu Dhabi, and Oman responded with traditional generosity. Even before the commando threat had been eliminated, repairs to the East Ghor Canal, badly damaged in an earlier Israeli reprisal raid, were begun.

The Jordanian budget showed a deficit of $25 million in 1971, but a large stride toward solvency was made with a United States aid agreement providing $15 million to help cover the debt. The greatest price Hussein paid for his policy was the loss of his most gifted and ruthless lieutenant. In November 1971, Prime Minister Wasfi Tal was assassinated while attending a meeting of the Arab League Joint Defense Council in Cairo. The three assassins described themselves as Palestinians and members of the "Black September" organization. In the perspective of history the loss of Tal may be considered a small price, but there are other bullets and other assassins who await their opportunity to deal with Hussein as the personification of treason to the cause of Palestine.

During the months of the antiguerrilla campaign, the Jordanians had been in contact with Israeli officials. As early as December 1970, Hussein stated that a general Middle Eastern settlement would permit a reexamination of the status of the West Bank. Establishment of a West Bank political entity independent of Israel and Jordan was indicated as a possibility. Following talks in London with Prime Minister Heath and Foreign Secretary Home, in Washington with President Nixon and Defense Secretary Laird, and in Bonn with Chancellor Brandt, Hussein announced through his Foreign Minister Abdullah Salah that, under certain circumstances, Jordan would consider recognizing Israel. The king was to further ingratiate himself with his American sponsors by attempting to organize Arab support, including military supplies, for Pakistan in its war with India over the future of Bangla Desh.

Although Hussein was willing to court the West for political and economic support to the extent that he gave lip service to an independent West Bank, he remained a Hashemite monarch, the last of the line, whose grandfather had transformed Jordan from an emirate to a kingdom by annexing that part of Palestine which was the West Bank. He was aware not only of Western proposals for a Palestinian entity but also of the extent to which Israel had consolidated its grip on the West Bank. By

March 1972 twelve new Israeli settlements had been founded there, while as many as forty thousand Arabs had foresaken agriculture and other pursuits to find more remunerative employment in Israeli industries. The result was a counsel of desperation. In the same month Hussein announced a plan for a "United Arab Kingdom" comprised of two regions, with Amman as the central and eastern regional capital and Jerusalem as the western regional capital. Predictably, he was denounced by every faction of the Palestinian movement. The plan also gave President Sadat an inexpensive means of refurbishing an image tarnished by his support of American, Four Power, and United Nations peace initiatives; hence the harsh condemnations which accompanied the severance of diplomatic relations with the Amman regime. The Israeli reaction was more muted, giving rise to speculation about further contacts between the two countries. The most emphatic rejection—not only of Hussein's proposals but also of the tactics and objectives of guerrilla organizations—came two months later when municipal elections were completed on the West Bank. Neither Hussein's pleas nor terrorist threats affected the voters. Over 85 percent of the electorate turned out to express a deeply felt desire for an opportunity to lead normal lives. The number of traditional leaders unseated in the elections was evidence that West Bank Palestinians wanted to find a means of coexisting with Israel under a leadership independent of both Hashemites and commandos. For the commandos, it was a defeat not less significant than that which they experienced at the hands of Hussein's soldiers in the months of September 1970 and July 1971.

Throughout 1972 Hussein continued his efforts to reestablish the Hashemite standard west of the Jordan River. Several thousand Jordanian passports were provided to Gaza residents, primarily to facilitate student travel to foreign institutions of higher learning. Attempts were made to secure the systematic passage of Gaza product to markets in Amman and other East Bank cities. There even may have been an element of *Realpolitik* in Hussein's divorce of his English wife and marriage to a lissome Palestinian, Alia Tuqan, although the Tuqans had lost some of their standing in the Palestinian community as a result of long, devoted service to the Hashemite house.

Yet by 1973 it was clear that a "United Kingdom" had eluded Hussein. Israeli progress in integrating the West Bank into its economy indicated that Jordanian planning should not be conditioned by the possibility of an Arab-Israeli settlement, but should be based upon the kingdom east of the river, supported by foreign subsidies, by the remittances of emigré workers, by tax revenues (which have climbed back to the 1968 level of $32 million), and by exports which reached a post-1967 high of $80 million in 1972.

In the final analysis, Hussein is not badly off in his garrison state. His security forces have been improved, his army reequipped and modernized in order to carry out its primary mission—preserving the Hashemite dynasty. Tourists are visiting Jerash and Petra once again (although in smaller numbers), the industrial and agricultural infrastructure of the country continues to expand, and the once bare hills of Transjordan are dotted with afforestation projects. The most accomplished walker of the political tightrope in the Arab world moves on, not daring to take a backward glance.

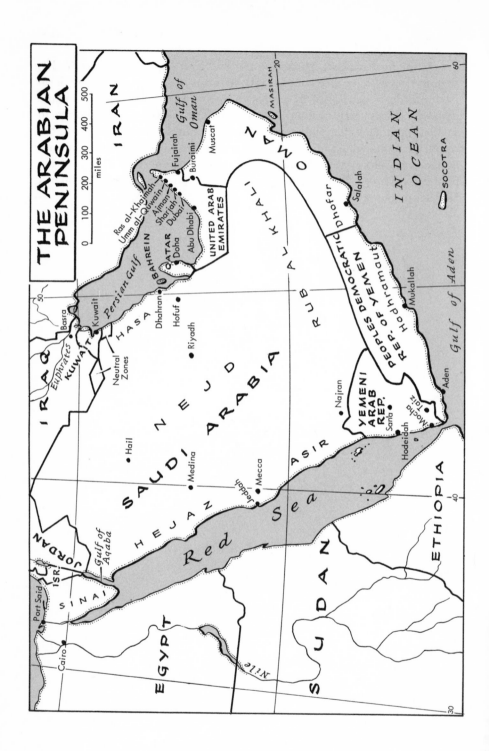

THE ARABIAN PENINSULA

5

THE ARABIAN
PENINSULA

The Arabic name for the Arabian Peninsula, *Jezirat al-Arabiyya*, "Island of the Arabs," is accurate in all but the strictest geographical sense. The land stretches more than a thousand miles south and east of the Wadi Sirhan, near Saudi Arabia's frontier with Jordan. It differs so utterly from countries of the Crescent described in the foregoing pages that it must be regarded as a place apart, differing as Malta differs from the two continental countries which are but a short air journey away—Libya and Italy.

It is not that one is the desert and the other is the sown. Considerable cultivation and verdant highland areas are found in the Arabian Peninsula just as extensive stretches of desert are found in the triangle between Damascus, Baghdad, and Amman. Moreover, there are strong links between the two—commercial ties that reach back to antiquity, Islam, more recent forms of political association such as the Arab League, and many other connections based upon modern transportation and communications. The Arabian Peninsula is the heartland of the Arabs and the heartland of Islam. In the view of peninsular Arabs, people north of the Wadi Sirhan have been Arabized and Islamicized. It matters not that Damascus and Baghdad were the seats of great caliphates, nor that for centuries the Prophet's viceroy on earth was a Turkish sovereign resident in Constantinople. The land trodden by Mohammed lies between Mecca and Medina.

Five times daily the Muslim faithful—a Hadhrami merchant in Sumatra perhaps, or a Berber in the Atlas Mountains of Morocco, a Turcoman in the Soviet Union, a Montenegrin near the Adriatic shore—orients himself to face the Ka'aba in Mecca before beginning the ritual prayer. Nor does it matter that the Hejaz, the province which contains two of the three most important shrine cities—Mecca and Medina (the third being Jerusalem)—has become, through thirteen centuries of pilgrimage, one of the most racially heterogeneous regions on earth. Those pilgrims who did not return to distant homelands have become Arabized as well and, by virtue of living near the Ka'aba, somehow more Arab than, say, an Iraqi or an Egyptian. The Island of the Arabs has clung to traditional methods and observances with more tenacity than other parts of the Arab world. This, too, has acted to make it a place apart.

This stronghold of tradition has been under assault since World War II and the pace of change, of modernization, has accelerated with each year since 1946. Many alterations in mode and outlook can be ascribed to the vast revenues derived from petroleum products. But change means more than jet aircraft, paved roads, schools, refrigeration, and air conditioning. Trade unions, republican regimes, and the introduction of alien ideologies also are working their influences on the Arabs of the Peninsula. The insular character of life in this great land mass cannot endure much longer.

Much more archeological evidence must be found and sifted before a comprehensive history of the Arabian Peninsula in antiquity can be written. Of the hundreds of sites in northern Hejaz alone, only a few, such as Medinat Salha, a well-known Nabatean settlement along the north-south caravan route, have been subjected to scientific investigation. The caravan route itself is often referred to as the Incense Road because of the important trade in frankincense produced in the South Arabian kingdoms of Ma'in, Qataban, and Saba (Sheba) for centuries before the birth of Christ. Mediterranean peoples envied these kingdoms because it was assumed that they were also the source of the silks and spices of the East that landed in the ports of South Arabia for onward transport overland. Before Hippalus instructed navigators in the art of using the seasonal monsoons on the passage to and from India, the imagined riches of South Arabia had lured the Tenth Legion of Aelius Gallus to its tragic destiny. Ethiopian and Achaemenid Persian occupation followed—the latter in about A.D. 570—before the tide of Islam swept over South Arabia in the seventh century.

The principal maritime trade route of antiquity conferred importance upon Oman and the Persian Gulf.[1] The head of the Gulf was linked with the Caspian, Black, and Mediterranean Seas by the Tigris and Euphrates and by caravan routes. The Persian Gulf was additionally important because the people along its shores lived from early times by pearling as well as fishing and plundering.

The Sumerians had trade relations with Bahrain, the southern Gulf, and Oman before 1800 B.C. These ties were reestablished in the Assyrian era. Recent excavations in Bahrain, Dubai, and the Buraimi Oasis indicate the great influence of the early Mesopotamian civilizations in these areas. Alexander the Great's admiral, Nearchos, entered the Persian Gulf through the Straits of Hormuz in command of vessels transporting part of his army homeward. At about this time Gerra ('Uqair), on the mainland shore west of Qatar, was developing as a commercial center and in the third century B.C. it became an outpost of the Chaldean civilization. Mesopotamian influence declined and the next imperial standard to be raised, further to the north of Gerra, was that of Trajan (A.D. 116). His stay was brief and had little effect on the coastal inhabitants.

Ancient Persia looked to Oman and the southern shore of the Gulf as areas to be conquered and exploited. The Persian southwesterly thrust has deep historical roots. The Achaemenid presence in the southern Arabian Peninsula extended from the sixth to the fourth century B.C., after which there was little activity until the Sassanid invasion early in the third century A.D. Sassanid efforts to establish a form of colonial domination over the fertile coastal area northwest of Muscat were only moderately successful until the fifth century, when Persian influence reached unprecedented heights. It remained at a high level until about one hundred years before Islam penetrated southeastern Arabia.

Arab tribal movement throughout the Peninsula is a story of bewildering complexity. Much of the migration had an economic motivation, such as the Yemeni invasion of Oman after the collapse of the Marib Dam northeast of San'a had rendered much land uncultivable. The shift of a large section of the Ka'b tribe from the southern Gulf to what is now Iranian territory, east of Abadan Island, followed seasons of poor fishing and unsuccessful pearling operations. The transformation of the nomadic 'Utub tribesmen of northern Arabia to urban mercantile pursuits in Bahrain and Kuwait came after their flocks had been carried off repeatedly by their Shammar rivals, whose growing strength in any

---

[1]The established geographic name for this body of water has fallen prey to nationalism. For centuries, the southern end of the Red Sea has been known as the Arabian Gulf, but in recent years the Persian Gulf has also become "Arabian" throughout the Arab world.

event threatened the 'Utub hold upon adequate grazing land. The promise of better economic opportunities took the ancestors of Saudi Arabia's King Faisal from Qatif on the Persian Gulf to central Arabia, where they founded Dar'iyah near the modern capital city of Riyadh. Arab movement throughout the Peninsula is explained to a great extent by the missionary fervor, or even militancy, with which the Prophet's followers fanned out from Hejaz once the Christians and Jews were no longer the only "People of the Book."

Christianity, a frail transplant in Arabia, quickly succumbed to Islam. There were churches in San'a, Aden, and several parts of Oman, but slight progress had been made against pagan indifference and polytheistic beliefs before the green banners of Islam were raised. The Jewish community survived because of its highly skilled artisans and merchants. A considerable Jewish population existed in Yemen until 1948 when, with varying degrees of reluctance, the great majority permitted themselves to be transported to the new state of Israel. Small Jewish colonies still live in northern Yemen, near Sada, proud of visage, content with their lot, and undisturbed by their Muslim neighbors.

The physical environment of the Arabian Peninsula renders the delimitation of boundaries difficult, and there are still many areas in dispute. Tribal allegiances, the levying and payment of tribute, access to water resources and grazing land figure prominently in boundary questions. Mountainous regions in the Peninsula have provided places of refuge for minor Islamic sects or even cultural or ethnic minorities such as the Dhofari people who live in the hills above Salalah near the western marches of the Sultanate of Oman. A brief sketch of the Peninsula's geographic features therefore might serve as a useful introduction to a country-by-country survey of this vast area.

The coastal plain along the Red Sea, long known as the Tihama (a Semitic word meaning "lowland"), is largely barren. Now only the coastal areas of Asir (a province of Saudi Arabia) and Yemen are considered to be the Tihama. To the north the coastal plain is considered as part of Hejaz, a word meaning "barrier," which in early times was applied only to the mountain range dividing interior Nejd from the coastal plain. The western slopes of the mountains rise precipitately and therefore support little agriculture. In Asir there are peaks reaching nine thousand feet and in the Yemeni Arab Republic they are higher still, giving credence to a description of prerevolutionary Yemen as "a series of tiny mountainside republics, each having little to do with the other." The mountains are responsible for an average annual rainfall of about twelve inches. Vegetation is rich, but in recent years drought conditions have prevailed, bringing further misery to peoples suffering the devastating effects of war.

The eastern slopes of the mountains drop off more gradually into Nejd, the heart of Arabia. There is much terracing for agricultural purposes and the water supply is usually adequate. Nejd is a plateau bounded by desert areas—the Great Nefud, north of Ha'il, and the vast Rub al-Khali or Empty Quarter in the south. There is also the smaller but equally barren region known as the Dahna, a narrow desert area on a northwest-southeast axis that lies across the direct route between Riyadh and Hofuf, the old capital of Hasa, Saudi Arabia's eastern province. A most important feature of Nejd is the oasis of al-Kharj, southeast of Riyadh, which supports considerable agriculture with its "water pits." Nejd slants gradually down to Hasa and the Persian Gulf.

The Hasa province of Saudi Arabia, Kuwait, the Neutral Zone jointly administered by the two countries, many of the coastal shaikhdoms, and the Sultanate of Oman are petroleum producers, some with offshore as well as mainland sources. In much of eastern Arabia and the southern Gulf, the derricks, gas-oil separator plants ("gosps"), and other machinery for oil production are the principal features of an otherwise lunar landscape. But the terrain is not completely unrelieved. Welcome exceptions are the well-watered oases of Hofuf, Qatif, and Sufwa in the province of Hasa.

Hofuf, with its four springs, supports vast date cultivation, has oleander-lined, aquamarine pools, and furnishes a striking contrast to the howling desert wilderness around it. Its Ottoman fort, a monument to Midhat Pasha's misspent energies, adds to its charm. However, in recent years the introduction of traffic lights, automated date packing plants, and a furniture factory (the wood, of course, is imported) has been hard on those who have fallen under the spell of the old Arabia.

East of the Yemeni mountains and highlands, east-northeast on the compass from Aden, is Hadhramaut, the high plateau bounded to landward by the Rub al-Khali, and extending for eight hundred miles through the People's Democratic Republic of Yemen. Associated with Britain until 1967, this area was formerly divided into the Western Aden Protectorate and Eastern Aden Protectorate. It is thought that the name Hadhramaut comes from a Himyarite term, which passed into classical Arabic, denoting an area both densely populated and under intensive cultivation. If so, it must refer to a highly developed riverine civilization of several thousand years ago, before the great Wadi Hadhramaut dried up and pushed its inhabitants outward to other pursuits, mercantile and maritime.

Bounding the Hadhramaut to the east are the forested and grassy slopes of the Qarah Mountains, rising little more than three thousand feet in the westernmost province of Oman, Dhofar. To Salalah, the provincial capital, on the Indian Ocean shore, the mountain people bring firewood to trade for products from the *suqs* of the city. The coastal region receives monsoon rains which support cocoanut plantations and some farming.

The coast east of Dhofar to the cape which bears the name of Ras al-Hadd is desolate and virtually uninhabited, for the life-giving monsoon does not reach that far. Rounding the cape and moving north to Muscat, the terrain roughens and the sparse population is supported largely by fishing. The principal settlement, Sur, just up the coast from Ras al-Hadd, was one of the great sally-ports for Arab pirates and slave traders before they succumbed to the forceful presence of the Royal Navy and Bombay Marine in the nineteenth century.

Muscat's tiny harbor, dominated by two Portuguese forts on promontories behind it, is no longer crowded with the ships whose crews for centuries have carved the names of their vessels into the stone cliffs which in many places rise almost vertically from its waters. Most modern vessels unload by lighter at Matrah, the commercial center of the Omani coast a few miles further north. A deepwater jetty is under construction there, alongside which six large freighters will be able to moor at one time.

Beyond Matrah the Batinah Coast begins, narrow and fertile, well watered by streams rushing down the slopes of the ten-thousand-foot *massif* behind it known as the Jebel Akhdar (Green Mountain). The mountains of Jebel Akhdar are without timber and nearly devoid of other vegetation, but in the high valleys there is rich soil for agriculture. The Batinah Coast is a succession of palm gardens and villages. Soon markets will be more accessible for the fish, fruit, and vegetables of the region, for a major road project to link Matrah and Sohar was begun in 1971. Another will cross the Hajar range, of which the Jebel Akhdar is the high southern portion, and will improve surface transportation between Sohar and the Buraimi Oasis.[2] A paved highway already exists between Buraimi (where partisans of the old Arabia are now tempted by the air-conditioned al-Ayn Hilton Hotel) and Abu Dhabi on the Trucial Coast.

The Batinah Coast, backed by the Hajar range, stretches north through the Shaikhdom of Fujairah, which divides Omani territory, to Ras al-Musandam where the southern shore of the Persian Gulf begins. The terrain is dramatic from Ras al-Musandam to Ras al-Khaimah.

---

[2] The oasis is at the Oman-Abu Dhabi frontier. Two of its eight villages are under Omani administration and the others are controlled by Abu Dhabi. All eight are claimed by Saudi Arabia.

Mountains slope down directly into the sea, broken by fjords and an occasional valley leading into confined areas of plain. In contrast to the other shaikhdoms of the Trucial Coast, Ras al-Khaimah is a fertile area. Wealthy citizens of Dubai, including the ruling shaikh, have purchased farmland there and have built villas as weekend retreats.

Beyond Ras al-Khaimah through the rest of the Trucial Coast, the Qatar Peninsula, Hasa, and Kuwait, the terrain is largely the same. Low-lying sandy beaches give way to gravelly deserts. There are many inlets, of which the Dubai Creek is the most picturesque. Teeming with colorful native craft, it is the most important entrepot port of the region. The Shaikhdom of Dubai has been well described as "the Venice of the Persian Gulf." Off the Arab shore of the Gulf are many small islands, some nothing more than sand banks and exposed coral reefs. An exception, both in size and in the availability of a good supply of fresh water, is Bahrain.

This, then, is the Arabian Peninsula. Not many years ago a correspondent described the Yemen of the Zeidi Imams as "rushing headlong into the tenth century." Now, in every corner of the Peninsula, the confrontation with the twentieth century is taking many forms.

Saudi Arabia

The beginnings of the ruling house of Saudi Arabia are traceable to the departure of King Faisal's ancestors from the Qatif Oasis in the middle of the fifteenth century. Their destination was Nejd in central Arabia where, through the beneficence of a relative, they were able to take possession of the lands upon which Dar'iyah, the old Saudi capital, was built. For many decades Dar'iyah was one of a number of independent city-states in central Arabia. Its inhabitants eked out a bare existence from the plantations they developed and by supplying provisions to caravans—the best profits coming from the great pilgrimage caravans between Hasa and Mecca. To the northwest of Dar'iyah was the more prosperous Buraida, on the caravan route to the Holy Places from Mesopotamia and Persia, from whence the *hadjis* followed the Wadi Rima after provisioning at Zubair (near Basra) or Kuwait. Prosperity, however, was an open invitation to raids by the Sherifian rulers of Mecca, who had been established in the Hejaz since the tenth century and who regarded Nejd as a hunting ground to be despoiled at will. Arabia's chroniclers and historians, such as the great ibn Bishr, were assisted by a well developed oral tradition in keeping alive the memory of such punitive and revenue-gathering incursions. It must have afforded Abdul Aziz ibn Saud of Nejd the greatest satisfaction to realize what a large and venerable score he was settling by driving the Sherifians, by then transformed into three Hashemite dynasties (Hejaz, Transjordan, and Iraq) out of Hejaz in 1925.

The expansionist activities of the founders of Dar'iyah were modest.

Sons grew up and went to other parts of Nejd where farming and grazing land was available. Raids and counter-raids were launched against rival claimants to land and water supplies. Alliances between clans were made and broken. Elsewhere, in what was to become the Kingdom of Saudi Arabia, competing forces were greater in numbers and resources. The Sherifian theocracy in Hejaz could control the Red Sea coastal area between Yenbo and Jizan only through appeasement of the Yemeni Imams and political vassalage to the Mamluk Sultans at Cairo. At various times Mamluk rulers stationed troops in Mecca and maintained representatives with proconsular powers at Jeddah.

With the arrival of the Portuguese in the Indian Ocean at the end of the fifteenth century, a new phase began. Vasco da Gama and his successors took control of a vast oceangoing *dhow* trade which had been dominated previously by the Arabs of Oman and South Arabia. Portuguese supremacy in the Indian Ocean and her use of the Cape route disrupted Arab trade with Europe via the Gulf of Aden, Jeddah, the Gulf of Suez, and Cairo. Nor was this threat to Mamluk prosperity all, for the conviction became widespread that the Portuguese thrust was directed against Islam and that it was no less important than the campaigns that had driven Muslims out of the Iberian Peninsula. These factors decided the Mamluks upon transforming southwestern Arabia into a defensive bastion against Portuguese imperialism. The people of the Hejaz, and of Jeddah in particular, suffered greatly from the excesses and exactions of the expanded Mamluk force.

The Red Sea campaign ended with the eclipse of the Mamluk Sultanate by the armies of Selim the Dread in 1517, when Egypt and Syria became Ottoman provinces.[1] The Sherifians then became satraps of the Ottomans, answerable, through Selim's delegate in Cairo, to the Grand Seigneur at Constantinople, in whose name prayers were read out at Mecca. A situation resulted which was to be repeated again and again into the twentieth century: the religious ties between Mecca and the great seat of Muslim learning, al-Azhar, and the commercial links between Jeddah and the port of Suez were not strong enough to prevent the poisoning of Egyptian-Hejazi relations. Suspicion and hatred arose from Cairo's policy of imposing political subordination upon Hejaz. In taking over the Mamluk challenge to Portuguese hegemony on the seas around the Arabian Peninsula, the Ottomans inflicted more injury on their Hejazi coreligionists than on the infidel, most notably in the Red Sea naval expedition of 1538.

---

[1]Mamluk forces thus cut off at Taiz, in Yemen, were joined by refugees from the force previously occupying Jeddah and in time entered the service of the Ottoman Sultan.

Because of the presence of the Holy Places, a greater measure of political organization existed in the Hejaz than in Nejd or Hasa. The latter had been dominated by tribal confederations ever since the Carmathians, the "military socialists" whose guilds were one of several heretical factions in early Islam, were driven out in 966. The Ottoman armies arrived in 1590; their occupation lasted only until 1669, when the Banu Khalid tribe expelled their weakened garrisons. The Sultan's banner would not fly again in eastern Arabia until Midhat Pasha's adventures in the 1870s. As the empire went into decline, the Sherifians paid only lip service to the authority of the Sultan-Caliph. Yemen, which had become an Ottoman Pashalic in 1537, was once more ruled by the Zeidi Imamate. Portuguese domination of the maritime routes around Arabia passed briefly to the Dutch and then to the British, who attempted—not entirely successfully, as will be seen—to avoid commitments "to landward" in Arabia. Such developments cleared the way, as it were, for the contest to determine who among the Arabs themselves would forge a transpeninsular political entity.

Close to Dar'iyah lay Uyainah, the town in which the House of Saud's great ally in conquest was born three or four years after the beginning of the eighteenth century. This was the remarkable theologian Mohammed ibn Abdul Wahhab, whose family's reputation as learned exponents of the *Shari'a* (Islamic law) was well established in Nejd. Abdul Wahhab was born into an Arabia in which the Islam of the Prophet Mohammed was not deeply entrenched. Pantheism and polytheistic practices abounded. Rocks and trees were worshiped as divine objects and many Nejdis were unrestrained by any form of religious observance. This situation horrified the young religious fanatic—as he had become—and he set about arming himself to combat it and to return Islam to the pristine purity of the seventh century. In arming himself, Abdul Wahhab also armed the House of Saud, although that did not become manifest until he was about forty years of age.

After religious instruction at home and a first pilgrimage to Mecca, this "Nejdi Oliver Cromwell" studied for a time in Medina, Basra, and various places in Hasa. He was appalled by the sumptuousness of Shiite pilgrims from Persia who passed through Nejd on the Basra-Buraida route of the *hijrah*. Driven out of Basra for attacking what he considered to be false accretions to Islamic doctrine, Abdul Wahhab made a name for himself after his return to Nejd by his vigorous espousal of the doctrine of God's Oneness. Wahhabism, as his detractors termed his beliefs and as it became known to Westerners, was in his view and in the view of his adherents an Islamic Unitarianism. The term *tauhid*, oneness, was more than a repudiation of all but the Islam propagated by the Prophet; it was a call to battle against the worship of saints and objects. Trees were felled, tombs destroyed, and in time Abdul Wahhab's militancy caused his expulsion from Uyainah. The greatest pressure for his expulsion came from the paramount shaikh of the Banu Khalid, the dominant tribe in Hasa, where there was still a considerable Shiite population.[2]

In resettling, Abdul Wahhab made the fateful choice of Dar'iyah. In 1744 the great reformer enlisted Mohammed ibn Saud to undertake *jihad*, the holiest of holy wars, for the purpose of imposing a purified Islam on Nejd and, in time, all of Arabia. Converts to Wahhabism swelled the population of Dar'iyah and raiding expeditions soon began. The beduin were plundered in the name of Islamic purity. In the twenty-one years before Mohammed ibn Saud died, much of Nejd fell under Wahhabi sway. An exception was Riyadh. But in 1765 Abdul Wahhab renewed the alliance of 1744, this time with Abdul Aziz, Mohammed ibn Saud's son, and in another eight years Riyadh surrendered.

The Sherifian response to Wahhabism was to place a ban on Wahhabi pilgrimages to the Holy Places. Raiding between the Banu Khalid of Hasa and the Wahhabis continued for many years. The Ismaelites, a sect which had evolved from the Shiite branch of Islam, invaded Nejd in the 1760s and 1770s from their stronghold in Asir, the region between Hejaz and Yemen. These attacks were repulsed with difficulty. The invasion of Nejd by the Muntafiq, the tribal confederation of southern Iraq, acting on the orders of a Georgian Mamluk Pasha of Baghdad, posed less of a problem. The Wahhabis defeated this expedition less through military skill than by the pervasive appeal of their doctrine. A number of converts from the Muntafiq ranks remained in Nejd.

When Abdul Wahhab died in 1792 his followers controlled a vast area from northernmost Arabia to the Rub al-Khali. The oases of Qatif and Hofuf in Hasa fell to Abdul Aziz shortly after the reformer's death. These were acquired by the sword, but to the south and east, in what is now known as the Trucial Coast, Wahhabism was widely accepted without recourse to such measures. By the end of the century a representative of Abdul Aziz was established in the strategic Buraimi Oasis. His presence there is one of the reasons for the continuing claim of modern Saudi Arabia to sovereignty over that area.

Hejaz remained closed to the Wahhabis. Before Abdul Wahhab's

---

[2]Today the only Shiites native to Hasa dwell in the Qatif Oasis, but economic development has attracted many other "schismatics" such as Persian, Pakistani, and Indian Shiites, Yemeni Zeidis, and Ibadhis from Oman, to say nothing of Goanese Catholics and Lebanese and Western Christians who are employed there in considerable numbers.

death, Sherif Ghalib ibn Musa'id began an anti-Wahhabi campaign during which Nejd was invaded. This war, for such it became, continued until the death of Abdul Aziz in 1803. But in his last days he had the satisfaction of knowing that the marcher lords of the Nejd-Hejaz frontier were swelling the Wahhabi ranks and that the Sherifians were in retreat.

The Wahhabis already had struck across the northern desert of the Euphrates, descending upon the Shiite shrine city of Karbala in 1801. After stripping off the silver and gold ornamentation on the tomb of Hussein, the Prophet's grandson, the city and surrounding district were thoroughly ransacked. Another Wahhabi column penetrated far into Syria, threatening Damascus. But the main effort was reserved for Mecca. It fell to Saud, son of Abdul Aziz, and his puritan fanatics in 1803. Anything associated with saint worship, earthly pleasures, or practices regarded to be idolatrous was destroyed. The same treatment was accorded to Medina in 1805. The Wahhabi campaigns had long been a subject of concern to the Sublime Porte, but the Ottoman Empire's embroilment in the Napoleonic Wars limited its response to the Pasha of Baghdad's pleas that it undertake punitive expeditions. Therefore, the House of Saud was untroubled by external forces for another decade. Recognizing that nine centuries of Sherifian control over the Hejaz should not be terminated until the Wahhabis had developed administrative abilities commensurate with their martial skills, Saud ibn Abdul Aziz permitted Sherif Ghalib to carry on in Mecca as his delegate. During the years following the fall of Medina, Wahhabi leaders placed much emphasis on improving the government of their territories, reforming the administration of *Shari'a* law, and eliminating petty squabbling and blood feuds between subject tribes.

The work of nation-building was ended by an Ottoman-sponsored invasion of Hejaz under the direction of the Sultan's viceroy in Cairo, the redoubtable Mohammed Ali. After initial successes against the invaders, the siege artillery and other advanced weaponry of the Ottoman levies broke Wahhabi resistance. By 1814 Medina and Mecca had fallen and Saud ibn Abdul Aziz was regrouping his forces on the Nejdi frontier. He died there before he could lead a counterattack. Abdul Aziz was succeeded by his ineffectual son, Abdullah ibn Saud. The young heir to the Wahhabi legacy was no match for the thrusting determination of Ibrahim Pasha, Mohammed Ali's son and field commander. Dar'iyah fell after a siege of five months and was destroyed on Mohammed Ali's orders, an action he regarded as symbolic of the eclipse of Wahhabi power in Arabia.

After the destruction of Dar'iyah, Abdullah ibn Saud and other Wahhabi leaders were carried off to Cairo, from whence Abdullah was taken to Constantinople to be exhibited to the Sultan and his ministers before being executed. The House of Saud was now taken firmly under the control of Abdullah's uncle, Turki ibn Abdullah, who set about organizing opposition to the force occupying Nejd. Although the occupation was in the name of the Ottoman Empire, it was regarded by the Nejdis as Egyptian. As such, it is a historical legacy which played a part in determining Saudi reaction to Egyptian policies and activities in the Arabian Peninsula during the era of Gamal Abdul Nasser.

By 1824, Turki controlled Riyadh, which from that day forward was recognized and fought for as the capital city of Nejd and such territories as became subject to Nejdi rule. The recrudescence of Wahhabi strength confronted the Egyptians with the prospect of being cut off from their home base. Accordingly, Mohammed Ali ordered the withdrawal of his near mutinous garrison to Hejaz. Turki's forces then reasserted the authority of the House of Saud in Hasa. The vigor of his rule found expression in his espousal of the stern religious principles of Wahhabism. His governors and other officials were strictly supervised and quickly remover if evidence of partiality or cruelty was produced.

The Saudi state was making an impressive recovery when Turki was struck down by a dissident family member. His son Faisal was no less vigorous than his father had been, and indeed was his superior in qualities of leadership, but he had difficulty asserting his authority in the chaos which followed his father's assassination. The Banu Khalid of Hasa and the Khalifahs (who were established in Qatar and Bahrain, and who paid *zakat*, or tribute, to the Saudis) attempted to throw off Nejdi rule. Mohammed Ali, who had sundered his ties with Constantinople, was also encouraged to undertake another Arabian venture. He envisioned a Muslim Empire, ruled from Cairo, stretching from the Arabian Peninsula to the Persian frontiers. His Syrian campaign was but one aspect of a larger strategy, and in 1834 he recommenced operations in Arabia.

Mohammed Ali's commanders had first to deal with the Egyptian garrison of Hejaz, which had mutinied and marched southward on a pillaging expedition through the Tihama, eventually taking over the Yemeni port cities of Hodeidah and Mocha. Fresh troops from Egypt were transported down the Red Sea to occupy the coastal plain and reincorporate the mutineers into the Egyptian force after exemplary punishments had been inflicted. The Zeidi Imam of San'a was compelled to recognize Egyptian paramountcy in Yemen until 1840.

The Egyptians now turned their attention to Nejd and by 1837 Riyadh was in their hands after they had effectively used Khalid ibn Saud, Abdullah's brother, as a rival claimant to Faisal ibn Turki. Khalid had been a prisoner in Cairo since 1818 when Abdullah went to his fate in Constantinople in 1837 it was Faisal's turn to go as a prisoner to Cairo. During this period Egypt's proconsul in Nejd and Hasa was the army commander Khurshid Pasha a tough Georgian Mamluk. It was transparently clear to the people of Riyadh by 1838 that Khalid ibn Saud was a cipher, answerable only to his Egyptian masters.

For Mohammed Ali, operations in Nejd and Hasa were steps along the way to Baghdad, perhaps as the southern pincer of a campaign in which another army in Syria would strike at Mosul and then the Mesopotamian capital. But in 1840 the Egyptian grand design collapsed. Moves on the European political chessboard, backed by a brief military campaign, restored Syria to Ottoman hegemony and Egypt to a nominal tributary relationship to the Sultan. For the second time in two decades an Egyptian expeditionary force evacuated Nejd.

Khalid ibn Saud did not long survive the departure of Khurshid Pasha. With Faisal ibn Turki still locked up in Cairo, rival claimants to the dominant position in the House of Saud came forward. For three years Nejd remained in the uncertain grasp of Abdullah ibn Thunaiyan, a member of a Saudi cadet branch. Then, in 1843, Faisal ibn Turki escaped or was released from prison. Contemporary writers hint that his freedom was brought about with the complicity of Abbas Pasha who would become Khedive in 1849. Faisal ruled until 1865 and his reputation as the most outstanding ruler of the House of Saud remained unchallenged until the reign of his grandson, Abdul Aziz ibn Saud. Stability, prosperity, and expansion are the key words to describe Faisal ibn Turki's era. At the end of his life, the Saudi writ ran firmly from Nejd through Hasa and far beyond the Buraimi Oasis to the interior of Oman. Faisal improved his father's administrative policies, stimulated the diversification of economic activities as never before, brought peace to his domains through the energetic application of rough justice, and succeeded in building a Saudi state—in every way but one.

No workable agreement on succession had been arranged by the time of Faisal's death. The resultant chaos must have impressed itself deeply on the great Abdul Aziz ibn Saud when he reached the end of his long life, for the impression quite obviously remains with his son, Saudi Arabia's present ruler. After 1865, the structure erected by Faisal ibn Turki was destroyed by the hostility of two sons who vied for primacy at Riyadh. Abdullah ibn Faisal, the eldest son, had given ample evidence of his unfitness to rule before his father died. Faisal's second son Saud took this evidence seriously and recruited support for his claim to succession in Asir and on the frontiers of Yemen. The first battle took place within months of Abdullah's accession and the challenger was narrowly defeated. Years of agitation and preparation followed, with Saud using the Buraimi Oasis as his base of operations. By 1870 Hasa had capitulated and in another year Abdullah was a fugitive and Saud established at Riyadh.

Saud's victory was accomplished at the price of spreading anarchy—to which famine was an acccomplice of appalling effectiveness—throughout the lands of which Faisal ibn Turki had been so firmly the master. Nor was that all. That energetic modernizer, Midhat Pasha, then Governor-General of the Pashalic of Baghdad, saw in the situation an opportunity to add military laurels to those he had earned as an administrator. Hofuf was besieged by the Pasha's troops landed from Basra at Qatif and supported by an overland column. By the end of 1871 the second Ottoman occupation of Hasa was established and Abdullah ibn Faisal was a prisoner of the Turks, to whom he had gone seeking refuge from his brother. In the ensuing two years the inhabitants of Riyadh revolted, forcing Saud to decamp. They welcomed the return of Abdullah, who had escaped from Hofuf, but within months the gates of the city were once again opened to Saud, who had recruited sufficient support to send his brother into exile.

The House of Saud was challenged not only to the east in Hasa but also in the northern reaches of Arabia. The Rashidis of Ha'il, capital of Jebel Shammar, had long governed that extensive territory on behalf of the overlords of Riyadh. It was to be expected that the Rashidis would not stand idle during the internecine strife in Nejd, and indeed throughout the 1870s they diligently removed stone after stone from the foundation of the House of Saud. Much help came from the Saudis themselves, for power in Riyadh changed hands with a bewildering rapidity not seen again until the era of the French Third Republic. Saud ibn Faisal died of fever in 1875, passing on his troublemaking proclivities in full measure to his sons. By contrast, Mohammed ibn Rashid combined patience, a capacity for intrigue, good generalship, and effective administration to carry forward his southern strategy. By the middle of the next decade he was the master of virtually all of Nejd. In 1891 the House of Saud collapsed and its survivors fled from Riyadh.

Abdullah ibn Faisal died in 1889 and his place was taken by Abdul Rahman, the youngest son of the great Faisal ibn Turki. Abdul Rahman might have tried to prolong his hold upon Riyadh, the defenses of which had been greatly improved over the years, but so completely had Mohammed ibn Rashid subjugated the surrounding territory that it would simply have been a matter of besieging the city until its inhabitants were starved into submission. Accordingly, he withdrew his family and, after short stays in Bahrain and Qatar, settled in Kuwait to wait upon developments in Nejd.

Nejd was not the only place where the old order was being changed. There it had been transformed by the traditional combination of warfare and tribal alliances, culminating in the triumph of the House of Rashid. But in other parts of the Arabian Peninsula the old order was being dismantled under the influence of altogether new factors—the forces of modernization and Western imperialism. The opening of the Suez Canal turned the Red Sea, a body of water which Muslims considered uniquely their own, into a heavily traveled Western commercial artery. Vessels of the British India Steam Navigation Company and its European competitors were arriving in ever-increasing numbers at ports on the Arabian shore of the Gulf. Germany was attempting to make up for a late start in the great game of empire, broaching plans for a railroad reaching from Berlin beyond Baghdad to the Persian Gulf shore. For not much longer would the chieftains of Arabia vie for power in isolation.

Mohammed ibn Rashid died at Ha'il in 1897, to be succeeded by lesser men. The news caused dismay in Ottoman councils, for the great Rashidi leader had collaborated faithfully with them. Quite another reaction occured in Kuwait, and not only among the exiled Saudis. The new ruler of that emirate, Mubarak ibn Sabah, also possessed political ambitions in full measure.

If Abdul Aziz ibn Rashid lacked most of the qualities of leadership with which his uncle and predecessor had consolidated his rule in Nejd, he did not lack aggressiveness. His raiding activities created alliances between the Sabahs of Kuwait and, among others, the great tribal confederation of the southern Euphrates, the Muntafiq. Not only did he beat off their counterattacks, in which the Saudis participated, but he also would have overrun Kuwait had not Mubarak's British allies held his forces at bay with a naval bombardment. The Rashidi siege of Kuwait was then broken off. At this time, with Kuwait and Muntafiq forces reduced and demoralized, Abdul Aziz ibn Abdul Rahman al-Faisal as-Saud burst upon the stage of Arabian history. He was a boy of eleven when his father, Abdul Rahman, took him from Riyadh to exile in Kuwait. Now, at twenty-one, he recaptured the capital of Saudi Nejd. Abdul Aziz —who would soon be more widely known by the patronymic ibn Saud— carried off this feat of daring with not more than fifty armed men. The Rashidi governor and many of his soldiers were cut down and a surprised citizenry joined in driving the remnants of the occupying force from the city. It was January 15, 1902.

The father of ibn Saud lived until 1928, but from the time of restored

Saudi rule in Riyadh it was as obvious to him as to any disinterested observer that his son should be at the head of the Saudi state. A simple solution was found. During the lifetime of Mohammed ibn Abdul Wahhab, the family of the great Imam had intermarried with that of Mohammed ibn Saud, and as a result, upon the death of the founder of Wahhabism, the title of Imam passed over to the Saudi ruling house. After 1920 it was employed to designate ibn Saud's father as head of the Saudi dynasty. Upon his father's death, ibn Saud became eligible for it, but he had already taken the title of Sultan in 1921 and then given it up five years later in favor of the title of King.

The harshness of Abdul Aziz ibn Rashid's rule permitted ibn Saud to reestablish Saudi authority over the Nejdi heartland with little difficulty. After a series of bloody affrays with ibn Rashid and his Turkish allies from Hasa, in which ibn Saud added to his reputation for bravery and leadership, Nejd was firmly in his control. In the decisive battle in April 1906, Abdul Aziz ibn Rashid was killed. When the House of Saud again confronted that of Rashid it would be on the latter's territory, the Jebel Shammar.

However, the Saudis were harassed from other quarters. The necessity to ransom his brother by acknowledging Ottoman suzerainty over Nejd was the bitter beginning of ibn Saud's relations with Sherif Hussein of Mecca, who had captured the boy while raiding the western marches of the Saudi domain. (Once he was released the Ottoman connection was quickly repudiated.) If the Wahhabis were to regain the vast lands once governed by Faisal ibn Turki and to decrease their vulnerability to Ottoman or Ottoman-sponsored attacks, traditional methods of warfare would not suffice. Thus ibn Saud was impelled to establish a large number of "military settlements" whose inhabitants, the *Ikhwan* (Brethren), were systematically trained and psychologically prepared, by the inculcation of Wahhabite principles, to be the spearhead of any Saudi campaign.

To the east of Riyadh, Hasa was thinly garrisoned by Ottoman troops. Long marches and a stealthy attack delivered up Hofuf to ibn Saud. The Qatif detachment did not contest the oasis. Two counterattacks mounted by sea from Basra were unavailing and at the end of 1913 the vast territory from Kuwait to Qatar was once again under Wahhabi control. Further expansion would call for greater efforts and would be complicated by a number of British "grand designs" for the Middle East—all of which were mooted by Foreign Office, War Office, and British Indian authorities shortly after the Ottoman Empire entered World War I on the side of the Central Powers. Because the Rashidis of Jebel Shammar had placed themselves under Ottoman suzerainty, British proponents of a forward strategy were quick to enter into a treaty relationship with ibn Saud, providing him with a subsidy and encouragement for an attack upon Ha'il. Such encouragement was hardly needed. Much skirmishing and several pitched battles took place in the Jebel Shammar with inconclusive results.

The British failed to incorporate ibn Saud's forces into their larger strategy. More decisive than their own wrangling over means and objectives was ibn Saud's refusal to commit forces to the Arab Revolt. (The term "revolt" could apply to the Sherif of Mecca and other Arab subjects of the Sultan-Caliph, but not to an independent central Arabian chieftain.) He would not weaken Nejd's defenses unless the House of Rashid was won over to participation in the campaign against the Ottoman armies. Nor would he countenance a position in the campaign subordinate to Sherif Hussein of Mecca—a condition upon which the Hashemite ruler of Hejaz insisted. Instead of cooperation there were clashes, with Saudi forces succeeding in supplanting Sherifian control over strategic villages in northeastern Hejaz. The British subsidy to ibn Saud, however, had the important result of preventing him from jeopardizing the Arab Revolt by expanding the conflict with Sherif Hussein—a desperate policy, arising from the need for booty to replace revenue from trade, principally in camels to Syria and Palestine—cut off by the war.

The redrawing of the map of the Middle East by the victorious Allied Powers offered little satisfaction to the House of Saud. Before 1921 the Nejdi state was bounded to the east, north, and northeast by territories unconnected except for a common, insubstantial obligation to the Ottoman sultan. By the end of that year the Hashemites were in authority not only in Hejaz but also in Transjordan and Iraq, supported by British arms, advisors, and subventions. In these circumstances the continuing if fragile relationship between ibn Saud and the British government proved to be of value to both.

The first phase of ibn Saud's postwar strategy called for the elimination of the House of Rashid. This was accomplished in a bloody *dénouement;* by the end of 1961 Jebel Shammar was firmly under Saudi control. The resulting extension of the frontier between what was now the Sultanate of Nejd and the Kingdom of Iraq caused a succession of crises, especially during ibn Saud's campaign against King Faisal's father and brother in Hejaz, but by 1930 a combination of British military force and diplomacy brought peace to the border area (see Chapter 2).

Firepower rather than diplomacy determined the frontiers between Nejd and Transjordan after *Ikhwan* raids into Emir Abdullah's territory in 1922.[3] The effectiveness of armored vehicles and Royal Air Force

---

[3]The British occupation of the district of Aqaba on behalf of Emir Abdullah was contested, and the district was not recognized as Jordanian territory until after ibn Saud's death in 1953.

bombing and strafing missions made a lasting impression upon ibn Saud and his young sons, who would in future build modern armed forces with revenues from oil production.

With respect to Kuwait, negotiations rather than force finally resolved a dangerous Saudi-Kuwaiti dispute. Shaikh Salim ibn Sabah's aggressiveness in claiming wells and grazing lands used by tribes subject to ibn Saud and his assertion of primacy over some of those tribes were in part due to confidence that his ancestral territory was protected by the Anglo-Kuwait Treaty of 1899. At 'Uqair in 1923 ibn Saud met with Shaikh Sabah and worked out the details of a Saudi-Kuwaiti administered Neutral Zone, with mutual access to its water and grazing resources assured. Neither the House of Saud nor the House of Sabah would have been so acquiescent in the 'Uqair formula had they known of the oil reserves which lay below the surface of the Neutral Zone. The 'Uqair meetings also provided for the establishment of a Nejdi-Iraqi neutral zone, but (as noted above) difficulties on that frontier were not to be fully resolved for nearly a decade.

The stage was now set for the final phase of ibn Saud's postwar strategy. Preparations for the invasion of Hejaz included the extension of Saudi control over Asir, formerly the domain of Sayyid Mohammed ibn Ali al-Idriss who, with British encouragement, had established himself at Hodeidah in coastal Yemen (see below). A force of *Ikhwan* led by ibn Saud's second son, Emir Faisal, took over most of what is now Saudi Arabia's southwestern province.[4] Many more preparatory moves were planned, for ibn Saud did not underestimate his enemy. But the actual outbreak of hostilities was precipitated by the response of King (formerly Sherif) Hussein of the Hejaz to Kemal Ataturk's decision, in 1924, to abolish the Caliphate. By asserting that he was the first Arab Caliph of all the Muslims since Mamluk and Ottoman times, King Hussein forced the hand of ibn Saud.

The ferocity with which the *Ikhwan*, acting without authority from Riyadh, had fallen upon the Hejazi summer capital of Taif in late 1924 was an indication to ibn Saud that the situation was getting beyond his control. The next indication came from Jeddah, the port and commercial center of Hejaz, whose inhabitants had no wish to risk their lives in defense of Hussein's pan-Islamic pretensions. Their opposition to Sherifian policy forced Hussein's departure and Ali, the eldest and least competent of the exiled king's sons, was left to preside over the dissolution of Hashemite rule in Hejaz. It was not long in coming, for ibn Saud knew

---

[4]The frontier with Yemen would be finally established by the Treaty of Taif (1934) after Imam Yahya's tribesmen had attacked Najran and other parts of Asir. Saudi troops under Emir Faisal penetrated the Tihama as far south as Hodeidah while Emir Saud, ibn Saud's eldest son, dealt with resistance in upland Asir.

that he would face the wrath of the *Ikhwan* himself if they were not sent against the Holy Cities.

Mecca was delivered up without the attendant massacre feared by its inhabitants, for the Wahhabis were content to loot and destroy tombs and other evidences of departure from an orthodoxy as stern as that of Praisegod Barebones. Medina was even less trouble for a Wahhabi force under Mohammed, another of the ruler's many sons. The gates were opened to the vanguard of the new dispensation. Memories of the Sherifian siege of the Ottoman garrison in 1917–18 were too fresh to allow for pointless heroics. Jeddah fell without bloodshed and without the *Ikhwan* being compelled to breach its weak defenses by assault. The kingship of Ali ibn Hussein ended on December 23, 1925, long before his first anniversary. British officials arranged Ali's sea passage to Basra, from whence he went on to Baghdad as the guest of his more durable and capable brother, King Faisal.

The change in Hejaz was carried off smoothly, in part because ibn Saud dispatched his more fanatical lieutenants to remote districts where they could exercise their zealous bigotry on startled tribespeople. Thus the Wahhabi Sultan, who was proclaimed King of Hejaz in January 1926, avoided early difficulties with Western nations represented at Jeddah and with Muslim leaders throughout the world. This would have provided scant comfort to the inhabitants of northern Hejaz, whose heads were bloodied in aid of Saudi external relations, but for the new king it was a small price to pay for international acceptance of the House of Saud's realization of its venerable aspiration.

British political support of the Hashemites in Hejaz was not easily transferable. Saudi Arabia continued to experience difficulties over the frontiers with Britain's Hashemite clients in Transjordan and Iraq and with its protégé, the ruler of Kuwait. Some of these problems—but not the Saudi claim to territory in Transjordan stretching northward from Aqaba to Ma'an—were settled in discussions between ibn Saud and Sir Gilbert Clayton as the Hejaz campaign drew to a close. Further negotiations led, in 1927, to the Treaty of Jeddah which acknowledged Britain's special position in the Persian Gulf and recognized, in language eminently acceptable to the king, ibn Saud's sovereignty from the Gulf to the Red Sea. But diplomatic *politesse* was not enough. Neither the tribes on the northeastern marches of ibn Saud's domain, nor their rivals in Iraq, nor indeed the British forces stationed there displayed a measure of the restraint which characterized the meetings between ibn Saud and Sir Gilbert Clayton.

Through 1928 and 1929 the threat of war with Iraq loomed large. Clash after clash occurred in the frontier area (incidentally providing young John Bagot Glubb with the experience of desert warfare which subsequently would be employed to develop Jordan's beduin legion-naires into an effective instrument of Hashemite policy). As Wahhabi tribesmen became uncontrollable, ibn Saud grew painfully aware that the sword he had forged in 1912, the *Ikhwan*, could not be sheathed and must be broken if his kingdom were to have the peace without which it could not approach the threshold of the modern world. He acted deci-sively. The result was the battle at Sibila in March 1929, in which the tribes which had defied his authority were crushed by a force which became the nucleus of a national army.

The basis for a final settlement with Iraq was thus established. A brief campaign against Imam Yahya led to the demarcation of the frontier with Yemen in 1934 (see below). Although the memory of the House of Saud's era of expansion into southeastern Arabia was kept green and led to the Buraimi crisis late in ibn Saud's life, the present borders of the Kingdom of Saudi Arabia were established by the end of 1934. It was in that year that the name Saudi Arabia was officially adopted.

Although ibn Saud's contacts with Britons, official and otherwise, had created the basis for mutual respect, the British-Hashemite connec-tion prevented a cordial relationship and did much to facilitate subse-quent "oil diplomacy" by the Americans. So did Britain's postwar eco-nomic slump, a by-product of which was the termination of Britain's subsidy to the desert king.

Ibn Saud surrounded himself with a small, capable group of officials drawn from all over the Arab world to administer an enlarged realm with greatly expanded international obligations. The king's shrewdness and pragmatism were reflected in the abilities of his appointees. Many of them served throughout his long reign, honorably and efficiently, except for the few who were to find latter-day oil revenues irresistibly tempting.

Difficulties with fractious subjects and provincial governors drawn from the proud band of brothers who had campaigned with him for a quarter of a century, and to whom centralized administration was vir-tually incomprehensible, forced ibn Saud to improve his country's com-munication system. The beginning of Saudi nationhood was signaled as much by purchases of motor vehicles and aircraft and the installation of a system of wireless telegraphy as by the eclipse of the *Ikhwan*. Shortly afterward came the rudimentary beginnings of telephone systems in the major towns. This was not simply a matter of purchase, instruction, and installation, for every instrument of infidel manufacture was viewed with suspicion or outright hostility by tradition-bound *ulema* and a people steeped in the austere principles of Wahhabism. In introducing these innovations, as in all else, ibn Saud maintained the balance between his role as the sovereign of a theocratic state and his plans for modernization and consolidation. His example has informed the reign of Faisal, his second son and ablest lieutenant. The oft-repeated tale of how ibn Saud introduced the telephone may be apocryphal, yet it bespeaks his level-headedness sufficiently well to bear yet one more repetition. He ordered a religious leader to man one instrument and read verses from the Koran to another divine some distance away. The second man then affirmed that the contraption was not an artifice of the Devil, for the same holy words which had been sent in at one one end had come out the other.

The beginnings of secular education and modern medical services were of even greater moment than the introduction of advanced communication methods. To be sure, these could hardly be introduced on a national scale, and relatively few of ibn Saud's subjects benefitted from them. But, lacking external subsidies and faced with a primitive economy and an income from the pilgrimage traffic which was unpredictable in all aspects except its chronic inadequacy, ibn Saud was hard pressed for the means to effect modernization. Improved administration had increased income from the provinces, but hopes for development were pinned to the search for mineral resources. The presence of oil in Bahrain, a part of the same geological structure as Hasa, brought concession-hunters to Riyadh as early as 1923. For a meager annual sum, an exploration concession was granted to a British firm, but relations between this firm and the king quickly soured. It was an American entrepreneur and Arabophile, Charles Crane, who was responsible for Saudi Arabia's entry into the world petroleum market.

Crane achieved his *coup* by underwriting an economic and geological survey which in turn encouraged the Standard Oil Company of California to negotiate for a concession. Agreement was reached in 1933 and soon a vanguard of hardy geologists were traversing barren wastes unknown either to Niebuhr, Doughty, or to many beduin for that matter. Their efforts were rewarded near Jebel Dhahran in 1935 and marked the beginning of what was to become the Arabian American Oil Company (Aramco), the source of funds for (and itself an agency of) modernization, and a major plus factor in the American balance of payments equation. But before Saudi Arabia could prosper, another period of crisis supervened. Production began in 1938 and in mid-1939 the first cargo of oil was shipped from Ras Tanura. Two months earlier, Nazi troops had occupied Czechoslovakia. And four months after the pioneering tanker steamed through the Straits of Hormuz, Hitler moved on Poland. Global war cut off the Saudi oilfields from Western markets and drastically limited the annual pilgrim traffic. Ibn Saud's financial situation would have deteriorated to pre-1917 standards had not Great Britain and the United States provided assistance.

Neither American aid nor President Roosevelt's meeting with ibn Saud on a cruiser in the Great Bitter Lake in early 1945 was the result of any American awareness of Saudi Arabia's growing importance. The former was simply an aspect of a general wartime policy, and the latter a fruitless effort to secure Arab support for the resettlement in Palestine of Jewish survivors of the Nazi holocaust. Indeed, proposals by American officials for United States government participation in constructing an oil pipeline from Hasa to the Mediterranean were dismissed by Secretary Harold Ickes, who asserted that Saudi Arabia was in the British sphere of influence. Tapline (the Trans-Arabian Pipeline) was completed as a privately financed and privately engineered American project in 1950. It was a vast undertaking, for the oil which reaches the refinery in Sidon, Lebanon, enters the pipeline system at Abqaiq, nearly 1,100 miles away. The problems of construction were solved in good time, but the complete pipeline remains at the mercy of politics, the more so since 1967, for Tapline traverses the Israeli-occupied Golan Heights.

By 1948 oil royalties to Saudi Arabia were mounting rapidly. Between 1949 and 1960 annual income rose from $85 million to $340 million. In 1969 the figure was $950 million and a more rapid rate of growth is currently being achieved because of renegotiated agreements with producing companies. Since 1960 the number of producers, both onshore and offshore—in the Red Sea as well as in the Persian Gulf—has steadily increased, in part due to Aramco's relinquishment of extensive concession areas.

A Lebanese contractor who had amassed a fortune in Saudi Arabia once referred to the last years of ibn Saud's rule as "the good old days, when the old king didn't know the difference between a thousand and a million." Ibn Saud's place in history must be determined by the totality of his long reign, not by those few years of rapidly deteriorating health prior to his death in 1953. But the fact remains that the latter period was one during which, because of the oil boom, worldwide attention was focused on Saudi Arabia and the king's public image was at its worst. Until a few years before his death, religious and tribal leaders were given a feeling of participation in the changing life of the country. The king moved with the times, evolving older forms of tribal democracy into a rough-and-ready Consultative Council which acted as a fairly effective safety valve. Occasionally the trend of events disturbed the traditionalists, especially extremists among the Wahhabi *ulema*, but ibn Saud's accessibility, willingness to consult, and obvious agreement upon fundamental issues of religious life brought Saudi Arabia to the threshold of modernization without internal upheaval.

In the five years before the king's death, millions of *riyals* were available for construction and development. This was precisely the period during which ibn Saud's failing health and unwise counsel destroyed the remarkable balance between religious fundamentalism and secular innovation. Widespread graft, corruption, and peculation involving the official who issued building and import permits, the contractor whose bid was successful, the businessman who supplied equipment and materials, and the agent who recruited the labor force meant that every project or acquisition was paid for several times. Development activity greatly enlarged the Western presence in a land about which the Prophet Mohammed had said, during his last illness, ". . . there shall not remain two religions in the land of Arabia." Caliph 'Umar responded to this injunction by expelling the Christians and Jews of Najran and Khaybar, but King Abdul Aziz ibn Saud, Imam of the Wahhabis, seemed willing to permit the breaching of the Islamic citadel.

Hence a recrudescence of religious extremism combined with a decline in standards of public conduct to create a pervasive atmosphere of hypocrisy. There were other problems for the regime. Little had been done to promote a Saudi Arabian national consciousness, although the king may have thought that his forays to distribute largesse among the beduin and urban poor had accomplished that vital task. But now, at the end of ibn Saud's long life, a king had been overthrown in Egypt and a Revolutionary Command Council was promising millenarian change in the Arab world. Already an idealized version of the new Egyptian regime was spreading through the ranks of younger officers and civil servants, and especially among young Saudis returning from programs of training and education abroad.

An atmosphere of insecurity and the enfeebled state of the king's physical and mental health secured his acquiescence to an external venture aimed at recovering popularity for the royal family through expanding the Saudi domain to its nineteenth-century frontiers in southeastern Arabia. Rumors of the discovery of oil-bearing strata in the Buraimi Oasis area were an additional inducement to adopt a new "forward policy." Several villages of the oasis were administered by the Sultanate of Muscat and Oman, but the major portion was controlled by the Shaikhdom of Abu Dhabi. Both Sultan Said ibn Taimur and Shaikh ibn Sultan were dependent upon Great Britain for the conduct of their external relations under the terms of long-standing treaties (see below). Therefore, when a small Saudi force occupied a portion of Buraimi in August 1953 and began promoting—in the conventional fashion—declarations of allegiance to Saudi Arabia, the Riyadh regime was immediately embroiled in a dispute with Great Britain.

Three months later, and over a half-century after his epic recapture of Riyadh for the House of Saud, the great king died. His kingdom was beset by domestic discord and mounting pressures in the international sphere. Such was the old warrior's legacy to his eldest son, Saud ibn Abdul Aziz. He was incapable of dealing with it.

The dozen years of King Saud's rule reveal a monarch increasingly capricious with the passage of time, unavailable for consultation, unmoved by public affronts to the moral code on the part of members of his own family, and surrounded by a royal oligarchy which replaced the Consultative Council. The high walls of the Nasriyah Palace at Riyadh and an omnipresent screen of fawning, grasping courtiers marked the separation of the royal family from its people. Rather than move among them, Saud sought to purchase their acquiescence to his rule by subsidies to leading townspeople and to tribes. The tribes in turn were called on to supply recruits for the growing "White Army," whose mission was to protect the royal family against attack from any quarter, including the regular armed force.

The vast scale of such subsidies, the size of the privy purse, large subventions to the Algerian revolutionary movement, and the Buraimi venture combined with an inefficient development program to lay siege to the value of the *riyal*. Saudi currency fell in value by nearly 80 percent early in the reign of King Saud, Aramco experienced its first major labor disturbances in October 1953, and nascent public opinion was further encouraged by the publication of the country's first daily newspaper, beginning in December of the same year. The rumblings of discontent grew louder.

In this threatening situation, Crown Prince Faisal ibn Abdul Aziz was cast in the role of Sisyphus. He was the motive force behind the establishment of a Council of Ministers, but control of key portfolios by some of Saud's and Faisal's more malleable brothers vitiated his efforts. There were distractions as well. Skirmishing between Saudi irregulars and the British-officered Trucial Oman Scouts in the Buraimi region led to an international arbitration agreement in 1954. It came to naught less than a year later with the adjournment of the tribunal amid charges that the Saudi delegate had attempted to secure a favorable decision through bribery. Then the Suez War led to a short-lived oil boycott and the rupture of relations with Great Britain and France. In such circumstances little attention could be given to ordered programs of social, economic, and administrative improvement.

By 1957, however, King Saud's profligate spending amounted to a sustained attack on the *riyal*. Crown Prince Faisal was unable to take effective steps to deal with the problem because of the king's newly gained, if short-lived, prestige as the "chosen instrument" of John Foster Dulles's Middle Eastern policy, a manifestation of the Secretary of State's anti-Nasserism rather than any rational appreciation of the situation. Faisal's opportunity finally came with the disclosures of a sensational "murder plot." It was described by the Cairo and Damascus news media as a conspiracy financed by King Saud and his advisors to assassinate President Nasser and frustrate an Egyptian-Syrian federation. The price for all this was alleged to be $53 million. In Damascus photostatic copies of canceled checks amounting to a down payment of one-tenth went on display. The humiliation of the king and his entourage strengthened Faisal's hand. In his capacity as Prime Minister, the Crown Prince took over full executive power and restructured the Council of Ministers. Control of finance and administration was vested in the Council and a program of fiscal retrenchment was implemented.

On this occasion another council, drawn from all sections of the royal family, called upon Saud to abdicate in favor of Faisal. Although the Crown Prince rejected this demand as a betrayal of a vow made to his father to never challenge Saud's kingship, he used the situation to extract from Saud a pledge to support the reform program. The program included such measures as the establishment of a monetary agency and a development board, the allocation of major financial support to the University of Riyadh, approval of a program to bring Saudi Arabian Airlines into the jet age, and authorization for Petromin, a government-sponsored firm for the programmatic exploitation of the country's petroleum and mineral resources.

But King Saud, his immediate family, and his small circle of Rasputinish advisors could tolerate fiscal realism and concurrent reductions in the royal household budget for only a limited time. Making the most of a dispute over his proposal to bestow full control of a projected Hejaz oil refinery upon one of his sons, King Saud secured Faisal's resignation as Prime Minister in January 1961. He assumed that portfolio himself and held it until October 1962, when Faisal returned to office.

On the face of it, Saud seemed to be making new departures in reform. The inclusion of commoners in the cabinet and the announcement that Islamic law would be supplanted in certain areas by modern decree legislation suggested a brave new world for Saudi Arabia. So did the establishment of a Supreme Planning Council and the invitation to a World Bank mission to make recommendations on budgetary and economic planning. But it was not to be. Much was promised and little delivered. The "interlude of Saud" was a period in which a weak-willed monarch was pulled in one direction by woolly-headed family members such as Prince Talal, whose thinking was done for him by Radio Cairo, and in another by a sordid assemblage of confidence men. When the latter group gained ascendancy, Talal and another prince, Nawaf, departed for Cairo. Their highly publicized defection was followed by that of several air force officers with their planes. Fear of losing further aircraft resulted in orders to impound fuel supplies and restrict training flights. King Saud's hysterical statements to the press accusing President Nasser of implementing Zionist plots and making war on Islam suggested that he had lost control of his government. Throughout this confused period, only strong Saudi support of Kuwait against the territorial claims of Iraq's Abdul Karim Qasim (1961) gave an appearance of decisiveness to the regime—although in fact what passed for decisiveness was more in the nature of a reflex action.

The outbreak of civil war in the Yemen and the dispatch of Egyptian forces to prop up the revolutionary regime of Colonel Abdullah Sallal were widely regarded as preliminaries to the destruction of the Saudi monarchy. It was at this point that Crown Prince Faisal returned to office and began a remarkable salvage operation. American government support for Faisal was a vital factor. Exchanges between Faisal and President Kennedy emphasized the United States commitment to maintain the territorial integrity of Saudi Arabia and favored the Crown Prince's plans for reform. When Egyptian aircraft based in Yemen bombed Saudi border villages and diplomatic relations between Cairo and Riyadh were sundered in November 1962, a squadron of F–100 jet aircraft was dispatched to Saudi Arabia from American bases in Germany to give point to Kennedy's assurances.

Faisal's success in restoring morale and securing the loyalty of the armed forces was testimony to his qualities of leadership. A program of "pragmatic development" was quickly implemented in areas in which the theocratic nature of the state was not challenged. Dozens of projects were finally taken off the drawing boards and moved into the execution stage. High priority was given to road, port, and airfield development, the currency was stabilized, and the government scholarship program was expanded. Quick action was taken to pay outstanding debts and diplomatic relations were reestablished with Great Britain and France.

Meanwhile King Saud and a huge entourage roamed throughout Europe. A Saudi commercial airliner laden with the King's luggage and retainers exploded and crashed in the Alps, a prince was murdered in a Paris hotel, and finally Faisal concluded that Saudi Arabia could afford neither this kind of expenditure nor this kind of notoriety. When the Egyptian challenge in Yemen made necessary an enormous budgetary allocation to reequip and modernize the armed forces, which in turn meant slashing the royal household budget, relations between king and crown prince were further embittered. It was not difficult to persuade Saud to return and reassert personal rule.

Faisal was extremely vulnerable. Firstly, he was balancing his program of military preparedness with a diplomatic campaign to promote Egyptian and Saudi disengagement in Yemen. A minor breakthrough had been achieved by the resumption of diplomatic relations with Cairo. King Saud condemned this policy as one of appeasement. Secondly, the strain placed upon a traditional society by Faisal's program of modernization made it possible for Saud and his supporters to accuse him of encouraging the spread of undesirable foreign influences. Now, however, Saud not only failed to secure the support of the royal family, the upper bureaucracy, and the military leadership, but was even unable to generate a significant amount of polarization. Faisal's measures had already brought about the recantation and return of Prince Talal, Prince Nawaf, and their followers from Cairo. Now a family council once again called for the abdication of King Saud, and on this occasion Faisal concurred, with the condition that the assent of the *ulema* be obtained. The appropriate *fetwa*, or religious decree, was published on November 2, 1964. Faisal entered upon the kingship as messages of congratulation poured into Riyadh from all over the world. None was warmer than that of President Nasser who, ironically enough, was to act as host to ex-King Saud when he tired of gilded exile in Greece.

It was obvious from the first that Faisal would employ his new powers decisively. Within a month his brother Prince Sultan, Minister of Defense, was authorized to make further expenditures (eventually amounting to $600 million) to modernize the army and establish an air defense system including jet fighters, ground-to-air missiles, radar, and a telecommunications network. The succession question was dealt with by designating Prince Khalid ibn Abdul Aziz as Crown Prince. A boundary agreement with Qatar was an early indication of Faisal's concern over the security of the Persian Gulf after the phasing out of the British military presence in 1971. The College of Petroleum and Minerals was opened in Dhahran and major financial support was provided to the new Abdul Aziz University in Jeddah. The central planning authority was thoroughly purged and reorganized. Oil revenues were at last being employed for the benefit of the country rather than the needs, real or imagined, of the royal family.

King Faisal did not confine to the military sphere his efforts to remove Egyptian influence from the Arabian Peninsula. In 1965 a major offensive against revolutionary Arab socialism began with his call for an

Islamic summit conference to reassert traditional values and to organize resistance to alien ideologies and concepts. Within eighteen months this usually contemplative and introspective ruler had traveled to Turkey, Pakistan, Iran, Morocco, Tunisia, and Mali to publicize his Muslim campaign. The volume of abuse directed at what Radio Cairo called the "Islamic Pact" and emanating from Egypt, Syria, and Iraq suggested that his policy was ill-conceived. Certainly the course of events in Baghdad and Damascus and the rising tide of discontent in Egypt indicated that the proponents of revolutionary socialism were greater threats to each other than to the Saudi monarchy. Yet one result was an Egyptian-financed campaign of subversion in the kingdom. Moreover, many Muslims regarded Faisal's policy as the exploitation of Islam for political purposes—which was perhaps not as offensive as the various attempts to establish an affinity between Islam and communism or to reinterpret the Koran on a socialistic basis, but was nonetheless an intrusion between man and his God.

Faisal's search for an Islamic renaissance did not diminish the prestige he had earned by providing Saudi Arabia with a modern infrastructure. His shrewdness in the realm of diplomacy, his position as Keeper of the Holy Places, and his well-established reputation as an implacable foe of Israel were factors which broadened his constituency of supporters throughout the Arab world and enabled him to function effectively in the Shatt al-Arab dispute between Iraq and Iran in 1966. More important to Saudi Arabia was his combination of military and diplomatic methods of containing Egyptian activities in Yemen while fostering disillusion and hostility between the Egyptians and Yemeni republicans, and his effective collaboration with the Shah to prevent an "Egyptian solution" for the Persian Gulf. President Nasser was reduced to placing former King Saud before a Radio Cairo microphone in January 1967 for the purpose of asserting that he was still the rightful ruler of Saudi Arabia and would return "to save the people and the country." Toward this end, however, Saud's principal activity during his stay in Cairo was his nightly tieup of the Hotel Semiramis switchboard with telephone calls to his aged mother in Riyadh. The year 1967 possibly marked the high point of Faisal's regime. The June disaster led to the Khartoum Conference, at which Nasser was placed upon the Saudi payroll. It was Saudi Arabian diplomacy that brought Arab leaders to the realization that the embargo on oil exports to the United States, Great Britain, and West Germany was more harmful to their own countries than to the alleged "collusionists." Faisal took the lead in obtaining agreement that oil revenues rather than oil embargoes were the basis upon which political concessions could be obtained from the West.

Budgetary support supplied to the war-ravaged economy of Egypt by Saudi Arabia (and other Arab oil-producing countries) not only turned off Nasser's sponsorship of Saud but curbed Egyptian activities in the Persian Gulf region. The return of the Egyptian expeditionary force from Yemen further facilitated *rapprochement*, leading to a Saudi-Egyptian trade and cooperation agreement in 1968. On the domestic front, the Saudi economy continued to develop. The 1967 gross national product increased 10 percent over that of 1966, and by 1971 oil revenues reached about $1.2 billion as the result of increased production and tough negotiations. This was over 80 percent of Saudi Arabia's total budget and had important implications for overall economic development.

Between 1968 and 1971 Faisal's capacity to guide and control policy began to weaken. Failing health and constant pressure took their toll. Extremely conservative advisors such as the two Syrians, Rashad Pharaon and Ma'ruf Dawalibi, confused Faisal's priorities, fostering indecision and a loss of momentum in the drive toward modernization. There were only a few officials to whom Faisal could delegate authority with any confidence—his two brothers, Prince Fahad (Interior) and Prince Sultan (Defense), and the Minister of Petroleum Affairs, Shaikh Zaki Yamani. More determinative was the fact that Faisal's expectations—and those of his people—were greater than were justified by Saudi Arabia's resources. The country was too vast and the population too small—probably about four million although seven million are claimed for political and strategic reasons—for rapid industrialization.

King Faisal held the underlying conviction that undesirable side effects of urbanization, industrialization, and other facets of modernization could be countered by reinforcing the foundations of the community with the ideological cement of Islam. He relied upon his ability to obtain the *ulema's* sanction for his programs and its cooperation in transmitting the ethical standards of the Muslim faith to the bureaucracy, the military, and the intelligentsia. Success would mean that Saudi Arabia would emerge as a state without precedent in the twentieth century—a modern theocracy.

Collaboration of Islamic religious leaders and massive infusions of oil income were not enough to assure steady progress in modernization; the need for technological skills, industrial diversification, and a large trained labor force required not only a major influx of Western experts but also a supplementary labor force recruited in other parts of the Middle East. A new freedom of movement for foreigners and foreign concepts was requisite, beyond Riyadh, Jeddah, and the "Aramco enclave" in Hasa to all parts of the country, with only Mecca and Medina sheltered from the infidel gaze. Yet thousands of Yemenis, Syrians, Palestinians,

Lebanese, and Egyptians were deported as undesirable elements between 1964 and 1972.

The blowing up of Tapline by Palestinian commandos in Israeli-occupied Golan Heights in 1969 cost Saudi Arabia $72,000 daily and convinced Faisal that he was being betrayed by the Palestinians whose cause he had supported since 1948. In the same year, the burning of al-Aqsa Mosque in occupied eastern Jerusalem was a shattering experience for the aging Keeper of the Holy Places. King Faisal refused to accept evidence that the fire was the work of a demented Australian and continued to assert that it was part of the "Zionist conspiracy." To observers, this fixation was a further indication that 1969 marked a serious loss of momentum for the reformist regime.

Two major plots to overthrow the monarchy were uncovered in September of that year. Government officials, Petromin employees, and high-ranking army officers were involved and widespread arrests resulted. Such events, together with the heavy fighting on the South Yemeni frontier that resulted from Saudi Arabia's effort to eradicate the socialist regime in Aden, gave Iran a clear field in which to organize its own preferred security arrangements for the Persian Gulf.

Further blows were dealt to Saudi Arabia in 1969. Revolutionary regimes emerged in Sudan and Libya. The former established an unsympathetic government across the Red Sea from the vulnerable Hejaz and Asir coasts of Saudi Arabia. Defeat of a second *coup* attempt by an openly communist and pro-Soviet group in Khartoum two years later brought little comfort to Riyadh, despite growing indications of conservatism in the Sudanese government. More important to the Saudis was the increasing cordiality between Khartoum and Peking.

As for the Saudi perception of Libyan developments, it mattered little that the erratic Colonel Qaddafi rejected socialism in favor of an Islamic fundamentalism. Another monarchy had fallen to the soldiers. By 1970 the atmosphere of Riyadh had a paranoid quality reminiscent of 1961. Faisal's "White Revolution" was a failure by any contrast with that of his Iranian counterpart.

Nonetheless, Saudi Arabia's income from oil continued to mount rapidly. Production rose nearly 25 percent in 1971. Increases in posted prices and other concessions were wrested from the major oil companies as a result of the agreement sponsored by the Organization of Petroleum Exporting Countries at a Teheran meeting in February 1971. These price increases were a portent of the multiple effects on income to be achieved through the concept of "gradual nationalization" introduced at the Beirut meeting of the organization in March 1972. The initial demand was for a minimum 20 percent national participation in the shares of the producing companies. Aramco agreed in principle, but long, complicated negotiations were predicted before a formula could be arrived at to determine the extent to which allowance could be made for investment, exploration, and capital equipment and for operating expenses.

It was King Faisal's concern and that of his gifted Minister for Petroleum Affairs Shaikh Zaki Yamani that "participation" negotiations not interrupt the flow of oil to Western markets (and Japan) where petroleum consumption was rising 10 percent annually. Shaikh Zaki was opposed to the high pressure methods employed against Western marketing companies by Libya and, until mid-1972, by Iraq. He knew that the Arab countries lacked the managerial and technical skills which had enabled the Shah of Iran to state flatly that renewal of his country's 1954 agreement with the Western producing and marketing consortium upon expiry in 1979 was not negotiable (while noting the Shah's assurances of ample supplies to Western marketing companies). Hence Shaikh Zaki took the lead in developing, on behalf of Saudi Arabia and the oil-producing shaikhdoms of the Persian Gulf, a formula for securing a controlling 51 percent interest in petroleum concessions by 1983. It would cost the Arab governments concerned $1 billion to purchase the controlling interest but the rising price of oil, the expanding market, and the steadily increasing share of profits made the price a bargain. The resulting agreement provided for the purchase of a 25 percent interest in January 1973 and subsequent purchases raising the Arab interest to 30 percent in 1979, then increasing by 5 percent annually until 1982, with a 6 percent increase the following year for a total interest of 51 percent. The Arab governments and Western oil companies could also hope that Shaikh Zaki had succeeded in depoliticizing Arab oil, at least in the producing countries.

Meanwhile, exploration continued to go forward, increasing the already staggering total of proved reserves. The most dramatic new oil strike came at the end of 1971 at Mazalij in the Aramco concession area. Mazalij could be the largest oil field anywhere in the world.

Hence vast sums were available for investment in the kingdom's infrastructure. The 1971–72 budget, the largest in Saudi history, amounted to over $2.5 billion. Highways, ports, airfields, telecommunications, and industrial development continued to be emphasized, but more attention was given to agriculture. A large irrigation project was inaugurated by King Faisal at the end of 1971 in Hasa province, which would bring about fifty thousand acres into cultivation. Yet advances in the fortunes of the hard-lining, military-oriented Sudeiri branch of the family, led by Fahad and Sultan, with the acquiescence of Khalid and other full brothers, assured that military modernization and expansion would continue to have a high priority.[5]

Whatever the domestic implications of the Sudeiri pressure group for an aging monarch whose health was failing, military expansion and the kingdom's wealth strengthened Faisal's already influential position in Arab councils. The polarization between Arab progressives and conservatives was no longer as marked as it had been in the lifetime of Gamal Abdul Nasser. President Anwar Sadat's deep commitment to Islam and his purges of pro-Soviet elements in the Egyptian government and party structure improved Saudi-Egyptian relations, as did Egyptian reliance upon subsidies from major Arab oil-producing states.

King Faisal welcomed President Sadat's invitation of June 1971 to visit Egypt, and the reception was cordial. His brother, Minister of Defense Prince Sultan, was dispatched on diplomatic missions to Arab capitals, while Faisal underscored his own position as monarch and Keeper of the Holy Places by a world tour which took him to Iran, Nationalist China, Japan, the United States, and France. Yassir Arafat, King Hussein, and Jordanian Prime Minister Wasfi Tal visited Riyadh to discuss the commando crisis and the broader ramifications of the Palestine situation. They were followed by President Sadat, whose visit in August 1971 highlighted Faisal's dilemma as a monarchist and legitimist who nonetheless held a deep commitment to the Palestinian cause and was therefore opposed to the negotiated settlement which the Egyptian president was working toward. Yet the two leaders established excellent rapport, based in some measure upon mutual, deeply held religious convictions. A year later, Faisal would influence Sadat's decision to expel the Soviet Military Mission to the UAR.

Among other questions discussed by King Faisal and his distinguished visitors was the future of the Persian Gulf. Sir William Luce, who had the unenviable task of overseeing the British military and political withdrawal, and many of the emirs and shaikhs ruling the states on the Arabian littoral of the Persian Gulf came to Riyadh to seek Faisal's

---

[5]Sudeiri influence was manifest in the military maneuvers of January 1971 in Asir province, near the South Yemen frontier. Operations were based on the large, modern military complex at Khamis Musheit, the construction of which began while an Egyptian military expedition was in Yemen. Jet aircraft, missiles, heavy artillery, and tanks were deployed in the maneuvers. From 1965 to 1972 the Saudis invested over $300 million in British aircraft, missile, and radar systems, $100 million in American ground-to-air missiles, and nearly as much to purchase one hundred French AMX–30 tanks; $180 million was allotted for naval modernization and expansion. In 1972 the Saudi Air Force's striking power was increased by fifty percent with the purchase of twenty-seven F–5 fighter-bombers from the United States.

advice and support. The king's journey to Teheran in May 1971 for discussions on the Persian Gulf with the Shah was indicative of Iran's predominant role in that important region, but by the end of 1972 there were significant Saudi initiatives in Gulf defense talks with Iran.

Saudi Arabia quickly entered into diplomatic relations with Bahrain and Qatar after their independence was proclaimed (see below), but Saudi recognition was withheld from the new Union of Arab Emirates because of the long-standing boundary dispute with its most powerful member, Abu Dhabi. Portents were favorable, however, as was indicated in December 1971 by the cordiality of talks between King Faisal and Sultan Qabus of Oman, despite a related boundary problem. The Sultan's visit concluded with the establishment of diplomatic relations between the two countries.

Both rulers were deeply concerned over developments in South Arabia. For Qabus, the threat was real and present in the form of the Dhofar rebellion. For Faisal, this was an aspect of a greater problem which had to do with the ideological commitments of the People's Democratic Republic of South Yemen. Saudi Arabia continued to employ its new and special relationship with the Yemeni Arab Republic to bring pressure on the Aden regime.

Such preoccupations were in some measure responsible for Faisal's tendency to neglect domestic programs of social benefit. Moreover, corruption, incompetence, distrust of foreigners, and at the same time reliance upon them continued to widen the gap between plan and execution in the development program. Since the removal of the Senussi monarchy in oil wealthy Libya, comparisons between that country and Saudi Arabia have become inevitable. The Libya of King Idriss, with its enormous territory, underdeveloped institutions, small population, and oil wealth was the Arab country most similar to Saudi Arabia. However, there is one major difference between Saudi Arabia and Libya. The young Saudi officers and their allies in the civil service and university may be considered the "Palestinians" of their country. Opposed to them is a fierce, well-armed beduin force, the National Guard—formerly known as the White Army. The junior officers who took power in Libya were unthreatened by any elite military force. In Saudi Arabia, however, the National Guard has been and is being trained by experts in repression, officers of the Royal Jordanian Army. The *dénouement* in Saudi Arabia, unlike Libya, is likely to be bloody.

South Arabia

1. THE YEMENI ARAB REPUBLIC

The fertile and usually well-watered soil of highland Yemen has always supported a denser population than any other area of the Arabian Peninsula. The term "Yemen" comprehends much more of southwestern Arabia than the highlands; included is the Tihama, a coastal plain stretching southward from Abu Arish near the Saudi frontier past the old coffee port of Mocha to the Bab-al-Mandeb. But there is still much more to Yemen. Historically, it embraces that part of the People's Democratic Republic of Yemen which, before 1967, constituted the Aden Colony and the Western Aden Protectorate. Beginning in the mid-fifties the statelets of the Protectorate and Aden were patched together (in several phases) to form the jerry-built South Arabian Federation. Until 1967 there was not much historical or geographical basis for including the former Eastern Aden Protectorate, which covered the geographical area of Hadhramaut, as part of this "Yemen." But its forced incorporation into the People's Democratic Republic of South Yemen by the National Liberation Front government after the British withdrawal of that year suggests that its future is as a part of a Greater Yemen, whether ruled from Aden, San'a, or Taiz, and whether or not a unitary state eventually emerges.

The claim to sovereignty over historic Yemen was put forward most energetically by two of the last three Zeidi Imams, Yahya ibn Mohammed (1904–48) and Ahmed ibn Yahya (1948–62). The third, Imam Mohammed Badr ibn Ahmed, fled San'a after the republican revolution of 1962 and in 1970 went into exile in London following the settlement between the republican regime and his royalist supporters, which concluded seven years of civil war. Thus ended the Hamid-ud-Din (Defender of the Faith) dynasty established in 1891 by Yahya's father, Imam Mohammed, whose piety in no way qualified the ferocity with which he opposed the Turkish occupation of Yemen.

The Zeidi Imamate existed in Yemen for ten centuries before the Hamidud-Din branch was founded. It was established in circumstances of adversity and persevered in adversity until it fell between the millstones of British colonialism (as exemplified by the South Arabian Federation) and Arab nationalism in 1962.

Zeid, who gave the Imamate its name, was the grandson of Ali, in turn the son-in-law of the Prophet and the progenitor of the Shiite sect of Islam. It was Ali who was sent by Mohammed to establish order among fractious converts in the Yemen in 631. The memory of Ali's generous nature and eloquence was kept green, and in 740, when Zeid met the same fate as his grandfather in asserting his claim to the Caliphate, it was in Yemen that the survivors of his following found refuge. Shiites of the highland Yemen looked to the Fatimid Caliph in Cairo for spiritual leadership; Sunnites of the coast and foothills looked to Abbasid Baghdad.[1] The first Zeidi Imamate was established at Sada in the northern highlands in the ninth century and gained sufficient influence to invite Abbasid punitive expeditions. More durable was the connection with Cairo. An immediate consequence of Saladin's victory over the Fatimids came in 1174 with the expedition of his brother Turanshah, which made Yemen an Ayyubid province whose capital was Taiz. Saladin's Turkish and Kurdish governates subsequently became independent as the Rasulid dynasty (1232–1441), centered upon Zabid, near Hodeidah. When the Ayyubid dynasty declined, it was replaced by the Mamluk rulers of Cairo. As soon as the armies of Selim the Dread occupied Cairo in 1517, Yemen became an outpost of the Ottoman Empire.

The tortuous road to San'a, nine thousand feet above the Red Sea coast, was the gauge used to measure the power of these invaders. At times, their authority was confined to the Tihama, but occasionally the chiefs of San'a and the uplands paid tribute and experienced direct rule. However, the Zeidi Imamate developed its own traditions and radiated

---

[1]The Ismailis, another Shiite sect which acknowledges the Agha Khan as its leader, were long established on the northern marches of Yemen before accepting Zeidism, falling under Wahhabi swords, or migrating to East Africa. Ismaili influence remained significant into the last quarter of the nineteenth century.

its influence from Sada in the north, protected by tribes of tough mountaineers.

Yemen experienced a rule of unprecedented severity under the Ottomans after 1517. Having sacked Aden in 1538 and conquered Taiz seven years later, the Ottoman army laid waste the country between the coast and San'a and brought the mountain capital under siege. But San'a held fast and there, as throughout the highlands, the Zeidis increased their following by the zeal with which they organized resistance to their Sunnite occupiers. A high point was reached in the last decade of the sixteenth century when the first of the Zeidi Imams of San'a became the personification of Yemen's struggle for independence from the Turks. Imam Qasim succeeded so well that many Shafais, the Sunnite natives of the Tihama, supported him, although Turkish cruelty was as much a factor in bringing this about as was Qasim's charismatic leadership. By 1598 the greater part of Yemen was under Imam Qasim's authority, but massive Ottoman reinforcements tipped the scales against him. He then recruited forces in the remote fastness of eastern Yemen (as would other Imams down to the last of the Hamid-ud-Din) and came back to fight the Ottomans to a standstill by 1608.

A year later the English began their long association with South Arabia when an East India Company vessel called at Mocha. English, and to a lesser extent Dutch, involvement in the coffee trade made Mocha the most flourishing port on the Arabian shores through the seventeenth and eighteenth centuries. It was a time of declining Turkish influence. In little more than two decades the last Ottoman soldier had left Yemen. Meanwhile the Zeidi Imams had extended their sway over the northern districts of what is now the People's Democratic Republic of Yemen. But there was nobody of the stature of Imam Qasim to take advantage of this long period in which Yemen was free from external pressures. The principal foreign contacts came by way of the coffee trade, which was a source of prosperity and, therefore, a factor of stability. However, division among the Zeidis, the challenges of pretenders, and the ravages of tribal warfare caused a steady decline of Imamic fortunes. By the end of the eighteenth century the Tihama was in rebellion against the Zeidis, whose authority remained unchallenged only in the San'a district. The Wahhabi "cleansing" of the Tihama in the decade after 1803 must have given its Sunnite inhabitants a certain amount of nostalgia for the old Zeidi dispensation. As noted earlier, Wahhabi zeal brought the Egyptians back to Arabia, first in a surrogate role for the Ottoman Sultan, and then in the name of Mohammed Ali, ruler of Egypt. By 1820 the Zeidi Imam at San'a was paying tribute to the Egyptians, and in 1833 Mocha was in the hands of Mohammed Ali's soldiers. The Egyptians remained in control of the Tihama until 1840, when defeat in Syria compelled their with-drawal, just as the "June setback" of 1967 would cause the evacuation of another Egyptian army from Yemen.

Having failed to rouse the Turks to deal with the Egyptian chal-lenge, the British took matters into their own hands and, in response to a provocation of questionable authenticity and slight dimensions, wrested Aden from the Sultan of Lahej in 1839. The news caused no great stir in San'a, where Imamic rule was in steep decline. This emboldened the Turks to attempt the recovery of past glories, for there was no longer an Ibrahim Pasha to stand in their way. In 1849 an Ottoman expedition took over the Tihama. That gauge of power, the route to San'a, found the Turks wanting. The people of the highlands united to drive out the hated Ottoman forces. When the invaders limped back down the mountain passes to Hodeidah, order dissolved into chaos among the Zeidis. It was a certainty that the Ottoman army would return, and from 1849 to 1918 there was always a Turkish military presence in Yemen.

The opening of the Suez Canal gave no greater importance to Yemen but it did bring a first-rate Ottoman fighting force down the Red Sea to Hodeidah. This time the polity of the Zeidis was so fragmented that San'a was taken without the slightest difficulty. Ahmed Mukhtar Pasha then turned his attention southward, past Taiz, and down the slopes to Aden. His forces penetrated as far as Lahej in the Adeni hinterland. Without realizing it, the Turks were strengthening the Zeidi Imams in their claims to rule over all of historic Yemen, for their invasion was made in the name of Imam Muhsin, who may have been a Turkish puppet but who was also a Zeidi Imam.

The highland people repaid this favor with widespread tribal rebel-lion, which increased in intensity after Imam Muhsin's death in 1891. The new Imam, Mohammed, in founding the Hamid-ud-Din dynasty, changed the Imamate from an electoral to a hereditary office and pre-pared the way for a full-scale challenge to the Ottoman occupiers. This was mounted by his son and successor, Imam Yahya, who was allied by marriage to the shaikh of the powerful Hashid tribe, which was to be-come known as one of the "Wings of the Imamate"; the other was the Bakil tribe, also from the northern district. The strength provided by these fanatic mountaineers permitted Yahya to besiege San'a in 1904, the first year of his Imamate. The Turks and civilian population alike suffered enormous casualties before the city fell. Yahya held it for part of 1905, but reinforcements kept pouring into what was becoming known as the "graveyard of the Ottoman army." San'a was recaptured and Yahya went to ground in the north. When he returned with over 100,000 men in 1911, the Turks were ready for him and the siege was raised after a relief column from Tihama reinforced the San'a garrison. An uneasy truce was observed until the Ottoman army evacuated Yemen in 1918. During World War I Turkish forces once again advanced far into the Aden Protectorate, strengthening Imam Yahya's conviction that his historic mission and religious duty was to secure all of Yemen under his rule.

Imam Yahya's retention of Turkish officials in important posts was indicative of Yemen's isolation during the interwar period. The governmental structure thereby fostered the illusion among the British that diplomatic negotiations with Yemen would be no different—if anything, less difficult—than, for example, with a Wafdist government in Egypt. The venerable tradition of friendly relations between the Imams and English traders at Mocha encouraged Aden and Whitehall. But Yahya regarded the various treaties with the shaikhs and petty sultans of the Western Aden Protectorate (see below) as encroachments upon Yemeni sovereignty. Nor would he recognize border demarcations worked out by Ottoman and Adeni authorities before World War I. A British mission to San'a in 1926 achieved nothing. The Imam subsidized tribal forays into the Protectorate, bringing the Royal Air Force into action. After the bombing of Taiz in 1928 the incursions stopped.

Turning his attention to Najran and other parts of the Asiri borderland, Yahya then became embroiled with ibn Saud. In 1934, with Prince Faisal ibn Abdul Aziz at the head of a victorious Saudi army in Hodeidah, the Zeidi mission to the north obviously had to await a better opportunity. The Treaty of Taif restored the Tihama to the Imam, bringing into question ibn Saud's Wahhabite missionary fervor but advancing his reputation as a statesman.

British and Italian warships anchored off Hodeidah to observe the movements of Prince Faisal's force. Italy's growing interest in Yemen and reports of Italian intrigues among shaikhs and townspeople gave rise to British fears that Mussolini might one day enforce a *mare clausum* policy in the southern Red Sea. This possibility, as much as the Treaty of Taif between Yahya and ibn Saud, brought about further British efforts to come to terms with the Imam. The resulting Treaty of San'a (1934) was a curious exercise in diplomacy. The British negotiator, Sir Bernard Reilly, returned to Aden satisfied that Britain's special relationship with the petty states of the Western Aden Protectorate was unimpaired. Yahya's interpretation was that, present "temporary arrangements" notwithstanding, he had been recognized as king of all Yemen, from the northern frontier right down to Jebel Shamaan and the port city of Aden which it dominated.[2]

---

[2]His secular title of "king" was employed in the document but never gained the currency that it did in Saudi Arabia after ibn Saud adopted it.

There were occasional disturbances on the frontier with the Protectorate down to 1948, but on the whole relations were correct. Internal policy, if it could be described as such, was limited to close supervision of the ruling family's various monopolies and tax collection, but no concerted opposition was aroused.[3] More vexed was the succession question. Throughout the Imamate's long history there had been pretenders whose claims had some degree of authenticity. In addition, the tradition of dynastic succession was not firmly implanted. Rival claimants were further encouraged by the well-established reputation for cruelty which Crown Prince Ahmed possessed and, indeed, enjoyed.

Seyyid Abdullah al-Wazir, descendant of an Imam of the late nineteenth century, struck first and hardest. The old Imam was gunned down in February 1948 by one of Abdullah's supporters and a government was formed which made a variety of concessions to popular opinion. It survived for a month before Ahmed, who had been governor of the province of Taiz, marched on San'a at the head of a vast force of tribesmen recruited in the northern mountains.

The beheading of Abdullah al-Wazir was an appropriate beginning for a regime marked by bloodshed. Not all the blood was shed within Yemen. Ahmed opened his campaign against the Western Aden Protectorate within months of his accession, having first moved his capital from San'a to Taiz to be more closely in touch with developments. Postwar changes in British colonial policy were a guarantee of the trouble Ahmed's guns and money provided. The "Northwest Frontier" system of tribal administration was abandoned. Among the thinning ranks of supporters of the imperial idea, social and economic betterment became the *raison d'être* of colonial governments. Protectorate treaties were supplemented with advisory treaties which in turn encouraged some form of collaboration between the states of the Western Aden Protectorate. The established rulers were as much interested in greater protection from Ahmed's agents and gunmen as in the economic and social advancement implicit in a federative arrangement. Whatever their motivation, acquiescence increased the British "presence" in tribal territory. This in turn increased dissidence, already present in large measure. The rulers in treaty relations with Great Britain might have been *primus inter pares* in the British view (and their own), but among the shaikhs who made up the *pares*, there were many who were willing to collaborate with Imam Ahmed for their own purposes.

---

[3]After World War II, a "Free Yemeni" movement was founded by emigré merchants in Aden. Contacts were established with opponents of the Hamid-ud-Din within Yemen, but no internal movement had been organized before Imam Yahya's death.

The vigor with which Imam Ahmed asserted his claim to territories which for centuries had been independent of any shadow of Zeidi authority advanced the date of Great Britain's departure. But it was also a harbinger of the end of the Hamid-ud-Din dynasty and an Imamate which reached back into the mists of history for a thousand years. British political agents, British-officered levies (latterly organized as a federation army), and Royal Air Force fighter bombers from Aden's Khormaksar Base made the protectorate treaties into much more than paper and sealing wax. To obtain the money, arms, and military technology required for his border war, Imam Ahmed broke the tradition of Yemeni isolation and entered a strange new world.[4]

Imam Ahmed's son, Mohammed Badr, was influential in the formulation of the new policy. He had won the designation of Crown Prince and the office of prime minister by placing himself at the head of a force of tribesmen and rushing to his father's rescue during an attempted *coup d'état* in April 1955 when the Imam was imprisoned in Taiz by army officers who supported the claim of a half-brother, Abdullah, to the Imamate. The rebels were dealt with faithfully. After a series of public beheadings, a frequent break in the tedium of everyday life in the era of Ahmed, the Imam and his son turned their attention to the Protectorate.

The concept of uniting the states of the Western Aden Protectorate in what was initially called the Federation of Arab Emirates of the South had been mooted by the Governor of Aden in 1954. The policy was condemned as violently by the Voice of the Arabs, *al-Ahram*, and other Egyptian news media as by the Imam himself. King Saud, whose anti-British enthusiasms had been increased by the Buraimi affair, joined the chorus. Quickly satisfied that Egypt and Saudi Arabia were prepared to go beyond reciting the standard anti-imperial litanies, Crown Prince Badr pressed his father to meet with Nasser and Saud. Badr's arguments were convincing, especially in view of the depleted state of the Imam's treasury.

---

[4]The deterioration of Anglo-Yemeni relations did not obstruct the departure of virtually the entire Yemeni Jewish community for the state of Israel. It numbered about forty thousand and was the oldest settlement of Jews outside Israel. Its traditions asserted that the community left ancient Israel before the destruction of the temple and at one time dominated parts of Yemen as a warrior class. Although Imam Yahya opposed the emigration of Yemeni Jews to Palestine before 1948, placing a high valuation on their contributions to the economy as jewelers, glaziers, leather workers, and builders, several thousand did succeed in departing in small groups. Imam Ahmed held the Jews in contempt. The historical accident of his accession to power at the time that Israel was founded—in addition to his reputation for tyranny —encouraged a mass migration to Aden. Large sums of money were extorted from the Jews before they left Yemen. In Aden a reception center was established through British collaboration with officials of the Jewish Agency. They were then transported by air ("Operation Magic Carpet") to another form of second-class citizenship in Israel.

In 1956, therefore, Imam Ahmed emerged on the international scene, leaving his country to confer with the Egyptian and Saudi leaders in Jeddah. There would be no turning back to the days of Zeidi isolation on the highland plateau.

Ahmed returned $30 million richer, praising the generosity of King Saud. Less was said about President Nasser, but soon Badr was in Cairo, dazzled by the Egyptian leader's prescriptions for the Arab world. He accepted the offer of military advisors and other specialists, and also the suggestion that contacts with the Communist bloc would have beneficial results. Moscow and Eastern European capitals were added to Badr's itinerary, and before the year was out a Soviet freighter was discharging military stores in Hodeidah.[5] The penetration of Yemen had begun. Modernization, it seemed, was to come through the barrel of a gun.

Nasser's plans for the Arabian Peninsula were facilitated by the conjunction of Badr's rise to power in Yemen and his own rise to the pinnacle of his influence in the Arab world between the Suez War of 1956 and the breakup of the United Arab Republic in 1961. Another factor was the declining health of the Imam. Although his ferocious character remained unchanged, the forcefulness with which he cowed the province of Taiz and, after 1948, the entire country was diminishing. In its place was indecisiveness. As much as the Imam disliked his son's reformist zeal and espousal of pan-Arabism, he shrank from replacing him.[6] A further deterioration of Ahmed's physical condition brought on the unprecedented measure of a journey to Rome for specialized medical treatment. This gave Badr the opportunity to press on with his neo-Nasserite program.

The opposition movement had expanded even before the Imam departed for Europe. The Free Yemeni movement in Aden, supported by the Arab Trade Union Congress and its political wing, the People's Socialist Party (led by Abdullah Asnag), was now coordinating its activities with Yemenis in Cairo. At that stage the Cairo branch of the movement had covert support from the Egyptian government. In 1959 both the Aden and Cairo Free Yemenis were in contact with a "Free Yemeni Army Officers' Movement" within Yemen. The only open manifestation of the latter organization was a sporadic distribution of crude anti-Imamate pamphlets in Yemen's cities.

---

[5] A subsequent visit to Peking by Crown Prince Badr resulted in an aid agreement through which the Chinese government carried out major road construction projects, built a textile mill in San'a and a hospital in Taiz, and provided funds for the construction of the Yemeni embassy in Peking. The agreement was renewed after the revolution of September 1962.

[6] But Ahmed did give some consideration to assigning the premiership to his brother, Hassan, Yemen's permanent delegate to the United Nations.

During the brief regency of the Crown Prince the situation changed radically. The Egyptian president had broadened the base of popular support in the early years of his revolutionary regime by emphasizing social services and army reform. In seeking to emulate him, Badr had the advice of a number of Yemenis who had returned from Cairo as well as of one who had been born there and had lived most of his life before 1959 in Egypt and Europe. This was Dr. Abdur Rahman Baidani, a German-trained economist who would figure prominently in the first republican government after the 1962 revolution. Infiltration by anti-Imamic elements was facilitated by Yemeni membership in the hybrid United Arab States, a vague confederative arrangement with Egypt and Syria which had come into being in 1958 after the formation of the United Arab Republic.

It was inevitable that powerful interest groups would oppose the new program, for as a result of it, the income of tribal shaikhs was affected, army commands were shifted, and officers and civil authorities were placed on the retired list. The border war against the South Arabian Federation, established in 1958, was temporarily shut down. Such wars always have been forms of outdoor relief for the wealthy, and the cessation of hostilities cut into the income of influential Yemenis engaged in gun-running and related activities. Soon the Crown Prince was confronted by an army mutiny and tribal revolt.[7] When the Imam returned from convalescence in Rome, the allegiance of a sizable proportion of the armed forces was in question and rebellion was spreading in the Sunnite Tihama.

Imam Ahmed returned to Yemen with health restored, and for two years his subjects felt the full force of his ruthlessness. The hostage system by which the country had previously been controlled was reinstituted. Some two thousand relatives of tribal shaikhs and other influential persons throughout the country were kept in the Imam's prisons. Taxes on agricultural products, farm animals, and capital became so onerous that landowners chopped down fruit trees in protest. War on the South Arabian Federation was resumed and Crown Prince Badr was placed under house arrest.

The old Imam abominated Nasserism, as he understood it, but admired and even improved upon one aspect of the Egyptian leader's tac-

---

[7]One aspect of the tribal unrest deserves elaboration. Some of the Zeidis who opposed the policies of a Zeidi Crown Prince took pride in asserting their special status as descendants of the pre-Islamic population of South Arabia. It is not difficult to see how tribal elements who could object—after a thousand years—to the "foreign domination" of Zeidi Sayyids, who were regarded as displaced Hejazis, would conceive a robust hatred and contempt for the Egyptians after their arrival in 1962.

tics. During the last years of his life he adroitly played the Eastern and Western blocs against one another. Yemeni students went abroad for training under grants from the American Agency for International Development and from the Soviet Union. The United States assisted road construction projects concurrently with similar projects underwritten by the Chinese People's Republic. There were West German and Eastern European activities on a smaller scale. Soviet aid to the reactionary Imamic regime was impressive. In 1961 the Russians completed their modernization of Hodeidah port, supplied two hundred trucks, two seagoing dredges, a complete power station, and many other valuable items of equipment.

In the same year, opposition to Ahmed's rule began to show some measure of organization. Government installations were bombed in San'a and Taiz, clandestine radios began functioning, and the Egyptian regime's support of the Free Yemeni movement became obvious. Two attempts were made to assassinate the Imam and in one of them, at Hodeidah, he was gravely wounded. Enough vitality remained for him to react to President Nasser's new socialization decrees by withdrawing his country from the United Arab States. As an institution, the UAS was a dead letter, but the rupture gave the Imam an opportunity to denounce Arab socialism—which he did, employing a remarkable combination of traditional and modern methods of communication. After composing a long poem on the evils inherent in socialist panaceas, the Imam read his literary masterwork on the Yemeni radio. The effect in the Arab world (for the poem was widely rebroadcast) was as spectacular in its way as that of the Bey of Tripoli, who declared war on the United States in the early nineteenth century by marching into the garden of a startled consul to chop down his flagpole.

It was a last grand gesture. The Imam never recovered from the wounds received at Hodeidah. The country was slipping out of his control and in mid-1962 there were major demonstrations in Taiz, supported for the first time by the merchants of the city. In September 1962, Imam Ahmed died in his bed, which was in itself a minor success.

In the last year of his life Ahmed reluctantly reconfirmed his son as heir presumptive. Badr immediately set out to implement the reform program he had outlined in 1959. A political amnesty was proclaimed and future foreign policy was described as based upon the principles of positive neutrality and nonalignment. An attempt to tranquilize the deeply conservative Zeidi oligarchy of Sayyids, or notables, the tribesmen, and the *ulema* took the form of disingenuous pronouncements that Egyptian concepts of social revolution were not applicable to Yemen. Badr further insisted that the Imamate was to be the wellspring of all reform. Judging from his efforts to deemphasize his father's insistence on the unity of the Arab south, he appeared to be favoring an Imamic version of "socialism in one country." The experience of 1959 suggested that he would have his hands full with domestic policy and that the war against the South Arabian Federation should be shut down, at least for a time.

Badr was not given time to initiate his policies. On September 26th, only eight days after his father's death, Imam Badr was overthrown by an army *coup d'état* led by Colonel Abdullah Sallal (soon, predictably enough, to become field marshal). The palace was heavily if not thoroughly bombarded and the death of the Imam and the establishment of the Yemeni Arab Republic were announced over San'a radio. Sallal became the new republic's first president. He also took the portfolio of prime minister.

Iraq, which twelve hundred years before had been the site of the Zeidi sect's bloody inception, was associated with the blotting out of the Zeidi Imamate. Abdullah Sallal had received his military training at the Baghdad Military College, where he imbibed the revolutionary philosophy which influenced his subsequent career. Although not a member of the Zeidi aristocracy—his father was a blacksmith—Sallal got onto friendly terms with Badr when the latter was a youth. To advance his own cause, Sallal became involved in Abdullah al-Wazir's attempt to secure the Imamate in 1948. He was sentenced to life imprisonment but released and reinstated in the army in 1955 through the intervention of Crown Prince Badr, with whom he worked closely while concerting his plans with younger officers. Any remorse Sallal might have felt about the fate of his royal benefactor was quickly dispelled by news that Badr had survived the bombardment and was organizing a tribal assault on San'a.

Before it was established that the Imam was alive and that civil war was in prospect, President Nasser had taken steps to "protect the revolution." The day after the Yemeni Arab Republic was proclaimed, UAR troops were flown into San'a and on the following day the first seaborne contingent landed at Hodeidah—a fact which suggested a certain amount of coordination between Cairo and the perpetrators of the *coup*. There were twelve thousand UAR soldiers in Yemen by December; the Egyptian occupation had begun, with Marshal Abdul Hakim Amer playing Ibrahim Pasha to Nasser's Mohammed Ali. Cairo was responsible for the installation of Abdur Rahman Baidani as deputy prime minister. The new republic's first foreign minister, Muhsin al-Ayni, was from northern Yemen, educated in France and active in the Aden Trade Union Congress and in the Free Yemeni movement in Cairo. The contribution of al-Ayni to the development of the Yemeni Arab Republic would be far more significant than that of Sallal.

By December 1962 the Yemenis had a republican government and no apparent policy, whereas the UAR had a base in the Arabian Peninsula and a policy, the first phase of which was to drive the British out of Aden. Once the South Arabian Federation had been replaced by an Arab socialist regime dependent upon Cairo, attention could be given to the second phase, which was to bring down the House of Saud and to apply the oil revenues of that country to other suitably "progressive" causes. Soon the South Arabian Federation was under attack by infiltrators and dissident tribesmen, armed and trained in Egyptian camps behind the Yemeni Arab Republic's frontier. Egyptians swarmed into San'a, Taiz, and Hodeidah, and in making Yemen a base for the operations, gave the fledgling republic a policy—to get rid of the Egyptians. What complicated matters for the republicans was increasing Saudi (and, to some extent, Iranian) support for Imam Badr, whose policy was to get rid of them as well as the Egyptians. Thus Badr and his followers provided the rationale which was to keep the Egyptians in Yemen until 1967, when Israel contributed to the rationale for their departure. But already in January 1963, Dr. Baidani's conduct as Cairo's man in San'a was so crude and overbearing that he was dismissed and sent back to Egypt.

Neither Saudi Arabia nor Jordan recognized the new republican regime. Nasser's appreciation of the situation was correct: the Yemeni army was hardly of a standard to be the shield of the republic, and Saudi Arabian aid to the royalists would be prompt and generous. The United Arab Republic's military intervention was accompanied by diplomatic recognition. The Soviet Union and most of the Communist bloc quickly established relations with the new regime. The United States and Great Britain held back, seeking more information on the developing situation. The first Western country to accord recognition was the Federal Republic of Germany, on October 23, 1962. British parliamentary missions visited both royalist- and republican-held Yemen. Negotiations with the latter were complicated by the expansion of hostilities against the South Arabian Federation and Sallal's bellicose proclamation in November that the Yemeni Arab Republic would be the nucleus of a Republic of the Arabian Peninsula which would arise from the ruins of "colonialist and feudal" regimes in southern and eastern Arabia and Saudi Arabia. But American policy planners concluded, during the first months of the new San'a regime, that Soviet interests were becoming so firmly entrenched as to necessitate the establishment of an American diplomatic mission to the republic in order to exercise a moderating influence.

In an exchange of letters with Crown Prince Faisal (see above), President Kennedy prepared the way for recognition of the Sallal regime by promising to come to the defense of Saudi Arabia if the kingdom were threatened by external aggression. The American policy of conciliation led to contacts with Prince Faisal, President Sallal, President Nasser, and King Hussein of Jordan. Imam Badr was not consulted, it being assumed by the Department of State, rather inaccurately, that Prince Faisal could represent his point of view. All parties to the American mediatory effort agreed that a settlement between the republicans and royalists was favored by both sides and would be facilitated by the withdrawal of external support. This was followed by American recognition of the Yemeni Arab Republic (December 20, 1962), resumption of the aid program, and membership in the United Nations for the San'a regime. The Kingdom of Jordan followed the lead of its American paymaster and performed the distasteful function of extending recognition shortly thereafter. Saudi Arabia waited upon events.

It soon became apparent that Sallal did not measure up to the task of heading a revolutionary government. The most striking evidence was provided by his increasing reliance upon Nasser's brother-in-law, Marshal Amer, and his large staff of officers and administrators. Under Amer's competent direction, the Saudi-UAR proxy war entered a violent new phase. By April 1963, over two-thirds of Yemen was controlled by the republicans, and royalist positions were under heavy bombardment by the Egyptian air force. This was the high point of the United Arab Republic's fortunes. Soon royalist counteroffensives caused withdrawals until each side held about one-half of the country.

Futile attempts to promote disengagement were made in missions to the Yemen by Ralph Bunche, United Nations Under Secretary for Political Affairs, and Ellsworth Bunker, special envoy of President Kennedy. These efforts were institutionalized in the United Nations Yemen Observer Mission, which lasted from June 1963 to September 1964, during which time it scarcely functioned at all. The wild terrain of northern and eastern Yemen was no place for peacekeeping missions whose experience consisted of United Nations operations on both sides of the well-defined communal boundaries of Cyprus or along the clearly delimited Israeli frontiers. The most hopeful activities were carried on by the Yemenis themselves. Secret meetings between royalists and republicans began as early as 1963, precipitated by the evolution of a political "third force" opposed to the republic's reliance upon and subservience to the United Arab Republic.

The Egyptians continued to use their special position in Yemen to strike at the South Arabian Federation. In early 1964 a major offensive was undertaken against the Federation, known as the Radfan Rebellion from the mountainous Radfan region where large numbers of Federation and British troops were tied down by Egyptian-trained and -financed guerrillas. During the campaign, in April 1964, President Nasser visited the Yemeni Arab Republic and pledged renewed efforts to eradicate British influence from Arabia and to replace "feudal" regimes with exponents of Arab socialism. Another motive for the Egyptian President's visit was to boost the flagging morale of Egyptian troops whose casualty rates were mounting from the hit-and-run tactics of Yemeni tribesmen. Nasser's speeches in fact spurred renewed Saudi efforts to provide logistical support for Imam Badr's tribesmen and a certain amount of clandestine British support for the royalists. In addition, the San'a regime was creating problems for itself by its treatment of the coastal and lowland Shafai community, which was no better than that accorded it by the Zeidi Imams and perhaps worse.

The next year, 1965, saw a decline in Egyptian influence, a marked erosion of Sallal's position, and a general weakening of the republican regime. In the field, royalist forces enjoyed one success after another. To retrieve the situation, Sallal and his Egyptian patrons were forced to turn to the veteran politician Ahmet No'man, relying upon him to form a government with a broader base of support. Prime Minister No'man was a Shafai with impeccable revolutionary credentials. He had come around to a moderate position, favoring a "normalization" of relations with Saudi Arabia and a search for a formula whereby royalist resistance could be terminated in exchange for the preservation of the Imamate as a strictly religious institution. He even spoke of a national referendum on the future form of Yemen's government. Such policies were too visionary for President Sallal, who therefore created a "Supreme Council of the Armed Forces" to monitor the activities of the civilian government. No'man submitted his resignation and in early 1966, accompanied by a number of other political figures, journeyed to Cairo to place his policy proposals before President Nasser. For his pains, No'man found himself in an Egyptian prison.

Although the casualty rolls grew and the cost of the Yemen operation mounted steadily, Nasser was determined to hold on in Yemen until the British were out of Aden; if he succeeded, it would go a long way toward refurbishing his image as a latter-day Saladin. In 1965 he went to Jeddah to negotiate with Faisal (who had replaced his brother as king in late 1964) and agreed to withdraw all Egyptian forces within thirteen months in exchange for a cessation of Saudi support for the royalists. The Jeddah agreement also called for a conference of all Yemeni factions to work out a provisional form of government pending the formulation of a constitution. When it was held at Haradh, in northern Yemen, in November 1965, the conference broke up in complete disagreement.

Nasser had no intention of honoring the Jeddah agreement, as was evinced by the continuously rising level of Egyptian troop strength in Yemen. By 1966 it had reached sixty thousand, and there were seventy thousand troops at the wrong end of the Red Sea when the Six Day War of June 1967 erupted.

As the war dragged on, moderate republican elements began calling for direct negotiations with Imam Badr and a speedy evacuation of the Egyptian armed forces. Throughout 1966 Sallal kept a tenuous hold on power by resorting to purges and executions. He employed the late Imam Ahmed's methods of rule while the Egyptian air force kept Ahmed's son from the gates of San'a. With the outbreak of the Arab-Israeli war, it appeared that the hour had struck for republican Yemen. The role of the Egyptian forces shifted from maintaining Abdullah Sallal in authority to a watching brief on the rapidly developing situation in the South Arabian Federation. More important, with the Egyptian economy in ruins, King Faisal found himself capable of dislodging the United Arab Republic from its base in the Arabian Peninsula. At the Khartoum Conference in August 1967, the oil-producing Arab states agreed to render financial assistance to the countries which had engaged in direct combat with Israeli forces or had experienced direct exposure to them. In this manner, Faisal purchased not only approval of renewed oil shipments to Western markets but also the evacuation of Egyptian troops from Yemen. By December the last units had departed. But the British evacuation of Aden had come earlier, so once again President Nasser was able to claim a victory.

So long as President Sallal had Egyptian support, he could keep republican Yemen under some degree of control and the royalists in their mountain caves. His sponsors realized that he could not long survive their departure, and that the republican government would have to be strengthened if it were to withstand the royalist tribesmen. A parting gesture, therefore, was the Egyptian-engineered ouster of Sallal. In Iraq, en route to Moscow, when the new dispensation was announced, Sallal decided to settle in Baghdad where he had earlier absorbed as much as he could of the military craft.

It was indeed a near thing for the Yemeni Arab Republic. The royalists brought San'a under siege in December, almost as the last Egyptian soldiers were embarking at Hodeidah. Only the most energetic measures by General Hassan al-Amri, who took over from Sallal as interim prime minister and commander-in-chief of the armed forces, ably supported by the widely respected Qadi Abdul Rahman Iryani, the provisional president, broke the royalist offensive. By mid-1968 the two sides were again at a standstill, each holding about one-half of the country. The search for the elusive formula for peace in this ravaged land continued.

Saudi Arabia's King Faisal was no partisan of revolutionary regimes, but neither could he be regarded as an enthusiastic supporter of the Hamid-ud-Din. Moreover, it was less important which Yemeni entity ruled in San'a so long as the Egyptians were pushed out of the Arabian Peninsula. Hence from early on in the civil war the need for Riyadh and San'a to make common cause was apparent to a few Saudi and republican Yemeni leaders. On the other hand, it was not easy for the Saudi dynasty to contemplate participating in the extinction of another royalist regime —a task normally undertaken by revolutionary command councils.

Three developments set the stage for a Saudi-republican Yemeni *rapprochement*. The first was the failure of the Yemeni royalists to utilize effectively the large Saudi (and other) subventions to drive the republicans out of San'a. The Hamid-ud-Din were unsuccessful in employing what has been called the "rent-a-tribe" system. The second was the Six Day War, which produced decisive arguments in favor of an Egyptian withdrawal. The third was the advent, also in 1967, of the National Liberation Front government in Aden. As far back as 1963, Crown Prince Faisal had remarked to a British diplomat that, although he was hardly in a position to say so openly, he hoped that Britain would hang on in South Arabia, because the successor regime would be wedded to radical ideologies and Aden would become a base for the spread of extremist "liberation" movements in the Arabian Peninsula, supported by Soviet and Communist Chinese grants of funds and military supplies. It was an accurate prediction. The war in Dhofar against the Al Bu Said dynasty of the Sultanate of Oman was the initial external result of NLF paramountcy in Aden. In Riyadh, as in Oman and the Trucial States, this was regarded as the first phase of a program with grave implications for all regimes in Arabia. Yemenis of every persuasion began to realize that the area of devastation was spreading inexorably over what had been the Arabia Felix of antiquity. The Saudis and republican Yemenis now had a basis for common action.

Thus, in March 1970, under the convenient cover of participating in an Islamic conference, the Yemeni Prime Minister and Foreign Minister Muhsin al-Ayni journeyed to Saudi Arabia to begin the negotiations which were ultimately to bring Yemeni royalist hostilities against the San'a regime to an end. There had been informal meetings between republicans and royalists before—in Beirut and Cairo and, following negotiations between Nasser and Faisal, in conferences at Jeddah and Haradh in northern Yemen.

For Saudi Arabia and, in the early stages, Egypt, contacts between the warring elements gave rise to hopes of reductions in financial support. There was also the standard rhetoric concerning the need to close the ranks of Arab peoples in the face of the Israeli challenge. In the event, the failure of the last major Saudi-sponsored offensive in February 1968, which fell just short of capturing San'a, coupled with disturbing developments in South Arabia, made possible al-Ayni's visit to Saudi Arabia.

Muhsin al-Ayni is a politician of consummate shrewdness and skill, educated, experienced, and well-traveled. A socialist of remarkable persuasiveness, he is greatly admired by the younger elements in the army, civil service, and educated classes. The ranks of his nonadmirers—and not all of them are traditionalists—are also numerous. There are no neutrals in Yemen on the subject of al-Ayni.

His most gifted adversary among the Hamid-ud-Din was Yemen's Talleyrand, the royalist Foreign Minister Ahmed as-Shami. Having witnessed the failure of his patrons to organize military victory, as-Shami worked assiduously to achieve a compromise whereby the Imamate, as a religious institution, could be preserved within the structure of the republican government. However, once the royalist siege of San'a was lifted, the republicans felt that to compromise on the Imamate would simply nurture the seeds of counterrevolution. Thus, as-Shami realized, the only alternative open to him was to find a formula by which the more progressive royalists could return to San'a to "work within the system." If he had chosen to do so, he could have placed major obstacles in the path toward a resolution of differences by continuing his support of Imam Badr. Discussions between al-Ayni and Prince Sultan, the Saudi Minister of Defense, must be viewed in this perspective.

Both al-Ayni and as-Shami were far more advanced in their thinking on reconciliation than the interests they represented, or, for that matter, than the Saudis. The ruling family in Riyadh was split between hard-line monarchists, those who felt that the Hamid-ud-Din were a spent force and unworthy of further support, and those who looked upon a settlement with San'a as a step in the direction of settling accounts with the leftist Adeni government. In his initial meeting with Prince Sultan, al-Ayni stated that even if Saudi Arabia provided him with a subvention of millions of *riyals*, cut off its subsidies to the royalists (mainly to the tribes whose loyalties had been thus purchased) and, for that matter, delivered up the entire Hamid-ud-Din family for execution at the Bab al-Yemen in San'a, he could not accept, for any deal with the Saudi supporters of the Imam would compromise his political future in republican Yemen. It was an adroit opening gambit, from which he went on to suggest that if the royalist attacks ceased, republican military operations also would end, and eventually the royalists could return to San'a to take part, as Yemenis, in the government and political life of the Yemeni Arab Republic.

That this strategy finally succeeded owes much to Ahmed as-Shami. Not only did he win over most of the hard-core royalists who wanted to continue the fighting, but he also participated in resolving differences among Saudi policy-makers. He accomplished the first by emphasizing the destructive effects of prolonged warfare on the economic and social fabric of the country, and the opportunities which could be seized by establishing a political base in San'a. The second was less difficult. In conversations with Prince Sultan and others, he urged that reconciliation would afford Saudi Arabia the best opportunity for undermining the Communist-oriented NLF regime in Aden. In effect, he was offering the Saudis an advance base from which to carry out this policy. Saudi incursions and air strikes into the former Eastern Aden Protectorate already had taken place and had proved unsatisfactory because they could not be mounted in sufficient strength to dislodge the South Yemeni garrisons, much less to cut the overland supply route from Aden to the rebels in Dhofar. Moreover, they were serving to generate sympathy for the NLF among the traditionally dissident tribesmen and townspeople of Wadi Hadhramaut. The possibility for a more successful strategy lay further westward in what had for a half-century been the jousting-ground between the British, aided by their wards in the petty shaikhdoms and sultanates of the Western Aden Protectorate, and the forces of Imam Yahya, Imam Ahmed, and latterly, under Egyptian tutelage, the Yemeni Arab Republic.

For such reasons, the Saudis finally decided to cut off financial support to the Hamid-ud-Din. A period of "no war, no peace" ensued, lasting about four months. During this time Prime Minister Muhsin al-Ayni made his greatest contribution to the eventual reconciliation, for it was one thing to maneuver the Saudis into a new position, but quite another to deal with the Yemeni army, educated classes, and tribal leaders who had cast their lot with the republican regime. Al-Ayni claims to have spoken to seven hundred officers as well as to military cadets, civil servants, and all other influential elements within the San'a-Taiz-Hodeidah triangle, within which the writ of the republic runs. Most difficult to convince was the army commander, Hassan al-Amri, who possesses some of the characteristics of the late Abdul Karim Qasim of Iraq and who, before he went into exile in September 1971, was given to summary executions of "wrongdoers" and other extreme actions. At first al-Amri withdrew to Taiz, but eventually he was reconciled to the extent that he served on a delegation which visited Saudi Arabia to work out the final details.

The embassies of the Soviet Union, the Chinese People's Republic, and other Eastern bloc countries were not enthusiastic over the reconciliation. Here al-Ayni bore down heavily on the themes of his commitment to socialism and his gratitude for Eastern bloc support, also suggesting that the rest of the Arabian Peninsula would be much more receptive to "progressive" ideologies once the teeth had been extracted from the royalist opposition. He also emphasized the need, in terms of effective diplomacy and the requirement for massive infusions of aid to the war-ravaged, drought-stricken country, for a more neutralist foreign policy. This implied the expansion of diplomatic relations on a limited scale with Western nations.

Earlier, in 1969, it had not been particularly difficult to overcome opposition to reestablishing relations with the Federal Republic of Germany. The ineptitude of Germany's Middle Eastern policy had done more to convince the Eastern bloc that this was a logical first step than had the Bonn government's willingness to follow diplomatic recognition with an economic aid program of significant dimensions. The scenes of violence which had accompanied the rupture of Yemeni-German relations were pushed to the background as Mohammed Ahmet No'man, the republican ambassador-at-large and son of the revered Ahmet No'man, skillfully played upon Bonn's desire to regain something of the position Germany had occupied in the Arab world before details were made public of the Israeli-German Agreements of 1958 and 1959 on reparations to Israel. (Under them Western Germany became a transmission belt for further American military aid to Israel, resulting in the severance of diplomatic relations with Germany by "progressive" Arab states and Lebanon in 1965.)

The exchange of ambassadors between Bonn and San'a and the return of the ex-royalists in May 1970 were followed by the resumption of relations with Britain and France (the ambassadors in Jeddah being accredited to San'a). It was too early to contemplate full-scale diplomatic relations with the United States but, largely through Yemeni initiative, a small interests section was established in 1970 under the protection of the Italian embassy, which historically has enjoyed a special position in Yemen. Somalia provided a "home" for the Yemeni interests section in Washington.

On the domestic front, it was with the greatest difficulty that the ex-royalists were brought into republican politics. The reform program included a cutback in tribal subsidies (with plans for diverting the 1.6 million Yemeni *riyals* disbursed monthly to programs of regional educational and social development) and put an end to the entirely autonomous status of the army by establishing a Ministry of Defense to which the commander-in-chief was responsible. Such arrangements caused widespread discontent among various interest groups and provided a point around which opposition to al-Ayni could rally, thus nearly upsetting the delicate process whereby the traditional shaikhs were being brought into a Republican Council. There were also obstacles to agreement on a constitution, which was not promulgated until December 28, 1970.

The threat of dangerous political polarization led to complicated negotiations resulting in al-Ayni's resignation from the premiership and foreign ministry in February 1971, after which he accepted an appointment as ambassador to France. (His rival, as-Shami, had in the meanwhile been forced to retire from domestic politics and took the post of ambassador in London.) But al-Ayni was in no hurry to leave San'a. He held court in his modest villa on the road to the airport, extolling the merits of his reform program and attacking the new government's argument that his measures could lead only to a renewal of civil strife by breaking abruptly with entrenched traditions and usages.

During al-Ayni's ministry, the Saudi Arabian government had approached him on the subject of working across the republic's southern frontier to purchase the cooperation of tribesmen in a campaign against the People's Democratic Republic of South Yemen. Al-Ayni contends that his position was that he had no views on the subject and did not want to be told about it. In other words, a blind eye was turned. Following his resignation, he implied that the Saudis also were arming and financing large numbers of South Yemenis currently in exile in the Yemeni Arab Republic. Although al-Ayni met with South Yemeni leaders in Taiz, no improvement in relations resulted. He spoke eloquently in favor of the reunification of "historic Yemen" but in doing so further alienated Adeni politicians who feared that ultimately San'a would dominate any federal or unified Yemeni state. Adeni suspicion and hostility subsequently were underscored by the change of the country's name from the People's Democratic Republic of South Yemen to the People's Democratic Republic of Yemen, an act that caused bitter resentment in the Yemeni Arab Republic. Meanwhile, the Saudi arms traffic continued to flow.

That al-Ayni's successors were not averse to closer relations with Saudi Arabia was evidenced by President Qadi Iryani's state visit to Yemen's northern neighbor in mid-June 1971. The new Prime Minister and Foregn Minister, Ahmet No'man, a man of over seventy, had served as prime minister in the early phase of the civil war; his efforts to ameliorate the effects of the Egyptian occupation by a mission to Cairo had earned him a long imprisonment there. He returned to Yemen with the prestige of a veteran opponent of the Hamid-ud-Din and an eloquent spokesman for the reconciliation of royalists and republicans and with the advantage of a long absence from politics during much of the process of polarization.

The No'man government sought a more rapid development of official contacts with the United States. Several non-Communist countries established or resumed diplomatic relations. In arguing for an enlarged American presence, the advantages and "access" of the Soviet ambassador were emphasized. Yet President Iryani received complaints from the Soviet ambassador, most notably over the foreign policy statement in June which omitted the ritual blast at "imperialism and colonialism." To No'man's disingenuous claim that he was following the Soviet lead in recognizing nonsocialist regimes, the Russian reply was that while the USSR was strong enough for such measures, the Yemeni Arab Republic was not and that No'man was therefore failing to "protect the revolution." The Soviet Union had become accustomed to unquestioning Yemeni support in the United Nations and was incensed when the prime minister insisted, when called upon to follow the USSR in voting against an American proposal concerning the International Labor Organization, that he be provided with an agenda well in advance of meetings with the ambassador.

Relations with the Chinese were less complicated. In their latest road-building project they had completed over sixty kilometers of excellent surface on the route north from San'a to Sada and were on schedule there as well as on their hospital project in Taiz. At every level, comparisons were drawn with the West German aid projects, which were over a year behind schedule and entangled in Bonn's bureaucracy. The No'man ministry exploited this situation as another argument in favor of an enlarged American role in Yemen.

But prestige, goodwill, and a considerable skill in handling external relations were not enough. In attempting to broaden the base of its support, the No'man government closed its eyes to financial realities, resuming payments both to the tribal confederations and to the army. It was a disastrous policy, which could not be kept up even with Saudi subventions, a Libyan loan of $3 million, and a trickle of external financing from other sources. The accelerating economic crisis forced No'man to resign in July. His principal contribution had been, through President Iryani's mission to Jeddah, a scaling down of the Saudi policy of providing arms and subsidies for use against the Aden regime. No'man argued that the weaponry could just as easily be turned against San'a and that a moderate, prosperous Yemeni Arab Republic was a more effective threat to the People's Democratic Republic of Yemen than hordes of rampaging tribesmen.

Neither the army, the tribal notables, nor the powerful Sudeiri faction in Saudi Arabia was willing to see Muhsin al-Ayni summoned to the republican palace as No'man's replacement. After a month of maneuvering, a coalition of traditional and army elements succeeded in installing General Hassan al-Amri as prime minister. This pointed to a militant policy, as did the appointment to the foreign ministry of Abdullah Asnag, the Adeni trade unionist and political leader who had founded the People's Socialist Party and the Front for the Liberation of South Yemen before 1967 and who was an arch-enemy of the National Liberation Front government. The Asnag appointment pleased Saudi Arabia, which now much more openly subsidized rebel tribesmen from the Radfan mountains eastward to the Saudi-South Yemen frontier. But General al-Amri's impulsive slaying of a rank-and-file political opponent two weeks after his installation in office precipitated his own exile and prevented a further deterioration of Aden-San'a relations.

Muhsin al-Ayni was now called upon to retrieve the situation, taking over the premiership on September 18. His appointment of army leaders to several important ministries was an indication, in the view of many observers, of the fragility of the new arrangements. Nonetheless, a majority of the political elites, including the young army officers, were banking on al-Ayni's shrewdness and experience to provide an extended period of political calm to facilitate economic recuperation.

Al-Ayni refrained from promulgating socialist economic doctrines and encouraged development of the private sector. A liberal policy on domestic and foreign investment in Yemeni private industry was announced. Early in 1972 a number of guarantees and incentives had been formulated, including customs and tax exemptions. Al-Ayni was willing to reap benefits for his country from Sino-Soviet contention for influence in Arabia. China's program was expanded in September 1971 with the arrival of experts charged with the planning and construction of a medical center in Taiz. More extensive Soviet commitments were made during President Iryani's Moscow visit in the following December. They included expansion of the harbor facilities at Hodeidah, a fish cannery, cement factories, grain silos, water development, and educational assistance. Military aid was discussed, but no details were made public. The Soviet program was based upon long-term loans, to be repaid after 1981 in minerals, food products, and other exports. The rate of economic development was slowed, however, by drought, a cholera epidemic, and continuing tension in relations with South Yemen.

By taking over the portfolio of foreign affairs and downgrading Asnag (with whom he had collaborated in the pre-1967 Aden Trade Union Congress) to the ministry of national economy, al-Ayni retained the services of a capable administrator while removing a source of abrasive relations with his southern neighbors. A conciliatory policy was almost impossible to achieve, because of Yemen's reliance upon Saudi Arabia for budgetary economic assistance. There was little popular sentiment in favor of a strong anti-Aden policy, however, and al-Ayni encouraged the resumption of talks between the two regimes. A South Yemeni delegation visited San'a in November 1971. Nothing was accomplished. Bombing and shelling across the frontier resumed. In February 1972 the murder of a number of North Yemeni tribal leaders who allegedly had entered South Yemen for peace negotiations provoked a public outcry in the north. But al-Ayni continued his efforts, meeting with South Yemeni officials in Cairo in March 1972 even as he was attempting to secure Saudi approval for a scaling down of its disbursements to tribal leaders and mercenaries. The fighting continued despite further negotiations between al-Ayni and the South Yemeni Minister of the Interior in Algiers in April.

By mid-1972 it was apparent that al-Ayni was employing Saudi financial support more effectively than his predecessors, and was following No'man's generally successful initiatives in balancing Yemen's relations with the West and the Communist powers. A high point in statecraft was reached in July, with the visit of Secretary of State William Rogers to San'a, a prelude to the establishment of full diplomatic relations between the United States and Yemen and the resumption of development programs. At stake is the future of all South Arabia, the "soft underbelly" through which not only the Yemeni Arab Republic but also the Sultanate of Oman, the Union of Arab Emirates, Qatar, Bahrain, Kuwait, and indeed Saudi Arabia may be subjected to Communist-directed subversion, terrorism, and guerrilla warfare, of which the civil war in the Dhofar province of Oman is the first phase (see below). Whether or not there will be a second depends largely on the stability of the San'a regime and its future relations with Aden.

Nobody was more aware than Prime Minister al-Ayni that normalization of relations with the major powers and the Aden regime was a prerequisite for stability. He was dismayed by increases in the scope and intensity of fighting on the YAR-South Yemeni frontier in the autumn of 1972. The South Yemenis brought tanks and jet aircraft into action, and the effectiveness of night bombing raids suggested that non-Yemeni pilots had been introduced into the conflict. The YAR government was pressed to mount a major invasion not only by the Saudis and Sultan Qabus of Oman but also by members of the former South Arabian League and the Front for the Liberation of Southern Yemen (led by ex-chief minister of Aden, Abdul Qawi Makkawee) who were numbered among the nearly 300,000 South Yemeni exiles and refugees in the YAR. The SAL and FLOSY veterans received additional financial support from Libya, for Colonel Qaddafi perceived the campaign as an anti-Communist crusade.

Al-Ayni regarded such developments as disastrous. With single-minded determination, he sought renewed negotiations with the Aden regime. Talks were held in various Arab capitals, and an agreement on troop withdrawals was reached in late October. An agreement on the unification of the two Yemens was signed by al-Ayni and a South Yemeni negotiator on November 28, 1972, in Tripoli, Libya. The state was to be unitary and to be guided by the "principles of Islamic socialism." San'a was designated as the capital. It was also agreed that final details would be worked out by committees of specialists before June 15, 1973.

Arrangements for military disengagement went forward, but strong opposition to the Tripoli agreement quickly developed in the YAR Consultative Assembly, which was dominated by tribal chiefs accustomed to the longtime patronage of San'a and to the more recent heavy subsidies of Saudi Arabia. Muhsin al-Ayni resigned in December. His successor, Abdullah al-Hajari, retained most of the al-Ayni cabinet and gave lip service to the need for implementing the Tripoli agreement but was known to be completely out of sympathy with the Aden regime. The new foreign minister, Mohammed Ahmet No'man, was well known for his conservative, pro-Western viewpoint.

Meanwhile, Soviet and Chinese military aid continue to pour into the otherwise impoverished People's Democratic Republic of Yemen. Only al-Ayni seems capable of averting prolonged hostilities, but his condition for returning to the premiership is that the power of the tribal chiefs must be broken.

It is important that his condition be met.

2. THE PEOPLE'S DEMOCRATIC REPUBLIC OF YEMEN.

The comingling since antiquity of the histories of the peoples of this South Arabian state and of its neighbors in what is now the Yemeni Arab Republic has already been described. Apart from small-scale fishing, animal husbandry, agriculture, and traditional trading activities, such economic and political organization as existed when the National Liberation Front took over Aden and its hinterland in 1967 was a British legacy. It is therefore with the account of 130 years of British presence and developments since the Union Jack was lowered that this section is concerned.

For nearly two centuries after the Portuguese opened the Cape route between Europe and the Indian Ocean, South Arabia was in a state of economic depression. Further decline was arrested in the seventeenth century by the development of the European market for the coffee of highland Yemen. At first the Dutch engrossed the trade, but at the end of the century the prosperous port of Mocha was an English preserve. In the eighteenth century vessels from the American colonies called there, but the strongest link was with the East India Company. Much of the cargo was carried in "country craft," lateen-rigged *dhows* and booms which transshipped merchandise in Bombay. Aden remained somnolent throughout this period, even after Napoleon's invasion of Egypt had given emphasis to the importance of the route to India via the Isthmus of Suez and the Red Sea. The rise of steam navigation made the difference. Coaling stations and provisioning bases were required. A convenient act of piracy near Aden in 1839 resulted in the transformation of that port into a dependency of British India in 1839.

The first of a long series of treaties with local rulers was made with the Sultan of Lahej after the Bombay Regiment and a detachment of sepoys had wrested Aden from his control. The miserable state of the port and town made the annual stipend conferred upon the Sultan preferable to retaining what then became the first of Queen Victoria's imperial acquisitions. Aden Colony became the administrative responsibility of the Bombay Presidency of the East India Company.[1]

Although Aden was declared a free port in 1853, economic revival was slow until the opening of the Suez Canal in 1869. This brought the promise of bustling commercial activity which Aden had known in ancient times, but before it could be fulfilled a greater measure of security had to be achieved in South Arabia. Local interest in British protection was stimulated after 1872 as a reaction to an aggressive Turkish policy culminating in an invasion of South Arabia. The Turks considered themselves the successors to the Imamic claim to all territory down to the shores of the Indian Ocean. These circumstances impelled Bombay to authorize the signing of formal treaties of protection, a number of which were concluded between 1886 and 1914, when agreement was reached with the Sultan of Qishn and Socotra. These treaties were the basis of the Aden Protectorate and took the standard form of a British guarantee of defense against external attack in exchange for an undertaking not to enter into relations with any foreign power nor alienate territory to any power other than Great Britain.

A demarcation of the frontier was worked out between Turkish and British authorities in 1904, but much of the protectorate was occupied by

---

[1]In 1932 Aden was transferred to the control of the central government of India and five years later it became a Crown Colony, directly linked with London.

Ottoman forces during the Great War. It has been noted that after the Ottoman withdrawal in 1918, the Imam, the traditional Arab authority, refused to recognize the 1904 arrangements. As a result, Yemeni invasions chronically disrupted the western protectorate until 1934, the Treaty of San'a stabilized the frontier. But there was still no renunciation of Imamic claims to the protectorate area. Border incidents and related disputes were not entirely eliminated, but for all its imperfections, the Treaty of San'a was a step forward. Reinforcement of the Aden Protectorate Levies by tribal guards and armed police as well as the establishment of the Hadhrami Beduin Legion in the eastern protectorate encouraged its observation until the death of Imam Yahya in 1948.

During the era of decolonization after 1945, British officials and a number of tribal leaders, concerned primarily with economic and social development, expressed interest in a more structured polity than that provided by the protectorate and advisory treaties. Informal discussions of a possible federative arrangement began early in the postwar period. A series of grants under the Colonial Development and Welfare Act, beginning with an £8 million allocation to the colony and protectorate in 1945, gave rise to hopes that the economic, social, and cultural disparity between Aden and its hinterland would decrease. The most ambitious projects were undertaken after 1947 in Abyan, on the Gulf of Aden east of the colony. Cotton, vegetables, and fruit were grown in significant quantities after the introduction of modern irrigation facilities.

But Aden's pace of development was also quickening. In 1947 a legislative council was established. Although its authority was strictly circumscribed, the very existence of such a body spurred political activism in the colony. The volume of traffic passing through Aden increased annually and was accelerated after the completion of a major refinery and bunkering facility in 1954.[2] Trade with East African and Indian ports, the influx of Yemeni and Somali laborers, the development of Khormaksar Field into an international airport, and passengers coming ashore from ocean liners to throng the Indian, Jewish, and Arab shops made Aden the most colorful and cosmopolitan city on the Arabian shore.

A technical school was established in 1951, a college two years later, and Aden's importance to Great Britain was underscored by Queen

---

[2]Before independence in 1967, the Bureikha or "Little Aden" refinery was producing five million tons of petroleum products annually and bunkering an average of eighteen ships daily. Six thousand ships, about 22 million tons of shipping, were calling at Aden every year. About two hundred ocean going vessels arrived each month, and in addition there were hundreds of smaller ships engaged in trade along the Arabian and African shores between Port Said and Dar as-Salaam. Specific figures on entries of vessels to Aden port in 1966 and 1969 (6,246 and 1,568) dramatically illustrate the decline in port activity since independence.

Elizabeth's official visit in 1954. The value of the colony derived not only from economic activities but also from its strategic significance as the most important British base between Cyprus and Singapore after the British withdrawal from the Suez Canal Zone in early 1956. Extensive army, air force, and navy facilities and the presence of thousands of service families provided employment for a large local work force and injected vast sums of money into the colony. If the polyglot population suggested to Western visitors that there was little that was Arab about Aden Colony, Arabic newspapers, an active union movement (coordinated by the Aden Trade Union Congress), reliance upon the countries of the Fertile Crescent to staff primary and secondary schools, and the Free Yemeni Movement provided ample scope for identifying with Arab causes and concerting opposition to British authority. Before the Suez War, the Aden Trade Union Congress had begun using the strike as an instrument of political warfare. By 1959 there were eighty-four strikes and close coordination had been achieved between the ATUC and the United Arab Republic's specialists in South Arabian affairs. In 1960 President Nasser announced his support for the aims of Abdullah Asnag, leader of the ATUC and founder of its political wing, the People's Socialist Party. He ignored the more moderate South Arabian League, which sought to achieve independence for Aden and the protectorates through constitutional means.

Political and social evolution was much slower in the western and eastern protectorates. Imam Ahmed's warlike policies created some of the difficulties, but the greatest obstacle was tribalism. In 1954 and 1956, however, conferences between various rulers called for closer association, and in 1958 discussions were resumed that led to the establishment of the Federation of Arab Emirates of the South in February 1959. The co-founders were the rulers of six states of the western protectorate.

In 1962 a site near Aden was selected for the federal capital, al-Ittihad, or "Unity." (The name was changed in 1967 to Medinat as-Shaab, or "People's City," by the National Liberation Front government.) The organization, now known as the South Arabian Federation, had increased its membership to eleven. The question of the relationship of Aden Colony to the federation then arose. The possible linking of a cosmopolitan center possessing an articulate, politically oriented, and economically advanced population to a cluster of traditional, undeveloped communities stirred controversy in London, throughout Aden Colony and the protectorate, and certainly in San'a and Cairo. Already changes in the colony's legislative council to include elected members (1955) and then an elected majority (1959) assured that Aden's political future would be fully debated by those most closely concerned with the question.

In mid-1962, when talks began between the government of Aden and the Federation of South Arabia, there was substantial agreement between Conservative government and Labor opposition on the strategic importance of Aden. The Conservative position was that Great Britain required the fullest safeguards for the unfettered operation of defense installations considered essential for the discharge of worldwide responsibilities as well as for the protection of the inhabitants of South Arabia. It was, in fact, a Labor Party spokesman who pointed out that Aden was the base from which the defense of Kuwait would be mounted if Abdul Karim Qasim persisted in claiming that emirate for Iraq.

The British tendency to emphasize strategy was understandable. Aden had become the largest bunkering port in the world and the steady sound of aircraft engines bespoke the importance of Khormaksar Field as a staging point. The Crescent business district continued to evoke the atmosphere of British India of bygone days when Aden looked to Bombay and Bengal for direction and supported British penetration of East Africa.

As for relations between Aden and the federation, a rosy picture was painted. The federal ministers were induced to emphasize common economic interests and to call for confederation in order to achieve greater prosperity and end "the unnatural division between them." It was predicted that Aden's entry into the federation would bring nearer the achievement of full independence. The federal ministers agreed that Aden's advanced political and social institutions entitled it to special considerations—including larger representation in federal assemblies—and that neither the governor's reserved powers nor British sovereignty over Aden was to be affected.

Was this a comfortable means of retreat, similar to more recent attempts to achieve federation in the Persian Gulf? The Colonial Office architects of the South Arabia Federation were specialists in indirect rule, in the tradition of Sandeman of India's Northwest Frontier and of Lugard, who set the pattern of governance for Britain's colonies in East and West Africa. Their handiwork, culminating in the accession of Aden to the federation, was seen by politically conscious Arabs as the employment of "feudal Arab conservatism" to stifle nationalist sentiments and ensure that Aden would continue to serve British interests by providing the structure to support a worldwide policy.

The proclamation of republican rule in San'a in September 1962 was greeted with enthusiasm by political oppositionists in Aden and the protectorates. Excitement grew with the arrival of the Egyptian forces. The transistor radio had long been the means of political education for the ordinary folk of this area. In Aden, in remote Hadhrami settlements—

as in every other part of the Arab world—the dial was set on Cairo. The United Arab Republic was the model for every Arab country. The small political elite which led the antifederation movement included several hundred graduates of Cairo University. As far as they were concerned, the means of creating a UAR in South Arabia was through emulation of the Algerian struggle against colonial rule. Now even the lowest stratum of the feudal hinterland society was inspired by the eclipse of the Imamate. What had been regarded as a rigid, even unchallengeable social order could be overturned. The National Liberation Front, the Front for the Liberation of Occupied South Yemen, and other oppositionist groups gained many new recruits and a renewed sense of purpose.

The spread of violence was predictable, for the Egyptian presence in Yemen provided the supporters of the federation concept with a new sense of urgency. The protectorate rulers regarded federation as a means of preserving their independence from Yemen, which now meant preventing Aden, with its large, transient Yemeni work force, from becoming a rallying point for an aggressive Arab socialism. For Cairo, Aden was the symbol *sans pareil* of British imperialism in Arabia and as such could not merely be permitted to achieve independence by constitutional process but must be liberated.

In January 1963 Aden joined the Federation of South Arabia. The government which agreed to its entry had been elected in 1959 when only 27 percent of 21,500 registered electors voted. The decision to go ahead with accession before a new election was prompted by British Labor Party pressure to recognize the new republican government in Yemen. Labor spokesmen took the position that historically and culturally South Arabia and Yemen were one and that Britain should not provide obstacles to unification. For its part, the San'a regime in Yemen called for an armed rising in Aden—a move which suggested that historical and cultural factors were likely to count for less than the politics of subversion and *coup d'état*.

The crisis of Aden's entry into the Federation of South Arabia was complicated by the rhetoric of representative institutions. Aden, with its rigged electorate, self-serving Indian, Jewish, and Arab merchants, and rootless Yemeni and Somali labor force, was described by a British socialist publication as "an oasis of political dignity and economic activity in a desert of medieval despotic rule and economic stagnation."

At this point the Aden Trades Union Congress and its political arm, the People's Socialist Party, provided the most effective opposition to the federation concept. Concurrently, a subcommittee of the United Nations Committee on Colonialism, made up of representatives of Iraq, Yugoslavia, Venezuela, Cambodia, and Madagascar, expressed interest in a visit to Aden to "ascertain the views of the population." The Soviet Union endorsed this proposal, which also called for the removal of all British troops.

After visits to Egypt, Saudi Arabia, Iraq, and Yemen, the UN mission found "a very strong movement in favor of the union of the [federated] territories with Yemen." Describing the situation in Aden as "dangerous and likely to threaten international peace and security," the mission recommended elections on the basis of universal adult suffrage.

The activities of Egyptian-staffed training centers near the Yemeni frontier and of the National Liberation Front, pledged to terrorism, prompted stringent security legislation by the federal council in mid-1963. British officers on secondment to the new federal army, fearing the emergence of a "Free Officers" movement, became especially interested in training manuals on antisubversion measures.

The shape of things to come was soon discernible. On December 10, 1963, a bomb thrown at Khormaksar Field killed two persons and injured forty-one as the High Commissioner, Sir Kennedy Trevaskis, was about to depart for talks in London on the extension of the Aden franchise. A state of emergency was declared and fifty-seven arrests were made. Most were members of the People's Socialist Party and the Aden Trades Union Congress.

Loss of perspective as the result of pressures from San'a and Cairo and lack of imagination and foresight cost the British authorities an opportunity to make Abdullah Asnag a party to a political solution of the developing crisis. He was intelligent and an admirer of British accomplishments, but did not appreciate their frequent and uncomplimentary comparisons between him, a soft and rotund townsman, and the lean, tough tribesmen of the hinterland. Eventually Asnag was forced into that hinterland where his physical condition and political methods were toughened. It was an example of the "T. E. Lawrence syndrome" at its worst. Moreover, the vigorous British crackdown on Asnag and his organizations gave him greater importance in President Nasser's estimation than subsequent developments would justify. The prestige of the National Liberation Front, closely patterned upon the Algerian FLN, was rising rapidly. Its leader, Qahtan as-Shaabi, a native of Lahej, had studied agriculture in Khartoum and had held minor official posts in the Western Aden Protectorate before moving to Cairo in 1958. He served briefly in the government of the Yemeni Arab Republic while training his followers in the techniques of the FLN.

Increased terrorism was accompanied by increased activity on the federation's border with Yemen. After nearly fifty Yemeni attacks, in-

cluding air strikes by MIGs with Yemeni markings, a federation attack
was ordered on Harib, a fort across from Beihan in Yemeni territory. In
the tradition of earlier days in the protectorate, leaflets were dropped in
Kurdistan and on the northwest frontier to warn off the inhabitants before the RAF Hawker Hunters destroyed the fort. On April 4, 1964, the
Security Council voted to "deplore" this action. The United States and
Great Britain abstained and France voted with the majority.

At the end of April, President Nasser visited San'a as noted above,
and in a major speech the Egyptian president identified his primary
mission: the expulsion of the British and the liquidation of the Aden
base. North Yemen increased its activity in the Radfan mountains, sixty
miles north of Aden, raiding the Aden-Dhala road. When two British
soldiers were killed and beheaded in an ambush, reinforcements (the
first battalion of the King's Own Scottish Borderers) were flown out from
the United Kingdom.

The Radfan campaign served to "unify dissidents," so the result
was a major strengthening of the National Liberation Front. On the international level, the United Nations Committee on Colonialism reopened
the Aden "case" on May 7, 1964, and a resolution called upon Great
Britain to cease military action in Aden and the protectorates "forthwith."

The intensification of hostilities caused a significant split in the
Labor opposition in the United Kingdom. Harold Wilson supported
military action in areas in which the British presence was secured by
treaty and urged that Aden be held because of its importance "for communications and as a centre of peace-keeping operations." Other Labor
members, however, described the Radfan campaign as "the war we cannot win" and attacked "the crusty old fallacy that our presence in Aden
keeps the Russians out of the Middle East." Backbenchers took the position that the People's Socialist Party was the only valid political grouping
in Aden and argued that if power could be quickly transferred to the PSP,
there should be little difficulty in arranging to retain some facilities on a
leasehold basis. Because the retention of military base rights was not
considered a likely possibility, separation of the military base from the
Persian Gulf Command was advocated. Much emphasis was given to
Masirah Island in the Sultanate of Muscat and Oman where an RAF base
had existed since World War II as a staging post for the Far East.

In this atmosphere, British officials pressed on with plans for the
political and economic advancement of the Federation of South Arabia.
The Ministry of Overseas Development invested a substantial proportion
of its miniscule budget in a development plan. In July 1964, after a conference at Lancaster House, federation ministers announced a new federal constitution which was immediately accepted by the British govern-

ment. This instrument provided for a bicameral legislature, a Council of State with one representative from each state, and a National Assembly chosen "whenever possible" by popular election, with special. arrangements for areas where tribalism made this impossible. The president was to be elected by the legislators and the prime minister would be dependent on a parliamentary majority. Aden, a Crown Colony, would become a protected state like the rest of the federation, with sovereignty divided between the federal government and the Aden state. The several states were to have more authority on the subject of internal security. Finally, it was announced that independence would be granted to the federation not later than 1968, with Britain retaining a military base both to protect the federation and to fulfill Britain's worldwide responsibilities. The British government then announced a grant of £9 million toward the federation's 1964–65 budget, £4 million of which was for defense.

In October, the long delayed Aden elections took place. Although a campaign of terrorism had reduced the electorate to just over eight thousand, 75 percent of whom voted, the cease-fire agreement in Yemen and the Labor electoral victory in the United Kingdom gave rise to ill-founded feelings of optimism among Adenis. But terrorism was soon on the upswing. On December 11, 1964, after a visit to the Arab south that was marred by NLF-sponsored bomb incidents, the new Colonial Secretary, Mr. Anthony Greenwood, reported to the House of Commons that: "In view of aggression and subversive activities from across the border, I took the opportunity to reaffirm that Her Majesty's government is determined to carry out to the full its treaty obligations in the area."

But Greenwood also reaffirmed that the Aden base would be retained, in agreement with the federation, "for so long as it is required to service the interests we have in common." The precise nature of the common interests was not identified. Whether or not this was an early intimation of the form Labor's East-of-Suez policy would take, it was certainly a clear indication that Mr. Wilson's economists were looking closely at the £20 million expended annually on the base.

The subject of Aden and the federation became an exceedingly emotional one by the end of the year. Terrorism prevented the implementation of the new constitution, which in any case the Labor government was reluctant to support. Greenwood's attempt to convene a new constitutional conference in March 1965 was a failure because of the NLF's threat to kill any "traitor" who attended it. Federation officials wanted to counter "radical" Adeni politicians by including rulers of the eastern protectorate states in the conference. But the latter felt that a link with the federation would bring on difficulties with Yemen. More important was their fear of "complications" if oil were discovered in their territories.

Nor were matters helped by the appointment of the opposition leader Abdul Qawi Makkawee as chief minister of Aden state. Makkawee had been outspoken in his opposition to Aden's link with the federation, but Greenwood felt that in office he would rally support for a new federal constitution. At the time, there was much discussion about the concept of a unitary state, it being felt that such a state would serve to promote a meaningful association of Aden and its hinterland by breaking the power of the sultans and naibs.

March 1965 witnessed another major increase in terrorism with further ambushes on the Aden-Dhala road as well as a pitched battle in Fadhli State in which thirteen gunmen were captured and Egyptian MIGs violated the federation border in their attacks on federal units in Beihan. The Aden-Yemen road remained open, however, because trade with Yemen and Yemeni immigrant labor were vital to the Adeni economy.

Concurrently, the Arab League Committee on South Arabia, established at the Arab "summit" of September 1964, met with Asnag, Mohammed al-Jifri of the South Arabian League, Qahtan as-Shaabi of the NLF, and a group of deposed sultans in Cairo. The committee had representatives from Egypt, Saudi Arabia, the Yemeni Republic, Tunisia, and Kuwait and a fund of £80,000 to support "liberation movements" in Aden and South Arabia. The NLF position was that only through violence could liberation be achieved, while Asnag, al-Jifri, and the ex-sultans saw the struggle in political as well as terroristic terms. A split among delegates followed the larger division in the Arab world, with Kuwait, as was so often the case, on the fence.

Makkawee's Aden government continued to pressure British authorities to end the state of emergency, release detainees, permit the return of exiles, end "provocations" against the Yemeni Republic, and, most important, support an immediate UN-supervised election along lines called for by the United Nations in 1963. This resolution called for the release of detainees, the return of exiles, and self-determination as soon as possible by a vote based upon universal suffrage. Further, it noted that "the maintaining of a military base in Aden is prejudicial to the security of the region and its early removal is desirable."

Greenwood held out for deferring independence until 1968, urging in May 1965 that the interim period was needed for planning the transfer of power. Having concluded that a constitutional conference was not feasible and casting about for a mechanism to give effect to his policy, Greenwood spoke of a commission made up of participants from countries other than Britain to visit South Arabia for consultations. This proposal was condemned not only by oppositionist groups but by Makkawee, who said ". . . we reject the commission and will boycott it."

Each group read some form of delay or sellout into the commission proposal.

United Nations Secretary-General U Thant found it "not feasible" to accede to Greenwood's request to nominate members of the commission. Commonwealth countries with large Muslim populations refused to participate after being contacted by the Aden government. The Conservative opposition in Britain suggested that Labor was extending its credibility gap to South Arabia in that the commission proposal ran counter to the government's undertaking to reach a settlement by direct negotiation. In the event, when the commission was formed, the Aden government banned its entry.

In late July 1965 Greenwood visited Aden to give the commission proposal a decent burial. He reaffirmed the principles of self-determination and independence as set out in the UN resolution of 1963—no mean accomplishment considering that Britain had voted against the resolution at the time. A "representational working party" was called for to prepare for a constitutional conference under his chairmanship.

The "working party" which met in London in August could reach no agreement on an agenda for the conference, the main obstacle being PSP and Aden government insistence on full and complete implementation of the 1963 UN resolution. Makkawee and Asnag then visited Cairo, after which, against a rising crescendo of terrorism and assassinations, Makkawee induced the Aden Legislative Council to call for recognition of the NLF as a legitimate Adeni political party.

Makkawee's proposal, the refusal of the Legislative Council to condemn terrorism, and the sharp decline of security brought about the suspension of the state constitution. Aden was placed under the direct rule of the High Commissioner. Members of the federal government assailed Makkawee, saying that the ending of Aden's colonial status was the penultimate step toward independence in 1968—a step which was being blocked "by politicians in Aden who act according to the wishes of outsiders rather than the needs of the people."

But the federal authorities were too kind to the departing colonial power. If the Yemeni revolution of late 1962 had sent the federation into sick bay, its death warrant was the Labor government's decision to abandon the Aden base after independence and to refuse to sign a defense agreement providing British military protection. With this decision the Labor government guaranteed that an orderly transfer of power, for which chances were admittedly slight, would be impossible.

Britain's decision, which violated a pledge made in July 1964 to continue to defend the federation after independence, strengthened Nasser's resolve to maintain his forces in the Yemen. The Labor government was made to look both devious and foolish by the assertion of Mr. Denis Heàley, Minister of Defense, that the pledge had been made to a government "which has now disappeared." This statement was later withdrawn in the House of Commons. In such circumstances, the publication of Sir Ralph Hone and Sir Gawain Bell's *Constitutional Proposals for South Arabia 1966* was of little more than academic interest. Recommended was a "united republic" of South Arabia, to include Hadhramaut, and with a "capital territory" made up of Aden, al-Ittihad, the islands of Perim and Kamaran, and the Kuria Murias. To be sure, the weaknesses of the federal structure caused widespread interest in the unitary alternative among federal ministers. But when the Labor government decided not to sign a defense agreement, it was clear that hand grenade and machine gun, and not the Hone-Bell proposals, would determine South Arabia's future.

The Wilson government defended itself by citing its agreement to provide £5.5 million at independence and £2.5 million annually for three years after 1968 for the federal armed forces and claimed that the army could thus be doubled in size and light aircraft acquired. Commenting on the life expectancy of light aircraft against MIGs, Sir Alec Douglas-Home called for a force of jets to "balance Egypt's ambitions." Most observers regarded his proposal as no effective substitute for a British presence.

On March 20, 1967, the Foreign Secretary, George Brown, told of his attempts to have President Nasser use his influence to halt terrorism in Aden, and concluded: "I must tell the House frankly and with considerable regret that President Nasser has not so far given me the undertaking for which I have asked." It was then being widely predicted that the takeover in South Arabia would follow the pattern of Yemen, beginning with seizure of power in the towns.

Between March and September 1967, the Labor government sought means to advance the date of British withdrawal. The families of military personnel had been evacuated and the economy was beginning to run down. The rolls of the unemployed rose to 25,000, many of whom were driven to accepting the standard ten pound fee for throwing an NLF grenade. In April, the United Nations Mission to Aden arrived on the scene. Comprised of representatives of Venezuela, Afghanistan, and Mali, its visit was "for the purpose of recommending practical steps for the full implementation of the relevant resolutions of the General Assembly." Particular interest was expressed in the preparation and supervision of elections.

But the visit was a short one. The mission was boycotted by terrorist groups who had no interest in ballot boxes, and in turn it boycotted the federal authorities who had agreed to receive it. The federal government then refused to accord radio broadcast facilities to the mission's leader, Señor Perez-Guerrero—a broadcast which was to have included a statement that the UN Mission did not recognize the authority of the federation's government. After five days in which no political contacts were made, the mission departed.

In mid-April, Lord Shackleton, Minister without Portfolio, arrived in Aden on the first of many visits which would culminate in a conference with NLF leadership in Geneva seven months later. At almost the same time, the UN Mission met with Foreign Secretary George Brown, after which the House of Commons was told, on April 13, 1967, of "the need accepted by all for a central caretaker government." It appeared that the full implications of his government's policy were beginning to dawn on Brown, for his statements hinted at a restructuring of the federal government and perhaps a separate solution for Aden, indicating a cabinet split over the headlong push to be finished with South Arabia.

Finally, in June it appeared that something other than a policy of "scuttle" had commended itself to Her Majesty's government. In a policy statement to the House of Commons, Brown announced January 9, 1968, as the date of independence. South Arabia was to be organized as a unitary state as proposed by the 1966 Hone-Bell report, with elections to be held "eventually" on the basis of universal adult franchise. Additional military assistance was to include eight Hawker Hunter fighters and a military training mission. To ensure the new government freedom from aggression while it was finding its feet, a V-bomber force was to be stationed at Masirah Island off the coast of Oman's Dhofar province, while a strong naval force, including an aircraft carrier, would cruise in South Arabian waters for at least six months. Moreover, trial by jury in cases involving terrorism was to be abandoned and the NLF would be encouraged to turn to peaceful politics through the lifting of the ban on its activities.

The NLF responded to its new freedom by taking over the Crater district of Aden. At this stage, NLF strategy to eliminate political groupings which might possibly challenge its claim to undivided authority after the British withdrawal was completed. The primary target was the Front for the Liberation of Occupied Southern Yemen (FLOSY) in which Makkawee had joined forces with Asnag. After a number of bloody clashes, a cease-fire was negotiated by representatives of the two groups. Terrorist activities against British military and civilian personnel were then intensified to advance the date of complete evacuation. British authorities attempted to use the South Arabian Federation Army to provide security in Aden, but it was already heavily infiltrated by NLF supporters. When mutinies occurred in the federal army and the South Arabian police, additional British troops were flown in to restore order. It was an impossible task. The port city's economic life was at a standstill. By the end of August 1967, the federal government had collapsed and the NLF took over one state after another by the simple and direct technique of gun law. The federal army's only contribution was to arrange a second cease-fire between NLF and FLOSY supporters in Aden.

September saw the shuttling forth and back of spokesmen between Aden, Beirut, Cairo, London, New York, and even Jeddah. The High Commissioner announced British recognition of nationalist forces as representatives of the people, which must have come as a surprise to some of them. He specifically mentioned the NLF and stated his readiness to enter discussions immediately. Such calm as was introduced by this declaration of intentions was shattered by Foreign Secretary Brown's statement that with the evacuation of Egyptian troops from the Yemeni Arab Republic, there was no further need for a Royal Air Force or Royal Navy presence in Aden. This precipitated a final NLF-FLOSY shootout, with the federal army supporting Qahtan as-Shaabi and his followers.

At the end of November 1967 the last British troops left Aden. In accordance with an agreement signed between as-Shaabi and the British government at Geneva, the National Liberation Front simultaneously was recognized as the government of the People's Republic of South Yemen.

Great Britain had neither the resources nor the inclination to provide the £100 million which the NLF regime demanded as compensation for "one hundred years of colonial oppression." There were further difficulties over the regime's refusal to pay the pensions due to civil servants and military personnel in Aden and the protectorate. Within six months after independence, the People's Republic of South Yemen was destitute. The closure of the Suez Canal and the consequent heavy loss of bunkering traffic and transit trade removed any hope of economic viability for the new state. The Soviet Union was approached but its Middle Eastern policy and those of its European neighbors were in considerable disarray following the June war and there was reluctance to assume further commitments. The view from Steamer Point was of a backwater and many Adenis wondered who the new colonizers would be.

Several factors helped the NLF retain its hold on power. The army was reorganized and discipline restored. When this was accomplished, its modern equipment—a British legacy—made the army a powerful weapon at the regime's disposal. Another valuable inheritance was in the field of social services. British "oppression" had provided thirteen hospitals, over four hundred primary and intermediate schools, twelve secondary schools, and six teacher training colleges, all of which now came under NLF administration and, more important for the junta, guidance.

In addition to imposing the name "Yemen" on the former Eastern Aden Protectorate, whose ties with historic Yemen were tenuous and whose relationship with Aden were more commercial than political, the NLF regime secured possession of the islands of Perim, Socotra, and Kamaran. The British returned the Kuria Muria islands to Sultan Sayyid ibn Taimur. The islands, which had been a present to Queen Victoria from the Sultan of Muscat and Oman in the nineteenth century, were administered by Aden, so that Britain's generosity, as might have been expected, elicited protests from the new Aden government. Had the British been on better terms with the Yemeni Arab Republic, other arrangements might have been made for Kamaran, which lies off the north Yemen coast far north of Hodeidah. But it was Socotra and Perim, as well as the facilities of Aden port, which did much to kindle Soviet interest in the People's Democratic Republic of South Yemen.

The government which took over in November 1967 was headed by Qahtan as-Shaabi as president and supreme commander of the armed forces—by decree—for a two-year period. His ministers were drawn from a thirteen-man NLF command, which was subsequently expanded to a membership of forty-three and was also referred to as a general council. The president was in his mid-forties; the rest of the general command were much younger NLF underground operatives and guerrilla fighters. The country was divided into six governates, each controlled by an NLF "popular council." Even as these arrangements were being made, the Front for the Liberation of Southern Yemen, still led by Asnag and Makkawee, was establishing its headquarters in Taiz and attempting to train cadres for operations against the NLF regime. Had the Egyptians been able to maintain their military presence in the Yemeni Arab Republic, their "chosen instrument"—FLOSY—might soon have developed into a formidable challenge for the NLF, which owed little to Nasser. But FLOSY was now on its own with no support from the San'a regime other than the right of asylum. Soon, and most ironically, Saudi Arabian money would revitalize FLOSY.

Before the East bloc would do much more than express sympathy with President as-Shaabi's frequent assertions that he was taking his country along the road to socialism, he had to prove that he was in effective control of the country. It was no easy task. By the end of March 1968, all frontiers, seaports, and airfields were closed and a curfew imposed following anti-regime outbreaks in tribal areas. At first these were centered in the territory of the former Federation of South Arabia, but they quickly spread eastward to the Hadhramaut where extremist NLF authorities brought on a full-scale rebellion among the Kathiri, Qa'aiti, and Wahhidi tribespeople in an area not pacified by the British until the late 1930s. It was a situation of almost complete chaos. NLF zealots in control of Hadhrami centers of population were in opposition to the Aden regime, which they considered to have betrayed the revolution. The traditional leaders were fighting to preserve their status and privileges. Those considered to be their inferiors in a stratified society resorted to arms in their search for social justice and economic betterment.

Tribal rebellion was expanded by the infiltration of FLOSY supporters financed, as-Shaabi predictably asserted, by the Central Intelligence Agency. It was not until August 1968 that the republican army was able to drive the rebels into mountain retreats in the northeast near the Saudi Arabian frontier. FLOSY might have made a better showing had not dissension developed within its ranks over cooperation with Saudi Arabia. The Aden regime's successful security measures in most areas and its progress in land distribution encouraged the Soviet bloc. A number of preliminary exchanges led to a Soviet technical and military assistance agreement. By 1970 South Yemeni pilots were being trained in the USSR civil and military air traffic through Khormaksar Field was handled by Soviet controllers, and assistance was being provided in the construction of three military airports. Soviet pilots and technicians were manning and maintaining MIG–17 and MIG–21 aircraft and training the People's Republic of Yemen army in operations with T–54 medium tanks, antitank and antiaircraft weaponry, mortars, rocket launchers, and heavy artillery. Younger members of the National Liberation Front were awarded scholarships at Komsomol Institutes in the Soviet Union. Since 1969, assistance also has been provided in irrigation and agricultural development, public health, and the building of a modern fishing fleet. The Soviet initiative led to visits by Bulgarian and Hungarian experts. North Korea also signed a technical assistance agreement and arrangements were made to send a South Yemeni delegation to Peking.

The Chinese were particularly interested in establishing cordial relations with South Yemen. In early 1969 a Chinese-sponsored delegation to Aden was headed by Sumarto, one of a number of Indonesian communists living in exile in Peking. And just as Aden had provided a base for Britain's forward policy in East Africa a century earlier, so it could now serve Chinese interests in that area. By 1971 the Chinese, many of them employed as laborers on the Aden-Abyan-Mukallah road project, outnumbered the Russians. Of the four hundred Soviet technicians present, about 150 formed a military mission to the republican army. Yugoslavia provided some pilot training. The North Koreans were involved in agriculture and the East Germans in the construction of flour mills and the planning of glass, plastic, and soap factories. The United Nations Development Program undertook projects in South Yemen, most notably improving technical facilities at Khormaksar Field. Of all Arab states, South Yemen has received the most aid and technical assistance from Kuwait and Iraq. Its principal trading partner, however, was Japan.

East Germany entered into aid agreements with South Yemen late in 1969 and by 1971 was behind only the USSR and the People's Republic of China in commitments to the NLF regime. A training program in heavy equipment operation, especially for road construction, was implemented as part of the aid agreement which also provides specialists in agriculture, administration, health services, and "popular education." There have been a number of exchanges between members of the ruling NLF and the Socialist Unity Party, the East German Communist Party. In 1971 the NLF's secretary-general, Abdul Fattah Ismail al-Jaufi, visited East Berlin under Socialist Unity Party auspices. The East German mission expedited the planning phase of the highway from Aden to Abyan and then along the coast to Mukallah, a distance of five hundred miles. In the public press, these efforts were explained by the fact that Abyan and Mukallah are important agricultural regions. But of more significance were the logistical advantages conferred by this highway upon the Aden government as the principal supporter of the revolution against the Sultan of Oman in the Dhofar province.

Qahtan as-Shaabi succeeded in obtaining East bloc underpinnings for his country's ramshackle economy, simultaneously making his regime less of an oligarchy and more of a one-man show. But his domineering tactics increased and emboldened opposition to him. Shortly after the Soviet navy and a Chinese delegation had paid goodwill visits to Aden in early 1969, he was overthrown and replaced by a presidential council composed of five members. It was subsequently reduced to three, but included a seven-man executive committee. There were cabinet changes aimed at broadening the regime's base. Emerging as the new strong man was Mohammed Ali Haitham, who commanded the army's support and was a close ally of President Salem Rubaya Ali. The goal of achieving popular support for the NLF regime continued to be elusive and the party was split by cabals and intrigues.

Further difficulties befell South Yemen in 1969. A drought ruined many crops, making the country even more reliant on external support. Moves toward a reconciliation between the Yemeni Arab Republic government and the royalists further strained relations between Aden and San'a. When the South Yemeni army took a bad mauling from Saudi Arabian air and ground forces at the frontier settlement of Wadiyah, some five hundred miles northeast of Aden late in the same year, there were major purges in the army and defense ministry.

Tribal unrest continued throughout 1970 and 1971. There were unsuccessful attempts to convince the leaders of FLOSY and other opposition movements to return to Aden and participate in the government. Many FLOSY members preferred to accept Saudi subsidies to infiltrate the Radfan mountains, the site of frequent clashes between British and guerrilla elements before 1967. Meanwhile, divisions in the NLF government grew. NLF Secretary-General Ismail, favored inclusion of Baathist and Yemeni Communist Party members in the government, direct ties with the Soviet Communist Party and the East German Socialist Unity Party, as well as the development of a people's militia.

Ismail's candidate for the premiership, Ali Nasser Hassani, replaced Mohammed Ali Haitham in August 1971 after President Rubaya Ali accurately assessed relative political strengths and shifted his support to Hassani. Ismail had recruited key personnel in the amed forces. The new government carried out its plans for the formation of militant worker groups charged with expunging private enterprise in South Yemen. A wave of arrests and a spreading atmosphere of terror drove large numbers of merchants and intellectuals into exile. Many took refuge in the Yemeni Arab Republic, lending their considerable ability to that country in its campaign to achieve economic viability. Even the infusions of development assistance from China, the Soviet Union, a number of East European countries, and Iraq could not offset this impoverishment.

On the fourth anniversary of independence, November 30, 1971, a new constitution—prepared with East German advice—came into effect. Despite earlier protests from the Yemeni Arab Republic against changing the name of the country to the People's Democratic Republic of Yemen, this step was now taken. The San'a regime immediately withdrew its representative from Aden, signifying that the possibility of a unified Yemen was more remote than in the days of Imam Ahmed. (The development of PDRY–YAR relations into 1973 has been described above, in Section 2 of this chapter.) The constitution called for the election of a 101-member People's Supreme Council to supersede the General Council of forty-one.

Such measures neither improved the standard of living nor satisfied the expectations of the people of South Yemen. Aden ceased to be a free port at the end of 1971 and within six months the population of the formerly bustling city, which stood at 220,000 at independence, had fallen to eighty thousand. Only one-third of the remaining work force was employed. Wages were cut even as the cost of living rose. The viability of the regime depended more than ever on the sufferance of the East bloc. While the Aden regime continued to channel Soviet, Chinese, and "progressive" Arab arms and supplies to the Dhofar revolutionary movement, there were confusion and indications of hysteria in its announcements of successes in uncovering "reactionary plots" and repelling invasions by mercenaries, allegedly financed by the United States and Saudi Arabia. The oligarchs of the People's Democratic Republic of Yemen must earnestly hope that Russia's Indian Ocean strategy will continue to develop, because their future, if not their country's, is bound up with continued Soviet interest in South Yemen's ports, airfields, and islands.

Eastern Arabia

1. THE SULTANATE OF OMAN.

Archeological evidence merges with written records of the history of this southeasternmost portion of the Arabian Peninsula to identify a number of constant factors. They are: the interaction between Persian and Arab, which is also a constant in the history of the principalities to the north of Oman on the Arabian shore of the Persian Gulf; tribalism in conflict with centralizing elements; rivalries between religious and secular institutions, Imamate and Sultanate; and centuries of European contact with the Omani coast. What emerges is also an account of a country influenced in equal measure by desert traditions and maritime opportunities. For not only have the ports of Oman lain athwart the trade routes between the Indian Ocean and the Persian Gulf, but in its mountains and the wilderness behind them to landward has developed a separate society characterized by its isolation, impregnability, and economic self-sufficiency.

Before the Arabs moved through Dhofar and into Oman in the second century A.D., a pattern of cultivation had been established by the Achaemenid Persians whose underground water systems (or *qanats*) are an enduring legacy to the people of Oman. Before the Arabs were present in significant numbers, a second (or Sassanid) period of Persian occupation extended the areas of cultivation from mountain slopes to the Batinah Coast.

The early Arab intruders came into conflict with the Persians before settling in the western foothills in the southern extremity of the Hajar range. These pre-Islamic Arab tribes were grouped together under the name of Qahtani. The other great migration of tribes entered' Oman through another gateway, the Buraimi Oasis. The tribes which migrated from north to south comprised a loose confederation known as the Adnani. Adnani-Qahtani rivalry has been a feature of Omani history for more than a thousand years.

As the Arab population grew, the Persians focused their energies on developing the ports of the Batinah Coast. Sohar was their capital and they manifested their authority in the Omani interior through Arab tributaries. Down through the sixth century A.D., the key to prosperity and stability for the various Arab groupings was good relations with the Persian coastal power. The Arabs themselves gradually infiltrated the coast to engage in fishing, seafaring, and trading. The Julanda Arabs, who entered Oman by way of Bahrain, became extremely powerful in the last years of the pre-Islamic period. With the rise of Islam, Oman experienced a brief interlude of direct caliphate rule, after which the Julanda ascendancy was reestablished and spread from Bahrain to Dhofar. Although their authority was well established on the coast, conditions of anarchy existed among tribes of the interior.

Significant external ventures by the coastal Arabs of Oman occurred during the Umayyad dynasty. When the Damascus Caliphate was at the height of its power, it enjoyed Omani assistance in campaigns against the Khawarij, the fanatic proponents of a electoral caliphate, and in the expedition which brought Islam to faraway Khurasan.

With the decline of Umayyad fortunes, the Omanis fell back upon their home ground, but very different Omanis they were. With them they brought the seeds of the Ibadhi movement. The name is that of a holy man of Nizwa, Abdullah ibn Ibadh, whose interpretation of Islamic doctrine most appealed to the tribespeople of the interior. In its early manifestation, this movement was an offshoot of Khawarij doctrine, but devoid of the fanaticism which made the latter movement such an object of fear and hatred. By the early ninth century Ibadhism in its domestic Omani form had developed into a minor sect of Islam. In its emphasis upon a puritanical religious observance and a return to the conditions which prevailed before the era of Caliph Othman, in its egalitarianism and its emphasis upon strict observance of *Shari'a* law, the Ibadhi heresy might be regarded as being very similar to Wahhabism. Yet the ferocity displayed by each of these sects toward the other served to set them apart.

The first Ibadhi Imam was elected after the overthrow of the Julanda state in the ninth century and his sway extended over an area stretching from southeastern Oman through the Hadhramaut. Although Ibadhi supremacy might be regarded as a victory of religious organization over primitive tribalism, their skill at promoting commerce and agriculture was equally important in explaining their success. The Ibadhi capital was established at Nizwa, high on the Jebel Akhdar. This interior site, well suited to exercising control over the various tribes, has remained the most important center of Ibadhi power and as such was the base from which the Oman Revolutionary Movement (ORM) of Ghalib ibn Ali challenged Sultan Said ibn Taimur in the 1950s and early 1960s. More recently there has been agitation against Sultan Qabus ibn Said in the Nizwa area by elements of the Popular Front for the Liberation of Oman and the Arabian Gulf (PFLOAG). By contrast to the earlier ORM activities and the current Dhofar war, it is as yet of little consequence.

Ibadhism, however, was but a veneer covering the tribalism which was the principal feature of Omani society. Such authority as the Imans could wield depended upon their success in organizing a decentralized form of military power. This meant that each tribal leader pledged his loyalty to the Imam and was responsible for maintaining order in his tribe. It was a good system so long as religious fervor existed. But peace brought prosperity, which in turn weakened religious appeal and caused a breakdown in the authority of the Ibadhi Imamate by the early tenth century.

In the ensuing chaos, Oman suffered a series of invasions during which Hadhramaut was lost and coastal areas were colonized successively by Abbasids, Carmathians, Buwayhids, and Seljuks. Yet the strategic situation was such that throughout 150 years of political disruption, trade with Persia, India, and East Africa continued to develop. Although the Omanis regained control of the coastal areas and Hadhramaut by about 1050, peaceful conditions did not long endure, largely because of the inroads of Sunni Islam in the northern part of the country. The ports of the Batinah Coast fell under the sway of the maritime principalities of the Persian Gulf, while the interior was dominated first by the rulers of Bahrain and, after a succession of other invaders, by the Wahhabis. But this is to anticipate. From the middle of the eleventh century, the center of Omani power shifted to the extreme southeast, an area whose natural defenses made it possible for the Omanis to develop further their maritime prowess. From the ports of Kalhab, Sur, and Muscat, trading and private vessels ranged the Indian Ocean as far as the Malabar Coast of India and the East African shore.

With the coming of the Portuguese, the situation changed. From 1507 until 1650 Omani maritime activity depended upon the extent to which they were able to collaborate with the Portuguese. The Europeans dominated the entire coast from Ras al-Hadd in the southeast to Khor Fakkan near the head of the Gulf of Oman. It was not a period of uninterrupted control, for the Ottoman Turks captured and briefly held Muscat in 1551 and returned to harass Portuguese and Omanis alike on several subsequent occasions.

Long before the eclipse of Portuguese control of the Omani shore, a new Imamate was gaining support in the interior. The Imamic renaissance began during the first quarter of the seventeenth century when the Ya'rubi tribe, after securing western Oman as far north as Buraimi, extended its control over the entire Hajar range under Imam Nasir ibn Murshid (d. 1649). For two decades prior to its rise, the principal challenge to the Portuguese had come from abroad. With English maritime assistance, the Persians returned after many centuries to Sohar and Khor Fakkan, which become their strongholds on the Batinah Coast. The Portuguese held fast to Muscat and their ships ventured forth from that fortified port in vain attempts to regain their dominant position in the Indian Ocean and Arabian Sea. Especially important in loosening Portugal's grip on Muscat were the sea wars between the Portuguese and the Dutch off the coast of India in the decade of the 1630s.

Meanwhile, the process of consolidation under the Ya'rubi Imams continued in the interior, and by 1643 Sohar was taken from the Persians. Two long sieges of Muscat followed and finally, in 1650, the Imam, Sultan ibn Saif, drove the Portuguese from their last bastion on the Omani coast.

Henceforth, the conflict between the Portuguese and Omanis was conducted at sea. It may be said that the Portuguese were the authors of their own destruction, for many Omanis had been trained in the seafaring arts through service on Portuguese vessels. By 1665 the Portuguese were very nearly swept from the Indian Ocean. Their East African port of Mombasa had fallen to the Omanis and their settlements in India had been plundered in a sea war that extended from the west coast of India to East Africa. The special relationship between Oman and Zanzibar began at this time.

The ports of Oman already had taken on the cosmopolitan character which they possess today. India and Baluchi merchants were active there. East Africa provided not only slaves but also ivory and gold. These commodities, for slaves were regarded as such, were transshipped at Muscat for sale further northward in all of the ports of the Persian Gulf. India provided rice, spices, and cloth, and from the Dhofar region came cargoes of dates to be consumed locally or shipped to Indian ports. The Omanis were active in the coffee trade and their prosperity in all branches of trade spurred the East India Company to greater efforts in expanding that profitable commerce. Omani control of the entrance to the Persian Gulf conferred further importance upon the Ya'rubi Imams and aroused the concern and jealousy of the Persians. Any observer of political developments in the Persian Gulf region in the 1970s would be inclined to describe such concern and anxiety as a constant factor in the history of southeastern Arabia.

The Ya'rubi Imams took full advantage of the resources of Muscat and were continually criticized by the *ulema* for wordly ways, in particular their heavy involvement in trade and commerce. Their supporters pointed to the prosperity which had been brought to Oman and a number of tribal leaders advocated their continuation in the Imamic office. Widespread unrest and desultory fighting between the several factions continued from the sixth decade of the seventeenth century until a major civil war broke out in 1719.

The Beni Ghafir rallied the northern tribes in support of the Ya'rubi who, although of the Ibadhi sect, did not hesitate to call in Sunnite tribes as allies in the conflict. The Beni Hina led the rebellion against the Imamate and the rest of the tribes took sides according to their appreciation of the situation. Out of this conflict came the most clearly defined split between the peoples of Oman—the Hinnawi-Ghafiri rivalry which has disrupted the peace of southeastern Arabia ever since. The youthful Ya'rubi Imam, Saif ibn Sultan II, and his supporters eventually prevailed but peace and stability did not follow. The general weakening of Oman as the result of civil conflict facilitated a Persian invasion and occupation of the Batinah Coast as far south as Muscat between 1737 and 1744.

This was a period in which generalship rather than piety became the criterion for the Ibadhi Imamate. A collateral branch of the Beni Hina came to power during the Persian occupation, their success due largely to their ability to unify the Ghafiri and Hinnawi in order to expel the foreigners. Thus was established, in 1749, the Al Bu Said dynasty which has ruled in Oman down to the present time. Ahmed ibn Said Al Bu Saidi, the first Imam of the line, was an important personage in commerce and maritime affairs before he took advantage of the leadership vacuum to gain control of Oman. The Imamate, as a religious institution, fell rapidly into desuetude and within a generation of their victory over the Persians the Al Bu Said were giving themselves the style and secular title of Sultan. By neglecting the duties of the Imamate, the Al Bu Saids invited trouble, for future political challenges would almost invariably wear the religious robes of an elected Imam who bore the standard of the peoples of the interior against Al Bu Said domination of the coast. The levying of customs on trade between Muscat and the interior, the taking of tribute, and the enforcement of restrictions on freedom of movement were, as much as the assumption of worldly ways, sources of resentment and opposition.

The death of Ahmed ibn Said in 1783 opened nearly a decade of fighting between his sons over the succession. One of the five rivals, Said, ruled initially but was quickly replaced by his own energetic and ruthless son Hamad. It was during this period that the capital was shifted from the interior to Muscat. Hamad did not long survive the move, and upon his death in 1792 his uncle Sultan became the effective ruler of coastal Oman. Following the contest for the succession after Ahmed ibn Said's death, Sultan had gone into exile on the Mekran Coast, across the Arabian Sea from Oman. This period of enforced residence abroad had stimulated territorial ambitions, the result of which was a series of expeditions that not only brought Gwadur, in Mekran, under Muscat's control, but also extended Sultan's authority to Bundar Abbas and the islands of Qishm and Hormuz near the entrance of the Persian Gulf. (Persian rule over the islands and Bundar Abbas would be reasserted in the middle of the nineteenth century; Gwadur was sold to Pakistan in 1958.)

It was inevitable that the strategic implications of these activities would be appreciated by the two great rivals for empire, France and Great Britain. British fears that France might use Muscat as a base for privateers or as a staging post for an invasion of India led to an Anglo-Omani treaty in 1798. It provided for the exclusion of French and Dutch nationals from the sultanate as long as hostilities continued.

In 1806, by the convenient method of murdering his cousin, the greatest of the Al Bu Said sultans, Sayyid Said ibn Sultan, came to power in Muscat and became the most influential Arab leader between Bahrain and the East African shore. His power was feared at Bundar Abbas and elsewhere on the Persian shore. Yet during Sayyid's reign, Sohar and interior Oman were virtually independent of Muscat and were involved in fighting off a Wahhabi attempt to occupy Buraimi. This was of little concern to the sultan, as was indicated by the transfer of the seat of his rule to Zanzibar.

Sayyid Said died in 1856 and his possessions were divided. One son, Majid, ruled at Zanzibar while coastal Oman was controlled from Muscat by another, Thuwaini. This arrangement was recognized and confirmed by Great Britain five years later. The Al Bu Said relationship with the British brought Thuwaini under strong pressure not only to desist from slave and arms trading, but also to cooperate with the British in eliminating it. Such collaboration created difficulties in Oman when a collateral branch of the Al Bu Said family joined forces with the Wahhabis in raiding into the sultan's territory from a base in Buraimi. The mutual desire to maintain the slave trade motivated the alliance. This concerted military offensive failed, whereupon the Wahhabis bribed Selim, a son of Thuwaini, who murdered his father at Sohar in 1866, an act which forestalled a descent by sultanate forces upon the Wahhabis via an invasion of Buraimi. Because of Selim's dependence upon the Wahhabis, the Ibadhi inhabitants of Oman would not give him their allegiance, and in 1868 the Beni Hina confederacy of tribes drove him out of Muscat. Azzan ibn Qais, a member of the Al Bu Said family, was elected Imam and it briefly appeared that the religious institution would win out over secular rule. But Azzan was in for a difficult time, some of it of his own making, for he oppressed the inhabitants of the coastal towns and villages, especially the Indian traders, who were effective in obtaining British support against the Imam. His failure to obtain British recognition and the interruption of British subsidies weakened him considerably. His principal contribution was breaking with the Wahhabis and organizing the assault which drove them out of Buraimi. In this effort, he was supported by Zaid ibn Khalifah, the powerful ruler of Abu Dhabi.

During these years, Turki ibn Said, the uncle of ex-Sultan Selim, was in exile. His return was financed by the Zanzibari Al Bu Saids, who also purchased the support of the Persian Gulf rulers of Ras al-Khaimah, Ajman, and Dubai. When Imam Azzan ibn Qais failed to pay the usual subsidies, Hinnawi tribesmen joined Turki ibn Said. Hostilities broke out and the Imam was killed in fierce fighting in Matrah in early 1871. Thanks to his skillful balancing of Hinnawi and Ghafiri factions, Sultan Turki ibn Said's authority soon extended beyond Muscat and the coast to the interior.

Faisal ibn Turki succeeded to the sultanate upon his father's death in 1888 and the first years of his rule were untroubled. In 1891 Anglo-French imperial rivalries spurred British Indian authorities to go beyond their commercial agreement of 1839 to negotiate a treaty by which the Sultan undertook never "to cede, to sell, to mortgage, or otherwise give for occupation" any part of Muscat and Oman or its dependencies, save to the British government.

In 1895 unrest developed in the interior, for the most part among the Hinnawi, because the sultan withheld traditional payments. Zanzibari funds were made available to the rebels in hopes of creating circumstances favorable to a restoration of the old sultanate of Sayyid Said's time. The tribes laid siege to Muscat until Faisal bribed and bought off some of the invaders and organized Ghafiri support. The defeated rebels, less interested in the Sultan of Zanzibar's ambitions than in his money, were frustrated in subsequent attempts to revive the Imamate in the Jebel Akhdar.

British determination not to become involved "to landward" led to a refusal to provide military support during the rebellion. This gave the French another opportunity in Muscat. Energetic diplomacy obtained the sultan's acquiescence in the establishment of a coaling station in 1891. The arrangement was suspended after strong British protests and the incident marked the beginning of an especially forceful phase of British policy in southeastern Arabia associated with the name of Lord Curzon, Viceroy of India. During these years, the Indianization of Muscat proceeded rapidly. In its streets one heard much more Gujarati, Baluchi, and other languages of Persia and the Indian subcontinent than one heard Arabic.

Although the tribes of the interior held Faisal in contempt for his "loose ways," including his permission to import spirits and tobacco into Oman, he did not again encounter opposition until 1912 when he co-operated with the British in an elaborate program of arms control. This led to the election of an Ibadhi Imam, Selim ibn Rashid, a descendant of the Imams of medieval times. Support for the new Imam was not based on otherworldly qualifications but on the desire for guns. The revolt began when Ghafiri tribesmen expelled the sultan's garrison from Nizwa. This was followed by an alliance between the Hinnawi and Ghafiri which proved to be the most formidable ever faced by the Al Bu Said dynasty. Although British support assured that Sultan Faisal would remain secure in Muscat, he lived in a coastal enclave in the fashion of the sixteenth- and seventeenth-century Portuguese and was completely out of touch with the peoples he claimed as his subjects.

Faisal died in 1913 and his son Taimur came under strong pressure from the British to improve his relations with the supporters of the Ima-mate. But in the interior, the opposition found still more reason for op-posing the sultanate. Taimur not only collaborated closely with the British but also made himself vulnerable to criticism for his lax administration of *Shari'a* law. The anti-sultanate movement did not coalesce until after the Imam was murdered in 1920. At that time, a member of the Hinnawi confederacy, Shaikh Isa ibn Salih ibn Ali, emerged as a strongman and secured the election of his candidate, the feeble and indecisive Mo-hammed ibn Abdullah al-Khalili, to the Imamate. At this point, Britain came down strongly on the side of Sultan Taimur and her intervention led to the Treaty of Sib in 1920. (Sib is a small town on the Batinah Coast north of Muscat.)

For the next forty years the terms of this treaty would be inter-preted, reinterpreted, and misinterpreted. Opponents of sultanate rule claimed that it provided for the complete independence of the interior under the Imam. In fact, it was a reasonable exchange of pledges which made for a period of peace and relative stability. By agreeing not to in-crease the duty on goods being sent into the interior by over 5 percent, by opening Muscat to free ingress and egress by tribesmen from the interior, and by an undertaking not to harbor fugitives from Imamate justice, the leaders of inner Oman agreed to leave the sultan at peace and recognized his paramount authority. There was no specific reference to the status of the Imamate in the treaty. The signatory on behalf of the interior was Shaikh Isa ibn Salih.

A new era was dawning in Oman. In 1925 the d'Arcy interests obtained a concession for a geological survey. This was followed twelve years later by the award of a concession for oil exploration to another British firm. In the interim, Sultan Taimur abdicated in 1932 in favor of his twenty-one-year-old son, Said ibn Taimur, who would control the affairs of Oman with increasing authority, severity, and intolerance from that date until he was deposed by his son Qabus in 1970. Sultan Said was an effective administrator and a good financial manager. In order to minimize British influence, he abandoned Muscat and took up residence in Salalah in the province of Dhofar, the southwesternmost part of his territory.

In the first decade of his rule, Said ibn Taimur continued his father's policy of considering the interior to be the fiefdom of Shaikh Isa ibn Salih. Only during World War II did the sultan actively seek to extend his influence in the Jebel Akhdar. Over the years the sultan's authority had increased and he had developed considerable skill in playing off the Hinnawi and Ghafiri factions, although the latter was slightly more powerful at the time of Shaikh Isa's death in 1946. There were, however, other factors which led to changes in the interior, including renewed oil exploration and a recrudescence of Saudi activity.

In 1949, as Imam Mohammed ibn Abdullah attempted to keep oil prospectors out of the interior and tribal unrest was increasing, the Saudi Arabian government formally put forth its claim to the Buraimi Oasis and to the loyalty of the tribes living beyond Buraimi in Omani territory. The resulting incursion into Buraimi by ibn Saud's nominee, Turki ibn Ataishan, has been described earlier.[1] The Imam regarded this as an opportunity to assert his authority and proclaimed *jihad* against the Saudis. Not to be outdone, Sultan Said assembled a large force at Sohar to march, as his ancestor Thuwaini had hoped to do in 1866, on Buraimi. A major clash was averted only by firm British measures which broke up the sultan's expedition. The most powerful tribal leader in the interior, Sulaiman ibn Himyar, waited upon events and eventually concluded that

---

[1] The Saudis were thereby instrumental in bringing about the Anglo-Omani Friendship Treaty of 1951, through which seconded British officers began the modernization of the Sultan's Armed Forces in exchange for extension of the Royal Air Force's rights to utilize staging facilities at Salalah and on Masirah Island.

his interests would best be served by an arrangement with the Saudi authorities. Sultan Said's hold upon inner Oman, tenuous at best, was further weakened after the death of the Imam. New factors then came into play.

After considerable maneuvering, Ghalib ibn Ali, the *Qadi* (*Shari'a* judge) of Rastaq, a member of the Beni Hina and a follower of the previous Imam, succeeded in obtaining election to the highest Ibadhi office. His policies were in fact those of his stronger and more intelligent brother, Talib ibn Ali, who until that time had been governor (*wali*) of Rastaq. It was Ghalib's contention that, should oil be discovered in interior Oman, the royalties therefrom should accrue to the Imamate. The Imam's attempts to enforce supervision of exploration activities led to a clash with the Sultan's army and tribal collaborators. The Imam and his supporters were pushed out of Ibri in 1954 and Al Bu Said authority was greatly extended in the interior. Ghalib then journeyed to Saudi Arabia to recruit support, but failed to make an alliance with Sulaiman ibn Himyar, who continued to seek a better opportunity.

In the same year, Ghalib ibn Ali proclaimed an independent Imamic state and then made the mistake of applying for membership in the Arab League. While this was regarded as good politics in Riyadh and Cairo, it broke the tradition of isolation which characterized the Ibadhi Imamate from its inception and eroded Ghalib's support in interior Oman. But Saudi money and arms flowed into the region and the Saudis even were able to facilitate visits by Egyptian military officers.

This growing threat led to a northern expedition by the sultan's forces, after which Ghalib and Talib returned to Dammam, Saudi Arabia, to organize what became known as the Oman Liberation Army. Full-scale revolution broke out in 1957 upon Talib's return to the interior by way of the Batinah Coast. But this time Sulaiman ibn Himyar had cast his lot with the Imam, who made his headquarters at the old interior stronghold of Nizwa. The rebellion continued until Muscati troops, heavily supported by British air and ground forces, dislodged the Oman Liberation Army in January 1959. In the years that followed, the Oman Revolutionary Movement was responsible for widespread terrorism and guerrilla warfare directed from Dammam and Cairo by Talib ibn Ali. But the sultan's forces were steadily improved and reinforced, with the result that Al Bu Said control of the interior became even more extensive.

Said ibn Taimur was perhaps the most skillful of all the Al Bu Said dynasty in taking advantage of tribal disarray. He developed an extremely effective intelligence system and knew how to play upon the feelings of dissidence which his operatives had discovered. He did not attempt to rule directly, but he was careful—and usually successful—in providing deputies to control various areas of inner Oman.

Oil was discovered in the early 1960s and production began in 1967. The first tanker called at Mina al-Fahah, north of Muscat, to take on a cargo of crude oil. This event, barely a month after the Six Day War and the resulting embargo of oil exports to the West, pointed up Oman's isolation and remoteness from the mainstream of Arab politics.

Said ibn Taimur's father had sent him to study in England, and on several occasions in recent years he was heard to state that, inasmuch as he had an education, it was not necessary to provide schools for his countrymen. As a result, young Omanis were obliged to migrate in search of economic and educational opportunities and eventually there were Omani enrollees in the universities of all the "liberated" Arab countries— Iraq, Syria, Egypt, and Algeria—as well as in Eastern Europe. Some went as far afield as Peking. (Only the sons of wealthy Baluchi and Indian merchants in Muscat and Matrah were able to attend Western schools.) In the late 1950s the Sultan dispatched his son Qabus to a preparatory school in Oxford, after which he attended Sandhurst, served with the Cameronians in the Rhineland, and learned rudimentary public administration as a functionary of the Bedforshire County Council. He then returned to Salalah and house arrest.[2]

The inhabitants of Dhofar were an especially depressed section of the population. Of Ethiopic origin, the Dhofari are taller and darker than the Omani, speak a different language, and have closer links with Aden and Hadhramaut than with Muscat and the Jebel Akhdar. Many Dhofaris journeyed northward to the Trucial States to find jobs, and a significant number enlisted in military units such as the Trucial Oman Scouts and Abu Dhabi Defense Force. They were quick to learn Arabic and their intelligence and industry earned them rapid advancement. But a trickle of remittances did little to improve the lot of the Dhofari, and the sultan's arbitrariness finally brought on rebellion in 1963. Their leader, Musallem ibn N'ufal, secured arms and financial aid from Saudi Arabia. It was all the Sultan's Armed Forces could do to defend Salalah because most of the army was pinned down by security duties in "Oman proper." After an assassination attempt nearly succeeded in 1966, the sultan shut himself up in his Salalah palace. It was widely believed that he was dead and Oman was under direct British control. However, his army obtained a major victory in 1967 and most of the rebels' equipment was captured or destroyed.

Saudi Arabian aid was cut off and the rebellion would have been crushed had not the Soviet Union taken over its sponsorship. The departure of the British from Aden made meaningful support possible by way

---

[2]The Sultan, mindful of the Omani tradition of political assassination, exiled three brothers and kept other family members under surveillance.

of a Ho Chi Minh trail from that port city through Mukallah into the Qarah Mountains. What had been the Dhofar Liberation Front became a Communist-led Popular Front for the Liberation of Oman and the Occupied Arabian Gulf. Soon China became involved in the Dhofar war, as did the neo-Baathist regime in Baghdad and the Marxist-oriented Popular Front for the Liberation of Palestine. A number of Dhofaris went to China, Russia, or Iraq for military training and indoctrination.

But 1967 was also the year in which major new income became available to the Sultan through oil production. A rapid expansion and modernization of the Sultan's Armed Forces began. Some economic development projects were started, such as the construction of a jetty and deepwater port at Matrah, but such undertakings were closely related to the military buildup. There were no programs of social betterment or educational improvement. The old American missionary hospital in Matrah remained the only source of medical care for the Sultan's subjects.

Disaffection spread and revival of the Oman Revolutionary Movement in the Jebel Akhdar became a definite possibility. Iraqi arms were filtering through Dubai to the Batinah Coast and up the *wadis* to Nizwa, Ibri, and other traditional centers of resistance to the Al Bu Said and the rule of the coast. Superior intelligence-gathering enabled the Sultan's army to defeat guerrilla forces at Wadi Jisim on the Batinah Coast in 1969. This was followed by another shootout near Nizwa in 1970, from which the Iraqi-sponsored rebels of inner Oman have never recovered. But these were areas in which the British-officered Arab and Baluchi levies were at home. Dhofar continued to drain the country's resources.

In July 1970 Qabus ibn Said emerged from the obscurity of house arrest to overthrow his father and send the old tyrant off to exile in England.[3] The extent to which the British facilitated this development may never be known. Their special interests and grave concern over the security situation were motivation enough, whatever their involvement. Britain's returns from oil and a developing market were extensive, but her commercial position in the Persian Gulf was an even more important aspect of her special interest in Oman. Wealthy statelets such as Dubai, Abu Dhabi, and Qatar would not long support Britain's balance of payments if a revolutionary alternative were provided to the Al Bu Said dynasty and Oman became an invasion base.

Before Sultan Qabus celebrated his thirtieth birthday in December 1970, he eliminated "Muscat" from his country's name to emphasize his conviction that divisions between the coast and the interior should be ended. A new flag was designed, adding green—for Islam—to the tradi-

---

[3]Sultan Said ibn Taimur died in England late in 1972.

tional red and white, reducing the size of the crossed *khunjars* (daggers), and shifting them to the upper right corner, presumably to deemphasize the Al Bu Said reputation for ferocity. About 160 political prisoners were released from Jalali Fort. (The chronic overcrowding in this ancient fortress built by the Portuguese and overlooking Muscat harbor had resulted chiefly in a high mortality rate that allowed Said ibn Taimur to add new inmates at a great rate.[4] Orders were given to modernize the old castle at Muscat and to strengthen its roof for helicopter landings. After preliminary arrangements were made for a new governmental structure, Qabus began to travel extensively through Oman and made himself available to all his subjects in his temporary residence in Muscat.

A more important aspect of the new regime's openness was the Sultan's call for the return of the Omani diaspora to work for the "new Oman." Although the country might thus be subjected to many new and often radical influences, the new regime felt that these would be compensated for by the talents and skills brought home by expatriates, and by the new opportunities they would discover upon their return. As might be expected, heavy emphasis was given to developing modern educational facilities and social services.

The new ruler was acutely aware that his country's oil revenues were limited and could very possibly be expended in two decades. This meant that an income of approximately $125 million annually would have to be spent on establishing an infrastructure for Oman, stimulating industry, agriculture, and fishing, and in other ways to assure that this vast country, with its population of just under one million, would possess the diversified economy and institutions necessary to survive and prosper in the modern world.

The young Sultan's grand design was jeopardized by the continuation of the Dhofar war, which had become a jousting-ground for the two major ideological rivals of the communist world. Peking claimed that the thoughts of Mao governed every Dhofar rebel action, while a prize-winning Soviet film, *The Hot Winds of War*, shot in the Qarah Mountains, assured that Lenin would be given equal credit.

The war in Dhofar intensified in the spring of 1971 and by the end of the year Sultan Qabus's government was investing about $50 million of its annual income (about $135 million) in the Omani armed forces, much against the wishes of his uncle, Prime Minister Tariq ibn Taimur. Under the leadership of a talented Peking-trained native of Salalah, Mohammed Ahmed Ghassani, a force of about 750 guerrillas had mounted a threat to the

---

[4]From the Mirani fort opposite a cannon is still fired after sunset (until 1969 the gunpowder was United States Civil War surplus) but it no longer means that the town gates will be closed to all who do not have written permission to be abroad.

coastal plain and especially to the Dhofari capital. The Omani army was then reinforced by additional British officers, either on secondment or in a regular contractual relationship, which assured that effective use would be made of newly acquired weapons, aircraft, and other equipment. Although the Dhofar war was responsible for Saudi-Omani *rapprochement*, it posed a threat to the Omani development program.

Military policy was but one of several subjects on which the Sultan disagreed with Tariq. Another was the scope of the development program. Qabus relied increasingly upon the advice of Robert Anderson, an American entrepreneur who had served in high official posts in the American government. Reverses in Dhofar and strikes by Omani workers in Muscat and Matrah, protesting the large influx of foreign workers, brought on a government crisis in January 1972. It was resolved when the sultan demanded and obtained his uncle's resignation from the prime ministership. Taking on those responsibilities himself, Qabus ordered a major offensive against the Dhofari rebels, hoping to stamp out resistance and enable his government to concentrate on the development program. The timing of the offensive was fortunate, for the majority of the mountain people, seeing their primitive economy jeopardized, no longer would be intimidated by guerrillas living in their midst. By March the Sultan was "winning the hearts and minds" of his Dhofari subjects. The opposition was reduced to casual forays from sanctuaries in South Yemen, and in May the Aden regime was charging that its air space had been violated and boarder outposts bombed by aircraft based in Salalah. It now appeared even more unlikely that Russia and China would support the rebellion on a scale which would invite the intervention of Qabus's ally, the Shah of Iran, in his historical role as policeman of the Persian Gulf and eastern Arabia. Yet the discovery of caches of mortars, automatic weapons, and ammunition near Muscat by Omani security forces in early 1973 seemed to justify the augmentation of anti-guerrilla experts in the form of a Jordanian military mission provided by the Qabus-Hussein agreement in 1972.

Development activity intensified in early 1972. Progress was made on the new airport north of Matrah, which was scheduled for opening in September 1972 and was to be large enough to receive jumbo and supersonic jets. Hospitals, clinics, and schools were opening in all parts of the country. Improved security permitted work to proceed on the highway linking Salalah with the new port of Raysut. The port itself will make sea communication with Muscat and Matrah possible during the monsoon season. This is important for political as well as economic reasons, for Qabus intends, like his father before him, to base himself at Salalah. Said ibn Taimur may have used Salalah to isolate himself from British and other proponents of progress, but Qabus, the son of a

Dhofari mother, has deeper roots there. There is hope that he will continue to maintain personal contacts with other parts of the country. Early evidence of his political astuteness indicates that this will be the case.

The ruler's *savoir faire* has been revealed not only by the unprecedented cordiality of relations with Saudi Arabia, but also by the high level of collaboration with the Iranian regime. The Sultan has demonstrated that the removal of "Muscat" from his country's name was more than a gesture symbolizing the unity of the country. Although the inhabitants of Jebel Akhdar remain deeply suspicious of people from the coastal lowlands and resent all forms of external authority, the ground has been cut from under a revolutionary movement based upon the Imamate. By appointing nephews of Imam Ghalib ibn Ali's revered predecessor to ambassadorships in Riyadh and Cairo, Qabus has increased his prestige among the mountain people.

More important will be the sultan's record of economic achievement. Among the many exiles who have returned are intellectuals educated in the Soviet Union and Eastern Europe. They have joined other articulate Omanis in criticizing the lack of a coordinated plan for development and have complained of the Sultan's arbitrariness. Yet Qabus has demonstrated willingness to conciliate his critics by "promoting" a powerful and greatly disliked minister to a post at the United Nations. More significant is his increasing reliance upon American advice. Former Secretary of the Treasury Anderson is the most visible manifestation of this policy, and much American developmental expertise is now being channeled to the sultanate by way of Saudi Arabia.

The principal fear of Oman's well-wishers is that failure to maintain the momentum of progress toward unification and pacification of the country will force Qabus, as he grows older, into the traditional behavior patterns of his Al Bu Said ancestors. That would be disastrous not only for eastern Arabia, but for the West as well. But Oman's isolation is ended. In 1971 the sultanate entered into diplomatic relations with Japan, Pakistan, Algeria, Morocco, Tunisia, Iran, and the United States, and was admitted to the United Nations and Arab League in October of that year. Tradition dies hard, but Oman is well launched into the complex modern world.

2. THE PERSIAN GULF SHAIKHDOMS.

The importance of the Persian Gulf region to maritime commerce and imperial communications in antiquity, briefly noted above, has recently been confirmed by archeologists working on various sites from

Kuwait to the southern shore. In 1970 the Shaikhdom of Bahrain sponsored an archeological congress at which evidence of Sumerian, Assyrian, and Sassanian activities was discussed. Like the rulers of Bahrain and Kuwait before them, the rulers of Abu Dhabi and Dubai have subsidized excavations in their territories. Interest in pre-Islamic Arabia, in the early Islamic period, and in tribal migrations has developed in the last decade to a point where scholarly investigations are no longer monopolized by institutions external to the area. Documents and oral tradition are being preserved in various centers along the Arabian shore, such as the manuscript collection in Qatar which concentrates upon Islamic jurisprudence. But it is symptomatic of the enormous influence wielded by Great Britain in the Persian Gulf that the Arabs must rely on British sources and compilations for much of the knowledge of their own past. The government of Qatar is now in the process of translating into Arabic the greatest single source of historical, geographic, social, economic, and cultural information on the region—J. G. Lorimer's *Gazetteer of the Persian Gulf, Oman and Central Arabia.*[1]

By the early nineteenth century, when Great Britain first entered into treaty relations with various Arab rulers, the indigenous political structure of the Arabian shore had been virtually completed. The Banu Khalid had given way to the House of Saud in Hasa, but not before their protection of the 'Utub peoples of northern Nejd had facilitated the transformation of a nomadic people into the two leading maritime and commercial families of the Gulf, the Sabahs of Kuwait and the Khalifahs of Bahrain. The ruling al-Thani family in Qatar, established after the Khalifahs had departed from that territory to extinguish Persian rule in Bahrain, derived some measure of security from their acceptance of Wahhabi doctrine, which spared them the evangelizing zeal of the Saudis. Nor were the Sunnites of the Beni Yas tribal confederacy of the southern shore and their piratical neighbors, the Qawasim, as vulnerable to Saudi attack. Instead, the brunt was borne by the Ibadhis of inner Oman, repeatedly attacked from the Saudi base in Buraimi until Ibrahim Pasha's advance on Dar'iyah from Hejaz in 1818 brought respite to eastern Arabia.

Although a relative calm descended upon the several shaikhdoms after 1818, the situation was quite different at sea as piracy continued to threaten the East India Company's trade with Gulf ports. Strategic considerations, of which the home government had been acutely aware following Napoleon's occupation of Egypt and his eastward design, gave further support to the new and forceful policy of "John Company."

---

[1]First published in Calcutta in 1915 and republished by the Irish Universities Press in 1970.

The English connection with the Persian Gulf was two centuries old before the first treaty was signed between Britain and an Arab shaikh. The earliest enterprise in the Gulf area was a commercial link between Surat, the East India Company's headquarters (until their move to Bombay in 1688), and Jask on the Persian Mekran Coast. English products were transported from thence to Isfahan. The Persians were receptive and initially trade returns were good. The coincidence of Sir Robert Sherley's success at the Persian court—a chronicler asserts that he "possessed the chiefest place in the King of Persia's wars against the Turks"—helped the East India Company. So did the English reputation for maritime prowess, earned in skirmishes with the Portuguese off Jask. In 1622, therefore, the British were authorized to settle at Bundar Abbas after cooperating with the Persians to end the Portuguese occupation of the strategic island of Hormuz which dominates the entrance to the Persian Gulf. Bundar Abbas was eight days closer to Isfahan than Jask.

In 1640 efforts were made to establish regular trade with the Pashalic of Baghdad via Basra. There were difficulties with government officials and fierce competition from Indian, Armenian, Jewish, Persian, and Arab traders, but the principal challenge came from the Dutch and the Portuguese. (The latter's agency in Basra had been founded 130 years earlier.) Eventually Holland succeeded in engrossing most of the Surat-Basra trade, with the English making slow but steady inroads until it was possible to establish a permanent agency at Basra in 1723. Long before this, Basra had become a communications link between England and India, but in the global wars in the latter half of the eighteenth century, maritime supremacy in the Persian Gulf and Arabian Sea became vital to the British Empire. When Basra was temporarily closed to British vessels, as in the Persian occupation of 1776, it was in Kuwait that the dispatch boxes were transferred between ship and shore.

Trade and imperial communications prompted the Indian government's orders to the Bombay Marine for punitive expeditions against the Pirate Coast, from Ras al-Khaimah to Dubai, in 1809 and 1819. The second of these expeditions was carried out by forces under Sir William Grant Keir with such thoroughness that the several shaikhs were compelled to foreswear piracy by treaty. Thus the East India Company's chief representative in the Gulf at Bushir took on new political responsibilities and a naval presence, varying in size from a single sloop to several squadrons, was established in the Gulf to assist the resident in supervising treaty observance. There were five Arab signatories to the treaty— the rulers of Abu Dhabi, Dubai, Ajman, Umm al-Quwain and Sharjah. (Dynastic strife led Ras al-Khaimah to break away from Sharjah in 1866 and its status as a separate shaikhdom was recognized in 1921. Fujairah, on the Gulf of Oman, asserted its independence of Sharjah in 1901 and Great Britain recognized it as a shaikhdom under the trucial system in 1952.)

All Arab inhabitants of the Gulf shaikhdoms were penalized by the arrangements of 1819–20. British and Indian shipping now passed up and down the Gulf in reasonable safety while pirates preyed upon Arab country craft and upon each other. The delicate economic balance of the region, to a great extent based upon returns from fishing, maritime trade, and the annual pearling season, was threatened. Each depredation brought bloody retaliation until 1835, when an unprecedented level of violence was reached both at sea and ashore. It appeared that the marginal economy either of the Beni Yas of Abu Dhabi or of the Qawasim of Sharjah and Ras al-Khaimah would be ruined. Elsewhere the situation was almost as serious. In these desperate circumstances, the British arranged a truce for the approaching pearling season. Pressure continued to be exerted from Bushir, supported by the Bombay Presidency, with the result that there were annual renewals of the truce for eight years, after which a ten-year truce period was negotiated. Upon expiry in 1853, a "Treaty of Peace in Perpetuity upon the Seas" was signed and what had been known as the Pirate Coast became the Trucial Shaikhdoms.

Thus the Persian Gulf was fitted into Britain's worldwide system of informal empire. The Arab rulers agreed that they and their subjects were responsible to British authority for any treaty violations. It was to be expected that the British would exploit their special position for commercial and philanthropic purposes. The legacy of Wilberforce and the Clapham sect, the leading British abolitionists, was present in "visit and search" agreements to end the seaborne slave trade entered into by Arab shaikhs. The French vice consul at Basra was reduced to lamentations to his government over commercial domination of the Gulf by British-protected interests. The advent of steam navigation increased the ubiquity of United Kingdom merchant and naval vessels, and the house flag of the "B.I."—the British India Steam Navigation Company—was a familiar sight in every Gulf port. (It was as a result of her special position on Persia's southwestern flank that Britain was able to exert pressure on that country when it appeared to be moving into the Russian orbit.) The British occupation of Kharg Island, Mohammerah (Khorramshahr), and Bushir during the Anglo-Persian War of 1856–57 was an especially forceful demonstration of her power over the Teheran government.

Naval supremacy was also a determining factor on the Arabian shoreline. In 1839, during Mohammed Ali's second Arabian campaign, the Royal Navy stood by to protect Bahrain from a possible Egyptian landing. Three years later the Political Resident's authority prevented a Persian attempt to reassert control over the Bahrain archipelago. The Wahhabis under Faisal ibn Turki also were kept from extinguishing Khalifah rule over the islands in 1852. But the Khalifahs seemed bent on self-elimination during much of this period. The family was deeply divided. One faction and its supporters took refuge in Hasa and attempted a number of small-scale naval operations until British pressure brought about a treaty in 1861 which fully incorporated Bahrain into the maritime peacekeeping system. In view of frequent Ottoman and Persian attempts to secure the allegiance of the Khalifahs, the British recognized the independent status of the shaikhdom in this instrument.

Kuwait maintained cordial relations with the British throughout this period. The principal concern of the ruling Sabah family was to avoid an extension of Ottoman control over the shaikhdom. On several occasions it was necessary for the paramount shaikh to go through the form of accepting the annual decree of investiture[2] and the ceremonial robes of an Ottoman government. This was a desirable alternative to invasion by sea or, in view of the derelict condition of the few naval vessels stationed at Basra, overland invasion by Turkish troops and their Muntafiq Arab clients. The Sabahs would have resisted any Ottoman attempt to collect customs and other taxes, but before 1871 the Baghdad and Basra authorities never marshaled enough strength to enforce such a demand. Only once did the Shaikh of Kuwait feel sufficiently threatened to request that vessels of the "B.I." temporarily suspend their service to his port. It was his contention that British steamers added an aura of prosperity which "excited the jealousy of the Turks." The Political Resident complied readily and the crisis soon subsided.

Sabah vassalage became less nominal in 1871 when one of the Ottoman Empire's most vigorous and distinguished public servants, Midhat Pasha, was governor-general of the Pashalic of Baghdad. Rather than devoting all of his considerable talents to much needed reform and modernization, Midhat essayed to regain the glories of Sulaiman the Magnificent in what became known as the Nejd expedition. To escape direct incorporation in Midhat's province, the Sabahs collaborated by providing much of the shipping and camel transport. This shadowy relationship between Baghdad and Kuwait throughout the Ottoman period was to be the basis of Abdul Karim Qasim's claim to Iraqi sovereignty over the shaikhdom in 1961.

Midhat Pasha considered the "Sanjak of Nejd" to include Nejd, Hasa,

---

[2]The Sultan's annual *firman* or decree was delivered to each province of the empire by a high-ranking official, usually with great ceremony. In Kuwait, however, there was an element of farce in the ceremony.

Bahrain, Qatar, the several Trucial States (also known as Trucial Oman), and all of the Omani territory ruled by the Al Bu Said. Ottoman armies landed at Dammam, now Saudi Arabia's principal eastern port, and at Qatif Oasis, some miles to northward, where the old Turkish customs house may still be seen. The Ottoman invasion was facilitated by Wahhabi dynastic strife but, as noted above, Nejd remained under the control of the House of Saud. The al-Thani rulers of Qatar clearly felt that Midhat Pasha represented the shape of things to come, and the paramount shaikh, who only three years before had taken Qatar into the British-supervised trucial system, now proclaimed his allegiance to the Porte.

Although a number of officials in London and Bombay favored turning over full responsibility for maritime peace to the Ottoman Empire, Britain protested Midhat's invasion to Constantinople. Those closer to the scene realized that Midhat's imperial ambitions were, in more ways than one, built upon sand and their counsels prevailed. The Royal Navy and Royal Indian Navy continued to patrol the waters of the Gulf, including the coast of Qatar. Turkish pressure upon Bahrain mounted from 1871, with the Khalifahs being repeatedly informed that their future security could best be assured by emulation of the al-Thanis of Qatar. Because of Bahrain's advanced commercial situation, Britain would not acquiesce to such an arrangement and in 1880 a new treaty was concluded. Under its terms, the Shaikh of Bahrain undertook, in effect, to confide conduct of his external relations to the British Political Resident at Bushir. The 1880 treaty also provided that no country other than Great Britain could establish a diplomatic mission or coaling station there, nor could the shaikh negotiate treaties without British advice and consent. The next natural step was British assumption of formal responsibility for the shaikhdom's defenses.

The Bahrain treaty became the model for subsequent informal agreements with the shaikhdoms of the Trucial Coast, beginning with Abu Dhabi in 1887. Once again Turkish pretensions were responsible for these arrangements.[3] But as the tempo of French activity on the southern shore of the Gulf increased, the British recognized the need for formal undertakings. These were signed with the Trucial Coast shaikhs in March 1892.

Closer ties with Kuwait were established at the end of the decade. Shaikh Mubarak Sabah, who had gained his paramount position by murdering his half-brother in 1896, hoped to secure his position through a "Muscat-type" agreement. The Political Resident was not disposed to

---

[3]Nasr-ud-Din Shah obtained two small naval craft from Germany in 1883 and his attempts to increase Persian influence in the Gulf were also an annoyance to the Political Resident.

oblige him, but fratricide was quickly forgotten when German and Russian interests in the shaikhdom as a railroad terminus became known. An Anglo-Kuwaiti treaty went into effect in 1899 and, until its abrogation in 1961, was the basis for relationships between the two countries.

Although a German shipping line began regularly scheduled service to Gulf ports at the end of the century and Russian commercial activity in southwest Persia became highly competitive, the Persian Gulf remained very nearly a British *mare clausum*. In 1900, 321 of the 327 steamers entering the Gulf were British. The weakening Ottoman position on the Arabian shore was exemplified by the "Blue Line Agreement" of 1913, wherein Turkey recognized that the Qatar peninsula was firmly within the British sphere of influence and renounced its claims to that shaikhdom and any of Arabia south and east of it. Although unratified, it was sufficient to encourage ibn Saud to push the Turkish garrison out of Hasa at the end of that year. In another five years the defeat of the Central Powers and the turning inward of post-Tsarist Russia—to which must be added the factors of internal dissension and disorganization in Persia—permitted *Pax Britannica* to remain unchallenged from the head of the Gulf to the Straits of Hormuz.

The development of Gulf oil resources began on the Persian shore before World War I. The prospect of income from petroleum in the shaikhdoms affected Britain's relations with their Arab rulers and with Saudi Arabia during the interwar period. Advances in communications also acted to confer greater importance on the special relationship. As the flying boats of Imperial Airways lumbered over the Gulf enroute to and from India, Sharjah became the most important refueling and maintenance base in the Gulf although military and local commercial aviation requirements enlarged the British presence in the other shaikhdoms as well. It was the search for oil, however, that was principally responsible for altering the essentially maritime character of British policy. Arab interest in the arcane science of petroleum geology, or at least in its results, was stimulated by the decline of a traditional source of income. At the same time the pearling industry lost its dominant position in world markets to the Japanese cultured pearl.

Oil was discovered in Bahrain in 1932 and in the great Dukhan field of Qatar seven years later. American oil companies joined British firms in developing these resources, and now American nationals joined the British in becoming familiar with Persian Gulf life through employment in oil camps, on geological surveys, and other activities connected with petroleum development. The Bahrain refinery began operations in 1939, only to have its production drastically cut back, as in Saudi Arabia, with the outbreak of World War II. If the infant oil industry did little to sustain the faltering economies of the shaikhdoms, it did provide employment for diplomats. Saudi Arabia claimed extensive territories to the east of the boundary delimited in the unratified Anglo-Ottoman "Blue Line Agreement" of 1913. After several years of negotiations, Britain, acting on behalf of Qatar and Abu Dhabi, put forth in 1937 a compromise proposal which became known as the Riyadh Line. It was unacceptable to Saudi Arabia, which sought extensive tracts where Wahhabi zealots had once raided and beneath which it was assumed there were oil-bearing strata. The boundary with Qatar was not settled until 1964 and Saudi Arabia continues to claim most of Abu Dhabi's hinterland all the way east to the Buraimi Oasis.

In the 1920s and 1930s Bahrain took the lead in breaking with tradition and seeking the means of modernization. The ruler appointed a British adviser in 1926 and two years later a modern educational system and health services program were begun. The Khalifah ruling family, divested of its nineteenth-century fractiousness, contributed to what has become a long tradition of orderly progress, exemplified in 1973 by arrangements for a Constitutional Council comprised of twenty Cabinet and twenty-two elected members. In Kuwait, the Sabahs were equally responsible but the difference was that after 1932 Bahrain had financial resources for development programs denied to Kuwait for much longer. In Kuwait, as in Qatar and the Trucial States, such educational and health facilities as existed were largely provided by Christian missionaries, true pioneers in ecumenicism who had stayed on in Arabia to teach and heal even after discovering the impregnability of Muslim belief.

The Royal Navy seldom had to invoke its "visit and search" authority because of piratical activity, but it did employ it often to combat arms smuggling. With the outbreak of World War II, the scope of naval activity in the Persian Gulf increased manyfold. It was at Khorramshahr on the Shatt al-Arab that vast shipments of American and British supplies and equipment were unloaded for transport to the beleaguered Soviet Union. In 1942 an Italian submarine was sunk by the Royal Navy south of Bahrain. The main island of the archipelago and the Arabian American Oil Company camp at Dhahran, Saudi Arabia, were targets of ineffectual Italian air raids from bases in Somaliland. (A Japanese submarine sank a British freighter off Muscat later in the same year.) While great convoys and occasional gunfire brought the war somehow closer to the peoples of the Gulf states, the overriding feeling was one of anticipation.

In 1945, therefore, the prospect of vast revenues derived from the exploitation of petroleum reserves, infrastructure development, and greatly expanded markets for British products on the Arabian shore combined with Iranian complaints over infringement of her sovereignty to bring about a decision to move the Political Residency from Bushir. Its reestablishment at Bahrain in 1946 hardly satisfied Teheran, which ever more forcefully asserted the Iranian claim to Bahrain through the newly founded United Nations Organization. But Bahrain suited Great Britain ideally. As the most advanced of the Arab shaikhdoms, with improving communications and influence in the southern Gulf, Bahrain provided facilities and examples which the Political Resident could utilize in advancing British political and commercial interests. From Bahrain he supervised a growing network of political agents, highly trained in Arabic language and culture at the Foreign Office's own institution (first in Jordan, then after 1949 in Lebanon) in all the Gulf shaikhdoms.[4] The pace of change rapidly accelerated.

The period between the conclusion of World War II and the abrogation or expiry of the British protectorate treaties in the southern Gulf in 1971 was truly the era of petroleum and prosperity. Several Persian Gulf states which had been receiving income from petroleum production for many years prior to World War II—Iran, Iraq, and Bahrain—were now joined by Kuwait, where large-scale oil production began in 1946. The future looked bright, for Kuwait's Burgan field contained a proven reserve as large as that of the entire North American continent. The emirate, which had previously relied on boatbuilding, small-scale maritime trade, and fishing for subsistence now looked forward to programs of extensive development. The situation was repeated in Qatar, based on production of the Dukhan field.

In the southern Gulf, border clashes between Abu Dhabi and Dubai continued into 1947 when a truce was arranged. Out of this strife emerged the determination by the ruling family of the larger shaikhdom, Abu Dhabi, that it must develop military resources which would permit it to play a dominant role in the affairs of the southern Gulf.

Dubai was the most prosperous of the shaikhdoms, with an extensive entrepot trade serving not only the Arabian but also the Iranian shore of the Gulf. Dubai would remain the principal transfer point for goods shipped into southwestern Iran until the modernization of the port of Bundar Abbas made it available for oceangoing vessels at the end of the sixties. Much smuggling activity centered in Dubai. After Pakistan and India achieved independence, the shaikhdom became the center for a vast gold smuggling operation based upon the inflated price of gold in those two countries. In 1971 high-powered *dhows* carried nearly 150 tons

---

[4]The Consul General in Muscat also reported to the Political Resident at Bahrain.

of legally purchased gold (usually brought from the Bank of England and deposited in Dubai banks) to the subcontinent.

The remaining shaikhdoms—Sharjah, Ajman, Umm al-Quwain, and Ras al-Khaimah—eked out an existence by fishing and primitive agriculture, although the latter shaikhdom had better supplies of fresh water and plant life and was slightly more prosperous. The economy of the last of the Trucial shaikhdoms, Fujairah, differed from the others only because its position on the Gulf of Oman gave it access to rich fishing grounds.

Bahrain possessed the most balanced economy at the beginning of the era. Oil production continued but leveled off so that a limited income, partly dependent upon profits from refining Saudi Arabian crude oil, dictated a fiscal responsibility not soon to be emulated in Saudi Arabia or the other two oil-producing shaikhdoms, Kuwait and Qatar. Bahrain remained an important trading center and continued its traditional activities, such as fishing, weaving, boatbuilding, and a small amount of pearling.

After several years of uncoordinated planning and expenditure by local authorities, the emirate of Kuwait turned to Great Britain in 1950 for assistance in achieving a more effective utilization of oil revenues. The anticipated results were not realized, for British advisers simply opened the emirate to penetration by five large British firms working on a cost-plus basis. Thus a greater degree of economic disarray and irresponsible expenditures resulted. Remedial measures ultimately were achieved through the World Bank and various United Nations agencies after the Suez crisis of 1956.

Between 1949 and 1954, the principal concern of the British authorities and their wards in the shaikhdoms of the southern Gulf was the Saudi Arabian challenge. The resolute opposition to Saudi activities at Buraimi which was manifested by the Abu Dhabian governor of the oasis, Shaikh Zayid ibn Sultan, conferred great prestige upon him. He was looked upon not only as a natural leader by the peoples of the smaller shaikhdoms—Dubai always being excepted—but also as a challenger to his half-brother, the ruler of Abu Dhabi, Shaikh Shakhbut.

Only one of the shaikhdoms experienced anything which might be described as political activity before the Suez War. This was Bahrain, which not only had made sufficient progress in education and health services to qualify as a miniature welfare state, but which also had a political oppositionist movement, the Committee of National Unity, which had a constituency of sorts, with which it worked with increasing success. (The emirate also had a free trade union movement, which was most active in the oil industry.) The Bahraini authorities, however, employed widespread rioting during the Suez crisis as the means of destroying the political opposition. A number of the movement's leaders, Bahraini intellectuals who looked to Cairo for inspiration, were deported to St. Helena, an action which the Khalifahs and their British advisers soon came to regret.

As oil production increased in the several Gulf states, deposits of royalties in British banks became a factor of vital importance to Britain's monetary position. By 1960 about half of Qatar's petroleum income, for example, was deposited in United Kingdom banks. A smaller percentage, but a larger amount, of Kuwaiti money found the same haven. Such deposits bolstered the pound at times when it was under siege and also acted to give the Persian Gulf shaikhs considerable political leverage in their dealings with the British.

At the same time, Kuwait was making better use of its financial resources. The United Nations provided experts from Great Britain, Lebanon, and several other countries to plan the establishment of a university in Kuwait which would open its doors in the middle of the decade. Like Bahrain, Kuwait had become a welfare state. It was necessary for the Kuwait government to provide the means by which immigrant workers, who were needed in great numbers, could become naturalized Kuwaitis. The requirements were stiff—eight years of continuous residence for Arabs and fifteen years for non-Arabs—but many immigrants chose to cast their lot with the small, wealthy shaikhdom.

In the early sixties young Kuwaitis and many non-Kuwaiti Arabs began to express their political attitudes through "social clubs," for political parties were banned. It was through this medium that the Arab Nationalist Movement, a pro-Nasser political grouping active throughout the Fertile Crescent, extended its activities to the Persian Gulf.

Kuwait took the lead in bringing the Japanese into oil exploitation through the granting of offshore concessions. Soon Japan, whose energy requirements have become almost entirely dependent upon Persian Gulf oil (90 percent in 1971), began a commercial penetration of what previously had been an almost exclusively British commercial domain. The day of the "N.O.C." (No Objection Certificate) by which British political agents were empowered to restrict the entry of non-British and non-Arab entrepreneurs into the area had come to an end in the northern Gulf and its knell was sounded in the Trucial States and Qatar as well.

The Anglo-Kuwaiti Treaty was abrogated in 1961. Kuwait joined the Arab League and subsequently the United Nations. The Iraqi claim to Kuwait (see Chapter 3) was put forward at this time, leading to the landing of a British force later to be replaced by a military formation hastily brought together under Arab League auspices.

Partly out of the realization of its vulnerability, but also because of a desire to play a role in Arab affairs, the emirate government established the Kuwait Fund for Arab Economic Development in the year that its independence was declared. In the following year the birth of a similar organization, the Gulf Permanent Assistance Committee, was an indication that Kuwait saw itself as *primus inter pares* in that region.

There was political evolution as well. A Kuwaiti constitutional assembly was established in 1962 which led to the institution of a partially elected National Assembly in 1963. In the same year, when Baghdad recognized its independence and sovereignty in exchange for a £30 million "development grant," the Iraqi claim to Kuwait finally was laid to rest.

In 1961 Shaikh Salman ibn Hamad Khalifah died in Bahrain and was succeeded by his son, Shaikh Isa, who followed his father's careful developmental policies. There were particularly heavy expenditures for educational projects and town planning in the following five years. The absolute necessity for fulfilling the rising expectations of the Arab peoples of the Gulf states was underscored by more than occasional strikes over redundancy dismissals in the Bahrain oil industry as well as by Arab Nationalist Movement agitation in Kuwait. In 1962 British Indian Steam Navigation's passenger vessel *Dara*, a symbol of the *raj* in the Gulf, was blown up and sunk off Sharjah with a loss of 236 lives. The act of sabotage, attributed to the Oman Revolutionary Movement, bespoke the increasingly fragile basis of *Pax Britannica* in the Gulf.

Qatar's long period of free-wheeling, expenditure and erratic development came to an end in 1964 when the ruler, supported by a tough-minded Egyptian adviser, Hasan Kamil, embarked upon planning for a modern fishing industry, petrochemical plants, a cement industry, and diversified agriculture. A reserve fund of £100 million was invested abroad as a hedge against any future economic reverses within the shaikhdom.

Development projects were instituted in the Trucial shaikhdoms as well, supported by subventions from the British government, Kuwait, and Saudi Arabia. A road project linking Dubai and Ras al-Khaimah, a public health service, education projects, and water development activities were initiated. Dubai, under the shrewd and imaginative rule of Shaikh Rashid ibn Said Maktum, was becoming the banking center of the southern Gulf. However, it was upon Abu Dhabi that most attention was focused because of its entry into the oil-producing ranks on a scale which was soon bringing in an annual income in excess of $200 million.

This vast income was more than Shaikh Shakhbut could contemplate, let alone effectively utilize. Thus it came as no great surprise to observers that a British-engineered *coup* should send the aging ruler into exile in 1966 and establish Shaikh Zayid ibn Sultan Nahhayan, his proconsul at Buraimi, as ruler of the shaikhdom. After all, the incompetent and anti-British Shaikh Saqr ibn Sultan of Sharjah had been deposed under similar auspices only one year before. This tiny shaikhdom, largely dependent upon income from British military installations, was given over to a cousin, Shaikh Khalid ibn Mohammed Qasimi.

It seemed that each oil-producing shaikhdom had to go through a period of irresponsible spending and uncoordinated planning. Abu Dhabi was no exception. However, the shaikhdom's admission to the Organization of Petroleum Exporting Countries in 1967 was an early indication of a more businesslike approach to financial management and relations with the Western-controlled marketing companies. By 1973, as noted above, Abu Dhabi had joined other Gulf shaikhdoms and Saudi Arabia in arrangements that would provide them with a 51 percent, controlling interest in petroleum concessions.

The capable Sir Abdul Salem Sabah, ruler of Kuwait, died in 1965, but as in Bahrain, the succession was unchallenged and the shaikhdom continued to make progress in social and economic development. Its airport was expanded and an enlarged harbor at Shuwaikh could now handle a greatly increased volume of freight from overseas sources.

Political activity increased in the crisis-filled days of 1967 when an open split between the Arab National Movement and the Kuwait government developed and was reflected at all levels of the population. It was natural that the June War of 1967 should intensify political activity throughout the area. Every oil-producing shaikhdom except Bahrain was dependent upon politically sophisticated Palestinians, Syrians, and Lebanese and it could hardly be expected that such immigrant workers would not bring their politics with them. Moreover, in the southern Gulf as well as in Kuwait, there was much illegal immigration, largely from Persia and Pakistan, and these immigrants were also vulnerable to political exploitation, more out of frustration over their economic plight than because of identification with the Arab cause.

The long-expected announcement of British military withdrawal from the Persian Gulf came at the end of 1968. Shaikh Zayid of Abu Dhabi and other rulers initially gave undertakings that the shaikhdoms themselves would be responsible for the payment of British military formations if they would remain. When it became clear that Her Majesty's government would not permit regular officers and men to be the Hessians of the modern Arab world, the shaikhs expressed great interest in forming a federation of Arab emirates. Unlike the South Arabian Federation, this project was supported by Egypt and other Arab states as well as London—by the former because it seemed the best means of ensuring a rapid withdrawal. In the new atmosphere of enforced cordiality, Abu Dhabi and Dubai reached agreement on offshore boundaries plus some minor territorial rectifications.

Shaikh Zayid of Abu Dhabi was determined to be the dominant political leader of the southern Gulf once the last note of the British recessional had been sounded. The Abu Dhabi Defense Force testified to his resolve. Four times the size and many more times the firepower of the Trucial Oman Scouts (the British-sponsored peacekeeping force) in 1969, the ADDF was at once a versatile air, naval, and surface force and a major drain on the shaikhdom's resources.[5] It could not, however, defend Abu Dhabi or any federation with which that shaikhdom might become associated either from Saudi Arabia, which continued to claim sovereignty over a vast expanse of Abu Dhabian hinterland east to the Buraimi Oasis, or from Iran.

A more immediate problem for the Abu Dhabi ruling family was British interest in promoting a nine-state federation, including Bahrain and Qatar. Shaikh Zayid realized that Bahraini experience in politics, public administration, and commerce outstripped that of any other prospective federation member. Qatar was second to Bahrain in achievement—not a close second, but with a record of impressive progress under an administration pledged to reform. There was a legacy of bad feeling between the al-Thanis of Qatar and the Nahayyan of Abu Dhabi, deriving from past disputes over boundaries, grazing rights, and other matters which would seem trifling to an outsider. Jealousy and suspicion assured that negotiations on federation would be prolonged. Not all the disruptions were provided by Bahrain, Qatar, Abu Dhabi, and Dubai, however, for the tough old ruler of Ras al-Khaimah, Shaikh Saqr ibn Mohammed Qasimi, regarded himself as entitled to a major part in the government of any federation, as a descendant of the Qawasim rulers whose tribesmen had dominated the southern Gulf in the early nineteenth century. Visitors to Ras al-Khaimah were told that the British had employed the trucial system to weaken the Qawasim but that there should have been only one Arab signatory, Saqr's revered ancestor. Saqr's demands slowed negotiations and on at least one occasion, in 1969, he succeeded in disrupting them completely. Observers variously saw Saudi, Iraqi, and Iranian influence behind the old shaikh's actions, but connoisseurs of Gulf politics asserted that he was in the pay of all three countries.

Nonetheless, the shaikhdoms were well embarked by 1969 upon at-

---

[5]In 1970, with seven thousand men under arms, the ADDF was one-fifth the size of Abu Dhabi's native population.

tempts to achieve economic diversification and infrastructure improvement. Telecommunications, radar, and improved airports were in the planning stage from one end of the Gulf to the other. Kuwait opened its supertanker terminal, the first in the world to handle efficiently the vast new tankers of the era in which the Suez Canal was closed to maritime traffic.

Great progress was also made in Bahrain. Isa Town, the first phase of a larger-scale town planning project, was completed in 1968. Two principal islands of the archipelago were linked by causeway, but the announcement of plans for a causeway between Bahrain and the nearby Saudi Arabian mainland caused sharp Iranian objections, put forth in such aggressive tones as to cause the plan to be shelved. Construction began on an aluminum smelter in 1969 and Bahrain reinforced its status as the communications center of the Gulf with the completion of an earth satellite station.

Qatar, Bahrain's traditional rival for primacy in the southern Gulf, also sought to achieve further diversification. Construction of a fertilizer plant began in 1969 and a major modernization program was implemented in the capital city, Doha. But the event of greatest economic significance in the southern Gulf during that year was the addition of Dubai to the ranks of major petroleum-producing nations.

In preparation for military withdrawal, British diplomats worked assiduously to achieve federation and to reduce tensions between the various shaikhdoms. Great efforts were made to obtain cooperation on Gulf issues between Iran and Saudi Arabia, which was considered the best guarantee of security and an effective restraint upon Iraqi enthusiasms. Saudi Arabia's internal distractions, however, plus involvement in inter-Arab politics in the Fertile Crescent and across the Red Sea, gave Iran the paramount position by default. The Shah's government removed an obstacle to full participation in Gulf diplomacy in 1970 by acknowledging the results of a UN-sponsored plebiscite of that year and formally renouncing its claim to Bahrain. (But a secret corollary of this action, communicated to Great Britain, asserted an Iranian claim to control, if not sovereignty, over the strategically located islands of Abu Musa and the Tumbs, near the Straits of Hormuz.)

The slow political evolution of Bahrain continued, with Shaikh Isa giving over some of his responsibilities to a Council of State. The high level of social and educational services provided by the Bahrain government acted to minimize political pressure on the regime, but such services could not produce permanent political tranquility. The emirate's expanding school system—over one hundred primary and secondary schools were in existence by 1971—contains many aspiring politicians.

Qatar also instituted a Council of Ministers and a large Advisory Council in 1970. The affairs of the shaikhdom were placed on an even more businesslike basis by the able deputy ruler, prime minister, and finance minister, Shaikh Khalifah ibn Hamad al-Thani. Gone were the days when one of the ruling family stored over fifty high-powered automobiles in a Beirut garage and several princes supported complete soccer teams, the players drawn primarily from Europe, handsomely paid and accommodated, in contests upon which thousands of *dinars* in bets changed hands. Fiscal accountability was gaining the upper hand.

By 1972, the days were long past when the name of Kuwait was synonymous with reckless spending in European spas. Income from oil revenues neared a billion dollars annually, but it was significant that only half the gross national product came from oil. There was extensive investment in banking, insurance, shipping, petrochemical industries, and fishing, and Kuwaitis embarked upon new airline and supertanker enterprises. The ruling family was so firmly in control as to permit the existence of a free-swinging press and a facade of democracy. In 1971 the Arab Nationalist Movement obtained seven members in elections to the fifty-seat National Assembly and an ANM deputy entered the cabinet. Less than half of Kuwait's population of 750,000 are Kuwaiti nationals. Non-Kuwaitis whose fortunes have been made there, and even the depressed migrant workers from western Iran, were aware that engaging in antiregime activities brought speedy expulsion. As much as a fifth of the country's annual budget was channeled into aid projects, some of which could be described as "protection money," through which Kuwait secured a voice in Arab councils far out of proportion to its size, if not its income. Good relations were cultivated with Soviet bloc nations and China, not so much out of any perceived need to achieve political balance between the two power blocs as because such relations made sense commercially.

By mid-1971, despite British efforts and Kuwaiti good offices, little progress had been made toward the establishment of a viable federation. Bahrain's insistence on ministerial representation based upon population was a major obstacle. Qatar's aspirations to leadership of a federation exclusive of Bahrain were defeated by Abu Dhabi obstructionism. It was clear that Shaikh Zayid would thwart any federation experiment in which he did not have the largest share of authority. He had succeeded in purchasing the support of smaller shaikhdoms, with the predictable exception of Ras al-Khaimah.

His enthusiasm for federation having evaporated, Shaikh Isa announced, on August 14, 1971, that Bahrain was an independent and sovereign nation. Membership in the United Nations and the Arab

League soon followed. The special relationship with Great Britain was maintained through a friendship treaty. The Bahraini lead was quickly followed by Qatar, which also gained UN and Arab League membership. On December 2, the Union of Arab Emirates was proclaimed, comprised of Abu Dhabi, Dubai, Ajman, Fujairah, and Umm al-Quwain.

Shaikh Saqr's obdurate opposition to Abu Dhabi domination was reinforced by the Iranian seizure of the Tumbs several days before the federation was announced. These islands were recognized in the trucial agreements as belonging to Ras al-Khaimah. Iranian forces also landed on a third island, Abu Musa, but they did so by prearrangement with Sharjah. It was therefore a peaceful occupation. Such was not the case of the Tumbs, where several Iranian soldiers and members of the minuscule Ras al-Khaimah defense force were killed in brief but fierce fighting. Britain was bitterly castigated by all the shaikhdoms along the Arab littoral of the Gulf and by Iraq, which severed relations with the London government. United Nations and Arab League membership provided platforms for the new federation to air its complaints. (Bahrain's criticism, however, was muted. It was now understood that when Iran dropped its long-standing claim to sovereignty over Bahrain, the price was a free hand with Abu Musa and the Tumbs.) Prearrangement between Iran and Great Britain was obvious, but it was also obvious that Britain expected the action to be delayed until the various protectorate agreements dating back to the nineteenth century had expired, with the proclamation of the federation and after friendship treaties similar to those negotiated with Bahrain and Qatar had been concluded. Iran, for its part, acted in advance of those events in order to use Great Britain as a lightning rod at the UN and elsewhere.

Shaikh Zayid of Abu Dhabi, as president of the new state, entered office for five years. His longtime rival, Shaikh Rashid of Dubai, became vice president and Rashid's son Maktum, prime minister. The overall income from oil for the Union of Arab Emirates in 1971 was $350 million. To further reinforce his bid for a permanent role in the affairs of the southern Gulf and a wider Arab world, Shaikh Zayid announced the establishment of the Abu Dhabi Fund for Economic Development almost at the same time. It was modeled on the Kuwait institution founded a decade earlier.

A less predictable result of the Iranian action was the assassination of the ruler of Sharjah in January 1972. His predecessor, Shaikh Saqr ibn Sultan, who had been deposed several years earlier, with British collusion, because of his pro-Nasser proclivities, was able to rally support based upon resentment over Shaikh Khalid's acquiescence in the Iranian action. But the attempt only provided an opportunity for the new political entity to demonstrate its viability and determination through quick and decisive intervention of federation troops. This in turn was instrumental in bringing Ras al-Khaimah into the UAE in the following month, although Shaikh Saqr would have held out if the search for oil in his territory had succeeded.

The Soviet Union was quick to establish diplomatic relations with the UAE, creating concern in Teheran, Riyadh, and Western capitals. The American response was to accredit its ambassador to Kuwait to the new federation and to announce an agreement to continue the use of Bahraini port facilities for another twenty-five years. Many of the communications facilities formerly operated by Great Britain on the island were taken over by the United States.

There was further political change in Qatar where the deputy ruler, Shaikh Khalifah, replaced his profligate and permissive brother, sending him into exile. Khalifah acted only after years of hesitation, for his efforts to use the shaikhdom's enormous oil revenues to diversify and strengthen its economy long had been resisted by the ruler. Increases in offshore oil production and the price increases obtained in the Teheran agreement of 1971 raised Qatar's oil income from that source to $250 million in 1971. The change in the rulership gave evidence of stability which encouraged greatly increased investment there.

The Shah's policy in the Persian Gulf is understandable. Iran—with its improved military, air, and naval facilities across the Straits of Hormuz—and the UAE control the narrow waterway between the Persian Gulf and Arabian Sea. In 1967 the Gulf region for the first time exceeded the total annual production of oil and natural gas in the United States. It did so by producing just under one-half billion tons of oil and natural gas. Most of this production reaches its markets on tankers, for which the only exit from the Gulf is through the Straits of Hormuz. On certain days in 1971 almost six million barrels of petroleum products were loaded aboard supertankers at the Iranian offshore bunkering facility at Kharg Island.[6] The factionalism and contentiousness of southern Gulf politics have strengthened the Shah's conviction that the "oil route" can be made

---

[6]Sixty percent of non-Communist oil reserves are located in the Persian Gulf region, which is responsible for over one-third of current non-Communist petroleum production. Approximate, rounded figures for Persian Gulf oil production (in barrels per day, 1971) are Iran 4,000,000, Kuwait 3,200,000, Saudi Arabia 3,500,000, Abu Dhabi 900,000, Qatar 400,000, Oman 350,000, and Dubai 200,000. Iraq is rapidly expanding facilities for production. The Iraq Petroleum Company now produces something less than one-half the Iranian total. There are smaller producers in the Gulf —Bahrain, for example—and offshore and onshore prospecting by American, British, French, Italian, Japanese, and local concession-holders continues at a high level of activity.

secure only if such a vulnerable passageway is under direct Iranian super-vision. Hence the resolute action of late 1971, quietly approved by Great Britain and the United States.

Although the political future remained clouded in mid-1972, the pace of economic development continued to quicken and the quality of planning and execution continued to improve, giving rise to hopes that Gulf Arabs of every station in life—and immigrant Arabs as well—would find a "stake in society" and abjure panaceas of revolutionary change. Bahrain, faced with a drying up of oil reserves by 1990, not only added to an impressive record of economic diversification with plans for exploita-tion of natural gas deposits but also made great progress with a modern fishing industry, a drydocking and ship repair facility, and additions to the jetliner fleet of its profitable airline, Gulf Aviation. Major industrial projects were advancing out of the planning stage in Abu Dhabi, Dubai, and other shaikhdoms of the southern Gulf. The most obvious evidence of modernization was provided by supermarkets, shiny consumer goods of all kinds, paved and divided highways, and luxury hotels in such formerly remote places as the Buraimi Oasis. More important were the schools, scholarship funds, hospitals, cement, sulphur, aluminum, and petrochemical plants which indicated the determination of Gulf Arabs to shake off the dead hand of feudalism.

Much is at stake in eastern Arabia and the Persian Gulf for Arabs, Persians, and the great powers, East and West. The *Pax Britannica* lived to a venerable age in this region, but now it is gone. The Sultanate of Oman and the Gulf shaikhdoms are open to every form of penetration, commercial, cultural, diplomatic, military—the list is extensive. Indeed, that penetration began earlier in 1971 when the search for trading part-ners and markets led Kuwait to establish diplomatic relations with Peking at ambassadorial level.

Overall American investment in the region surpassed that of Great Britain over a decade ago. But Britain's returns from her commercial involvement are vital to her economic survival. Because it can no longer be protected by British armed might, her policy now emphasizes the need for friendship with the Arab peoples based upon long and in-timate association. British statesmen also call for an increased awareness on the part of the United States of its own vital interests in the region. Most obviously, some of these are commercial. But others are strategic, for the Peninsula and Gulf lie athwart major lines of global communica-tions and contain targets of opportunity, most notably for the Soviet Union in the present phase of its Indian Ocean policy. Some are political, especially the problem of keeping peace in the region. There are also "ideological interests," which relate to maintaining the viability of moderate Arab governments.

Various authorities have assessed Soviet naval policy in the Indian Ocean and Mediterranean as being opportunistic, as a means of countering or placing constraints upon the fleet carriers and Polaris submarines of the United States Navy. It has been established that the Polaris A–3 missile can be delivered to more major targets in the USSR from the Persian Gulf than from any other body of water except the Arctic Ocean. The policy is also assessed as a continuation of the late Chairman Khrushchev's attempts to stimulate national pride and exemplify the USSR as a global rather than merely a continental power, and as "showing the flag" in support of political and economic objectives. It is all of these, and more. A basic requirement of Soviet doctrine is the capability to wage limited warfare, to intervene decisively and profitably in local insurrections. The development of helicopter carriers and naval infantry supports this requirement. So do the extensive familiarization and acclimatization cruises by Soviet units in the Indian Ocean area since 1968, with visits to Aden and to Red Sea and Persian Gulf ports. With the expiration of the protectorate treaties at the end of 1971, the Persian Gulf, which for so long had been a British lake, was thrown open to Soviet penetration.

Although the Six Day War of June 1967 provided the Soviet Union an opportunity to increase its leverage on Syria and Iraq and to entrench its position in the United Arab Republic, the Soviet naval buildup in the Mediterranean and in the coastal waters of the Arabian Peninsula resulted from decisions taken much earlier and enshrined as official doctrine with the 1967 publication by the Soviet Ministry of Defense of *Naval Warfare in the Atlantic and Mediterranean*. The term "Indian Ocean" may well have been added to the title, and future historians may mark 1967 as the year of the great shift in Soviet strategic emphasis from Europe to the wider world. As far as the Indian Ocean is concerned, its lonely sea lanes are becoming a focus of concern not only for the two superpowers, but for Japan and mainland China as well. Japanese interest is understandable enough, with 90 percent of the nation's petroleum requirements being met by Persian Gulf sources. Units of the Maritime Self Defense Force have appeared in these waters and participated in joint maneuvers off the Straits of Malacca. The close identification of Japanese and American interests and the near life-or-death aspect of Japan's reliance upon Persian Gulf oil suggest that the United States must give close attention to contingency planning in this area. There are indications that Japanese naval planners are in advance of their American counterparts in this important regard. Only at great peril can China's interest in the Indian Ocean area be dismissed as a manifestation of her rivalry with the Soviet Union for ideological hegemony in the Third World. The *Nan Yang* or Southern Ocean was heavily penetrated by the Chinese in the fifteenth century, when their vessels frequently passed the Straits of Malacca to and from the Persian Gulf and East African ports. The burdens of history and the concept of destiny lie heavily upon the Peking regime. China is now the third naval power in Far Eastern waters, its ships have been sighted in the Indian Ocean, and in three or four decades the harbor facilities which the Chinese are currently providing for Tanzania may have a place in its own maritime strategy. For the present, however, it is the Soviet Union which has replaced Great Britain as the principal maritime power in the Indian Ocean.

The specific course of Soviet strategy in the Persian Gulf may be unpredictable, but what is at stake is not. Two-thirds of the world's proven oil reserves are in this area, a fact which takes on increased importance in view of the uncertainty of long-term production from north-of-Suez sources (Libya, Algeria, and the United Arab Republic) and of the difficulties faced in the production and marketing of Alaskan oil.[7] Still further importance is conferred upon the Gulf's oil resources by the growing market for its products in the Soviet Union, Rumania, and mainland China. With respect to the USSR, a short-term objective may be to secure less expensive Middle Eastern oil for domestic consumption while marketing its own production at higher prices in Eastern Europe and in exchange for hard currency and advanced technology in Western Europe. In the long term, expanding energy requirements within the Soviet Union itself may become a prime determinant. One may safely conclude that the Persian Gulf is on the threshold of another era in many ways reminiscent of the seventeenth century when the English, Dutch, and Portuguese sought preeminence there.

---

[7]The 1971 meeting of the Organization of Petroleum Exporting Countries (OPEC) at Teheran heard discussions of the feasibility of enlarging the tanker fleets of OPEC countries (to include the construction of drydock facilities in the Persian Gulf) as another means of limiting the role of Western oil marketing interests. Adding to what might be considered as the normal profit incentive is the continued pressure of Palestinian and other Arab interests for funds to support measures against Israel.

SUGGESTED
READINGS

The specialist resorts to bibliographies which, in the era of computer printouts, all but assures saturation coverage insofar as printed sources are concerned. Yet this book depended very heavily on oral tradition, personal observation, and two decades of conversation with Arabs of great estate and small, all of them aware of a heritage, all of them holding certain truths to be self-evident. Especially important is the latter, for nowhere is it more patent that history is determined by what people *believe* to be true than in the Arab lands of Western Asia.

The student, the informed layman, and the generalist for whom this book was written will not be receptive to the microhistory referenced in the specialists' bibliographies. And it would be an impertinence to suggest that they take time out from their careers to go and live among the Arabs for four or five years—however wonderful and mind-expanding an experience it might be. Hence the following suggestions, in the categories of general works, books relating to one or another of the Arab lands of Western Asia and, lastly, relevant periodicals.

General

The best source of information on the physical environment of the Arab East is W.B. FISHER, *The Middle East: A Physical, Social and Regional Geography* (London: Methuen, 1961, and republished with extensive revisions in 1971).

The labors of gifted scholars may be drawn upon for an understanding of Islam as a religion and way of life. Particularly recommended are SIR HAMILTON A.R. GIBB, *Mohammedanism: An Historical Survey* (New York: Oxford University Press, 1962); ALFRED GUILLAUME, *Islam*, 2nd ed. (Baltimore: Penguin Books, 1964); CARL BROCKELMANN, *History of the Islamic Peoples* (London: Routledge and Kegan Paul, 1949, translated from the German edition of 1939); and GUSTAVE VON GRUNEBAUM, *Medieval Islam* (Chicago: University of Chicago Press, 1961).

To a remarkable extent this is a history of cities—a Baghdad, or Beirut, Riyadh or Muscat. Therefore there is important background material available in IRA LAPIDUS, *Muslim Cities of the Later Middle Ages* (Cambridge, Mass.: Harvard University Press, 1967), which deals with the Mamluk era, and in the collection of papers edited by A.H. HOURANI and S.M. STERN, *The Islamic City: A Colloquium* (Oxford: Bruno Cassirer, 1970).

Ample coverage of those intrusions which were the Crusades is provided in W.B. STEVENSON, *The Crusaders in the East* (Beirut: Librairie du Liban, 1968), a reprint of an early study; and, in richer detail, by SIR STEVEN RUNCIMAN's *A History of the Crusades*, I, *The First Crusade and the Foundation of the Kingdom of Jerusalem*, II, *The Kingdom of Jerusalem and the Frankish East 1100–1187*, III, *The Kingdom of Acre and the Later Crusades* (Cambridge: Cambridge University Press, 1954).

For the Ottoman era there is PAUL WITTECK's seminal *The Rise of the Ottoman Empire* (London: Luzac for the Royal Asiatic Society, 1965); *Islamic Society in the Eighteenth Century*, which is volume I, part I, of SIR HAMILTON A.R. GIBB and HAROLD BOWEN, *Islamic Society and the West: A Study of the Impact of Western Civilization on Moslem Culture in the Near East* (London: Oxford University Press, 1951); and *The Central Islamic Lands*, volume I of P.M. HOLT, ANN K.S. LAMBTON, and BERNARD LEWIS, eds., *The Cambridge History of Islam* (Cambridge: Cambridge University Press, 1970).

Of the many studies of great power rivalries in the Arab East during the Ottoman period, particularly recommended are M.S. ANDERSON, *The Eastern Question* (New York: St. Martin's Press, 1966); VERNON J. PURYEAR, *France and the Levant: from the Bourbon Restoration to the Peace of Kutiah* (Berkeley: University of California Press, 1941); DEREK HOPWOOD, *The Russian Presence in Syria and Palestine 1843–1914: Church and Politics in the Near East* (London: Oxford University Press, 1969); and, P.M. HOLT, *Egypt and the Fertile Crescent 1516–1922* (London: Longmans Green, 1966).

The stirrings of nationalistic feelings among Arab peoples, anti-

Turkish sentiment, and resistance to European arrangements for Arab lands in the post-Ottoman era are described in GEORGE ANTONIUS, *The Arab Awakening* (Philadelphia: Lippincott, 1939) which should be read in tandem with ZEINE N. ZEINE, *The Emergence of Arab Nationalism: With a Background Study of Arab-Turkish Relations in the Near East* (Beirut: Khayat's, 1966) for the important qualifications—and explications—the latter provides. Very important are A.H. HOURANI, *Arabic Thought in the Liberal Age* (London: Oxford University Press, 1962) and SYLVIA HAIM, *Arab Nationalism: An Anthology* (Berkeley: University of California Press, 1962), which is especially recommended for its brilliant introduction. An outstanding survey that defies categorization but may be listed here for its interpretations of various aspects of Arab nationalism is ARNOLD HOTTINGER, *The Arabs: Their History, Culture and Place in the Modern World* (London: Thames and Hudson, 1963).

On European arrangements for the post-Ottoman period, suggested are ELIE KEDOURIE, *England and the Middle East: The Destruction of the Ottoman Empire, 1914–1921* (London: Bowes and Bowes, 1956); JUKKA NEVAKIVI, *Britain, France and the Arab Middle East 1914–1920* (London: Athlone Press, 1969); BRITON C. BUSCH, *Britain, India and the Arabs, 1914–1921* (Berkeley: University of California Press, 1971); AARON S. KLIEMAN, *Foundations of British Policy in the Arab World: The Cairo Conference of 1921* (Baltimore: Johns Hopkins University Press, 1970); ELIZABETH MONROE, *Britain's Moment in the Middle East, 1914–1956* (Baltimore: Johns Hopkins University Press, 1963); and, HARRY N. HOWARD, *The King-Crane Commission: An American Inquiry into the Middle East* (Beirut: Khayat's, 1963). Taking the account of great power rivalries into the Cold War era is GEORGE LENCZOWSKI, *The Middle East in World Affairs* (Ithaca: Cornell University Press, 1962).

The Arab response to the technological and communications revolutions is described in MORROE BERGER, *The Arab World Today* (New York: Doubleday, 1962); J.H. THOMPSON and R.D. REISCHAUER (eds.), *Modernization of the Arab World* (Princeton: Van Nostrand, 1966), and interpreted in GUSTAVE VON GRUNEBAUM, *Modern Islam: The Search for Cultural Identity* (Berkeley: University of California Press, 1962).

Most of the material made available in the works listed above emphasize the "sown." There are important general works on the desert portion of the Arab lands of western Asia and the waters that surround them. Suggested are THOMAS E. MARSTON, *Britain's Imperial Role in the Red Sea Area 1800–1878* (Hamden, Connecticut: Shoe String Press, 1961); R.B. SERJEANT, *The Portuguese off the South Arabian Coast* (London: Oxford University Press, 1963); SIR ARNOLD TALBOT WILSON, *The Persian Gulf: A Historical Sketch from the Earliest Times to the Beginning of the Twentieth Century* (London: George Allen and Unwin,

1928); J.B. KELLY, *Britain and the Persian Gulf 1795–1880* (Oxford: Clarendon Press, 1968); RAVINDAR KUMAR, *India and the Persian Gulf Region 1858–1907* (London: Asia Publishing House, 1965); BRITON C. BUSCH, *Britain and the Persian Gulf 1894–1914* (Berkeley: University of California Press, 1967); JOHN MARLOWE, *The Persian Gulf in the Twentieth Century* (London: Cresset, 1962); the valuable republications of S.B. MILES, *The Countries and Tribes of the Persian Gulf* (London: Frank Cass, 1966) and of the indispensable J.G. LORIMER, *Gazetteer of the Persian Gulf, Oman and Central Arabia*, 6 vols. (Shannon: Irish Universities Press, 1970). For the recent period, valuable background material is to be found in J.B. KELLY, *Eastern Arabian Frontiers* (London: Faber and Faber, 1964) and DEREK HOPWOOD (ed.), *The Arabian Peninsula: Society and Politics* (London: George Allen and Unwin, 1972).

Many are the accounts of Arabian exploration. Among the best are the selections from the writings of the nineteenth-century adventurer CHARLES M. DOUGHTY, published as EDWARD GARNETT, ed., *Passages from Arabia Deserta* (Harmondsworth: Penguin Books, 1956); the account by Doughty's Italian contemporary, CARLO GUARMANI, *Northern Najd: A Journey from Jerusalem to Anaiza in Qasim* (London: Argonaut Press, 1938); the compendium by D.G. HOGARTH, *The Penetration of Arabia* (London: Alston Rivers, 1906); R.E. CHEESMAN's *In Unknown Arabia* (London: Macmillan, 1926), the story of a trek from Hofuf to Jabrin in the Empty Quarter; the indefatigable H. ST. JOHN (ABDULLAH) PHILBY's *Forty Years in the Wilderness* (London: Robert Hale, 1957); and WILFRED THESIGER's epic *Arabian Sands* (Harmondsworth: Penguin Books, 1964).

Literature on the Middle Eastern oil industry is vast and expanding. Suggested are H. ST. JOHN (ABDULLAH) PHILBY's *Arabian Oil Ventures* (Washington, D.C.: Middle East Institute, 1964); S.H. LONGRIGG, *Oil in the Middle East: Its Discovery and Development* (London: Oxford University Press, 1954); DAVID H. FINNIE, *Desert Enterprise: The Middle East Oil Industry in its Local Environment* (Cambridge, Mass.: Harvard University Press, 1958); and, GEORGE LENCZOWSKI, *Oil and State in the Middle East* (Ithaca: Cornell University Press, 1960).

Lebanon

Two outstanding general accounts are available*, K.S. SALIBI, *The Modern History of Lebanon* (New York: Praeger, 1965) and A.H.

---

*Several titles, as will be obvious, relate as much to Syria as Lebanon but are only cited in this section.

HOURANI, *Syria and Lebanon: A Political Essay* (London: Oxford University Press, 1946). An important investigation of the "political sociology" of the country is ILIYA F. HARIK, *Politics and Change in a Traditional Society: Lebanon, 1711–1845* (Princeton, N.J.: Princeton University Press, 1968). Also recommended is WILLIAM R. POLK, *The Opening of South Lebanon: A Study of the Impact of the West on the Middle East* (Cambridge, Mass.: Harvard University Press, 1963). Indispensable for an understanding of the interwar period is S.H. LONGRIGG, *Syria and Lebanon under French Mandate* (London: Oxford University Press, 1958) a book that takes on the labyrinthine quality of its subject. LEONARD BINDER (ed.), *Politics in Lebanon* (New York: Wiley, 1966) is a collection of papers presented to a conference held at the University of Chicago, almost inevitably uneven in quality, but with important insights. Three excellent works on contemporary Lebanon are MICHAEL HUDSON, *The Precarious Republic: Political Modernization in Lebanon* (New York: Random House, 1969); MICHAEL SULEIMAN, *Political Parties in Lebanon: The Challenge of a Fragmented Political Culture* (Ithaca, N.Y.: Cornell University Press, 1967); and JOHN SYKES, *The Mountain Arabs: A Window on the Middle East* (London: Hutchinson, 1968). The latter does not suffer and, indeed, gains for being impressionistic and based upon personal observation before and during the Six Day War of June 1967, a time when the fabric of Lebanese society was nearly rent asunder.

Syria

Two books on the Ottoman era are suggested. They are ABDUL-KARIM RAFEQ, *The Province of Damascus 1723–1783* (Beirut: Khayat's, 1966) and AVEDIS K. SANJIAN, *The Armenian Communities in Syria under Ottoman Dominion* (Cambridge, Mass.: Harvard University Press, 1965). The shattered hopes of Arab nationalists after World War I are evoked in SATI AL-HUSRY, *The Day of Maysalun: A Page from the Modern History of the Arabs* (Washington, D.C.: The Middle East Institute, 1966). The best study of independent Syria is PATRICK SEALE, *The Struggle for Syria: A Study of Postwar Arab Politics* (London: Oxford University Press, 1965). Also recommended are LABIB ZUWIYYA YAMAK, *The Syrian Social Nationalist Party: an Ideological Analysis* (Cambridge, Mass.: Harvard University Press, 1966) and INTERNATIONAL BANK FOR RECONSTRUCTION AND DEVELOPMENT, *The Economic Development of Syria* (Baltimore: Johns Hopkins University Press, 1955).

Iraq

Major historical eras are portrayed and interpreted in S.H. LONGRIGG, *Four Centuries of Modern Iraq* (Beirut: Librairie du Liban, 1968); *Iraq 1900 to 1950: a Political, Social and Economic History* (London: Oxford University Press, 1953) by the same author; P.W. IRELAND, *Iraq: a Study in Political Development* (London: Jonathan Cape, 1937); and MAJID KHADDURI, *Independent Iraq, 1932–1958* (London, Oxford University Press, 1960).

British military and political involvement are detailed in A.J. BARKER, *The Neglected War: Mesopotamia 1914–1918* (London: Faber and Faber, 1967) and in SIR ARNOLD TALBOT WILSON's important two volumes, *Loyalties: Mesopotamia 1914–1917* and *Mesopotamia 1917–1920: A Clash of Loyalties* (London: Oxford University Press, 1930, 1931).

The transition from "old guard" to revolutionary government is described in LORD BIRDWOOD, *Nuri as-Said: A Study in Arab Leadership* (London: Cassell, 1959); "Caractacus," *Revolution in Iraq: An Essay in Comparative Public Opinion* (London: Gollancz, 1959); and in URIEL DANN, *Iraq under Qassem: A Political History 1958–1963* (London: Pall Mall Press, 1969) a remarkable accomplishment by an Israeli scholar. A comprehensive work, INTERNATIONAL BANK FOR RECONSTRUCTION AND DEVELOPMENT, *The Economic Development of Iraq* (Baltimore: Johns Hopkins University Press, 1965) evaluates the economic potential of the country in a more optimistic era.

Sectors of Iraq's heterogeneous population are dealt with in WILFRED THESIGER, *The Marsh Arabs* (London: Longmans Green, 1964); C.J. EDMONDS, *Kurds, Turks and Arabs: Politics, Travel and Research in Northeastern Iraq 1919–1925* (London: Oxford University Press, 1957); and THOMAS BOIS, *The Kurds* (Beirut, Khayat's, 1966), which covers Syria's Kurdish population as well as Iraq's and emphasizes society and culture. Other books dealing with Kurds beyond Iraq's frontiers as well as those settled since antiquity in "Iraqi Kurdistan" are HASSAN ARFA, *The Kurds: A Historical and Political Study* (London: Oxford University Press, 1966) and DEREK KINNANE, *The Kurds and Kurdistan* (London: Oxford University Press, 1964). JOHN JOSEPH, *The Nestorians and their Muslim Neighbors: A Study of Western Influences on their Relations* (Princeton, N.J.: Princeton University Press, 1961) might also be consulted.

Jordan

Among the better general accounts are PAUL W. COPELAND, *The Land and People of Jordan* (Philadelphia: Lippincott, 1965); GEORGE L. HARRIS, *Jordan: Its People, Its Society, Its Culture* (New York: Grove Press, 1958); and F.G. PEAKE, *A History of Jordan and its Tribes* (Coral Gables, Fla.: University of Miami Press, 1958). Important aspects of the country's recent history are covered in P.J. VATIKIOTIS, *Politics and the Military in Jordan: A Study of the Arab Legion 1921– 1957* (London: Frank Cass, 1967) and a trifle subjectively in HUSSEIN IBN TALAL, *Uneasy Lies the Head: the Autobiography of His Majesty King Hussein of the Hashemite Kingdom of Jordan* (New York: Geis, 1962). Also recommended is INTERNATIONAL BANK FOR RECONSTRUCTION AND DEVELOPMENT, *The Economic Development of Jordan* (Baltimore: Johns Hopkins University Press, 1957).

The Arabian Peninsula

A good assessment of the shape of change in the Peninsula is DAVID HOLDEN, *Farewell to Arabia* (London: Faber and Faber, 1966). Saudi Arabia's rise to nationhood can best be comprehended by reading H. ST. JOHN (ABDULLAH) PHILBY, *Saudi Arabia* (New York: Praeger, 1955); R. BAYLY WINDER, *Saudi Arabia in the Nineteenth Century* (New York: St. Martin's Press, 1965); K.S. TWITCHELL, *Saudi Arabia: with an Account of the Development of its Natural Resources* (Princeton, N.J.: Princeton University Press, 1953); and the best biography of the person who made it all possible, *The Desert King: a Life of Ibn Saud* by DAVID HOWARTH (London: Collins, 1964).

The best book on what is now the Yemeni Arab Republic (North Yemen) is HAROLD INGRAMS, *The Yemen: Imams, Rulers and Revolutions* (London: John Murray, 1963), followed at some distance by ERIC MACRO, *Yemen and the Western World since 1571* (London: C. Hurst, 1968) and Manfred W. Wenner, *Modern Yemen* (Baltimore: Johns Hopkins University Press, 1967). Special aspects are covered in HANS HELFRITZ, *The Yemen: A Secret Journey* (London: George Allen and Unwin, 1958); DANA ADAMS SCHMIDT, *Yemen: the Unknown War* (London: The Bodley Head, 1968); and EDGAR O'BALLANCE, *The War in the Yemen* (London: Faber and Faber, 1971).

British involvement in the modern history of Aden and what were the artificial entities bearing the names of Western Aden Protectorate and

Eastern Aden Protectorate (the latter being primarily the geographical area known as Hadhramaut), parts of which were willingly or unwillingly incorporated into the Federation of Arab Emirates of the South (South Arabian Federation) some years before being translated, largely at bayonet-point, into the People's Democratic Republic of Yemen (South Yemen) has insured a rich literature on that area. Good background is provided in GORDON WATERFIELD, *Sultans of Aden* (London: John Murray, 1968); JAMES LUNT, *The Barren Rocks of Aden* (London: Herbert Jenkins, 1966); and the very important third edition of HAROLD INGRAMS, *Arabia and the Isles* (London: John Murray, 1966), which includes a long, valuable introduction on recent developments in southwestern Arabia. Specialists interested in irredentism may turn to J. PLASS and U. GEHRKE, *Die Aden-Grenze in der Suedarabienfrage 1900–1967* (Opladen: Leske Verlag, 1967). The best account of the declension of British authority is TOM LITTLE, *South Arabia: Arena of Conflict* (New York: Praeger, 1968) and readers may also be interested in the *apologia* of SIR KENNEDY TREVASKIS, *Shades of Amber: a South Arabian Episode* (London: Hutchinson, 1968), whose role was to make the worst of a bad job. The tasks facing the rulers of post-British South Arabia are identified in A.S. BUJRA, *The Politics of Stratification: A Study of Political Change in a South Arabian Town* (London: Oxford University Press, 1971).

On eastern Arabia, readers may wish to consult R.G. LANDEN, *Oman Since 1856: Disruptive Modernization in a Traditional Arab Society* (Princeton, N.J.: Princeton University Press, 1967) which, despite imperfections, is informative; JAMES MORRIS, *Sultan in Oman: Venture into the Middle East* (New York: Pantheon, 1957); Research Division, Arabian American Oil Company, *Oman and the Southern Shore of the Persian Gulf* (Cairo: Imprimerie Misr, 1952), an unsuccessful attempt to demonstrate that in oil politics the pen is mightier than the sword; DONALD HAWLEY, *The Trucial States* (London: George Allen and Unwin, 1970), an informed work by Britain's first ambassador to the Sultanate of Oman; HUSAIN M. AL-BAHARNA, *The Legal Status of the Arabian Gulf States: A Study of their Treaty Relations and their International Problems* (New York: Oceana, 1969); AHMAD ABU HAKIMA, *History of Eastern Arabia 1750–1800: the Rise and Development of Bahrain and Kuwait* (Beirut: Khayat's, 1965); and H. R. P. DICKSON, *Kuwait and her Neighbours* (London: George Allen and Unwin, 1956). Valuable information is available in H. MOYSE-BARTLETT, *The Pirates of Trucial Oman* (London: MacDonald, 1966); CHARLES BELGRAVE, *The Pirate Coast* (London: Bell, 1966); RODERIC OWEN, *The Golden Bubble: Arabian Gulf Documentary* (London: Collins, 1957), an accurate representation of the sights and smells of the southern Gulf in the days of Shaikh Shakhbut ibn

Sultan of Abu Dhabi; and the encyclopedic work of H. R. P. DICKSON, *The Arab of the Desert: A Glimpse into Badawin Life in Kuwait and Saudi Arabia* (London: George Allen and Unwin, 1949).

Annual, Occasional, and Serial Publications

Among annual publications enabling students to remain abreast of current developments in the Arab East are *The Middle East and North Africa: Survey and Directory* published since the early 1950s by Europa: London, and the yearly *Survey of International Affairs* and *Documents on International Affairs* which since 1920 have been published in London by the Royal Institute of International Affairs (Chatham House). The Department of State's publications on United States foreign relations are valuable. An important occasional publication dealing with a wide variety of topics in modern Arab history and politics is *Middle Eastern Affairs*, edited by A. H. HOURANI, a part of the series of *St. Antony's Papers* published by the Oxford University Press.

Students of the modern period are in the debt of HARRY N. HOWARD for his bibliographies, frequently revised and brought up to date, published by the Middle East Institute (Washington, D.C.). Another valuable contribution is HARRY N. HOWARD, "The Middle East in Paperback," *Middle East Journal*, vol. 18, no. 3 (summer, 1964) and vol. 23, no. 3 (summer, 1969).

Serial publications on current developments are *Middle East Monitor* (monthly), Washington, D.C., *Arab Report and Record* (monthly) and *Middle East Economic Digest* (monthly), both published in London. Very important for statistical data and analysis are the relevant quarterly publications and annual supplements of the Economist Intelligence Unit, London.

The following are some of the specialized publications that run articles with informed analyses of contemporary events in the Arab East as well as bibliography, by scholars in the humanities and social sciences disciplines: *Der Islam, Die Welt des Islams, Europa-Archiv, International Affairs* (London, although the Moscow publication of the same name occasionally contains articles on the Arab East of interest for their perspective if not their scholarship), *International Journal of Middle Eastern Studies, Islamic Culture, Jeune Afrique, Middle East Journal, Middle Eastern Studies, Mizan Newsletter, Muslim World, New Middle East, New Outlook* (the Israeli publication, not to be confused with others of the same name), *Oriente Moderno, The World Today,* and the publication of the Faculty of Oriental Studies of St. Joseph's University, Beirut, *Travaux et Jours.*

APPENDIX

POPULATION, LAND, and PRODUCTIVITY

Information has been compiled from numerous sources. Where precise data are not available, the best estimate is indicated by an (E).

	POPULATION	AREA	GRAZING AND ARABLE LAND	GNP (per capita)
Lebanon	2,700,000	4,000 sq. mi.	36%	$ 500
Syria	6,300,000	72,335	76%	$ 210
Iraq	9,050,000	172,000	24%	$ 260
Jordan	2,420,000	37,500*	12%	$ 270 (E)
Saudi Arabia	5,600,000 (E)	873,000	15%	$ 577
Yemeni Arab Republic	5,500,000 (E)	75,000	20%	$ 58
Peoples Democratic Republic of Yemen	1,300,000	112,000	32%	$ 106
Sultanate of Oman	710,000	82,000	21%	not available
United Arab Emirates	201,000	32,000	Insignificant	" ... "
Qatar	115,000	4,100	"	$ 833
Bahrain	215,000	231	"	$ 242
Kuwait	782,000	7,780	"	$3,000

*Including West Bank (2,000 sq. mi.)

AFTERWORD

Past retained its role as prologue in 1973 in the Middle East, as evidenced by violence and terrorism (Israeli commandos ranging throughout much of Lebanon in punitive raids in February and April, destruction of a Libyan airliner over Sinai, murders of Western diplomats in Khartoum, Lebanon on the brink of civil war in May); riots resulting from confessional tension in Syria; Iraq's menacing of Kuwait; royal dictatorship in Jordan; bloodshed on the border between the two Yemens; renewed subversion in Oman; and the mounting accumulation of oil revenues and foreign currency reserves in the Persian Gulf states.

Lebanon's abiding search for stability was already jeopardized by social unrest before Israel's forward policy added another dimension to its permanent crisis. Strikes for higher wages, the underscoring of corruption in high places by a senior army officer's flight to asylum in Syria, and an Iraqi ban on imports or products produced in or transhipped through Lebanon[1] produced pressures from many quarters. In Lebanon's open society, with its capacity for compromise, its free press, and its excellent communications, it is to be expected that such crises will be transitory. But such characteristics, since that Black September of 1970 in Jordan, have made Lebanon increasingly attractive as a base for Palestinian organizations. An army of 18,000 had neither the firepower nor the monolithic popular support requisite to control 300,000 Palestinians, much less to cope with the surgical precision of the Israeli force that moved into Beirut on April 10. Fifty Palestinians had died in the north Lebanon raid two months earlier—now the toll was more than doubled and included high-ranking PLO officials.

That Israel hoped to provoke a Black May in Lebanon appeared to

---

[1]Retaliation for nationalization of the IPC refinery in Tripoli without compensation, but in accordance with a 1931 agreement.

257

be borne out by bitter fighting between Palestinians and the army after Popular Democratic Front for the Liberation of Palestine (PDFLP) extremists abducted two noncommissioned officers. Heavy weaponry was engaged, and Lebanese aircraft strafed refugee camps, occasioning the resignation of Premier Saeb Salam and the institution of martial law. Successive truces were unenforceable, and the state of emergency continued for three weeks before civilian government was restored under a new premier, Dr. Amin Hafez. The closure of frontiers crippled commerce and tourism, but by June the conciliatory efforts of the Kuwaiti foreign minister brought President Frangieh and PLO leader Yassir Arafat together to renew the uneasy *modus vivendi* by which the Palestinians continue to live in something less than a state within the state of Lebanon. Had not the Muslim population of Lebanon resisted Phalangist provocations and Palestinian exhortation, such politics of compromise would have been impossible.

Syria's domestic concerns and fear of an Israeli response blunted enthusiasm for intervention in the Lebanese crisis. The Yarmuk Brigade (Palestine Liberation Army) was unleashed to march up the hill into Lebanon and down again with, as expected, little consequence. The regular army found employment securing the regime against the Sunnite traditionalism of the Syrian citizenry when a new constitution was put forward in January. Concerned with locking in the special position of the Baath Party as his own instrumentality, President Hafez Assad neglected the ritual gesture toward Islam as the state religion. It was inevitable that this neglect would be interpreted as Alawite particularism. After shooting cleared the streets of Hama and Damascus in February, the missing provision was added to the constitution, which was approved by referendum in March. This facilitated the first election in a decade, two months later, in which the Baathists and their allies predictably captured 70 percent of the seats in the legislature.

The special relationship with the USSR assured continued military and economic aid, but did not inhibit Syrian pragmatism, as manifested by relaxation of restrictions on trade. Italy replaced the Soviet Union as the principal market for Syrian cotton, and steps were taken toward reestablishment of diplomatic relations with Great Britain.

In Iraq the contrast between realism and adventurism was more sharply defined. A Western market for oil from the nationalized Kirkuk fields was assured by compensating the Iraq Petroleum Company with 15 million tons of crude oil and recognizing the company's rights in the Basra concession area. (In Basra, production costs are lower and the production of Kirkuk will be surpassed.) Moreover, it was announced that barter agreements involving Iraqi oil would be suspended, a suggestion that the regime was dissatisfied with the level and quality of Soviet technological, economic and military assistance.

Iraq provided credibility, however, for the massive program of American military assistance to Iran by channeling arms through its embassy in Pakistan to dissident elements in Iranian Baluchistan. Iraqi incursions into Kuwaiti territory opened another market for American military hardware—$500 million worth. The occupation of Samitah, a border post, and the deployment of Iraqi troops on two islands (Warbah and Bubiyan) ended in May. The islands interdict Umm Qasr, under development as an Iraqi naval base and outlet for oil produced under Soviet auspices in the neighboring Rumeilah field.

Yet another recipient of American military assistance, estimated at $100 million in 1972–73 was Jordan. If King Hussein's ritual visit to the White House assured him of the means to impose stringent security measures after the disclosure of an anti-regime conspiracy and assassination plot, a measure of economic aid at least facilitated the resettlement of agriculturalists in the Jordan Valley. The commutation of the death sentences (after intercession by the ruler of Kuwait) on seventeen Palestinians and the installation, in May, of Ziad Rifai as prime minister improved relations with Egypt[2], which had already accepted the Royal Jordanian Army back into the joint military command of Arab "confrontation" states. But by June, the Jordanians heard concern for their national integrity expressed, *mirabile dictu*, by Israel after Egyptian hints of support for a Palestinian entity east of the Jordan.

The emphasis on military buildup extended also to Saudi Arabia— a $625 million air defense package purchased from Great Britain in May, and the disclosure of a $2 billion American program, including the sale of Phantom jets. The volume of the arms trade prompted strong Israeli protests, with little immediately discernible effect.

Discussion of eventual unification between the two Yemens was muted as the death toll on the frontier mounted. The assassination of Shaikh Mohammed Ali Osman (in San'a in May) of the YAR ruling council by Adeni terrorists, and PDRY "revelations" of Saudi-American plans for an invasion of Hadhramaut were surface indications of strong forces opposing the concept of a United Yemeni Republic.

The shooting once again intensified in Oman, spreading out of Dhofar as far afield as the Batinah Coast and encouraging the Shah of Iran, in an action which dramatized the seriousness with which he regards the surrogate role conferred upon him by Britain and America, to move Iranian air and commando forces across the Straits of Hormuz. The Iranian deployment also emphasized the extent to which Sultan Qabus has lost the initiative in his country. His Arab neighbors in the United Arab Emirates and Saudi Arabia, for reasons both contemporary and

---

[2]The former UAR's current official name is the ARE—Arab Republic of Egypt.

rooted in history, were deeply troubled by the presence on Arab soil of troops whose allegiance was to the defender of the Shiite faith.

But not even Clio, history's muse, would assert that the full measure of the present can be understood through knowledge of the past. In 1973 there were developments which suggested a break with the past or at least the emergence of new and unpredictable forces. The year in which events in East Asia seemed, after more than a century, to place a boundary upon the concept of Manifest Destiny also heard American voices calling for a more "forward" policy in the Middle East. The sale of raw commodities increased Third World foreign currency reserves, purchasing new respect (and concern) in industrialized states. Nowhere was the change more dramatic than in the Arab world. New men walked the corridors of power, calling for an Arab reserve currency to ensure against the repetition of losses on oil royalties consequent upon two devaluations of the dollar. Even as the Organization of Petroleum Exporting Countries demanded an 11 percent price increase as compensation for devaluation, Shaikh Zaki Yamani warned of the danger of American or other Western attempts to form an organization of petroleum importing countries. The indications, most clearly provided by Japan, were that such a combination was not in prospect.

The Arabs were hardly alone in contemplating the implications of vast holdings in reserve currencies, external demands for increased production, internal pressures to limit production and make income proportionate to the capability (in manpower and technology) to implement programs of development. If the oil was kept in the ground, it seemed that its value would increase. If transformed into currency reserves far in excess of the potential for rational investment, at home or abroad, it could be a factor of political instability. But even at 1973 levels, returns from oil production purchased arms in vast quantities and financed extensive development.

There was irony that in the year in which Israel celebrated a quarter century of nationhood and Palestinian fortunes were at a low ebb, the Arab world should secure an influence in world affairs unrivalled since the Umayyad Caliphate. The activities (noted above) of a conservative Kuwaiti regime on behalf of Palestinians may provide a clue as to how this leverage could be employed. Increased production of Middle Eastern oil may yet depend upon the response to the question—"What do you propose to do for the Palestinians?" The answer may be found in a century or more of bitter Saudi-Hashemite relations. Saudi Arabia has learned how to live with a Yemeni republic on its southern border. A Palestinian republic to northward would pose no great problem.

INDEX

A

Abbasid Caliphate (*see* Caliphates)
Abu Dhabi (*see* United Arab Emirates)
Abu Musa and the Tumbs, Iranian
　seizure of, 110, 113, 239, 241
Agha Khan, 38, 84, 170
Ajman (*see* United Arab Emirates)
Al-Aqsa Mosque, 109, 118, 165
Algeria, 58, 59, 60, 64, 65, 96, 98, 100,
　130, 159, 197, 198, 245
Ali (son-in-law of Prophet), 4, 74, 75,
　170, 174
Ali, Mohammed, 50
Amer, Marshal Abdul Hakim, 54, 104,
　179, 181
American University of Beirut, 12–13
Anderson, Robert, 224, 225
Anglo-Iranian Oil Company, 112
Anglo-Persian War, 228
Arabian American Oil Company
　(ARAMCO), 91, 156–57, 159,
　164, 166, 232
Arab League, 21, 35, 46, 93, 99, 118,
　120, 130, 131, 135, 220, 235, 240,
　241
Arab League Committee on South
　Arabia, 201
Arab League Joint Defense Council, 131
Arab Legion (*see* Jordan)
Arab Nationalist Movement, 56, 65, 100,
　234, 236, 237, 240
Arab Revolt, 2, 14, 41, 152
Arab Revolt in Palestine, 86, 87
Arab socialism, 30, 53, 56, 163, 178, 182

Arafat, Yasir, 29, 32, 33, 69, 128, 130,
　167
Ataturk, (Mustafa Kemal Pasha) 43, 153
Ayyubid dynasty (*see* Mamluks)

B

Baban dynasty, 78
Baghdad Pact, 90, 92–93, 94, 96, 121
Bahrain, Shaikhdom of:
　Britain and, 228–29, 232–33, 240–41
　Independence, 240–41
　Iranian claim to, 232–33, 239, 241
　Khalifah dynasty:
　　Khalifah, Shaikh Isa ibn Salman,
　　　236, 239, 240–41
　　Khalifah, Shaikh Salman ibn Hamad,
　　　236
　Modernization, 232, 236, 239, 243
　Oil, 231–32, 233, 234, 243
　Political development, 234–35, 239
　Treaties
Balfour Declaration, 41
Bangla Desh, 131
Basra Petroleum Company, 110
Bayar, Celal, 92
Bell, Gertrude, 84
Ben-Gurion, David, 61
Bismarck, Otto von, 41, 62
Black September (*see* Commando
　movement)
Brandt, Willy,131
British Petroleum Corporation, 110
Brockelmann, Carl, 37
Brown, George, 203, 204, 205

Bunche, Ralph, 181
Bunker, Ellsworth, 181
Buraimi Oasis, dispute, 154, 155, 158–
    159, 175, 212, 216, 219–20, 232,
    234, 238, 239, 240–41, 243
Buwayids, 75, 213

C

Cairo conference (1921), 116
Caliphates:
    Abbasid, 4, 37, 74–75, 85, 91, 170, 213
    Fatimid, 4, 5, 37, 170
    Ummayad, 4, 14, 37, 74, 85, 116, 212
Carbillet, G., 43–44
Carmathians, 144, 213
Catroux, Gen. Georges, 46
Chesney expedition, 82
Churchill, Sir Winston, 17, 84, 90, 92,
    116
Clayton, Sir Gilbert, 154
Commando movement, 28–31, 32–33, 34,
    35, 59–60, 61, 67, 70, 72, 107,
    121, 126, 128–30, 132, 167
Commando organizations:
    Black September, 32, 35, 131
    Fatah, 28, 29–30, 32, 125, 128, 130
    Palestine Liberation Army, 66
    Palestine Liberation Organization
        (PLO), 28, 32, 47, 59, 60, 65, 66,
        70, 125–26, 128, 130
    Popular Democratic Front for the
        Liberation of Palestine, 130
    Popular Front for the Liberation of
        Palestine (PFLP), 28, 32, 67, 125,
        129, 130, 222
    Sa'iqah, 24, 29, 66–67, 133
Compagnie Francaise des Petroles, 111
Cox, Sir Percy Z., 83, 84
Crane, Charles, 156
Crusades, 4–5, 6, 38–39, 116

D

Da Gama, Vasco, 6
Damascus Pact, 121
Darazi, Ismael al-, 5
deGaulle, Gen. Charles, 17–18, 25, 46,
    106
deJouvenal, Henri, 15
deMartel, Damien, 15, 16
Dentz, Gen. Henri, 17, 46
deRedcliffe, Stratford, 82
Douglas-Home, Sir Alec, 131, 203
Dubai (See United Arab Emirates)
Dulles, John F., 25, 124, 160

E

East India Company, 80, 171, 193,
    214–15, 226–28
Eden, Sir Anthony, 92, 122

Eisenhower Doctrine, 23, 25, 51, 123–24
Eisenhower, Dwight D., 120
Epic of Gilgamesh, 73
Eshkol, Levi, 61, 62, 63

F

Faisal, Emir (ibn Hussein), 14, 41, 42
    116
    (see also Iraq, King Faisal I of, and
        Syria, King Faisal of)
Farouk, King, (see Mohammed Ali
    Dynasty)
Fatah (see Commando organizations)
Fatimid Dynasty (see Caliphates)
Fedayeen (see Commando movement)
Federation of Arab Republics, 70
Fujairah (see United Arab Emirates)

G

Glubb, Sir John Bagot, 121–22, 155
Golan Heights, 30, 60, 63, 64, 67, 72,
    125, 127, 157, 165
Gouraud, General Henri, 13, 14, 15, 17,
    42
Greenwood, Anthony, 200, 201–2
Grobba, Dr. Fritz, 86

H

Habbash, George, 130
Hawatmeh, Naif, 130
Healey, Denis, 203
Heath, Donald, 131
Hejaz Railway, 116
Hitti, Philip K., 39
Holland, 78, 144, 171, 193, 227
Hone-Bell proposal, 203, 204
Hussein (grandson of Prophet), 74, 75,
    146
Hussein, Sherif of Mecca (later King of
    Hejaz), 41, 151, 152, 153

I

Ickes, Harold, 157
Ikhwan, 69, 151, 152, 153, 154, 155
International Monetary Fund, 131
Iraq:
    Britain and, 78, 80–82, 83, 88, 89–90,
        92–93, 98, 99, 106, 112–13
    British mandate in, 82–85
    Claim to Kuwait, 87, 99, 161, 196,
        229, 235, 236
    Development Board, 91, 92, 94
    Egypt (UAR) and, 91, 93–94, 95,
        96–97, 98, 100–102, 104, 105,
        106, 107
    Germany and, 86, 87–88
    Golden Square uprising, 87–88, 89
    Hashemite dynasty:

Iraq *(cont.)*
  Hashemite dynasty *(cont.)*
    Abdul Illah (regent), 50, 87, 89, 94,
      95, 123
    Faisal I (previously King of Syria),
      42, 84–85, 88, 154
    Faisal II, 50, 95
    Ghazi I, 86, 87
  Iran and, 87, 104, 106, 110, 112–13
  Iraqi Revolt of 1920, 82–83
  Israel and, 95, 106, 107, 108, 112
  Jordan and, 93, 94, 106, 112–13
  Kurds, 76, 77, 78, 83, 85, 89–90, 96,
    97, 98–99, 101–2, 103, 104, 105,
    106, 107, 108, 109, 110, 114
  Oil, 86, 89, 90, 91–92, 94, 95, 99, 103,
    105–6, 107, 110–12
  Persian conquests of, 75, 77, 78–79
  Political leaders:
    Ammash, Gen. Saleh Mahdi, 57, 108,
      109
    Aref, Gen. Abdul Salim, 57, 94, 97,
      101–4, 108
    Aref, Gen. Abdur Rahman, 104–8
    Askeri, Ja'far Pasha, 84
    Bakr, Brig. Ahmed Hassan, 101,
      108–9, 110, 112
    Barazani, Mullah Mustafa, 98,
      101–2, 107, 109, 110
    Bazzaz, Dr. Abdur Rahman, 102–5,
      109
    Ghaidan, Col. Sa'dun, 108
    Ghaylani, Rashid Ali, 87–88, 117
    Husri, Sati al-, 42, 86
    Hussein, Saddam (formerly Saddam
      Hussein al-Tekriti), 108, 109–10,
      111–12
    Jabr, Salih, 89
    Jawad, Hashim, 56
    Kubbeh, Ibrahim, 97
    Mahdawi, Col. Fadil Abbas, 96
    Mahmud, Shaikh, of Sulaimaniyah,
      83
    Midfai, Jamil, 88
    Naqib, Sayid Taleb Pasha, 84
    Qasim, Brig. Abdul Karim, 53, 56,
      57, 94, 95–100, 103, 108, 109,
      124, 161, 186, 196, 229
    Razzak, Brig. Aref Abdul, 102, 104
    Said, Nuri Pasha, 24, 48, 53, 55, 84,
      86, 88–95, 96, 100, 124
    Shaikly, Abdul Karim, 109
    Shawwaf, Col. Abdul Wahhab, 97
    Sidqi, Gen. Bakr, 86
    Sulaiman, Hikmat, 86
    Talabani, Jalal, 101–2, 105
    Taleb, Maj. Gen. Naji, 105, 106
    Tekriti, Gen. Hamad Shihab al-, 108
    Tekriti, Gen. Hardan al-, 108
    Yahya, Gen. Taher, 107
  Political parties:
    Baath, 30, 56, 95, 100, 101, 102,

Political parties *(cont.)*
  Baath *(cont.)*
    103, 105, 107, 108, 112, 113, 114
    Iraqi Communist, 56, 95–96, 97–98,
      99, 101, 113
    Kurdish Democratic, 101, 105, 114
  Religious and minority groupings:
    Armenians, 76, 78
    Christians, 76, 78, 82, 85, 89
    Indians, 76, 84
    Jews, 75, 76, 78, 89–90, 109
    Nestorians, 2, 78
    Shiites, 74, 75, 76, 78, 81, 84, 87, 89
    Sunnites, 74, 76, 77, 84, 87
  Revolution of 1958, 24, 94–95, 124
  Revolution of 1963, 99–100
  Russia and, 87, 93–94, 98, 101–2, 104,
    105, 110–13
  Saudi Arabia and, 84–85, 93, 96, 104
  Syria and, 93–94, 100, 101, 102,
    105–6, 107
  Treaties:
    Anglo-Iraqi (1930), 85, 89, 92
    Portsmouth (1948), 89
    Soviet-Iraqi (1972), 113
    Turko-Iraqi (1955), 50, 92–93
  Tribes:
    Al Bu Mohammed, 81
    Anezah, 76, 81
    Beni Lam, 81
    Ka'b, 81, 137
    Muntafiq, 76, 81, 145, 150, 229
    Shammar, 76, 81, 137
  Turkey and, 92–93, 106
  United States and, 89, 92, 93, 106,
    112, 113
Iraq Petroleum Corporation, 51, 60, 91,
  94, 103, 105, 106, 107, 109, 111,
  112, 124
Islamic Pact, 163
Ismaelis, 145, 170

J

Janissaries, 39, 78
Japan, 112, 225, 232, 235, 244
Jarring, Gunnar, 65, 127
Johnson, Lyndon B., 63
Johnston plan, 120–21
Jordan:
  Arab Development Society, 120
  Arab Legion, 117–18, 119, 121, 122,
    127
  Britain and, 119–20, 121–22, 123, 124,
    126, 128
  British mandate, 116–17
  Egypt (UAR) and, 120, 121, 122, 123,
    124, 126–27, 130
  Germany and, 131
  Hashemite dynasty:
    Abdullah, Emir (also King), 116–17,
      118–19, 152–53

Jordan *(cont.)*
  Hashemite dynasty *(cont.)*
    Hussein, King, 32, 59, 60, 67, 107,
      119–32, 167, 181
    Talal, King, 119
    Zayn, Queen, 119
  Iraq and, 119, 123, 124, 130
  Israel and, 115, 117–18, 120–21, 124,
    125, 126, 127, 128, 131, 132
  Jordan Development Bank, 119
  Palestine and, 115, 116, 117, 118
  Palestinian commandos, defeat of,
    128–30, 132
  Palestinian population of, 118, 119,
    125, 126
  Palestinians in occupied West Bank,
    127, 131–32
  Political and religious leaders:
    Alami, Musa, 120
    Husseini, Hajj Amin, 118
    Nabulsi, Sulaiman, 123
    Nasser, Sherif, 125
    Nuwar, Abu Aly, 122, 123
    Rifai, Samir, 122, 123, 125
    Salah, Abdullah, 131
    Tal, Wasfi, 125, 131, 167
    Talhouni, Bahjat, 122, 125
    Tuqan, Sulaiman, 123
  Russia and, 123, 126
  Saudi Arabia and, 117, 121, 123, 130,
    131
  Syria and, 117, 120, 121, 122, 123,
    124, 126, 129, 130
  Treaties:
    Anglo-Jordanian, 117, 123
    Jeddah (1927), 116, 154
  U.S. aid, 131
  U.S. technical assistance, 119
  United States and, 119–21, 122–23,
    124, 126, 128, 131, 132

K

Kamil, Hasan, 236
Keir, William G., 227
Kennedy, John F., 125, 161, 180, 181
Khartoum conference, 64–65, 107, 163,
  183
Khrushchev, Nikita, 51, 244
King-Crane commission, 41
Kosygin, Aleksei N., 113
Kuwait:
  Anglo-Kuwait treaty, 99, 153, 231, 235
  Britain and, 229, 230, 234, 235
  Fund for Economic Development,
    99, 236
  Germany and, 231
  Iraqi claim to, 87, 99, 161, 196, 229,
    235, 236
  Modernization & economic develop-
    ment, 232, 235, 236, 237, 238–39,
    240

Kuwait *(cont.)*
  Oil, 233, 234, 235, 240, 242
  People's Republic of China and, 240,
    243
  Political development, 235, 236, 237,
    240
  Russia and, 231, 240
  Sabah dynasty:
    Sabah, Shaikh Abdul Salem, 153, 237
    Sabah, Shaikh Mubarak, 150, 230

L

Laird, Melvin, 131
Lawrence, T.E., 41, 60, 84, 88, 90, 116
League of Nations, 21, 43, 45, 46, 84
League of Nations Permanent Mandates
  Commission, 43, 44
Lebanon:
  Agreement of 1936, 16
  Britain and, 8, 9, 10–11, 17–18,
    22–23, 28, 34
  Cairo agreement, 30
  Civil war, 1958, 24–25
  Confessionalism, 10, 11, 14–15, 16, 19,
    26, 28, 30–31
  Egypt (UAR) and, 12, 21, 23, 24, 25,
    27, 29–30
  France and, 2, 4, 7–8, 10–12, 21,
    22–23, 25, 34, 35
  French mandate, 13–19
  Intrabank, failure of, 27, 28, 34
  Iraq and, 16, 24, 30
  Israel and, 28–29, 31, 32–33, 35
  Ma'ni emirate, 6–7
  National Covenant, 18–19, 20–21
  People's Republic of China and, 34–35
  Political leaders:
    Ammoun, Fuad, 23
    Arslan, Majid, 19
    Chamoun, Camille, 18, 20, 21–25,
      26, 30, 31, 34
    Chehab, Faud, 20, 24, 25–27, 30,
      31
    Debbas, Charles, 15
    Edde, Emile, 17, 18
    Edde, Raymond, 30, 31
    Frangieh, Hamid, 23, 31
    Frangieh, Sleiman, 30, 31–32, 34,
      67
    Gemayel, Pierre, 26–27, 30, 31
    Helou, Charles, 23, 27–31, 32
    Junblatt, Kamal, 19, 20, 23, 25, 26,
      31, 34
    Karam, Yusuf, 10, 11
    Karami, Abdul Hamid, 19
    Karami, Rashid, 25, 28, 30
    Khuri, Bishara al-, 17, 18–21, 24
    Meouchi, Paul Cardinal, 23
    Muqaddem, Farouk, 30
    Saadeh, Antun, 16, 20

Political leaders *(cont.)*
  Sadr, Shaikh Musa, 30
  Salam, Saeb, 23, 24, 31, 32
  Sarkis, Elias, 31
Political parties:
  Communist, 16–17, 32, 34–35
  Constitutional Bloc, 17
  Hentchak, 23
  Najjada, 16, 25
  National Bloc, 17
  National Front, 24
  National Liberal, 24
  Partie Populaire Syrienne (PPS), 16,
    20, 26
  Phalange, 16, 25, 26, 30
  Progressive Socialist, 19
  Tashnak, 23
Religious and minority groups:
  Armenians, 13, 17, 19, 21, 23, 26
  Assyrians, 5
  Druzes, 4–5, 6–7, 8–9, 10–11, 13,
    14, 16, 17, 19, 21, 23, 26
  Greek Catholics, 13, 15, 19, 21, 26
  Greek Orthodox, 5, 13, 15, 16, 19,
    21, 26
  Jacobites, 5
  Jews, 8, 10
  Maronites, 4, 6–8, 9, 10–11, 13, 14,
    15, 16, 17, 18, 19, 21, 23, 25,
    26, 27, 30, 31
  Protestants, 8, 12, 16, 21, 26
  Shiites, 4, 5, 14, 16, 19, 21, 22, 26,
    30, 31
  Sunnites, 4, 14, 15, 16, 18, 19, 20,
    21, 22, 23, 24, 25, 26
  Russia and, 34–35
  Syria and, 10, 16, 23, 24, 29, 30,
    32–33, 35
  United States and, 8, 12–13, 18, 23,
    24–25, 28, 34
Libya, 32, 60, 70, 72, 107, 110, 130,
  165, 166, 168, 191, 245
Luce, Sir William, 167

M

Mamluks:
  Egyptian, 5, 6, 38, 143, 170
  Georgian, 79–80, 148
  Origins, 38
Marun, Yahanna, 4
Mohammed (the Prophet), 1, 37, 74,
  138, 144, 158, 170, 222
Mohammed Ali dynasty:
  Ali, Mohammed, 8–9, 10, 40, 80,
    146–48, 171–72, 228–29
  Farouk, King, 20
  Ibrahim, 8, 10, 40, 80, 146, 172, 226
Mongols, 5, 38, 75
Movement of Arab Liberation, 49
Munqidh, Usamah ibn, 39

N

Nasser, Gamal Abdul, 20, 23, 25, 29, 48,
Nassar, Gamal Abdul *(cont.)*
  53–55, 56, 57, 59, 62–63, 67,
  93–94, 95, 96–97, 104, 107, 124,
  129, 160, 161, 163–64, 175–76,
  179–83, 184, 199, 202–3, 206
Nixon, Richard M., 113, 131

O

Oman:
  Al Bu Said dynasty (1749 to 1920),
    215–18
  Al Bu Said dynasty, 1920 to present:
    ibn Faisal, Sultan Taimur, 218–19
    ibn Taimur, Sultan Said, 158, 206,
      219–22, 224
    ibn Said, Sultan Qabus, 168, 191,
      222–24
  Britain and, 213, 216, 217–18, 220,
    221, 222, 224
  Dhofar rebellion, 184, 186, 191, 208,
    210, 213, 221–22, 223–24
  Ibadh, Abdullah ibn, 212
  Ibadhi sect, 212–13, 215
  Iran and, 224
  Iraq and, 222
  Jordan and, 224
  Oil, 219, 221, 222, 223
  Oman Liberation Army, 220
  Oman Revolutionary Movement, 213,
    220, 222, 236
  People's Democratic Republic of
    Yemen and, 224
  People's Republic of China and, 222,
    224
  Popular Front for the Liberation of
    Oman and the Arabian Gulf, 213,
    222
  Russia and, 224
  Saudi Arabia and, 219–20, 221–22,
    224, 225
  Sultan's Armed Forces, 219, 221, 222
  Treaties:
    Anglo-Omani (1798), 216
    Anglo-Omani commercial agreement
      (1839), 217
    Anglo-Omani friendship treaty
      (1951), 219
    Qabus-Hussein agreement (1972),
      224
    Sib (1920), 218–19
  Tribes:
    Adnani, 212
    Beni Ghafir, 215, 217, 218, 219
    Beni Hina, 215, 217, 218, 219, 220
    Julanda, 212
    Qahtani, 212
    Yar'ubi, 214, 215
  United States and, 224, 225

Organization of Petroleum Exporting Countries (OPEC), 33, 165, 237, 245
Ottoman empire:
Eastern Arabia and, 229–30
Hejaz and Nejd and, 143–44, 149, 151–52
Iraq, rule in, 75–78, 79–82
Lebanon, rule in, 6–13
Oman and, 214
South Arabia, siege of, 193–94
Syria, rule in, 39–41, 116
Yemen, rule in, 170–73
Ottoman pashas:
Abbas, 148
Ahmed, 79
Ahmed Mukhtar, 172
Ali Rida, 79
Buyuk Sulaiman, 79
Daud (Baghdad), 79, 80
Daud (Lebanon), 11–12
Jamal, 41
Jazzar, 40
Khurshid, 148
Midhat, 81, 139, 144, 149, 229, 230
Mohammed Rashid, 11–12
Othman, 79
Sulaiman, 79
Ottoman sultans:
Abdul Hamid, 11, 40, 116
Abdul Majid, 9, 40
Mahmud, 11, 40
Murad IV, 77
Selim the Dread, 6, 16, 38, 75, 143, 170
Selim III, 40
Sulaiman the Magnificent, 75, 76, 81, 229

P

Palestine, 8, 16, 37, 58, 61, 70, 87, 89, 116, 117, 118, 131
Palestine Defense Fund, 90
Palestine Liberation Army (see Commandos)
Palestine Liberation Organization (see Commandos)
Palestine War, 48, 58, 59, 72, 89–90, 118, 119, 125
Palmerston, Lord, 9
Paris Peace Conference, 116
People's Democratic Republic of Yemen (formerly Aden Colony & the Aden Protectorates):
Aden Trades Union Congress, 176, 179, 190, 195, 197, 198
Britain and, 193–95, 196, 197, 198–206
Egypt (UAR) and, 195, 196–97, 199
Federation of Arab Emirates of the South (South Arabian Federation),

People's Democratic Republic (cont.)
Federation of Arab Emirates of the South (cont.)
177, 195, 196, 197–98, 203, 204, 237
South Yemen, 190, 191, 197, 204–5, 206, 207, 209
People's Republic of China and, 207–8, 209, 210
Political leaders:
Ali, Salem Rubaya, 208, 209
Asnag, Abdullah, 176, 195, 198, 201, 202, 204
Haitham, Mohammed Ali, 208, 209
Hassani, Ali Nasser, 209
Jaufii, Abdul Fattah Ismail al-, 208
Jifri, Mohammed al-, 201
Makkawee, Abdul, 191, 201–2, 204
Shaabi, Qatan as-, 198, 201, 205, 206–8
Political parties:
National Liberation Front, 169, 184, 186, 190, 192, 195, 197, 198, 199, 200, 201, 202, 204–7, 208
People's Socialist Party, 195, 197, 199. 202
Radfan rebellion, 181–82, 190, 199, 209
Russia and East bloc and, 198, 205, 206, 207–8, 201, 210
South Arabian League, 191, 195, 201
Treaties:
British protectorate, 193
San'a, 194
Persian Gulf shaikhdoms (see Bahrain, Kuwait, Qatar and United Arab Emirates)
Pharaon, Rashad, 164
Philby, H. St. John (Abdullah), 84
Podgorny, N., 64
Pompidou, Georges, 111–12
Ponsot, Henri, 15, 16
Popular Front for the Liberation of Palestine (see Commando Organizations)
Portugal, 78, 140, 143, 144, 192–93, 213–14, 227
Pre-Islamic influences:
Achaeminid, 74, 136, 137
Aelus Gallus, 136
Akkadian, 73, 74
Alexander, 3, 36, 137
Amorite, 3
Aramaean, 36
Assyrian, 3, 36, 74, 115, 137, 226
Babylonian, 74
Belisaurius, 74
Byzantine, 3, 36, 116
Canaanite, 3, 36
Chaldean, 3, 115, 137
Constantine, 116
Cyrus, 74
Darius, 3

Pre-Islamic influences *(cont.)*
  Egyptian, 36
  Ethiopian, 136
  Greek, 3, 36
  Hammurabi, 74
  Hebraic, 36
  Heraclius, 74
  Hittite, 36
  Hyksos, 3
  Julian, 74
  Medean, 74
  Nabatean, 116, 136
  Nearchos, 137
  Nebuchadnezzar, 74
  Parthian, 3, 74
  Persian, 3, 36, 74, 115, 137, 211, 212
  Philadelphus, 115
  Phoenician, 3, 36
  Pompey, 3
  Ptolomaic, 3, 36, 115
  Roman, 3–4, 36, 74, 116
  Sargon, 74
  Sassanid, 36, 74, 137, 211, 216
  Seleucid, 3, 36, 74, 115
  Sennacherib, 74
  Sumerian, 3, 73–74, 116, 226
  Trajan, 116

Q

Qaddafi, Moammar, 32, 72, 130, 165, 191
Qatar, Shaikhdom of:
  Britain and, 230, 232
  Economic development, 236, 239, 240, 242
  Oil, 231, 235, 242
  Thani, Khalifah ibn Hamad al-, Shaikh of, 240, 242

R

Ras al-Khaimah *(see* United Arab Emirates)
Rashid, Harun el-, 75
Rawlinson, Sir Henry, 81
Reilly, Sir Bernard, 173
Riad, Mahmud, 65
Rogers, William P., 129, 191
Roosevelt, Franklin D., 157

S

Sadat, Anwar, 72, 130, 132, 167
Sa'iqah (see Commando organizations)
Saladin, 5, 38, 39, 170
Sanjak of Alexandretta, 17, 42–43, 46, 49, 93
San Remo conference, 83, 91
Sarrail, Gen., 15, 44
Saudi Arabia:
  Britain and, 144, 151–53, 154–55, 157,

Saudi Arabia *(cont.)*
  Britain and *(cont.)*
    158–59, 161, 167
  Egypt (UAR) and, 158, 160, 161–64, 167
  Germany and, 156–57, 163
  Iran and, 163, 165, 168
  Kuwait and, 153, 161
  Modernization of. 155–56, 162, 166–67
  National Guard (White Army), 159, 168
  Oil, 156–57, 164, 165–67
  People's Democratic Republic of Yemen and, 165, 168
  Rashid, House of, 149–51, 152
  Saud, House of (1744–1902), 145–47, 148–50
  Saud, House of (1902 to present):
    Fahad (ibn Abdul Aziz), 164
    Faisal (ibn Abdul Aziz, Crown Prince, later King), 60, 130, 153, 159, 160, 161, 162–68, 180–81, 182, 183, 184
    Khalid (ibn Abdul Aziz) Crown Prince, 162
    Saud, Abdul Aziz ibn Abdul Rahman al Faisal as- (King "ibn Saud"), 85, 142, 150–59, 173
    Saud (ibn Abdul Aziz, Crown Prince, later King), 159–62
    Sultan (ibn Abdul Aziz), 162, 164, 186
  Sherifian era (Hejaz), 142–44, 145–46, 152, 153–54
  Treaties:
    Jeddah (1927), 117, 154
    Jeddah (1965), 182–83
    Neutral Zone agreement (1923), 153
    Taif (1934), 173
  Tribes:
    Banu Khalid, 144, 145, 147, 226
    'Utub, 137–38, 226
  United Arab Emirates and, 162, 166, 167–68
  United States and, 156–57, 159–60, 161
  Yemen Arab Republic and, 161–62, 163, 168
Seljuk Turks, 37–38, 75, 213
Sharjah *(see* United Arab Emirates)
Sherley, Sir Robert, 227
Shukairy, Ahmed, 59, 60
Six Day War, 27–28, 34, 37, 51, 55, 63–64, 66, 106, 107, 126–28, 163, 183, 205, 221, 237, 244
Spears, Gen. Sir Edward, 18
Strategic Arms Limitation Talks, 113
Suez War, 22–23, 51, 94, 159, 176, 195, 234
Syria:
  Britain and, 46–47
  Druze rebellion, 15, 43–44, 45, 57, 83

Syria (cont.)
  Egypt and, 51, 52, 53, 55, 56–57,
    58–59, 60, 62–63, 67, 70–72
  French mandate in, 42–46
  Hashemite rule in, 41–42
  Iraq and, 48, 50–51, 53, 56, 57, 60,
    66, 69
  Israel and, 48, 59, 60, 61–64, 66
  Jordan and, 59–60, 64, 66, 67–68, 69
  Lebanon and, 66–67, 68, 69, 70
  People's Republic of China and, 69, 70
  Political leaders:
    Aflaq, Michel, 49, 52, 56, 57, 68,
      69
    Assad, Gen. Hafiz, 65–70
    Atassi, Hashim al-, 45
    Atassi, Nur al-Din al-, 58, 59, 64,
      66, 67–68
    Azm, Haqqi al-, 45
    Azm, Khalid al-, 48
    Baqdash, Khalid, 51, 52
    Bitar, Salah al-Din al-, 49, 52, 56,
      65
    Dawalibi, Ma'ruf, 56, 65, 164
    Hafiz, Lt. Gen. Amin, 57, 58
    Hinnawi, Col. Sami, 48, 49
    Hurani, Akram, 49, 54, 56, 65
    Jedid, Col. Salah, 64, 65, 67
    Khuri, Faris al-, 45
    Makhus, Ibrahim, 58, 64, 66
    Mardam Bey, Jamil, 45
    Qudsi, Nazim al-, 56
    Quwatli Shukri al-, 45, 46, 47–48
    Serraj, Col. Abdul Hamid, 52, 53,
      54, 97, 122
    Shahbandar, Abdur Rahman, 45
    Shishakly, Col. Adib, 48–50
    Zaim, Col. Husni, 48, 49
    Zu'ayyan, Yusuf, 58, 64, 66
  Political parties:
    Arab Baath, 49, 52–53
    Arab Socialist, 49, 50, 56, 65, 72
    Arab Socialist Baath, 51, 52, 53, 55,
      57–58, 60, 67, 68. 69
    Communist, 51–52, 69, 70, 72
    National Bloc, 45, 49, 50
    National Progressive Front, 69
    People's, 45, 48
    Social Unionist, 69, 72
  Religious and minority groupings:
    Alawites, 38, 47, 52
    Christians, 47
    Druzes, 38, 47, 48, 50, 52, 68
  Russia and, 51–52, 55, 63, 64, 65,
    66, 67, 68, 70, 72
  Treaties:
    Agreement of 1936, 44, 45–46
    Syro-Egyptian Military Alliance
      (1955), 51
  Turkey and, 42–43, 49, 50, 51
  UAR era, 53–55, 57
  United States and, 46, 49, 52, 70
  Vichy government, 46

T

Tamerlane, 5, 38, 39
Teheran agreement, 165–66, 242, 245
Trans-Arabian Pipeline (Tapline), 60,
  67, 68, 123, 157, 165
Treaties and agreements:
  Anglo-Egyptian, 45
  Blue Line agreement, 231, 232
  Franklin-Bouillon, 42
  Hussein-McMahon, 41
  Israeli-German agreements, 187
  Riyadh Line, 232
  St. Jeanne de Maurienne, 41
  Sazanov-Paleologue, 41
  Sevres, 42
  Sykes-Picot, 41
Trevaskis, Sir Kennedy, 198
Trucial States (see United Arab Emirates)
Turanshah, 38, 170
Turcomans, 6, 75, 76

U

Umm al- Quwain (see United Arab
  Emirates)
Ummayads (see Caliphates)
United Arab Emirates (formerly Trucial
  States, Trucial Oman):
  Abu Dhabi, 227, 230, 232, 233,
    237–38, 241, 243
  Abu Dhabi Defense Force, 221, 238
  Abu Dhabi Fund for Economic
    Development, 241
  Ajman, 227, 234, 241
  Britain and, 226 ff.
  Dubai, 227, 233–34, 236, 238, 239,
    241, 243
  Fujairah, 227–28, 234, 241
  Germany and, 230–31
  Iran and, 232–33, 239, 241–43
  Oil, 233, 237, 239, 241–42, 243, 245
  People's Republic of China and,
    244–45
  Ras al-Khaimah, 227, 234, 236, 238,
    240, 241–42
  Russia and, 231, 242, 243–44, 245
  Saudi Arabia and, 230, 232, 234, 236,
    238, 239, 242
  Shaikhs (rulers) of:
    Khalid (ibn Mohammed al- Qasami)
      of Sharjah, 237, 241
    Maktum (ibn Rashid) of Dubai, 241
    Rashid (ibn Said Maktum) of
      Dubai, 236, 241
    Saqr (ibn Mohammed al-Qasami) of
      Ras al-Khaimah, 238
    Saqr (ibn Sultan) of Sharjah, 237,
      241, 242
    Shakhbut (of Abu Dhabi), 234,
      236–37
    Zayid (ibn Sultan al- Nahhayan) of

Shaikhs *(rulers)* of *(cont.)*
Zayid (ibn Sultan al- Nahhayan)
   of *(cont.)*
     Abu Dhabi, 234, 236–37, 238,
      240, 241
     Sharjah, 227–28, 231, 234, 241
     Tribes:
      Beni Yas, 226, 228
      Quwasim, 226, 228, 238
      Trucial Oman Scounts, 238
      Umm al-Quwain, 227, 234, 238, 241
United States and, 242, 244
United Arab Kingdom, 132
United Arab States, 177, 178
United Nations, 29, 33, 47, 63, 95, 120,
   127, 129, 132, 176, 201, 202,
   203, 225, 233, 235, 239, 240
United Nations Committee on
   Colonialism, 197–98, 199
United Nations Development Program,
   208
United Nations Emergency Force, 61–62,
   63
United Nations Israeli-Syrian Mixed
   Armistice Commission, 61
United Nations Mission to Aden, 203–4
United Nations Relief and Works
   Agency, 119
United Nations Resolution No. 242, 29,
   70, 127
United Nations Security Council, 199
United Nations Truce Supervisory
   Organization, 61
United Nations Yemen Observer
   Mission, 181
U Thant, 65, 202

W

Wahhab, Mohammed ibn Abdul,
   144–45, 151
Wahhabis, 78, 81, 117, 145–47, 151,
   154–55, 157–58, 213, 216–17,
   229, 230, 232
Wahhabism, 145, 147, 151, 155, 173,
   212, 226
Walid, Khalid ibn, 4, 74, 116
Weygand, Gen. Maxime, 15, 17, 44
Wilson, Sir Arnold T., 82, 83, 85
Wooley, Sir Leonard, 73–74
World Bank, 131, 160, 234

Y

Yamani, Zaki, 164, 166

Yemeni Arab Republic:
   Britain and, 171, 172, 173, 174, 175,
     180, 181–82, 187
   Civil war in, 179–84
   Egypt (UAR) and, 175–77, 178,
     179–80, 181–83, 184–85
   Free Yemeni Officers Movement, 174,
     176, 178, 179
   Germany and, 180, 187, 189
   Hamid ud-Din dynasty, 1891 to 1970:
     Ahmed, 174, 175–76, 177–78
     Mohammed, 172
     Mohammed Badr (Crown Prince,
      later Imam), 175–76, 177, 178–79,
      181, 182, 183
     Yahya, 169–74
   Jordan and, 180, 181
   People's Democratic Republic of
     Yemen and, 179, 181–82, 184,
     186, 188, 190–92
   People's Republic of China and, 176,
     178, 184, 187, 189, 190
   Political leaders:
     Amri, Gen. Hassan al-, 183, 186, 190
     Asnag, Abdullah, 176, 190
     Ayni, Muhsin al-, 179, 184–86, 187,
      188, 189–92
     Baidani, Dr. Abdur Rahman, 177,
      179
     Haraji, Abdullah al-, 192
     Iryani, Qadi Abdul, 183, 188, 190
     No'man, Ahmet, 182, 187, 188–89,
      191, 192
     No'man, Mohammed, 187
     Sallal, Col. Abdullah, 179, 180–81,
      182, 183
     Shami, Ahmed as-, 185, 186, 188
     Wazir, Seyyid Abdullah al-, 174, 179
   Russia, East bloc and, 176, 178, 180,
     184, 187, 189, 190
   Saudi Arabia and, 173, 175–76,
     180–81, 182, 184–85, 186, 188,
     189–90
   Treaties:
     Jeddah (1965), 182–83
     San'a, 173
     Taif, 173
     Tripoli, 192
   Tribes:
     Bakil, 172
     Hashid, 172
   United States and, 178, 180–81, 187,
     189, 191
   Zeidi Imamate to 1891, 169–72

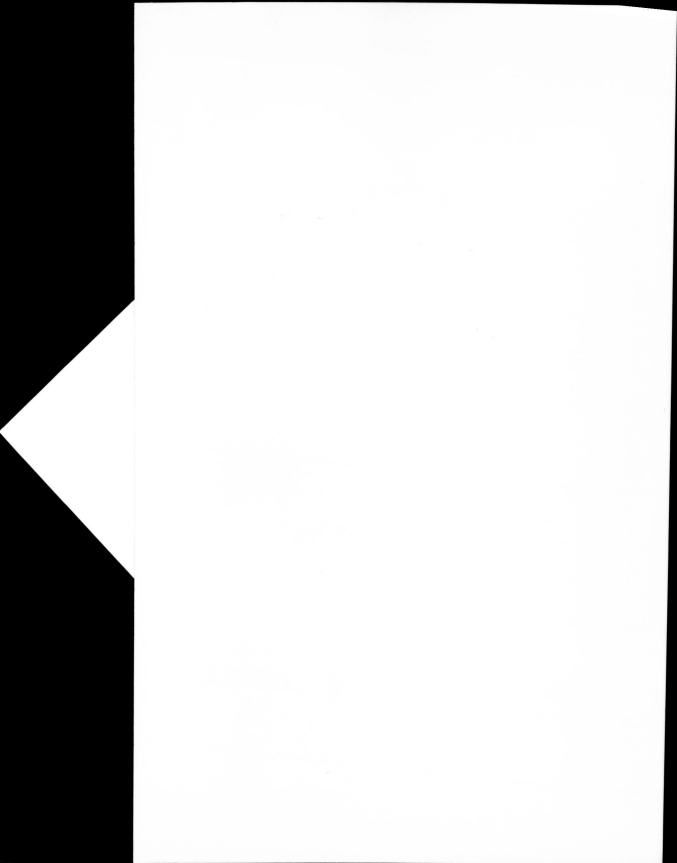

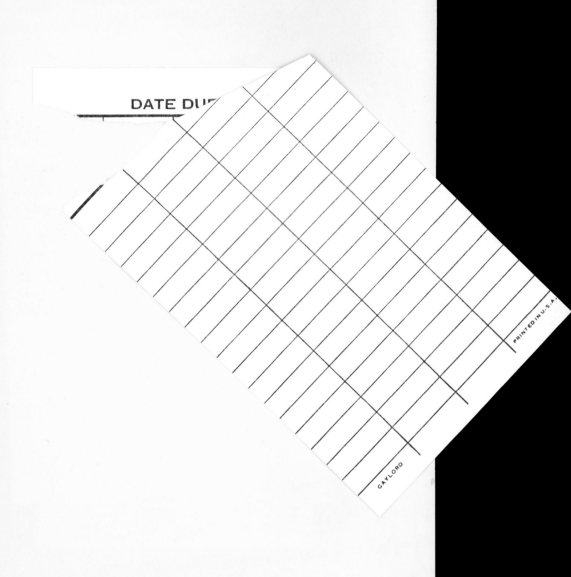

DATE DUE